PREDATORY STATES

750,000 to 1,000,000
1,000,000 to 5,000,000
5,000,000 to 10,000,000
greater than 10,000,000
Capital cities
Capital cities under 750,000
Atlantic Ocean
Gulf of Mexico
Caribbean Sea
Pacific Ocean
MEXICO
Tijuana
Mexicali
Ciudad Juárez
Culiacán
Torreón
Monterrey
San Luis Potosí
León
Guadalajara
Querétaro
Mexico City
Toluca
Puebla
Mérida
BELIZE
Belize City
GUATEMALA
Guatemala City
EL SALVADOR
San Salvador
HONDURAS
Tegucigalpa
NICARAGUA
Managua
COSTA RICA
San José
PANAMA
Panama City
CUBA
Havana
Nassau
JAMAICA
Kingston
HAITI
Port-au-Prince
DOMINICAN REPUBLIC
Santiago
Santo Domingo
PUERTO RICO
San Juan
ANTIGUA & BARBUDA
St. John's
GUADELOUPE
Basse-Terre
DOMINICA
Roseau
MARTINIQUE
Fort-de-France
ST LUCIA
Castries
ST VINCENT
Kingstown
BARBADOS
Bridgetown
GRENADA
St George's
TRINIDAD
Port-of-Spain
GUYANA
Georgetown
SURINAME
Paramaribo
FRENCH GUIANA
Cayenne
30°N
20°N
10°N
110°W
90°W
70°W

75°W
60°W
45°W
0°
15°S
30°S
45°S
Barranquilla
Cartagena
Maracaibo
Maracay
Caracas
Barquisimeto
Valencia
Cucuta
Bucaramanga
Ciudad Guayana
VENEZUELA
Medellín
Bogotá
COLOMBIA
Cali
Quito
ECUADOR
Guayaquil
Amazon R
Manaus
Belém
São Luís
Fortaleza
Teresina
Natal
Recife
Maceio
Salvador
BRAZIL
PERU
Lima
Brasília
La Paz
Santa Cruz
BOLIVIA
Goiânia
Belo Horizonte
Campo Grande
Campinas
São José dos Campos
PARAGUAY
São Paulo
Santos
Rio de Janeiro
Asunción
Curitiba
San Miguel de Tucumán
Pacific
Ocean
CHILE
Córdoba
Porto Alegre
Mendoza
URUGUAY
Santiago
Rosario
Montevideo
Buenos
Aires
ARGENTINA
Atlantic
Ocean
750,000 to 1,000,000
1,000,000 to 5,000,000
5,000,000 to 10,000,000
greater than 10,000,000
Capital cities

PREDATORY STATES

Operation Condor and Covert War in Latin America

J. Patrice McSherry

ROWMAN & LITTLEFIELD PUBLISHERS, INC.
Lanham • Boulder • New York • Toronto • Oxford

ROWMAN & LITTLEFIELD PUBLISHERS, INC.

Published in the United States of America
by Rowman & Littlefield Publishers, Inc.
A wholly owned subsidiary of The Rowman & Littlefield Publishing Group, Inc.
4501 Forbes Boulevard, Suite 200, Lanham, Maryland 20706
www.rowmanlittlefield.com

PO Box 317
Oxford
OX2 9RU, UK

British Library Cataloguing in Publication Information Available

Library of Congress Cataloging-in-Publication Data

McSherry, J. Patrice
Predatory States : Operation Condor and covert war in Latin America / J. Patrice McSherry.
p. cm.
Includes bibliographical references and index.
ISBN 0-7425-3686-6 (cloth : alk. paper) — ISBN 0-7425-3687-4 (alk. paper)
1. Operación Cóndor (South American countersubversion association) 2. State-sponsored terrorism—Latin America. 3. Political crimes and offenses—Latin America. I. Title.
HV6433.L32O64 2005
980.03'3—dc22
2004029817

∞™ The paper used in this publication meets the minimum requirements of American National Standard for Information Sciences—Permanence of Paper for Printed Library Materials, ANSI/NISO Z39.48-1992.

To the memory of my dear friend Beth, who, in the most difficult of times, kept urging me to write this book, and to Raúl, my *compañero,* and the people of Latin America, who know the meaning of political repression.

Contents

Illustrations

COVER: MURAL AT THE OFFICE of Asociación Madres de Plaza de Mayo (whose president is Hebe Bonafini), painted by the mothers, in Buenos Aires, Argentina. Reprinted with the permission of Anya Maria Mayans, U.S.-Uruguayan photographer and writer. © Anya Maria Mayans 2003.

6. Monument in Villa Grimaldi engraved with the names of the disappeared, with a fragment from the renowned Uruguayan poet and novelist, Mario Benedetti: "What is forgotten is full of memory." © J. Patrice McSherry 1998.

Foreword

I WAS A VICTIM OF OPERATION CONDOR and the one who discovered its secret archives in Asunción, Paraguay, in December 1992.

During the night of November 29, 1974, I was abducted by the political police of the dictator Afredo Stroessner and taken directly before a military tribunal in Paraguay made up of the military attachés of Argentina, Brazil, Bolivia, Chile, and Uruguay, also with the presence of Paraguayan civil and military authorities.

A Chilean officer questioned me about my supposed link with Chilean university people because I had taken a course in the sociology of education at Catholic University. The police chief of the province of Córdoba, Argentina, wanted to know of my links to the "subversives" of the University of La Plata, where I had graduated with a doctorate in the science of education.

The interrogation lasted thirty days, with terrible tortures. Finally, they categorized my crime as "intellectual terrorism": for the so-called subversive content of my doctoral thesis; for having promoted the campaign "A Roof of Your Own" for each Paraguayan educator in my capacity as a unionist fighting in the national teachers association; and for having put into practice the methods of Paulo Freire's *Pedagogy of the Oppressed* in the Juan B. Alberdi Institute, where I was director.

My wife, the educator Celestina Pérez, died as a consequence of the psychological tortures to which she was subjected, being forced to listen on the telephone, systematically for ten days, to my cries and screams from the torture chamber. On the tenth day, at midnight, she received a call announcing my death, with someone asking her "to come to retrieve the cadaver of the subversive educator." The call provoked a heart attack, and she died of pain.

I was transferred among various police stations for "bad conduct," eventually ending up at the concentration camp called Emboscada. In Police Station No. 1, the headquarters of INTERPOL, I learned of the existence of Operation Condor for the first time, seven months before the intelligence conference promoted by the Chileans Augusto Pinochet and Manuel Contreras in Santiago in November 1975. My informant was a police officer who was imprisoned with us for not having denounced his son, also a student at the University of La Plata, who had been a member of the rebellious Centro de Estudiantes (Student Center). This policeman became aware of Plan Condor because he worked in the telecommunications office of the police.

In my prison in Police Station No. 3, "Tomb of the Living," I shared a cell with the Argentine Amilcar Latino Santucho, who told me that he and Jorge Fuentes Alarcón, a Chilean leader of MIR (Movimiento de la Izquierda Revolucionaria, Movement of the Revolutionary Left of Chile) also had been taken before a military tribunal composed of military attachés of the Southern Cone countries of South America.

In September 1976, I was transferred to the concentration camp Emboscada, where I met the Paraguayan doctor Gladys M. De Sannemann, who told me that she was a victim of Operation Condor. She was abducted by the Paraguayan police in Argentine territory, in Misiones, Posadas.

After completing three years of prison I began a hunger strike, which lasted for thirty days, and thanks to the urgent action campaign by Amnesty International, I recovered my freedom in September 1977.

I went into exile in Panama. There, the United Nations Educational, Scientific, and Cultural Organization (UNESCO) in Paris, contracted me to be a consultant of UNESCO for Latin America, a position I held from 1978 to 1992.

For almost fifteen years, I carried out an investigative project on Operation Condor, based on the testimonies of my prison companions and on the *Revista Policial Paraguaya* (Paraguayan Police Magazine).

For these reasons, I value the research investigation on Operation Condor, *Predatory States*, realized by J. Patrice McSherry. She presents the U.S. and Latin American scenario in which this criminal pact developed and shows us how the Southern Cone countries were strongly politicized, with the rise of social mobilization after the triumph of the Cuban revolution. Professor McSherry also portrays the energetic response of the United States via the Pentagon, the CIA, and other security agencies, especially under the charge of National Security Advisor and Secretary of State Henry Kissinger in the 1970s. "No more Cubas" was the official policy underlying Washington's unconditional support for the military coup against the constitutional government of Salvador Allende in Chile on September 11, 1973.

This book is a serious historical work with abundant documentation.

Professor McSherry shows us the dynamics of Operation Condor, with the interchange of intelligence information among the member states, the targeting of the "subversive" or "terrorist" element, and the torture, execution, or transfer of the subversives to any other signatory country. She also sheds light on the consequences of U.S. military intervention in the region: the era of state terrorism; the reduction of spaces for democratic participation; the physical elimination of militants and leaders of revolutionary movements; the control of civil society; and the disarticulation of political society.

Using documents declassified by the U.S. State Department, the author points out that U.S. officials regarded Operation Condor as a legitimate counterinsurgency organization. She shows that the state terrorists of Condor counted on Washington for technical assistance in torture, for financing, and even for a system of telecommunications.

Thanks to this important work of historical investigation, we learn of the magnitude of the violations of human rights committed in this epoch against Latin American societies that had aspirations for freedom. Another important element of Professor McSherry's analysis is the contribution of French military officers, based on their counterrevolutionary experience in Algeria as well as Vietnam, to the training of U.S. soldiers in torture and other grave violations of human rights. This occurred under the administration of President John F. Kennedy.

Shortly before the publication of *Predatory States*, Paraguay established, through a law passed by Congress (Law 2225 of 2004), the Commission of Truth and Justice, to investigate enforced disappearances, extrajudicial executions, torture and other serious abuses, involuntary exile, and other grave violations of human rights. I am sure that Professor McSherry's work will bring valuable clues to the Commission of Truth and Justice for the clarification of so many crimes against humanity.

Recovering the past is a significant undertaking, indispensable for countering the impunity that continues to reign and for ensuring that justice is made effective in the face of the appalling violations of human rights committed in the decade of the 1970s. The importance of not forgetting what happened has nothing to do with a thirst for revenge. On the contrary, the act of remembering serves the need to keep historical memory alive and allows us to analyze, with some distance, how an organized and deliberate plan existed to do the greatest possible harm to defenseless Latin American societies. In fact, Professor McSherry demonstrates that there was such a plan, systematic, organized, and planned in order to prepare the ground for the critical economic and political situation in which we find ourselves today, with the imposition of neoliberalism, political domination, and an unpayable external debt.

Predatory States is a genuine scientific addition to the clarification of a history that never should have befallen Latin America and an invaluable contribution to the culture of peace.

Martín Almada
The Right Livelihood Award (Alternative Nobel Prize) Laureate, 2002
Asunción, Paraguay, 2004

Preface

I BEGAN TO FOLLOW THE TRAIL of Operation Condor in the early 1990s, as the Cold War was beginning to fade into history. It was a time of some hope, when global concerns with human rights and international justice emerged with new strength. The limits set by Cold War geopolitics had begun to crack and new demands arose to hold accountable Cold War violators of human rights on the Western, as well as the Eastern, side. New political and social forces—relatives of the victims, citizen organizations, human rights groups, nongovernmental organizations, international lawyers and judges, and networks of activists and truth-seekers—made their voices heard in the halls of the United Nations (UN) and in their own countries. In this new climate, General Augusto Pinochet was arrested for human rights crimes, the International Criminal Court (ICC) was established to prosecute war crimes and crimes against humanity, and other important advances were made in international law and government accountability. Unfortunately, this forward motion, which represented the beginnings of the globalization of justice and the rule of law, was set back by the horrific terrorist attack in September 2001 and the ensuing "war on terrorism."

The events of September 11 traumatized and pained me deeply, as a New Yorker and as a witness. The posters of missing people that sprouted everywhere in the city evoked jolting images of the disappeared of Latin America and their grieving families. The response of the Bush administration to 9/11 filled me with foreboding, however.

George W. Bush had already abandoned several international conventions on environmental protection and arms control and, in an unprecedented act, had revoked former President Bill Clinton's signature of the ICC treaty. As he unleashed the war on terror by bombing Afghanistan, President Bush declared that prisoners would be considered "illegal combatants" not eligible for protections afforded under the Geneva Conventions or the U.S. Constitution. In 2003, the administration undertook a unilateral invasion of Iraq, arguing that Iraq had weapons of mass destruction and implying that Saddam Hussein was linked to 9/11. Both claims were baseless. The administration also set out to sabotage the substance of the ICC by forcing individual governments to sign bilateral agreements to exempt U.S. military and civilian personnel from criminal charges covered by the court. The administration announced a new doctrine of "preemption," based on the presumed prerogative of the United States to wage war against potential, or hypothetical, enemies, even in the absence of hostile action or an imminent threat. Aggressive, unprovoked war, however, is illegal under international law and the UN Charter.[1] The stage was being set for new wars in which the ends justified any means, mirroring the Cold War.

The war against terrorism had important parallels to the Cold War anticommunist crusade, also led by the United States. For this reason, I believe a new examination of the deepest secrets of that era is useful and timely. During the Cold War, highly politicized and ruthless militaries in Latin America, aided and abetted by Washington, used the methods of terror to wage their anticommunist wars in secrecy. Counterinsurgent forces created a vast parallel infrastructure of clandestine detention centers and killing machinery to avoid national and international law and scrutiny, and utilized disappearance, torture, and assassination to defeat "internal enemies." The horrors of that time still reverberate in Latin America and in the world.

I have long been concerned with hidden power, the kind that operates parallel to democratic processes and in the recesses of military regimes, invisible and unaccountable. The parastatal structures I discuss in this book were an integral component of the national security states of Latin America and a key element of the terror the militaries used to control their societies. Six military states in South America extended these parastatal structures and extralegal methods across borders—with a "green light" from the U.S. government—in a transnational repressive program known as Operation Condor (or Plan Condor). The militaries in Argentina, Bolivia, Brazil, Chile, Paraguay, and Uruguay were the key protagonists of Condor, spreading dirty war throughout the region and beyond. For them, the ends justified the means; torture, extrajudicial executions, and abductions were considered legitimate if employed against "subversives." During the Cold War, tens of thousands of Latin American men, women, and children were tortured and murdered as a result of such methods, hundreds of them killed within the framework of Operation Condor.

One striking aspect of Condor was that it represented a secret alliance among militaries that had been historical adversaries, even enemies. Each country had a unique history, with its own social and political structures and social forces, yet the militaries came to share the same ideological concepts and counterinsurgency strategies. Clearly, such a situation leads the analyst toward system-level explanations. What were the commonalities and linkages that led to such striking ideological consensus and clandestine collaboration?

In this book, I begin the study of Condor from a global perspective, providing the international context of the Cold War and outlining the impact of U.S. and French counterinsurgency doctrines and training on Operation Condor, as well as the heritage of earlier parallel armies. Any attempt to analyze a transnational operation such as Condor necessitates a global scope, although it is an approach that inevitably limits a detailed focus on each member country. My objective here thus differs from that of my first book, which was an in-depth political history of Argentina's difficult transition from military to civilian rule. In a study such as the present one, the analyst cannot do justice to the complex and distinctive national situations of so many countries. I hope that the panoramic view of Condor presented here and the comparative analysis provided compensate for the unavoidably schematic discussions of each country's unique history.

Although survivors of Condor and some human rights observers began perceiving Condor's existence in the mid-1970s, the clandestine system remained shrouded in secrecy for another decade, a well-kept secret of the Cold War. The 1992 discovery of the police files known as the Archives of Terror in Paraguay (archives I studied in 1996) provided new documentation of Condor, confirming earlier testimonies of victims and hitherto fragmentary evidence. The investigation of Condor initiated by the Spanish judge Baltasar Garzón, whose extradition request led to the 1998 arrest of Pinochet in London, produced new revelations. Then, in June 1999, President Bill Clinton ordered the release of the first of three tranches of declassified U.S. documents. Until that time, the extent of U.S. government information regarding Condor had been unknown. The only document on Condor in the public domain had been a cable by FBI agent Robert Scherrer, sent from Buenos Aires to Washington in September 1976. In recent years, a veritable flood of information on Condor has emerged.

Structure of the Book

In chapter 1, I present an overview of Condor and discuss its key characteristics. I place Condor in the context of counterinsurgency warfare and show how it fit within U.S. and French counterinsurgency theory and practice.

Chapter 2 examines the international environment shaped by the Cold War and demonstrates that Condor actually operated in concert with paramilitary groups linked to the so-called stay-behind armies in Europe. This chapter also situates Condor within the inter-American military system, which was focused on counterinsurgency and covert operations beginning in the 1960s. The evidence strongly suggests that Condor grew out of earlier transnational programs set up in the Conferences of American Armies and elsewhere. I detail the role of Brazil in organizing early, pre-Condor cross-border collaboration among the armies and describe the role of the U.S. Central Intelligence Agency (CIA) in instigating and laying the foundation for Condor.

Chapter 3 discusses the early years of Condor and describes the nuclei of the Condor Group within military intelligence organizations. An important Condor meeting took place in February 1974, a year and a half earlier than the November 1975 meeting usually cited as the founding assembly of Condor.

In chapter 4, I discuss Condor operations during the network's later years as well as the role of the U.S. Congress in trying to discontinue U.S. assistance to the military regimes. The relationship of Secretary of State and National Security Advisor Henry Kissinger to Condor is also examined.

Chapter 5 analyzes a range of data on Condor assassinations, known as Phase III operations, and includes interviews with a member of the Michelini family.

Chapter 6 presents profiles of key Condor operatives and discusses their particular roles in the repressive system.

Chapter 7 documents the extension of Operation Condor to Central America in the 1980s.

Finally, in chapter 8 I review the conceptual framework of the book, assess the evidence, and draw some conclusions.

* * *

As I was making final changes to this manuscript, the CBS program *60 Minutes* released graphic photographs of U.S. forces abusing and sexually humiliating Iraqis in Abu Ghraib prison, igniting a worldwide uproar. Previous reports by human rights organizations such as Amnesty International and Human Rights Watch had documented U.S. use of torture and ill treatment of prisoners in Afghanistan, Iraq, and Guantánamo, Cuba, and the *Washington Post* had published stories about the use of torture by U.S. forces in 2002. The International Committee of the Red Cross had taken the extremely rare step of publicly condemning the illegality of the Guantánamo detentions and the persistent refusal of the U.S. government to respect the Geneva Conventions.[2] But the explicit nature of the photographs caused, for the first time, a public furor around the world and in the United States.

The scandal, and its sequels, underscored the concerns of this book, especially as new reporting revealed brutal methods and secret operations with eerie similarities to Operation Condor. The *Washington Post*, for example, reported that top Bush officials had approved a classified list of some twenty "techniques" for coercive interrogation of prisoners, including use of sensory deprivation, humiliation, and pain.[3] One method used by U.S. interrogators, with the grotesquely Orwellian name of "water-boarding,"[4] was identical to the *submarino* torture used by Condor militaries in the 1970s: near-drowning of a bound prisoner.

U.S. army documents showed that some thirty-seven prisoners had died in custody—a number of them of "smothering," "lack of oxygen," and "strangulation" during interrogation by U.S. intelligence officers—and an internal army report found that U.S. personnel had moved "ghost detainees" (essentially disappeared persons) to different areas of Abu Ghraib to escape the notice of the Red Cross. This army report, which was leaked to the media, said that "numerous incidents of sadistic, blatant, and wanton criminal abuses" had been inflicted on prisoners, and declared the abuse "systemic." The report also found that the harsh methods had been approved by military intelligence officers higher in the chain of command.[5] Later the press reported that the Justice Department had produced a legal memo in 2002 justifying torture and aggressive interrogations.[6] But virtually no U.S. media connected the torture and killing of prisoners with earlier historical examples of U.S. approval, use, and dissemination of "dirty war" methods, as evidenced by the CIA and army "torture manuals" released in the mid-1990s, numerous Latin American sources, and previous journalistic and scholarly investigations.

Journalist Seymour Hersh, citing high-ranking intelligence sources, wrote in May 2004 that the roots of the torture scandal lay in a decision by Secretary of Defense Donald Rumsfeld to expand a highly secret operation, already in use against Al Qaeda in Afghanistan, to Iraqi prisoners.[7] This decision gave blanket preapproval to elite U.S. Special Forces to kill, capture, and use harsh interrogation methods against prisoners—that is, torture. The "black operation" involved commandos and operatives from CIA paramilitary units, the army's Delta force, and other special forces, and it operated with no traceability and no (official) budget. Commandos were authorized to cross borders without visas, to essentially disappear and hold prisoners in secret CIA detention centers, to operate outside the normal chain of command, and to create an environment in which "no rules applied." The operation bore a striking resemblance to the Cold War program known as Operation Condor.

Loud voices have continued to argue that the only response to international terrorism is to suspend lawful methods and expand unchecked military and intelligence power. Indeed, some have claimed that the democratic limits and controls placed on such secret powers previously were the cause of 9/11. But as this book shows, U.S. sanctioning of extralegal and aberrant methods during the Cold War led to widespread human rights violations and crimes against humanity in Latin America and elsewhere. Reflecting on the destruction wrought by Operation Condor is, therefore, more important than ever today.

The lessons of the Cold War have been forgotten—if, indeed, they were ever learned by those in power. The methods and strategies of terror, once they are approved by political leaders and adopted by armed, security, and intelligence forces, are not easily unlearned or controlled. Unless governments and militaries, particularly those that profess to be democratic, explicitly repudiate the use of terror (or counterterror) in the name of a higher cause, the world's people will be threatened by the specter of new Condor-like organizations and new dirty wars. This book critically analyzes the pathologies of Operation Condor. I hope that it makes a contribution to understanding its causes and to advancing the search for truth and justice.

Notes

1. For a lucid exposition on U.S. policy in the context of just war criteria, see Patrick Hayden, "The War on Terrorism and the Just Use of Military Force," in Patrick Hayden, Tom Lansford, and Robert P. Watson, eds., *America's War on Terror* (Burlington, Vt.: Ashgate Publishing, 2004), 105–121.
2. Afsane Bassir Pour, "The Red Cross Accuses: 'The Photos Are Shocking, But Our Reports Are Worse,'" *Le Monde* (France), May 5, 2004.
3. John Mintz, "Britons Allege Guantánamo Abuse in Letter to Bush," *Washington Post*, May 14, 2004.
4. James Risen, David Johnston, and Neil A. Lewis, "Harsh CIA Methods Cited in Top Qaeda Interrogations," *New York Times*, May 13, 2004.
5. Major General Antonio M. Taguba, "Article 15-6 Investigation of the 800th Military Police Brigade," (internal U.S. Army report on Iraqi prisoner abuse), accessed by author on May 14, 2004 at www.msnbc.msn.com/id/4894001, pp. 16, 28; Julian Borger, "Jailed Iraqis Hidden from Red Cross, Says U.S. Army," *The Guardian* (U.K.), May 5, 2004. For information on prisoner deaths under interrogation, see Steven Lee Myers, "Military Completed Death Certificates for 20 Prisoners Only after Months Passed," *New York Times*, May 31, 2004.
6. See, for example, Dana Priest and R. Jeffrey Smith, "Memo Offered Justification for Use of Torture," *Washington Post*, June 8, 2004.
7. Seymour M. Hersh, "The Gray Zone," *The New Yorker*, May 24, 2004. Much of his report was substantiated by John Barry, Michael Hirsh, and Michael Isikoff in "The Roots of Torture," *Newsweek*, May 24, 2004. See also the *Washington Post*

editorial "Mr. Rumsfeld's Responsibility," of May 6, 2004, fixing blame on the defense secretary for fostering a lawless environment by indiscriminately designating prisoners as beyond the reach of the law; and Seymour M. Hersh, *Chain of Command: The Road from 9/11 to Abu Ghraib* (New York: HarperCollins Publishers, 2004).

Acknowledgments

THE RESEARCH FOR THIS BOOK was conducted over more than a decade. I began to gather information on the shadowy repressive system while living in Buenos Aires in 1992. My investigations over the next years took me back to Argentina many times and to five more Latin American countries (Brazil, Chile, Honduras, Paraguay, Uruguay), several more than once. During these years, numerous people assisted me. First, I wish to thank all my sources and interviewees, many of whom are cited in the study and some of whom wished to remain anonymous. Next, with apologies to those inadvertently omitted, I gratefully acknowledge those who helped me at various stages of this project: Pierre Abramovici, Martín Almada, Matt Armstrong, Beatriz Barrera, Giulia Barrera, Longino Becerra, Samuel Blixen, Oscar Bolioli, Jo-Marie Burt, Pat and Barbara Carney, Elaine Carey, Stella Calloni, Lilián Celiberti, Pablo Chargoñia, Margaret Crahan, Ramón Custodio, the late José D'Andrea Mohr, María Delgado, Ximena Erazo, Manuel Flores Silva, Donald Fraser, Mireya García R., Roberto Garretón, "Tex" Harris, the Institute for Policy Studies, Saul Landau, Brian Loveman, Miriam Malina, João Roberto Martins Filho, Anya Maria Mayans, Michael McClintock, Sara Méndez, Felipe Michelini, Rafael Michelini, the late Emilio Mignone, Osman Morales, Joseph E. Mulligan, Bertha Oliva, Raúl Olivera, Ramón Oquelí, Rosa Palau, Susan Peacock, Tania Pellegrini, Jaime Pizarro, Marcial Riquelme, Francisco Rivera, Marie-Monique Robin, Paz Rojas, Milton Romani Gerner, Graciela Romero and SERPAJ-Uruguay, Christine Turner, Juan Angel Urruzola, Douglas Valentine, Leo Valladares Lanza, and Robert White. Special thanks to Ariel Armony and Raúl Molina Mejía, who read the entire manuscript, and to Rose Muzio

Dormani, John Ehrenberg, I. Leonard Markovitz, and Rafael Michelini, who read sections of it. I also thank the anonymous reviewers for Rowman & Littlefield and my editor, Susan McEachern. All of them helped make this a better book. As always, I am responsible for any errors of fact or interpretation that remain. Finally, I am grateful to Long Island University, and to Guillermo Kerber Mas and the International Programme of the World Council of Churches, for their generous support of my research.

Note to Readers on Sources

WRITING A BOOK ON COVERT OPERATIONS is fraught with methodological dangers and complicated judgment calls. The first difficulty is the inherent problem of documenting covert operations. Covert operations are designed to be plausibly denied, their sponsors concealed. Such operations may employ contract agents, who are not official employees of any intelligence agency and whose links to the sponsoring entity can be denied. A key element of counterinsurgency strategy is psychological operations (PSYOPS or PSYWAR), which use propaganda to muddy the waters and deliberate misrepresentation to conceal a covert operation's perpetrators.

Clearly, reconstructing the secret history of Operation Condor is a difficult task, especially for researchers without abundant resources or subpoena power. Top Latin American officers, as well as knowledgeable U.S. officials, are still reluctant to discuss Condor, and some still deny its very existence. Declassified U.S. documents must be used with care; the selective nature of the documents approved for release may in itself constitute a manipulation of the historical record. Likewise, selective deletions in each document may leave an impression that is actually contrary to the meaning of the document. Sensitive information is often left out of official documents completely. As one foreign service officer put it, "the most significant diplomatic exchanges rarely get into official documents in this age of secure telephones and overwhelming fear of leaks." He emphasized the importance of oral histories and said that without them, "tomorrow's scholars would get much of the history wrong."[1] Official statements by government officials cannot be taken at face value, either. Such statements must be critically evaluated, factoring in the interests of the individual and his or her credibility. Finally, many testimonies about intelligence operations come from persons whose credibility is questionable. Military and security officers who participated in Condor operations, cited in this study, may have mixed truth with lies—known as gray propaganda—making it hard to decipher the accuracy of their accounts. I have tried in this book to surmount these problems by triangulating confessions and statements by Condor operatives who have come forward with the oral histories of survivors and a large assortment of documents from declassified U.S. archives, from the Paraguayan Archives of Terror, from CELS (Argentina), from Arquivo Ana Lagôa (Brazil), from the reports of the Sábato Commission (Argentina) and the Rettig Commission (Chile), from the files of SERPAJ-Uruguay and Comisionado Nacional de los Derechos Humanos de Honduras, from the websites of Equipo Nizkor and the National Security Archive, and from numerous secondary sources. Undoubtedly, key elements of the history of Operation Condor remain hidden or obscure, however, to be excavated and analyzed by contemporary and future scholars.[2] Partially understood events will, I hope, be clarified through the release of new documents or new disclosures by participants.

To assess the available evidence the scholar of covert operations must use care, judgment, and experience and apply knowledge and expertise to draw plausible, if sometimes tentative, conclusions. Legal proof is one thing, but political historians are also required to use common sense, reasoned logic, and knowledge of intelligence methods and operations to discern the "fingerprints" of their sponsors. As Thomas Powers, a noted analyst of U.S. intelligence organizations, once wrote,

> Despite all the evidence gathered by the Church Committee, it never found anything like an order to kill Castro in writing, and it never found a witness who would confess explicitly that he had received such an order. The committee's response to the incomplete record was to leave the question of authority hanging. Must we do the same? Lacking a smoking gun in the form of an incriminatory document or personal testimony, we can reach no firm conclusion, but at the same time the available evidence leans heavily toward a finding that the Kennedys did, in fact, authorize the CIA to make an attempt on Castro's life.[3]

Lawrence Barcella, who prosecuted the case of a Condor double assassination—that of Chilean Orlando Letelier and his aide Ronni Moffitt in 1976—had the following to say about this dilemma:

> One must distinguish between two groups of appreciations. One corresponds to the evidence that may legally constitute proof in a trial. The other is common sense. The admissable proof that we gathered during our investigation permit-

> ted us to arrive at Contreras. There were other pieces that truly and strongly pointed toward the culpability of General Pinochet, as the person who ordered and directed the assassination. . . .The idea that General [*sic*] Contreras and DINA could have ordered and executed an operation of this magnitude—the attack against Letelier in the United States—without the authorization and approval of General Pinochet, is laughable.[4]

Douglas Valentine, whose research on the Phoenix Program (a ruthless Vietnam-era counterinsurgency operation) required him to interview many former intelligence personnel, had the following comment to make on this question:

> After spending 20 years studying the CIA, I feel entitled to make judgment calls. This extends into other areas, such as whether or not to believe someone. I think I have a good reason for feeling entitled to do this: by keeping its major operations secret, the CIA cannot be documented in certain situations. Its system of ascending security classifications and clearances is a direct assault on the First Amendment and the most insidious form of censorship in America. The CIA trusts that academics will abide by the rules (and most do), and it has suborned the major media lock, stock, and barrel. So major portions of our history have fallen into the black hole of official secrecy, and journalists are merely stenographers for the secret services.[5]

In sum, the scholar faces a set of daunting problems when attempting to unravel secret intelligence relationships and covert operations. In this study of Operation Condor, I have investigated a variety of sources, searching for patterns in operational methods and transnational associations and linkages. None of the available sources is infallible, though, and with sources that inspire particular skepticism I have made extra efforts to confirm or disconfirm their veracity, counterchecking against credible sources and seeking out experts. Some Condor operations remain clouded in controversy and mystery, however. In such cases, I have presented the available documents and conflicting testimonies, along with the context of the situation. I believe it important to acquaint U.S. readers with information already familiar to Latin Americans and to allow readers to draw their own conclusions. Needless to say, the historical record, not to mention the cause of justice, would be advanced by serious, government-funded investigations of Operation Condor and its crimes.

Notes

1. The quote is from Samuel Lewis, in *Foreign Service Journal* (July–August 2003): 49.

2. Another book on Condor by John Dinges, *The Condor Years*, was published as I was making final revisions to this manuscript; I was unable to incorporate a reading of it into this study.

3. Thomas Powers, "Inside the Department of Dirty Tricks," *Atlantic Monthly*, Vol. 244, no. 2 (August 1979): 14–15.

4. Alejandra Matus, "Lo de Letelier fue terrorismo internacional," *Página/12* (Argentina), September 26, 1999.

5. E-mail communication from Douglas Valentine to author, August 8, 2003.

1

What Was Operation Condor?

OPERATION CONDOR WAS A SECRET INTELLIGENCE and operations system created in the 1970s through which the South American military states shared intelligence and seized, tortured, and executed political opponents in one another's territory. Inspired by a continental security doctrine that targeted ideological enemies, the military states in the Condor system engaged in terrorist practices to destroy the "subversive threat" from the left and defend "Western, Christian civilization." The Condor apparatus was a secret component of a larger, U.S.-led counterinsurgency strategy to preempt or reverse social movements demanding political or socioeconomic change. Operation Condor embodied a key strategic concept of Cold War national security doctrine: the concept of *hemispheric defense* defined by *ideological frontiers*, superseding the more limited doctrine of territorial defense. "Subversives" were defined as those with dangerous ideas that challenged the traditional order, whether they were peaceful dissenters, social activists, or armed revolutionaries. As Argentine general Jorge Rafael Videla put it, in a much-quoted 1976 comment, "A terrorist is not just someone with a gun or a bomb, but also someone who spreads ideas that are contrary to Western and Christian civilization." To the anticommunist militaries and their U.S. sponsors, the Cold War was World War III, the "war of ideologies."

Winds of Change in Latin America

After World War II, social discontent spread throughout Latin America as large numbers of people began demanding new rights. Inspired by Franklin D.

Roosevelt's "Four Freedoms"—freedom of speech, freedom of religion, freedom from want, and freedom from fear—new leaders and movements called for justice and a "new deal." Latin America was then, as it is now, the world region most unequal in terms of distribution of wealth and income and patterns of land ownership. The legacies of the colonial hacienda system, with its tiny land-owning elites and vast rural worker and peasant sectors, contributed to this persisting inequality. So did traditions in many countries of autocratic and elitist governments that remained indifferent to the plight of their poor. Millions of people among the rural and urban laboring classes lived in bad housing, in conditions of illiteracy, malnutrition, and high infant mortality, with little opportunity to express grievances politically or effect peaceful reform. Movements for change were often met with repression. Foreign governments also played a role, especially the United States, which had supported "friendly" dictators in the region and often sent in the Marines to secure U.S. economic and political interests.

Combined with postwar social dissatisfaction was the growing tide of Third World nationalism. Prominent Latin American leaders and intellectuals linked underdevelopment in the Third World to neocolonial practices by the major Western states and demanded self-determination and control of national resources. Revolutionaries and nationalists in Latin America issued passionate calls for nationalization of foreign-owned businesses, along with greater political participation, agrarian reform, an end to repression, free education, and equality and justice for the oppressed.[1] The leftist vision of a socially just society found deep echoes in Latin America. In Guatemala, progressive nationalist Jacobo Arbenz, elected president in 1950, represented the new brand of reformist leader. He established new rights for workers and the indigenous majority and enacted an agrarian reform. The government bought unused lands and redistributed them to landless peasants in an effort to raise standards of living and modernize the economy. Unfortunately, Arbenz's program collided with the anticommunist agenda of the Eisenhower administration. The Guatemalan land reform led to the first U.S. covert operation in the Western Hemisphere.

Arbenz's agrarian reform affected the largest landowner in Guatemala: the U.S.-based United Fruit Company. The Eisenhower administration viewed Arbenz with suspicion, and the president authorized the Central Intelligence Agency (CIA) to organize his ouster. In 1954, working with right-wing forces in the country, the CIA secretly orchestrated Arbenz's overthrow. The U.S.-approved colonel installed as the new president reversed Arbenz's reforms and began a repressive sweep to crush Arbenz supporters. The putsch against Arbenz sent a message to those who sought social reform in Latin America: even moderate, constitutional change affecting U.S. interests would be opposed by the colossus of the north as well as by local oligarchies. Some concluded that armed struggle would be necessary to overcome the power of dominant classes and restructure elitist and exclusionary systems.

In 1959, the Cuban revolution erupted, forcing the exit of U.S. anticommunist ally Fulgencio Batista and dramatically challenging U.S. hegemonic presumptions. The Cuban revolution sent shock waves through the region, igniting new social movements (including several guerrilla organizations) as well as right-wing reactions. Newly politicized sectors—workers, peasants, students, intellectuals, and religious—demanded a new social order. Radical and nationalist projects galvanized masses of people throughout Latin America, who called for solutions to persisting underdevelopment, lack of democracy, and injustice. The Catholic Church, long allied with regional elites, began to change as well, with a new doctrine of Liberation Theology. The doctrine proclaimed "a preferential option for the poor" and legitimized the struggle against "institutionalized violence," the everyday brutalities that human-made inequality and poverty inflicted on the dispossessed. Latin American intellectuals formulated theories of dependency, a complex of ideas positing that foreign extraction of natural resources and imperial exploitation had robbed the region of its wealth and distorted its possibilities for development. Hunger for change was everywhere.

In the midst of this social mobilization, U.S. national security strategists (who feared "another Cuba") and their Latin American counterparts began to regard large sectors of these societies as potentially or actually subversive. They especially feared leftist or nationalist leaders who were popularly elected, thus giving their ideas legitimacy. Washington responded to the Cuban revolution by strengthening Latin American military-security forces and honing a security doctrine that targeted "internal enemies." National security doctrine—a politicized doctrine of internal war and counterrevolution that targeted the enemy within—gave the militaries a messianic mission: to remake their states and societies and eliminate "subversion." Political and social conflict was viewed through the lens of countersubversive war. The counterinsurgents believed that world communism had infiltrated their societies, and the doctrine advocated and legitimated an expansive and politicized role for the armed forces to combat it. Moreover, harsh, extralegal methods were considered legitimate in a total war against subversion.

In the 1960s, '70s, and early '80s, U.S.-backed armed forces carried out military coups throughout Latin America, moving to obliterate leftist forces and extirpate leftist ideas. The militaries installed a new form of rule, which I have previously termed the national security state,[2] founded on the new security doctrine. These repressive systems transformed the political, economic, and cultural landscape in their countries, quite unlike previous coups and regimes.

A key aim of these states was to depoliticize and demobilize politically active groups and movements of workers, students, peasants, and intellectuals, which were identified as "internal enemies." The militaries acted to change the mentality of their people and quash democratic pressures from below. Their objectives went far beyond eliminating "guerrillas" or "communists."

Operation Condor, formed in the 1970s, extended the dirty wars across borders. The system's key members were the military regimes of Argentina, Chile, Uruguay, Paraguay, Bolivia, and Brazil, later joined by Ecuador and Peru in less central roles. Condor also enjoyed organizational, intelligence, financial, and technological sustenance from the United States, acting as a secret partner and sponsor. The Condor militaries made use of a highly sophisticated system of command, control, and intelligence in their counterinsurgency war against leftist and progressive forces. Within the framework of Operation Condor, military and paramilitary commandos "disappeared" refugees and exiles—including democratic leaders—who had fled coups and repression in their own countries. Some were targeted in Europe and the United States, and in 1980 Condor operations and methods appeared in Central America. Condor was a secret strike force of the military regimes, and it signified an unprecedented level of coordinated repression in Latin America.

The Condor System

The Condor system linked together secret units within the military intelligence forces of member countries into one transnational group or organization, focused on extraterritorial action. A former agent of Chile's secret police referred to the organization's commanders as the Condor Group. In each country, Condor operatives were drawn from branches of the military, intelligence organizations, and police, and also included right-wing civilians, all operating under centralized military command. Covert Condor operations were state policy under the military dictatorships of the era but were carried out largely by special squadrons that were top secret and not known to all government or military officials. Within the framework of Operation Condor, the military states implemented a calculated policy of extermination of their political enemies around the world. The fact that Condor was, in essence, a transnational criminal operation, has led judges and prosecutors in a number of European and Latin American countries to initiate legal cases against numerous Condor officers in recent years.[3]

The Condor system consisted of three levels. The first was mutual cooperation among military intelligence services, to coordinate political surveillance of targeted dissidents and exchange intelligence information. The second was covert action, a form of offensive unconventional warfare in which the role of the perpetrator remains concealed. Multinational Condor squadrons carried out covert cross-border operations to detain-disappear exiles and transfer them to their countries of origin, where most disappeared permanently. The third and most secret level was Condor's assassination capability, known as "Phase III." Under Phase III, special teams of assassins from member countries were formed to travel worldwide to eliminate "subversive enemies." Phase III was aimed at political leaders especially feared for their potential to mobilize world opinion or organize broad opposition to the military states.

Condor assassinations were so top secret that the military dictatorships took pains to publicly deny their involvement in them. In one notorious case in Buenos Aires in 1976, two exiled Uruguayan legislators known for their opposition to the Uruguayan military regime, Zelmar Michelini and Héctor Gutiérrez Ruiz, were abducted separately by sizable groups of armed men in broad daylight, at about the same time. Both were found dead several days later. The week before, they had organized a meeting in Buenos Aires of notable civilian and military Uruguayans to discuss the launching of a campaign to press for elections and the return to democracy in Uruguay. After their assassinations caused political shock waves in the region, several officials of the Argentine junta expressed their condolences, and junta leader Jorge Rafael Videla ordered a police investigation of the crimes.[4] In fact, the abductions-assassinations were covert Condor operations involving both Argentine and Uruguayan forces, with carte blanche from the junta. The Argentine state dissociated itself from the parallel forces that carried out the assassinations to preserve the covert nature and deniability of its involvement in Operation Condor.

Other victims of Phase III included constitutionalist Chilean general Carlos Prats, who had opposed the 1973 military coup in Chile, and his wife Sofía Cuthbert, in Buenos Aires (1974); Chilean Christian Democrat leader Bernardo Leighton and his wife, Ana Fresno, in Rome (1975); Chilean Orlando Letelier, foreign minister in the socialist Allende government and a fierce foe of the Pinochet regime, and his U.S. colleague Ronni Moffitt, in Washington, D.C. (1976); and nationalist former president of Bolivia Juan José Torres, in Buenos Aires (1976). Condor officers used irregular forces—essentially death squads acting on military orders—in these cases. In the Leighton and Letelier-Moffitt cases, respectively, agents of Chile's fearsome Directorate of National Intelligence (Dirección de Inteligencia Nacional, DINA) "contracted" neofascist organizations in Italy (Ordine Nuovo and Avanguardia Nazional) and right-wing Cuban exiles in the United States to collaborate in carrying out the crimes. In the Prats assassination, members of a neofascist group linked to Argentine military intelligence, Milicia, worked with DINA and Argentine security forces. Michael Townley, a U.S. expatriate and DINA assassin often linked to the CIA, admitted his operational role in these three terrorist acts (both DINA and the CIA denied that he was their agent and said he was working for the other).

Operation Condor was not a rogue or ad hoc operation, but a well-organized, sophisticated, and well-equipped network with systematized planning and training, operations and communications centers, and a chain of command in each country. A former DINA officer, Marcelo Moren Brito, testified that Condor operated "at the strategic level and was managed by the President"—Pinochet—and his subordinate, Manuel Contreras, chief of DINA. A Chilean court referred to Condor as "an extraofficial ("*no institucional*") organism that unified the secret police" of member countries. Condor operatives utilized dedicated communications networks and received specialized instruction. Several clandestine detention and torture centers were established in Buenos Aires explicitly for Condor's foreign prisoners. The most notorious was Orletti Motors, an abandoned garage equipped with torture devices and staffed by Uruguayan and Argentine military officers and former torturers of the Triple A (death squads sponsored by the previous Peronist government). Hundreds of Uruguayans, Bolivians, and Chileans were held in Orletti Motors, and Orletti survivors said that combined operations were conducted by military personnel of Argentina, Bolivia, Chile, Paraguay, and Uruguay.[5]

When, and why, do states turn to terrorist methods when faced with perceived threats? In his landmark study, E. V. Walter argued that state elites manipulate fear as a means of controlling society and maintaining power.[6] Terror is used to engineer compliant behavior not only among victims, but also among larger target populations. While victims suffer direct consequences, broad sectors of society are the principal target. The underlying goal of state terrorism, Walter suggests, is to eliminate potential power contenders and to impose silence and political paralysis, thereby consolidating existing power relations. The proximate end is to instill terror in society, the ultimate end is control. Condor's targets were persons who espoused political, economic, and social programs at odds with the ideologies and plans of the military dictatorships, their elite allies, and their sponsors in Washington. Through the use of terror, the military states sought to extinguish the aspirations for social justice and deeper democracy held by millions of people during the 1960s and '70s. The evidence suggests that Operation Condor, and the generalized repression of the Cold War years in Latin America, represented a military "solution" to an age-old problem: the distribution of power and wealth in human society, who gets what, how, and why.

Characteristics of Operation Condor

What were the defining features of Operation Condor? First, its specialization: *cross-border and foreign operations against exiles.* In this sense, Condor was a subset of the broader repression carried out by the militaries within their own territories, although they used the same methods. Condor squads carried out cross-border surveillance, targeting, abduction, torture, and transfer of exiles, working with counterpart intelligence apparatuses or with extreme-right paramilitary networks in member countries. Operations were directed by specialized units within larger intelligence organs of the Condor countries, such as the Foreign Department of the gestapo-like DINA and the Extraterritorial Task Force (GTE) of the Argentine army intelligence apparatus, Battalion 601. Condor member governments aided one another by supplying agents with passports and visas, funds, cars, aircraft, personnel, and other logistical assistance. The existing system of military attachés was used as a convenient posting for Condor agents, who then acted as conduits for intelligence and communications and supervised covert operations. Condor allowed the militaries to act with impunity against exiles in associated countries, erasing traditional principles of asylum and political sanctuary long honored in the region.

A second trait of Condor was its *multinational character.* Operation Condor united militaries that had previously considered themselves adversaries and had long histories of suspicion and conflict. On the operational level, Condor units included specially trained men from two or more countries, organized into squadrons or task forces based on the model of Special Forces teams, with expertise in unconventional warfare and "counterterror" operations (the use of "terror to fight terror"). One 1976 Defense Intelligence Agency (DIA) report stated, for example, that one Condor unit was "structured much like a U.S. Special Forces Team" and was preparing to carry out Phase III assassination operations.[7] Condor utilized psychological warfare (PSYWAR or PSYOPS), especially use of black propaganda, deception, and disinformation to control and manipulate the "hearts and minds" of the population. One common tactic was to make Condor acts appear to be committed by the left, to confuse the public, achieve political goals, increase terror, disrupt and discredit opposition forces, and absolve the state of responsibility. As parallel structures of the state, Condor units usually reported directly to a top army or intelligence commander, outside of ordinary command channels. Finally, Condor interrogation teams consisted of intelligence officers from two or more countries.

A third defining feature of Condor was its *precise and selective targeting of dissidents.* Unlike the broader, more arbitrary disappearances of thousands of civilians in the Condor countries, Condor specialized in the "decapitation" of exiled leaders or members of leftist, popular, and revolutionary organizations, and the elimination of actual or potential leaders of resistance to the military regimes. Some of Condor's victims were guerrillas, but not all; it is important to emphasize, additionally, that armed insurgents, like all individuals, were entitled under international law and civilized norms to due process and to freedom from torture and extrajudicial execution. Condor also targeted union leaders, social democrats, Christian democrats, nationalists, dissident generals, former presidents and congressional representatives, and others who were opposed to military dictatorship and repression in their countries.

A fourth distinguishing feature of Condor was its *parastatal structure*. Javier Giraldo has pointed out that the prefix "para" carries several meanings: (1) approximation, (2) transposition, and (3) deviation or irregularity. It signifies something next to, adjoining, similar to, but at the same time beyond, outside of, combining the senses of proximity and deformation.[8] A state-sponsored paramilitary force is one supplemental to regular military forces or serving as a proxy for them, parallel to the official military institution. The U.S. Defense Department defines paramilitaries as "distinct from the armed forces of any country, but resembling them in organization, equipment, training, or mission." Paramilitaries act as both intelligence assets and as instruments of terror and coercion in so-called black or black world operations (in military terminology). At the same time, they afford regular militaries and governments secrecy and plausible deniability. The use of paramilitary forces was an important instrument within the counterinsurgency strategies of the Condor militaries—and a central feature of U.S. counterinsurgency doctrine.

In this book, I define parastatal structures as the forces and infrastructure of "black world" special operations. This hidden part of the state—what I term the parallel state—includes parapolice and paramilitary forces, harbored and directed by the state, with access to a vast shadow infrastructure including secret prisons, fleets of unmarked cars and unregistered aircraft, unofficial cemeteries, secure communications systems, and other parallel structures funded by "black budgets." In Latin America, the parallel state augmented the lethal capabilities of the military dictatorships while allowing them to retain the appearance of legality and a certain legitimacy. Parastatal structures permitted the militaries to avoid international law and human rights guarantees, prevent public scrutiny, expand the powers of the state over society, and give the militaries free rein to utilize extreme and lawless methods against "subversion." The parastatal forces created by the counterinsurgents included the clandestine groups, secret intelligence organizations, "task forces," and civilian informant networks acting covertly on behalf of the state.

One of my central arguments is that Operation Condor was an offensive weapon of the parallel state and a component of it. Under Operation Condor, military intelligence organizations created special clandestine detention centers for foreign prisoners outside of the normal prison system, hidden in military bases or abandoned buildings. Torture and execution were rife in such centers. Exiles and refugees who were legally arrested could be passed into the covert Condor system, at which point all information available to the outside world about the person ceased. Prisoners were transferred across borders without passports, on unregistered flights, and like the other disappeared, their detention and imprisonment were denied by the state. To avoid detection, Condor disposed of victims by burning their bodies or throwing them into the sea. The pervading sense of ambiguity, unreality, and dread created by the parallel state was a key element of the terror used by the militaries to consolidate power over society. In subsequent sections of this chapter I further develop the concept of the parallel state and discuss the impact of U.S. security doctrine and training on its formation.

A fifth characteristic of Condor was its *advanced technology* and its access to substantial national and international resources. Condor employed a computerized database of thousands of individuals considered politically suspect and had archives of photos, microfilms, surveillance reports, psychological profiles, reports on membership in organizations, personal and political histories, and lists of friends and family members, as well as files on all manner of organizations. Several sources indicate that the CIA provided powerful computers to the Condor system (and, in fact, no other country in the region was technologically capable of doing so). An Argentine military source told a U.S. Embassy contact in 1976 that the CIA had played a key role in setting up computerized links among the intelligence and operations units of the six Condor states.[9] A former Bolivian agent of Condor, Juan Carlos Fortún, told a Bolivian journalist in the early 1990s that an advanced system of communications was installed in the Ministry of the Interior in La Paz, along with a telex system interlinked with the five other Condor countries. He said that a special machine to encode and decode messages was made especially for the Condor system by the Logistics Department of the CIA.[10]

The Condor network's secure communications system, Condortel, enabled Condor controllers to exchange data on suspects, track the movement of individuals across borders on various forms of transport, and transmit orders to operations teams, as well as share and receive intelligence information across a large geographical area. Condortel allowed Condor operations centers in member countries to communicate with one another and with the parent station in a U.S. facility in the Panama Canal Zone. This link to the U.S. military-intelligence complex in Panama is a key piece of evidence regarding secret U.S. sponsorship of Condor, a discussion to which I return in chapter 3. Operation

Condor had access to an encrypted (or encoded) system within the secure U.S. communications network based in the Canal Zone.

A final characteristic of Condor was its *use of criminal syndicates and extremist organizations and networks* to carry out operations, especially Phase III assassinations. While Condor was an alliance among military states, it employed civilians and paramilitaries, another aspect of its parallel nature. Right-wing civilians formed part of Condor "hunter-killer" squads and tortured prisoners in secret detention centers such as Orletti Motors. In Argentina, such civilians became known as *inorgánicos* (inorganics, versus organic members of the intelligence forces). Declassified U.S. documents confirm this dimension of Operation Condor. According to a 1976 DIA report based on information provided by FBI attaché Robert Scherrer, "Source stated that team members [of Phase III death squads] would not be commissioned or non-commissioned officers of the armed forces, but rather 'special agents.'"[11]

Assassin Michael Townley, for example, worked within the fascist paramilitary organization Patria y Libertad in Chile during the leftist Allende administration (1970–1973) and collaborated in Argentina with both extremist army officers and right-wing death squads linked to them such as Milicia, Libertadores de América, and Triple A. Townley joined DINA in 1974. In Argentina, a group of former Triple A death squad operatives led by right-wing gangster Aníbal Gordon ran Orletti Motors in 1976, under the command of General Otto Paladino, the head of state intelligence agency SIDE (Secretaría de Inteligencia de Estado) and a Condor officer. Later, in Central America, Argentine Condor officers and the anticommunist militaries in Honduras, El Salvador, and Guatemala worked closely with the Nicaraguan contras, an antistate paramilitary army, to overthrow the revolutionary Sandinista government. In the latter case, Condor as an interstatal organization made shrewd use of antistatal networks to carry out operations, camouflage its activities, and broaden its rightist base.

Finally, officers linked to Condor, from the most aggressive and fanatical sectors of the military, also moved to purge constitutionalist officers from their own ranks in order to consolidate the power of the counterinsurgency sector and move military institutions to the far right in the service of the anticommunist cause. The Brazilian military purged its own forces after the 1964 coup, and in Chile, DINA carried out significant repression against constitutionalist officers within the Chilean armed forces after the 1973 coup.

Analytical Framework

Operation Condor emerged in the context of a new form of warfare in world history: counterinsurgency. This book argues that this new form of warfare transformed the nature of state and society just as conventional, "industrial" warfare had done in the early twentieth century. Omer Bartov defines industrial killing, which first emerged in World War I, as "the mechanized, impersonal, and sustained mass destruction of human beings, organized and sustained by states."[12] Modern industrial warfare, he asserts, resulted in the expansion of the state and its penetration of society.[13] Counterinsurgency war—conducted in the shadows, using paramilitary forces and secret armies operating outside lawful state action—greatly deepened this penetration and control of society through its explicit targeting of the civilian population rather than an opposing army.

I frame the argument of this book around several central conceptual propositions. First, counterinsurgency warfare restructured state and society in profound ways. Second, intrinsically linked to the counterinsurgents' reshaping of the polity was their creation and mobilization of a parallel or shadow state apparatus engineered to implement and extend the state's repressive power over society. This parallel apparatus was created to carry out covert or secret policies, to avoid legal constraints, and to circumvent any form of accountability. Third, Operation Condor as a transnational state terror system was a product of counterinsurgency doctrine and training, a cross-border component of the parallel state created by the military regimes.

A fourth proposition, suggested by patterns in the data, provides an explanation for the first three phenomena: the Latin American militaries, normally acting with the support of the U.S. government, overthrew civilian governments and destroyed other centers of democratic power in their societies (parties, unions, universities, and constitutionalist sectors of the armed forces) precisely when the class orientation of the state was about to change or was in the process of change, shifting state power to non-elite social sectors. That is, political resources and power appeared to be within the grasp of previously marginalized social sectors. Preventing such transformations of the state was a key objective of Latin American elites, and U.S. officials considered it a vital national security interest as well. According to one important study, death squads are most prevalent "in societies where an authoritarian alliance between the military and a powerful economic elite is faced with a serious challenge to its legitimacy and authority. What the ruling elite fear most is an opposition movement that can mobilize the rural and urban poor behind efforts to redistribute political power and economic resources."[14] My research indicates that Condor death squads were created as an integral part of a broader counterinsurgency or "counterterror" campaign condoned by elite groups as well as their key foreign ally, the United States. We now turn to a fuller discussion of each element of the analysis.

The Role of Counterinsurgency

The emphasis on counterinsurgent political action represented a major change in U.S. military doctrine and mission and had profound effects in Latin America. Counterinsurgency doctrine advocated: (1) the organization and use of closely controlled indigenous paramilitary and irregular forces, networks of informants, and other civilian auxiliaries as "force multipliers" and intelligence gatherers; (2) the expansion of state intelligence organizations to monitor and control society; (3) the use of political-ideological criteria to determine friendly and hostile sectors of society; (4) the use of terror (later called "counterterror") to control society and eliminate opposition leaders; (5) the use of psychological warfare (PSYWAR) to manipulate the political climate and prepare a population for violence through black propaganda and/or the use of fear. The reorganization of the state to implement these objectives profoundly altered government's relation to its citizens and deeply transformed both the state itself and society. Rather than serving its citizens, as in the modern Western model, government became a predatory force that instilled fear, confusion, and disorientation among its citizens. Moreover, covert action and the use of paramilitaries—both central to counterinsurgency warfare—constituted what Human Rights Watch (HRW) once called "a strategy of impunity." Militaries carried out dirty wars and terrorist acts, while officials—often with the complicity of Washington—were able to deny them.

Counterinsurgency warfare in its modern form is often identified with the French military, which developed new methods to fight anticolonial insurgencies and independence movements in Indochina and Algeria in the 1940s and 1950s. Military strategists defined counterinsurgency warfare as "low intensity" warfare, below the threshold of conventional war and employing specially trained commando units. The aim of counterinsurgency forces was to defeat guerrilla insurgencies seeking to change the political system and to deter social unrest through political, ideological, economic, social, and psychological as well as military means. The French emphasized that insurgency was political and ideological, not just military, in nature. As French expert Bernard Fall put it, "revolutionary warfare equals guerrilla warfare plus political action,"[15] and to defeat guerrilla movements, counterinsurgent militaries needed to confront them in the political and ideological realms. The counterinsurgents aimed to forcibly assert government control over the population, using irregular or paramilitary forces in conjunction with military units. Moreover, counterinsurgency war was dirty war. As French theorist David Galula argued, "If the counterinsurgent wishes to bring a quicker end to the war, he must discard some of the legal concepts that would be applicable to ordinary conditions."[16]

During the Cold War, U.S. policymakers and counterinsurgency specialists argued that behind all dissent or political opposition in the developing world was a ubiquitous communist movement directed by Moscow, a movement that relied on terror to achieve its goals. The East-West paradigm and assumption of Soviet subversion utterly failed to explain many popular struggles in Latin America and elsewhere, however. Concurrent with the rise of the Cold War was the eruption of nationalist sentiment in the Third World, as we have seen. While the USSR and Cuba were sympathetic to indigenous revolutionary movements, they did not create them. Most scholars concur that social protest and revolutionary movements in the Americas were the product of indigenous conditions coupled with a crisis of state legitimacy. Unequal socioeconomic structures and skewed distribution of wealth, poverty and economic hardship, lack of democracy, repression, and truncated freedoms for the vast majority of the populace: these conditions reflected excessive and undemocratic concentrations of political and economic power. The appeal of radical change to many people in Latin America was based not on terror by insurgents (as counterinsurgents supposed), but on the dream of social justice and better lives for their children. For those living in intolerable conditions, the realization that change was possible was deeply liberating.

Early U.S. Guerrilla Operations

D. H. Berger, McClintock, and others have shown that early anticommunist operations by U.S. and allied forces in the 1940s utilized guerrilla rather than counterguerrilla forces. As fear of Soviet power expanded among U.S. policy circles in the late 1940s, veterans of special operations during World War II moved to apply them again against the USSR. As Berger notes, "covert paramilitary activity has its genesis *as a policy tool* of the US in the latter stages of World War II and the immediate post-war period."[17] Berger describes the use of indigenous paramilitary forces by allied nations behind enemy lines in World War II and the ways in which similar parallel formations were organized to fight communism in the late 1940s and early 1950s. The newly formed CIA conducted and led paramilitary operations throughout Europe and Asia during the early part of the Cold War. Covert action allowed Washington to secretly move beyond its stated strategy of containment to employ aggressive, offensive action against perceived communist threats. General William Donovan, founder of a special operations branch of the military in 1941, especially promoted the use of physical subversion, sabotage, and guerrilla warfare in support of conventional military operations. He forcefully advocated the formation of quasi-military guerrilla forces and the establishment and support of small paramilitary groups in targeted countries.[18] The U.S. security apparatus invested massive resources to create and develop anticommunist organizations throughout the world, including "stay-behind armies" throughout Western Europe, parallel forces discussed in chapter 2.

By the 1960s, as McClintock shows, strategists decided to fight revolutionaries and guerrillas by creating *counterguerrilla* forces made up of military officers and paramilitary irregulars who used the methods of terror.[19] The U.S. Army Special Forces worked in tandem with the CIA to form paramilitary forces from minority groups in Vietnam, for example, for two basic reasons: to broaden and strengthen the counterinsurgency effort and to prevent the Vietnamese revolutionaries from recruiting these social sectors and gaining control of their strategic lands. Some 17,000 people were incorporated.[20] This practice—also used in Central America with the organization of ORDEN, Organización Democrática Nacionalista, or Democratic Nationalist Organization, in El Salvador and, later, the Civil Patrols in Guatemala—ensured military control of the population, forced civilians to mobilize for combat and intelligence functions, and disrupted ordinary community life by militarizing civil society. The divisions in society were made clear: one was forced to make a choice between the insurgents and the government. Neutrality was not an option; often, it was considered a sign of incipient subversion. Thus, this component of counterinsurgency warfare—the creation of parallel military formations—was a key factor in the radical reorganization of state and society.

Modeled on the special operations forces of the U.S. military, counterinsurgent guerrillas used repressive methods to control target populations. One 1968 U.S. Army manual detailed ways to create irregular forces to counter subversion and gave instructions in the use of psychological warfare, countersabotage, and repression[21] in the cause of "internal defense." The manual instructed officers to periodically photograph all residents in an area, conduct surprise relocations of residents, and "register" individuals or houses in counterguerrilla sweeps, among other tactics. The secrecy associated with counterinsurgency warfare was directly related to its objective to dominate civilian populations, using the methods of terror if necessary. As General Paul Gorman, then chief of the U.S. Southern Command (SOUTHCOM, the military headquarters for the Western hemisphere based then in the Panama Canal Zone), said in 1984, counterinsurgency is "a form of warfare repugnant to Americans, a conflict which involves innocents, in which non-combatant casualties may be an explicit object."[22] One 1962 U.S. Army PSYOPS manual stated:

> Civilians in the operational area may be supporting their own government or collaborating with an enemy occupation force. An isolation program designed to

> instill doubt and fear may be carried out, and a positive political action program designed to elicit active support of the guerrillas also may be effected. If these programs fail, it may become necessary to take more aggressive action in the form of harsh treatment or even abductions.[23]

McClintock found that a classified U.S. Army Special Forces manual of December 1960, *Counter-Insurgency Operations*, was one of the earliest to mention explicitly, in its section "Terror Operations," the use of counterinsurgent terror as a legitimate tactic.[24] Other secret U.S. Army special operations handbooks and articles from the 1960s endorsed counterterror, including assassination and abduction, in certain situations. A March 1961 article in *Military Review* stated, for example, "Political warfare, in short, is warfare . . . [that] embraces diverse forms of coercion and violence including strikes and riots, economic sanctions, subsidies for guerrilla or proxy warfare and, when necessary, kidnapping or assassination of enemy elites."[25] The Special Forces in Vietnam received orders in 1965 to "conduct operations to dislodge VC-controlled [VC was Viet Cong, the Vietnamese communists] officials, to include assassination" and specified that small commando units would be "ambushing, raiding, sabotaging, and committing acts of terrorism" against the insurgents.[26] In short, the use of terrorism was an integral part of U.S. counterinsurgency operations and training in the 1960s.

The counterinsurgents perceived that revolutionary war was primarily a political struggle.[27] But counterinsurgency theory assumed that revolutionaries triumphed through the skillful use of manipulation, control, and terror. Thus, in what McClintock calls a "mirror imaging" effect, such methods formed the central thrust of counterinsurgency doctrine. An example of such mirror imaging appeared in a January 1965 letter from the Headquarters of the U.S. 5th Special Forces Group (Airborne) to commanders:

> Definition: The SF [Special Forces] Counterinsurgency program is a phased and combined military-civil counterinsurgency effort designed to accomplish the following objectives: (a) destroy the Viet Cong and create a secure environment; (b) firm governmental control over the population; and (c) enlist the population's active and willing support of, and participation in, the government's programs.[28]

The U.S. objective to gain control over indigenous peoples and forcibly "enlist" their allegiance failed in Vietnam, and not only because people everywhere resent foreign domination and coercive methods. As outlined earlier, the roots of social movements and nationalist insurgencies were more complex than military orthodoxy perceived. "Friendly" pro-U.S. governments were often deeply repressive, corrupt, and hostile to social reforms. The counterinsurgents misunderstood the essential human motivations and real grievances that drove millions of people to protest their conditions and join popular or insurgent struggles. As two early critics of counterinsurgency theory argued, "For years French officers, who have become the leading theorists of 'revolutionary war,' persisted in ignoring the simple fact that most Algerian Moslems were not interested in becoming part of the greater French nation."[29]

The U.S. government launched counterinsurgency programs throughout the developing world in the 1960s. Counterinsurgency warfare, directed against insurgents and broad civilian sectors of society, was, above all, a mechanism to secure social control and "stability," protecting the interests of the counterinsurgent forces and the political-economic system that fostered them against a real or potential challenge from below. As the mechanization and depersonalization of combat resulted in industrial killing in the two world wars, as Bartov notes, so counterinsurgency warfare, in practice, produced "industrial repression." Counterinsurgency militaries organized massive new state and parastatal apparatuses for intelligence, surveillance, and social control, including secret torture-disappearance-killing systems and new technologies of violence to terrorize whole populations.

Counterinsurgency Warfare in Latin America

In Latin America, both the French and U.S. governments were key proponents and sponsors of counterinsurgency doctrine and the unconventional warfare model of organization for military forces. In 2003, Manuel Contreras, the former chief of DINA, said that the French had trained DINA operatives in methods of dirty war and counterrevolution based on their experience in Algeria. Additionally, he said, the French terrorist group named the Secret Army Organization of France (OAS)—which staged a coup attempt and an assassination attempt against President Charles de Gaulle in Paris in 1962—was a model for DINA. French officer Paul Aussaresses, who had participated in torture in Algeria and whose descriptions and justifications of torture resulted in a criminal conviction in France in 2001, also trained U.S. officers in Fort Bragg, North Carolina, and Panama in the early 1960s. He instructed Latin American officers in interrogation techniques in Manaus, Brazil, in the 1970s when he was a military attaché there. The training in French methods of counterrevolutionary war included torture techniques and the formation of death squads, Aussaresses said. Indeed, the Frenchman said he had translated French manuals on torture into English during his time in the States.[30] Aussaresses was named military attaché in Washington, D.C., in 1961. One of his U.S. trainees, Robert Komer, later became one of the organizers of the

Phoenix Program, the deadly counterinsurgency campaign that resulted in tens of thousands of civilian deaths in Vietnam.[31]

The French impact was crucial, but given the status of the U.S. government as the hemispheric hegemon, and its enormous resources, U.S. military influence was ultimately the more powerful in Latin America. U.S. national security doctrine and training were imparted to tens of thousands of Latin American officers through U.S. training centers (such as the Army School of the Americas) and in-country Mobile Training Teams (MTTs), equipped and financed through Military Assistance Programs (MAP) and, later, International Military Education and Training (IMET). The Latin American Special Action Force (1st Special Forces, 8th Special Forces Group) was stationed in the Panama Canal Zone in 1962 and was the main source of MTTs to disseminate the U.S. doctrine in Latin American countries.[32] MTTs specializing in counterinsurgency warfare advocated unconventional tactics such as subversion, sabotage, and terrorist activities against insurgents. The diffusion of the new security doctrine and organizational model was accompanied by massive U.S. expenditures to reshape the hemispheric security architecture and mobilize its military partners in a U.S.-led anticommunist crusade.

Recently declassified documents have shown that U.S. military trainers taught techniques of assassination as early as the 1950s in Guatemala and elsewhere.[33] U.S. national security doctrine, especially after the 1959 Cuban revolution, increasingly encouraged a concept of unconventional war subject to no rules or ethics, a "dirty war" to be won at all costs. U.S. military study plans and manuals from the 1960s were suffused with suspicion of popular movements, demonstrations, and public gatherings, assuming communist origin. Moreover, U.S. military and CIA training manuals declassified in the mid-1990s provided documented evidence that army and CIA instructors taught torture methods, such as the use of electroshock; the use of drugs and hypnosis to induce psychological regression; the sequential use of sensory deprivation, pain, and other means in interrogations; assassination methods; and the use of threats against and abduction of family members to break down prisoner resistance.[34]

The Latin American militaries, many of which had long occupied a dominant role in their societies and some of which had used torture before, began to characterize domestic conflicts as international communist conspiracies and portray themselves as the front lines in a global holy war. Over time, important sectors of the armed forces throughout the region were converted from conventional to unconventional forces that adopted counterinsurgency warfare and covert operations to combat "internal subversion." Covert paramilitary actions were a proactive tool allowing the counterinsurgents to prevent (or cause in other situations) the overthrow of a government in power.[35]

U.S. personnel assisted in the formation of special elite units to conduct aggressive, covert, offensive operations against domestic opposition, accompanied by CIA-designed PSYWAR programs. Significantly, such covert activity was to be used not only in situations of unrest or revolution, but as a preventive means to assure that such a situation would never materialize. As a secret U.S. national security policy document stated in 1962:

> Where subversive insurgency is virtually non-existent or incipient (PHASE I), the objective is to support the development of an adequate counter-insurgency capability in indigenous military forces through the Military Assistance Program, and to complement the nation-building programs of AID [Agency for International Development] with military civic action. The same means, in collaboration with AID and CIA, will be employed to develop a similar capability in indigenous para-military forces.[36]

Thus, even in peaceful Third World societies, it was U.S. policy to develop military counterinsurgency forces and add to their capabilities by creating paramilitary auxiliaries. Clearly, targeting people who *might* become insurgents was a strategy with deeply authoritarian and repressive implications. The assumption was that civilian populations were potentially subversive, even in the absence of lawless behavior. The creation of paramilitary forces served to "provide visible and effective demonstrations of the power of the state," as one U.S. Army study noted.[37] Thus, civilian sectors were weakened and progressive social change halted or reversed in numerous countries. The repressive forces of the state exponentially expanded in Latin America and elsewhere in the developing world, in many cases deployed against all forms of political opposition. U.S. doctrine and training deeply shaped the strategic perspectives, organization, logistics, operations, intelligence, and deployment of the Latin American armed forces. It was a policy that contributed to new forms of mass repression in Latin America.

Impact of Counterinsurgency on State and Society

The new security doctrine produced an expansion of the military role in Latin America as the armed forces inserted themselves in political, economic, social, psychological, and cultural spheres, and internationalized domestic conflicts by linking them to the "international communist movement." CIA personnel worked closely with SOUTHCOM and U.S. military intelligence structures to develop new intelligence organizations in Latin America that would integrate all countersubversive efforts—by police, military, and intelligence forces—under one command. These new organizations were central to the new counterinsurgency model, and they had access to sophisticated U.S. surveillance and communication technology. Organizations such as DINA (Chile), La Técnica (Paraguay), and Serviço Nacional de Informações (National Information Service—SNI, Brazil), all formed with CIA advice and support, became SS-like political policing organizations that were the main instruments of state terror in their societies. As the intelligence apparatus of the Latin American state expanded, the ideological assumptions of the new security doctrine guided its operations. Increasingly, a person's ideas—not illegal acts—were the criteria used in decisions to detain or disappear him or her. Counterinsurgency specialists also reengineered police forces and changed their mission from a law enforcement to a militarized model.[38]

An article based on declassified intelligence sources regarding the U.S.-led transformation of the Colombian military reveals much about the U.S. role in the militarization of state and society through counterinsurgency training, and the ensuing creation of parallel state structures. A U.S. military advisory team went to Colombia in 1959 to construct a new internal security infrastructure, develop "counter-guerrilla training, civil action programmes, intelligence structures, and communications networks" and aid the Colombians "to undertake offensive counter-insurgency and psychological warfare operations."[39] U.S. advisors led the reorientation of the army from conventional to unconventional warfare and the reorganization of its forces to focus on internal security. The U.S. team helped to create and organize Ranger commandos based on the special forces model, a new national intelligence structure, and new PSYWAR and civil action units.

The more sensitive U.S. efforts to bolster Colombia's internal security were "sterile and covert in nature" to avoid charges of imperialist intervention.[40] The U.S. team recommended the use of "third country nationals, covertly under U.S. control, but apparently contracted by the host government" to work with the Colombian forces. In 1961, with U.S. assistance, the Colombians created a new intelligence organization named Departamento Administrativo de Seguridad to perform both intelligence and counterintelligence functions and coordinate all the countersubversive operations of various security forces in the country. Also recommended by the U.S. program were "civilian registration programmes and other populace control measures" as well as "exhaustive interrogation of captured bandits and guerrillas using sodium pentothal and polygraph." U.S. Mobile Training Teams, composed of Special Operations Forces and intelligence advisors, assisted in the creation of "Intelligence/Hunter-Killer teams" to pursue subversives, which included both military and civilian operatives.[41] Such hunter-killer teams later characterized Operation Condor.

The U.S. team presented its final report to the U.S. Special Group (Counterinsurgency) with a secret supplement that advised extreme measures if Colombia's internal security faced heightened threats. Quoting the report, Dennis M. Rempe summarizes:

> Civilian and military personnel, clandestinely selected and trained in resistance operations, would be required in order to develop an underground civil and military structure. This organization was to undertake "clandestine execution of plans developed by the United States Government toward defined objectives in the political, economic, and military fields" . . . [including] "counter-agent and counter-propaganda" functions as well as "paramilitary, sabotage, and/or terrorist activities against known communist proponents."[42]

This revealing proposal exposed a U.S. policy to encourage and develop secret underground units—parallel structures that were essentially death squads—to carry out terrorist acts.[43] Moreover, such units operated not only in the service of their own military, but also to advance U.S.-defined plans and objectives. Later, Operation Condor fit the profile of such a covert structure; therefore, this secret document sheds light on the reasons why contemporary U.S. military and intelligence documents portrayed Condor as a legitimate and valuable counterterror organization.[44]

National security doctrine's emphasis on the internal enemy and the extralegal methods it advocated had profound ramifications in Latin America. Far from focusing only on communist guerrillas, the militaries increasingly targeted broad sectors of society as subversive. New internal security systems erased the boundaries between war and peace, guilt and innocence, deeply rending the social fabric and destroying the bonds of trust between government and society and within society. The focus on war by stealth, against civilian populations, gave rise to strategies of state terror that led to the brutalization, torture, and murder of tens of thousands of people. As Jaime Malamud Goti vividly described state terror in Argentina:

> Repression targeted vast social segments. Indeed, the generals' speeches revealed that the social areas they considered contaminated by subversion were the religious, the political, the educational, the economic, and cultural. Except for a few citizens who stood beyond suspicion, the rest of society was considered to be vulnerable to the inviting advances of this enemy with infinite shapes. Among those mentioned as "subversives" by state's officials of the 70s's [*sic*] impassioned speeches were . . . "contractualists," "empiricists," "utilitarians," "positivists," "rationalists," and "Freudians." To quell this infinite threat, terror became the regime's principal political tool.[45]

Military terror atomized and traumatized society and caused citizens to retreat to private life. The overwhelming presence of the terrorist state created fear, dissolved social networks, and paralyzed collective political action. In some countries, meetings of any kind (including birthday parties) required state permission. Many witnessed armed squadrons of men break down a neighbor's door and drag him or her away. Overall, counterinsurgency warfare against "internal enemies" produced a dramatic enlargement of military political power in state and society. Moreover, this form of warfare led directly to the creation of the parallel state.

Utility of the Concept of the Parallel State

To secure at least a minimal acceptance of their legitimacy, the national security states needed to mask the involvement of the state in the atrocities being carried on. Thus, the military rulers created shadow systems to carry out illegal acts that were, on the one hand, visible—part of the strategy of terror—but on the other, deniable. The parallel state allowed the military rulers to claim that the waves of torture, disappearance, and assassination that engulfed their countries were the work of "out-of-control death squads" or "internecine conflicts within the left." And, at some times, these regimes were able to achieve a partial legitimacy, especially vis-à-vis elite groups, based on regime policies that favored elite economic interests and eliminated the "leftist threat."

The parallel state apparatus was thus the invisible side of the military state but closely linked—if secretly—to its visible face. Parastatal death squads carried out disappearances, torture, assassination, and extrajudicial execution covertly, as an appendage of the visible state and under its orders, while affording the military governments deniability and disclaimability. Parastatal structures were, therefore, an integral part of the internal security apparatus of the military states. While appearing to be out-of-control forces, paramilitary units were actually more dangerous and more powerful because they acted under the secret direction of a military command, backed by the full resources of the state.

The parallel state was an instrument to accomplish secretly what could not be accomplished legally or politically. It was created to carry out policies that violated all laws and norms and to circumvent any limits on the coercive power of the state, allowing the state to use extreme violence against "internal enemies" beyond all civilized boundaries, with no lawful constraints and with total impunity. Parallel state structures were "state owned," but they were a deformation of a legitimate state.

Some analysts have used the term "parallel power" to refer to autonomous social networks that compete with legitimate state power, such as drug traffickers or gangs.[46] My concept is clearly different: I mean the state-created secret machinery of repression to carry out illegal operations and dirty wars. In one useful typology,[47] paramilitaries are defined along a spectrum of two key variables, loyalty to the state and level of autonomy, depending, respectively, on their political allegiance (or lack thereof) to the ruling elite and their level of self-sufficiency. Condor's parallel formations ranged between two categories, "Loyal/Dependent" and "Loyal/Semiautonomous," because they operated under military command, as arms of the state, albeit with a broad mandate.

The creation or use of parallel power structures always poses a risk to the state, however. Parallel organizations necessarily operate with substantial independence and may escape military command and control. By involving themselves in crime, drug trafficking, and other illicit operations to become self-financing, parallel groups can avoid accountability to their original masters. Structures of the parallel state may become powerful and independent forces within the state or outside of it, developing their own agendas and using their significant power to obtain self-defined objectives. Indeed, there have been examples of this phenomenon in Latin America, most recently in Colombia. The potential always exists that such groups will become "Frankenstein's monsters," further corrupting state and society.

Some might protest that the structures I am describing were not parallel at all, but rather comprised a new form of state apparatus. I myself have written extensively on the national security states and used that term to capture the idea of a new form of state based on Cold War national security doctrine. Nevertheless, I believe it valuable to delineate, name, and analyze the structures of the invisible state and to highlight their linkages to central organizational tenets of counterinsurgency doctrine. The concept of the parallel state sheds light on the ways in which states—both undemocratic and democratic—may resort to the use of parallel armies and covert operations in the name of a higher cause. Indeed, because parallel structures are fundamentally unaccountable and undemocratic whether they are used by states that are "democratic" or "undemocratic," the distinction between the two becomes blurred. An analysis of the parallel state highlights the dangers to democracy, the rule of law, and rights posed by such structures. Parallel structures drain power from traditional, representative state institutions. Power is exercised outside the legal framework in the most primitive forms. In Latin America, hidden and illegal formations of the state were expanded, while the security of the populace was erased. The parallel state facilitated the destruction of the democratic regimes, however imperfect, that had existed previously in Latin America. In Eric Nordlinger's terms, such shadow structures were a tool to expand state capacity and autonomy vis-à-vis society and to force society to conform to military rule.[48] They allowed the militaries to use the enormous capacities of the modern state to "transform the mentality" of their people through terror. The parallel state represented the growth of a new form of state power, a hidden component of newly rationalized and bureaucratized military dictatorships. It represented, in fact, the dark side of modernization, the application of science and technology to the ends of social and political control. This development evokes the concept of the garrison state proposed by Harold Lasswell in the 1940s. He then considered the possibility that military institutions—the "specialists in violence"—with access to powerful new technologies emerging in the scientific world, could exert new forms of control and repression that would dwarf previous tyrannies.[49] The parallel state was a key weapon with which the militaries achieved total power and engineered an enforced consensus, and silence, in their societies.

Condor as the Transnational Arm of the Parallel State

As suggested previously, Operation Condor was a manifestation of both counterinsurgency theory and practice and parallel state structures. As a transnational arm of the parallel state, the secret Condor system concealed the policy of the allied militaries to carry out coordinated abduction, torture, and assassination operations across borders. Some persons targeted by Condor were under UN protection as refugees and others were prominent prodemocracy leaders. The Condor system thus enabled the military states to camouflage international acts of terror. Such aggressive actions by U.S.-backed militaries would have been very difficult to carry out without the support or consent of Washington. In fact, evidence demonstrates that top U.S. leaders and national security officials considered Condor to be an effective weapon in the hemispheric anticommunist crusade. Key branches of the U.S. state, namely the executive, the State Department, the Defense Department, and the CIA, were not only closely informed of Condor operations but also supplied significant assistance and sustenance to the Condor system, and, indeed, actively collaborated with some of Condor's hunts for exiled political activists.

As part of the parallel state, Condor exercised unchecked power. Like other parastatal structures, it had a dual character: it was both invisible and visible—but deniable—at the same time. Condor served several functions: (1) it allowed the military states to eliminate political opponents who had escaped national jurisdiction, disregarding due process, while maintaining a quasi-legal face to domestic constituents and the international community; (2) it camouflaged the use of criminal methods, which might estrange actual and potential national and international allies or disrupt economic relations; (3) by operating in the shadows and attributing Condor atrocities to out-of-control groups, the military rulers made it difficult for survivors, human rights monitors, and critics to protest the Condor system, place responsibility on the military states, or take definitive action to stop them; and (4) Condor and the other elements of the state terror apparatus instilled terror and disorientation throughout the region.[50]

The Condor system takes on deeper meaning when viewed alongside the secret European "stay-behind" armies discovered in 1990, part of a U.S.-led, covert effort to set up secret structures parallel to (and sometimes opposed to) elected governments and democratic institutions at the dawn of the Cold War. The creation and utilization of parallel security structures long predated Condor, suggesting that Operation Condor was not an anomaly but rather a counterinsurgency weapon with historical roots.

The Class Orientation of the State

Finally, I argue that counterinsurgency was applied in countries where power seemed likely to shift to nonelite sectors associated with leftist, nationalist, or populist agendas, and away from traditional ruling elites. Such a shift was clearly unacceptable to the elites in question and, usually, to U.S. political leaders. Washington identified a series of nationalist, populist, and progressive movements and leaders in the developing world as "communist" and targeted them for neutralization or destruction.

It is important to note that U.S. policy in Latin America was not simply a series of mistakes based on misperceptions but was the continuation of a historical pattern of intervention and expansionism in the region aimed at protecting growing economic, political, and military interests. In 1823, U.S. leaders had proclaimed the Monroe Doctrine to discourage European influence in the Western hemisphere. Over time, the doctrine was reshaped, as in the 1904 Roosevelt corollary, to justify an expanding array of U.S. interests and "international police power" in the region.[51] The early U.S. seizure of Mexican lands (1846-1848) and acquisition of Spain's colonies in Puerto Rico, the Philippines, and elsewhere (1898) were driven by economic and security interests as well as ideas of national and racial superiority. In the first half of the twentieth century, U.S. leaders looked to right-wing autocrats worldwide as the best guarantors of stability, order, anti-Bolshevism, and openness to U.S. capitalist expansion.[52]

As U.S. investors increasingly sought raw materials and markets in Latin America, the U.S. government expanded its military reach to the Panama Canal and beyond, setting up military bases across the region. The early part of the twentieth century was marked by U.S. intervention in much of Central

America and the Caribbean (Cuba, Nicaragua, Honduras, Puerto Rico, the Dominican Republic, and elsewhere). In many cases, the marines created proxy forces, such as the national guards in Nicaragua and the Dominican Republic, to maintain "order" after their departure, and a series of pro-U.S. autocrats ruled for decades. The pattern of U.S. interventionism in Central America and the Caribbean in the twentieth century illuminated Washington's urge to control these regions and incorporate them within the U.S. political economy. Even during Franklin Delano Roosevelt's "Good Neighbor" period, the U.S. government maintained supportive relations with such dictators as Anastasio Somoza in Nicaragua and Jorge Ubico in Guatemala, ruthless men who willingly protected U.S. investments and generally accepted U.S. political orientations.

With the close of World War II and the establishment of the UN, U.S. policymakers increasingly shifted their foreign policy strategy in the developing world: from *overt* to *covert* intervention. By the 1960s, U.S. covert operations reached Brazil, Chile, and Uruguay, among other South American countries. The Cold War ideological focus on the evils of communism was a useful strategy for justifying U.S. support for anticommunist (and antidemocratic) dictators; it also provided a rationale for the pursuit of U.S. economic interests in the developing world. U.S. foreign policy during the Cold War was more than an anti-Soviet project. It was an expansionist effort to globalize the U.S. sphere of influence and expand U.S. hegemony, spreading free market capitalism and U.S.-style liberalism under "a military shield" worldwide.[53]

Washington's foreign policy in Latin America and elsewhere in the developing world is best understood through the analytical lens of hegemony, a broad concept that allows us to avoid single-issue explanations for U.S. behavior, such as the communist threat or corporate investments. To maintain and advance its hegemony, a dominant country pursues political, economic, and military/strategic interests in its sphere of influence and acts to stifle any challenge to them. The previously cited secret State Department document of September 1962, "United States Overseas Internal Defense Policy," made clear the economic, security, and political interests invested in U.S. security doctrine:

> The broad U.S. interests in the underdeveloped world are as follows: 1. A political and ideological interest in assuring that developing nations evolve in a way that affords a congenial world environment for international cooperation and the growth of free institutions. 2. A military interest in assuring that strategic areas and the manpower and natural resources of developing nations do not fall under communist control. . . . 3. An economic interest in assuring that the resources and markets of the less developed world remain available to us and to other Free World countries.

In this context, it is vital to acknowledge the class nature of the national security doctrine and its definition of the internal enemy. In all cases under discussion, hard-line military institutions acted, with local and U.S. support, when control of the state was contested by social sectors and political leaders seeking structural change in political or socioeconomic arenas. Washington's interests in maintaining pro-U.S., pro-capitalist governments merged with the interests of economic and political elites in these countries who were anxious to retain their privileges. During the turbulent 1960s and '70s, poor and working-class movements and their allies among intellectuals, students, teachers, and other sectors stood to gain important influence over national policy and socioeconomic resources. In response, the military states, with the support of traditional elites in the region, employed harsh methods of social control. Terror was used to diminish society's expectations for social change and the pursuit of alternatives to the existing socioeconomic and political systems. As noted by Tulio Halperín Donghi, the military regimes "tended to represent the interests of three very specific groups: the military hierarchy, the national economic elite, and the transnational corporations . . . the subordinate classes lost many of the rights of citizenship."[54] In short, the militaries acted to bolster or install systems that lacked the support of a majority of their people.

In Chile, for example, socialist Salvador Allende was pursuing structural change through the democratic framework, empowering non-elite social groups and nationalizing key industrial sectors such as the U.S.-owned copper mines. In Brazil, President João Goulart challenged foreign control of natural resources, endorsed radical peasant leagues and a broad agrarian reform, and encouraged leftist and populist sectors of society to participate politically. In Argentina, while two guerrilla organizations were certainly alarming to the military and their allies, even more so were the Peronists and broad sectors of society that were demanding radical change. In Bolivia, army officer Juan José Torres, who won the presidency in 1970, embarked on a populist program before he was overthrown in a 1971 coup (he was a Condor victim in 1976). In Uruguay, the new leftist Frente Amplio party, which enjoyed substantial support, entered the electoral process in 1971, in part as a progressive political alternative to the Tupamaro guerrillas. The Frente was met by repression and plotting not only by the Uruguayan military but by allied militaries as well. In all of these cases, the U.S. government provided significant assistance to the antidemocratic militaries, whose anticommunism was viewed as their most important asset. Throughout Latin America, Washington instigated "regime change" in numerous cases in the 1960s and '70s, whether overtly or covertly.

The trigger for military coups was less elite fear of Soviet encroachment or guerrilla threats (the stated rationales) than fears of popular demands for social reform and democratic change. U.S. intelligence analyses from the 1970s acknowledged that no guerrilla force in Latin America had the strength to seriously endanger any government. As one 1970 CIA report stated, "Cooperation among Latin American revolutionary groups across national boundaries is not extensive. . . . Insurgency movements thus far have remained essentially national in scope. . . . Most revolutionary groups in Latin America have struggled merely to survive." A 1976 CIA memo similarly acknowledged that "guerrilla groups in South America have never posed a direct challenge to any government. Most of the groups have been too small and weak to engage security forces directly."[55]

Yet in 1971, President Richard Nixon mused that he wished Brazilian military dictator Emilio Garrastazu Médici "were running the whole continent."[56] Nixon and National Security Advisor (later Secretary of State) Henry Kissinger wanted to punish the Chilean people for electing Allende and send a warning to other Latin Americans who dared to defy U.S. imperial preferences. As Nixon put it in a National Security Council meeting of November 6, 1970: "Latin America is not gone, and we want to keep it. . . . If there is any way we can hurt him [Allende] whether by government or private business—I want them to know our policy is negative. . . . No impression should be permitted in Latin America that they can get away with this, that it's safe to go this way."[57] Clearly, the prospect of *elected* progressive and socialist leaders was unacceptable to Nixon and Kissinger—not only the specter of communist guerrillas.

Nevertheless, some analysts have argued that the violence of guerrilla movements provoked, or justified, the crushing responses of the counterinsurgency militaries (an approach known as the "theory of the two demons" in Argentina). A few brief observations must suffice. First, the violence unleashed by the military regimes targeted their societies at large, not only relatively small guerrilla movements. By using mass, disproportionate terror against their populations, abandoning legal methods, destroying the freedoms and revoking the constitutional rights of all citizens, the militaries demonstrated that their strategic goals were much broader than eliminating guerrillas. In practice, they dismantled the institutions of democracy in their countries and eradicated all constitutional guarantees and rights under law. The military regimes treated the exercise of rights such as freedom of speech and assembly as national security threats. Messianic military officers viewed democracy itself as incompatible with national security because it gave voice to "subversive" elements.

Second, revolutionaries and guerrillas sometimes served as a convenient pretext for massive military intervention. Guerrillas appeared *after* coups had already installed military regimes in Brazil and Paraguay, and guerrilla organizations were virtually defeated before coups were carried out in Argentina and Uruguay. Revolutionary groups in Chile such as MIR or the Socialist Party, while believing armed struggle was justified, were primarily political and did not carry out armed activities before the 1973 coup. At times, the militaries' alarmist warnings of guerrilla threats were fabricated to justify repression, as in Chile with the incident of "the 119 missing" (see chapter 3). In Brazil, the Catholic Church's report on torture referred to the tendency of the military to inflate subversive threats: "all suspect political activities were allegedly planned by the Communist Party, which became hundreds of times more powerful in the minds of the military authorities than was in fact the case."[58]

Third, there was no equivalency between the systematic state terror of the military regimes and the more limited violence carried out by guerrilla bands in various countries. While a detailed analysis of these groups cannot be undertaken here, they generally did not engage in indiscriminate terrorism. (Che Guevara and other influential revolutionary thinkers specifically rejected terrorism—acts of random violence against civilians to create panic and fear—as a tactic.) Finally, as we have seen, the national security states targeted elected leaders, priests and nuns, and supporters of governments they had ousted, as well as unionists, students, peasants, and other activists, and moved to obliterate all traces of leftist thought in their societies. In short, the anticommunist crusade was not restricted to guerrillas or to communists.

In conclusion, the origins of Operation Condor can be traced to counterinsurgency doctrine and practice. Condor's characteristics reflected the tenets of counterinsurgency warfare, a type of warfare that deeply reshaped Latin America, producing predatory states led by military, security, and intelligence forces that believed themselves engaged in an ideological holy war. Counterinsurgency warfare and its extralegal methods produced "industrial repression." Such warfare was utilized to demobilize popular challenges to existing political and socioeconomic structures, thus preserving the interests of ruling elites in Latin America and advancing the hegemonic interests of Washington, which wished to keep Latin America within its sphere of influence and control.

The formation and use of shadowy parallel structures was part and parcel of counterinsurgency warfare, and the concept of the parallel state provides a frame of reference with which to understand the hidden apparatus of terror and social control used by the military states, with the assistance, financing, and direction of a powerful foreign ally, the U.S. government. Operation Condor was the transnational arm of the parallel state and was perfectly consistent with counterinsurgency doctrine.

The conceptual framework of this study connects the interests of national and international actors to the use of counterinsurgency warfare and to the creation of the parallel state, allowing us to bridge the gap between international and comparative politics and link the system and state levels of analysis. Washington's counterinsurgency strategy of creating and working through parallel state structures in contested countries enabled anticommunist forces to gain and wield preponderant power and install regimes that largely advanced the security agenda (as well as the political and economic interests) of the U.S. government.[59] In short, the conceptual framework offered here provides a lens with which to understand a central paradox underlying this study: why the self-proclaimed leader of the free world would ally itself with brutal military dictatorships, and Operation Condor, as they were killing thousands of their own people.

Notes

1. See, for example, Daniel Castro, *Revolution and Revolutionaries* (Wilmington, Del.: Scholarly Resources, 1999); Brian Loveman and Thomas M. Davies, eds., *Che Guevara and Guerrilla Movements*, 3rd ed. (Wilmington, Del.: Scholarly Resources, 1997).

2. See my *Incomplete Transition: Military Power and Democracy in Argentina* (New York: St. Martin's Press, 1997).

3. The most well-known case was Spanish judge Baltasar Garzón's against Chilean dictator Pinochet, which resulted in the general's arrest in London in 1998. Garzón also charged dozens of Argentine, Uruguayan, and Chilean officers with human rights crimes committed within the Condor framework. See "Sumario 19/97: Terrorism and Genocide, OPERATION CONDOR, Rogatory Letter from the Fifth Central Magistrate of the National Court of Justice in Madrid, Judge Baltasar Garzón Real, to the Competent Judicial Authority of the United Kingdom," November 27, 1998. Prosecutions and investigations of Condor are underway in Italy, France, Chile, and Argentina. Several judges have asked Henry Kissinger, former national security advisor and then–secretary of state during the Nixon and Ford administrations, to testify about his knowledge of Operation Condor.

4. Gerardo Irusta M., *Espionaje y servicios secretos en Bolivia y el Cono Sur: Nazis en la Operación Cóndor*, 2nd ed. (La Paz, 1997), 595.

5. "El juicio público a los dictadores," *Dignidad* (Argentina), June 25, 1985, reproduces the testimony of a Uruguayan survivor of Orletti, Enrique Rodríguez Larreta. See also "Operación Cóndor: Pinochet tenía 'conocimiento cabal,'" *La Nación* (Chile), July 7, 2004.

6. E. V. Walter, *Terror and Resistance: A Study of Political Violence* (New York: Oxford University Press, 1969).

7. U.S. Army, DIA, "Subject: (U) Special Operations Forces (U)," October 1, 1976, available on foia.state.gov.

8. Javier Giraldo, *Colombia: Genocidal Democracy* (Monroe, Maine: Common Courage Press, 1996), 77; see also his "Corrupted Justice and the Schizophrenic State in Colombia," *Social Justice*, Vol. 26, no. 4 (1999): 31–54.

9. Saul Landau, *The Dangerous Doctrine: National Security and U.S. Foreign Policy* (A PACCA Book. Boulder, Colo.: Westview, 1988), 119; personal correspondence with author, February 13, 1999.

10. He may have meant the Technical Services Department of the CIA. Irusta, *Espionaje*, 547–550. Much of the information in this book seems credible, but some is impossible to verify, although it meshes with that of other sources. The author, and the agent he cites here, are both deceased.

11. DIA, "Subject," 2.

12. Omer Bartov, "Industrial Killing: World War I, The Holocaust, and Representation," presentation at Rutgers University, March 1997, at http://muweb.millersville.edu/~holo-con/bartov.html. See also Bartov, *Murder in Our Midst: The Holocaust, Industrial Killing, and Representation* (New York: Oxford University Press, 1996).

13. Omer Bartov, *Mirrors of Destruction: War, Genocide, and Modern Identity* (New York: Oxford University Press, 2000).

14. T. David Mason and Dale A. Krane, "The Political Economy of Death Squads: Toward a Theory of the Impact of State-Sanctioned Terror," *International Studies Quarterly*, Vol. 33 (1989): 178. See also Bruce B. Campbell and Arthur D. Brenner, eds., *Death Squads in Global Perspective: Murder with Deniability* (New York: St. Martin's Press, 2000).

15. Bernard B. Fall, "The Theory and Practice of Insurgency and Counterinsurgency," *Naval War College Review* (April 1965): 1, at www.nwc.navy.mil/press/Review/1998/winter/art5-w98.htm. See also David Galula, *Counterinsurgency Warfare: Theory and Practice* (New York: Praeger: 1964); Bernard Fall, "Counterinsurgency: The French Experience," presentation to students at the U.S. Industrial College of the Armed Forces, Publication No. L63-109 (for official use), January 18, 1963.

16. Galula, *Counterinsurgency*, 126.

17. D. H. Berger (Major, U.S. Marines), "The Use of Covert Paramilitary Activity as a Policy Tool: An Analysis of Operations Conducted by the U.S. Central Intelligence Agency, 1949–1951" (Decatur, Ga.: Marine Corps Command and Staff College, n.d.), 2.

18. Berger, "The Use of Covert Paramilitary Activity," 4.

19. Michael McClintock, "American Doctrine and Counterinsurgent State Terror," in Alexander George, ed., *Western State Terrorism* (New York: Routledge, 1991): 121–154; Michael McClintock, *Instruments of Statecraft: U.S. Guerrilla Warfare, Counterinsurgency, Counterterrorism, 1940–1990* (New York: Pantheon Books, 1992), especially chapter 2.

20. U.S. Army, *Vietnam Studies: U.S. Army Special Forces 1961–1971*, Part Two, "The Middle Years: 1965-1968. Chapter II, Beginnings of the Civilian Irregular Defense Group," at www.ehistory.com/ vietnam/books/spfor/0077.cfm. See also Michael McClintock, *The American Connection*, Volume I, *State Terror and Popular Resistance in El Salvador* (London: Zed Books, 1985), 26.

21. U.S. Army, Escuela de las Américas, Ejército de los EEUU, Fuerte Gulick, Panama, "FM 31-16, Operaciones de contra-guerrilla," June 1968 (replaced FM 31-16 of February 16, 1963).

22. Cited in Douglas Valentine, *The Phoenix Program* (New York: William Morrow, 1990), 425.

23. Cited in Doug Stokes, "US Military Doctrine and Colombia's War of Terror," *Znet*, September 25, 2002.

24. McClintock, "American Doctrine," 132.

25. McClintock, "American Doctrine," 131.

26. McClintock, "American Doctrine," 138–139.

27. See, for example, Fall, "Counterinsurgency," 3–4.

28. U.S. Army, *Vietnam Studies.*

29. Peter Paret and John Shy, "The Theory and the Threat," in Lt.-Col. T. N. Greene, ed., *The Guerrilla and How to Fight Him* (New York: Praeger, 1962).

30. These dirty war commanders spoke in a French documentary called "Death Squadrons: The French School" (2003) by filmmaker Marie-Monique Robin, a film that caused a stir in the Southern Cone. I am grateful that she shared a copy of the film and the transcript with me. See also *La Tercera* (Chile), September 2, 2003; Marie-Monique Robin, "La letra con sangre," *Página/12* (Argentina), September 3, 2003; "La siniestra porfía del maestro de la DINA," *La Nación* (Chile), September 3, 2003, among other articles.

31. Robin, "La letra"; Horacio Verbitsky, "Discurso del método," *Página/12*, August 31, 2003.

32. Dennis M. Rempe, "Guerrillas, Bandits, and Independent Republics: US Counter-insurgency Efforts in Colombia 1959–1965," from *Small Wars and Insurgencies*, Vol. 6, no. 3 (Winter 1995), 304–327. Published by Frank Cass, London. (www.derechos.net/paulwolf/colombia/smallwars.htm), 6 (Internet version).

33. "CIA and Assassinations: The Guatemala 1954 Documents," Electronic Briefing Book no. 4, and "U.S. Policy in Guatemala, 1966–1986," Electronic Briefing Book no. 11, National Security Archive, 1997.

34. I studied the manuals in the National Security Archive, Washington, D.C., in 1999. See also Sandra B. McPherson, "The Misuse of Psychological Techniques Under U.S. Government Auspices: Interrogation and Terrorism Manuals," in Harold V. Hall and Leighton C. Whitaker, eds., *Collective Violence: Effective Strategies for Assessing and Intervening in Fatal Group and Institutional Aggression* (New York: CRC Press, 1999), 621–632; Latin American Working Group, "Inspector General's Report on Army Manuals a Feeble Response: What the Recently Declassified Manuals Contain," report, Washington, D.C., 1997; J. Patrice McSherry, "Tracking the Origins of a State Terror Network: Operation Condor," *Latin American Perspectives*, Vol. 29, no. 1 (2002).

35. Berger, "The Use of Paramilitary," 11.

36. U.S. State Department, "United States Overseas Internal Defense Policy," (SECRET), September 1962: 10, 28.

37. McClintock, *The American Connection*, 35.

38. See, for example, Martha K. Huggins, *Political Policing: The United States and Latin America* (Durham, N.C.: Duke University Press, 1998).

39. Rempe, "Guerrillas," 1.

40. Rempe, "Guerrillas," 2.

41. Rempe, "Guerrillas," 3–5, 8.

42. Rempe, "Guerrillas," 8.

43. The U.S. military continued to encourage the use of paramilitaries in Colombia in the 1990s. See Human Rights Watch (HRW), *Colombia's Killer Networks: The Military-Paramilitary Partnership and the United States*, New York: HRW, November 1996.

44. See McSherry, "Tracking the Origins," and "Operation Condor as a Hemispheric 'Counterterror' Organization," in Cecilia Menjívar and Néstor Rodríguez, eds., *When States Kill: Latin America, the U.S., and Technologies of Terror* (Austin: University of Texas Press, 2005).

45. Jaime Malamud Goti, "State Terror and Memory of What?" *University of Arkansas at Little Rock Law Review*, Vol. 21, no. 1 (Fall 1998): 107. While I find Malamud Goti's descriptions of state terror and its impact on society to be profound, I strongly disagree with his conclusion: that the trials of the military juntas later, under democratic rule, were counterproductive.

46. See, for example, Elizabeth Leeds, "Cocaine and Parallel Politics in the Brazilian Urban Periphery: Constraints on Local-Level Democratization," *Latin American Research Review*, Vol. 31, no. 3 (1996): 47–84.

47. Andrew Scobell and Brad Hammitt, "Goons, Gunmen, and Gendarmerie: Toward a Reconceptualization of Paramilitary Formations," *Journal of Political and Military Sociology*, Vol. 26, no. 2 (Winter 1998): 5–6 (Internet version, available on ProQuest).

48. Eric Nordlinger's response to Gabriel Almond, "The Return to the State," *American Political Science Review*, Vol. 82, no. 3 (September 1988): 875–902.

49. Noting that there were "no examples of the military state combined with modern technology," Lasswell warned of the dangers of this new modern and technical military class to democratic polities. Harold D. Lasswell, "The Garrison State," *The American Journal of Sociology*, Vol. 46, no. 4 (1941): 455–468; see also his "The Garrison-State Hypothesis Today," in Samuel P. Huntington, *Changing Patterns of Military Politics* (New York: The Free Press, 1962), 51–70.

50. This conceptualization draws from Steven Metz, "A Flame Kept Burning: Counterinsurgency Support after the Cold War," *Parameters* (Autumn 1995): 31–41.

51. The next section draws from J. Patrice McSherry, "Challenges to U.S. Hegemony in Latin America," *Journal of Third World Studies*, Vol. 20, no. 2 (Fall 2003): 235–242. See also Gaddis Smith, *The Last Years of the Monroe Doctrine* (New York: Hill and Wang, 1994).

52. See David Schmitz, *Thank God They're on Our Side* (Chapel Hill: University of North Carolina, 1999), especially his excellent conclusion.

53. See, for example, Melvyn P. Leffler, *The Specter of Communism: The United States and the Origins of the Cold War, 1917–1953* (New York: Hill and Wang, 1994); Thomas G. Paterson and Robert J. McMahon, eds., *The Origins of the Cold War*, 3rd ed. (Lexington, Ky.: D.C. Heath, 1991); Thomas G. Paterson and J. Garry Clifford, *America Ascendant: U.S. Foreign Relations since 1939* (Lexington, Ky.: D.C. Heath, 1995); Benjamin Schwartz, "Permanent Interests, Endless Threats: Cold War Continuities and NATO Enlargement," *World Policy Journal*, Vol. 14, no. 3 (Fall 1997).

54. Tulio Halperín Donghi, *The Contemporary History of Latin America*, John Charles Chasteen, trans. (Durham, N.C.: Duke University Press, 1993), 312.

55. CIA Directorate of Intelligence, intelligence memorandum, "Cooperation among Latin American Terrorist and Insurgent Groups," no. 1464/70, September 21, 1970; CIA, "Terrorism in South America," August 9, 1976. John Dinges has made the argument that the guerrilla alliance Junta Coordinadora Revolucionaria (JCR) was seen as a significant threat by the militaries and was a primary impetus for the organization of Condor. My research has found little evidence that the JCR was ever a very significant organization or a credible threat, however. Declassified U.S. documents label the JCR as fairly ineffective, and secret Argentine and Chilean military documents and testimonies from former intelligence operatives do not place any special priority on the JCR as opposed to other leftist and guerrilla groups. Dinges made this argument as a participant in a panel on Condor organized by this author at the Latin American Studies Association congress in September 2001; see also John Dinges, *The Condor Years* (New York: New Press, 2004).

56. Conversation 16–36 between Nixon and Secretary of State William Rogers, December 7, 1971, in National Security Archive Electronic Briefing Book no. 71, Document no. 11.

57. White House Memorandum of Conversation: NSC Meeting-Chile [NSSM97], 1970, www.gwu.edu/ ~nsarchiv/ news/2000113/.

58. Catholic Church, Archdiocese of São Paulo, *Torture in Brazil*, trans. Jaime Wright (Austin: University of Texas Press, 1998), 131.

59. Martha Huggins provides a rich case study along similar lines in *Political Policing*.

2

Cold War Security Coordination: The Global Context

BEGINNING IN THE 1940S, U.S. and allied commands created and financed paramilitary armies in Europe, and later in Asia, and Latin America, to advance the anticommunist cause. A brief review of this history shows that Condor was not an anomaly, but a manifestation of a broader anticommunist strategy adopted secretly by Western leaders. The genesis of the strategic concept and model of Condor may be found in these earlier military and intelligence networks, especially the clandestine anticommunist "stay-behind armies" formed throughout Western Europe in the 1940s and 1950s.[1] In fact, the 1975 assassination attempt in Rome by Condor agents against Christian Democrat leader Bernardo Leighton and his wife, Ana Fresno, was undertaken by Italian neofascists linked to Italy's stay-behind network, providing an explicit connection with Condor.

Condor specifically grew out of Western hemisphere relationships and programs forged in the School of the Americas and elsewhere, a product of inter-American doctrine and strategy disseminated through the continental military system. In training programs, U.S. officers transmitted techniques of counterinsurgency warfare honed in Vietnam and elsewhere, diffusing them throughout the region. In U.S.-led military and intelligence conferences, officers from Latin America and the United States studied and shared methods of combating "subversion" and ways to unify and combine their counterinsurgency efforts. Operation Condor was organized from within this developing system of cross-border coordination. In fact, the Latin American militaries, encouraged and assisted by their U.S. partners, began to collaborate to repress leftists and even oust leftist governments long before Condor was officially instituted and code named. The military regime of Brazil, which took power through a coup in 1964, played a key role in these operations, as did the CIA. CIA officers secretly laid the groundwork for Operation Condor by stitching together the Latin American intelligence organizations, as I show in this chapter. Thus, Condor's cross-border disappearance-torture-execution operations against exiles, like the other campaigns of state terror carried out by the Latin American national security states during the Cold War, cannot be seen in isolation from the inter-American counterinsurgency regime.

The U.S.-USSR Battle for Hegemony

By the late 1940s, the perceived threat of international communist revolution obsessed U.S. national security officials and guided U.S. foreign policy around the world.[2] U.S. leaders interpreted internal conflicts, social unrest, and insurgencies in the developing world as manifestations of the primary strategic threat, the USSR.[3] U.S. officials and their allies increasingly couched the struggle with communism as an ideological war, "a global confrontation between communism and freedom, a confrontation unlimited in scope and magnitude."[4] The most influential U.S. statement of this new perspective was National Security Council Paper No. 68 (NSC-68) of 1950, an alarmist policy document that portrayed the Cold War in terms of a global struggle between the United States and a menacing enemy "animated by a new fanatic faith, antithetical to our own, and seek[ing] to impose its absolute authority on the rest of the world." It frankly portrayed U.S. rivalry with the Soviet Union as a battle for world hegemony, and stated that "our overall policy at the present time may be described as one designed to foster a world environment in which the American system can survive and flourish" and to develop "a successfully functioning political and economic system" in the noncommunist world, which required "an adequate military shield" under which it could develop.[5]

The U.S. government solidified an international anticommunist military coalition through the Treaty of Reciprocal Assistance (or Rio Pact) in the Western hemisphere (1947) and the North Atlantic Treaty in Europe (1949). U.S. policymakers pursued three key strategic objectives in the Third World, seen as a major battleground between the superpowers: containment (or reversal) of communism; expansion of capitalism and prevention of the spread of noncapitalist systems; and ensuring political alignment with the United States.[6] As the Cold War heated up in the 1950s with the Korean War and McCarthyism in the United States, the secret 1954 Doolittle Report argued that dirty methods would be required to win, making the case that the United

States faced a total war against "an implacable enemy whose avowed objective is world domination." It continued:

> There are no rules in such a game. Hitherto acceptable norms of human conduct do not apply. If the United States is to survive, long-standing American concepts of "fair play" must be reconsidered. . . .We must learn to subvert, sabotage and destroy our enemies by more clever, more sophisticated, and more effective methods than those used against us.[7]

Such official attitudes gave rise to a ruthless security doctrine in which the ends justified the means.

Through its Cold War lens, U.S. policymakers saw the "loss" of Latin American allies as a de facto benefit to the USSR in the geopolitical game. The USSR tacitly accepted the Western hemisphere as a sphere of U.S. influence, however, with the obvious exception of its strong support for Cuba.[8] The USSR did nothing to aid nationalist-leftist forces in Guatemala during the U.S.-sponsored 1954 coup nor in the Dominican Republic during the 1965 U.S. invasion, nor did it assist the Allende government during the 1973 U.S.-backed coup in Chile. The U.S. also implicitly accepted the hegemony of the USSR in Eastern Europe, as witnessed by its unwillingness to openly aid the revolts in Hungary in 1956 and Czechoslovakia in 1968. The USSR refrained from provocative military moves in the hemisphere after the 1962 missile crisis, as did Cuba after 1967, the year that Che Guevara was killed in Bolivia by U.S.-trained Bolivian forces assisted by the CIA. Both the USSR and Cuba then exerted political influence largely through the Communist Parties in Latin American countries and via direct government-to-government relations. Washington's real concern seemed to be indigenous radical movements in Latin America that challenged U.S. hegemony, and the spread of the revolutionary idea.

The so-called stay-behind armies set up by U.S. and British intelligence officers after World War II were an early example of the formation of parallel military forces to fight communism. Nominally a first line of defense against a Soviet invasion, the secret forces were unknown to all but select leaders, and they escaped democratic accountability. Moreover, over time the stay-behind forces were linked to destabilizing and terrorist acts against the legal left and against constitutional governments, thereby presenting a threat to democratic systems and human rights. Unlike Operation Condor, , the stay-behind armies operated within states that were democracies, which limited their power to some extent. But the European stay-behind formations, led and financed by the U.S. government within the NATO framework, resembled Condor as a counterterror system, and Condor actually operated in concert with groups linked to the stay-behind armies in more than one case.

The European Stay-Behind Armies

After World War II, U.S. policymakers initiated a secret, multibillion dollar project to develop global covert warfare and propaganda machinery to wage the Cold War against communism.[9] National Security Council Directive 10/2 of June 1948 authorized a vast program of clandestine

> propaganda, economic warfare, preventative direct action including sabotage, anti-sabotage, demolition, and evacuation measures . . . subversion against hostile states, including assistance to underground resistance movements, guerrillas, and refugee liberation groups, and support of indigenous anti-Communist elements . . . [to be done so that] any U.S. government responsibility for them is not evident to unauthorized persons and that if uncovered the U.S. government can plausibly deny any responsibility.[10]

U.S. and British officials organized clandestine anticommunist commandos throughout Western Europe and Scandinavia even before the formation of NATO. Washington also made extensive use of covert paramilitary forces, run by the CIA, in Eastern Europe during the early years of the Cold War, in an effort to subvert communist governments.[11] After NATO was established, the secret stay-behind projects in Western Europe were housed under the Clandestine Coordinating Committee of the Supreme Headquarters Allied Powers Europe (SHAPE).[12] The covert paramilitary networks (known as Gladio in Italy, Operation Stay Behind in the United Kingdom, and Sheepskin in Greece, among other names) encompassed even countries that were officially neutral. They incorporated members of various security services as well as anticommunist partisans, fascist networks, and former Nazis. One NATO source told Searchlight (a British nongovernmental organization) that the two-pronged strategy of Britain's Stay Behind was "to destabilize any left-leaning government, even a Social Democratic one, and in the event of a Warsaw Pact attack to function as a guerrilla army using classical guerrilla tactics."[13] Units were trained in secret facilities at U.S. and other bases in Europe, where they took part in "simulated exercises," and stay-behind organizers from Italy, Britain, and France exchanged visits in the 1970s.[14]

The earliest U.S. covert operations were in the Greek civil war in the 1940s and in the Italian elections of 1948, when the Italian Communist Party (PCI) stood poised to gain power. In Greece, popular opposition to the Nazi occupation, and later to the return of the authoritarian, pro-Nazi monarchy, was led by the Greek National Liberation Front, a leftist force that commanded widespread support. It included communists. In 1943, British and U.S. military units entered Greece specifically to combat the Front, and in 1946 they worked with royalist and rightist forces to prevent an election victory by the

Front and to repress all leftist activity.[15] In the late 1940s, after defeating the Front, the CIA established a large station in Greece. One of the most important in Europe, it served as a staging area and communications center for CIA operations throughout the Middle East.[16]

Clandestine Services officers of the CIA station in Greece organized a section called the Paramilitary Group in the early 1950s, and it was closely associated with Greece's stay-behind army. The CIA officers trained Greeks in guerrilla operations to prepare for a leftist coup or electoral victory and supplied the paramilitaries with automatic weapons and small mortars, which were hidden in caches to be dug up for use when the stay-behind forces deployed.[17] The guerrilla formations were trained to be autonomous and self-mobilizing. When social protest again arose in the 1950s, a new intelligence agency named Kentriki Ypiresia Pliroforion (Central Information Bureau, or KYP) was formed in Greece with the assistance of the CIA. The KYP was deeply involved in the colonel's coup of 1967 and the ensuing Greek dictatorship.[18] Key coup leaders were operationally responsible for the secret Prometheus Plan, a military strategy against "internal subversion" approved by NATO. The Greek putschists utilized the shadow Prometheus command structure during the military overthrow. Some 300 senior officers in a brigade which was part of NATO and trained by the United States carried out Prometheus and overthrew the democratically elected government. They imposed martial law and arrested thousands of persons.[19] Greece's secret army was apparently dissolved by the colonels after the 1967 coup, as it was no longer needed.[20]

In Italy, the PCI was respected domestically for its central role in the antifascist resistance in World War II. It was subject to a covert U.S. campaign of political manipulation, paramilitary action, and black propaganda to undermine its popularity, a campaign that set a precedent for CIA covert operations and dirty war methods elsewhere.[21] Former CIA director William Colby claimed credit for the defeat of the PCI in the 1958 elections as well (when he was Rome station chief), commenting that it was "one of the most beautiful achievements of our organization."[22] Much information has emerged about Operation Gladio in Italy, some from former members of Gladio and former military officers, discussed in a subsequent section.

Washington insisted on a secret clause in the North Atlantic Treaty requiring the secret services of all joining nations to establish their own branches of the secret army—and to oppose communist influence, even if the population voted for communist candidates in free elections.[23] Charles de Gaulle pulled France out of NATO partially due to the secret protocol, which he regarded as a violation of sovereignty, and he regarded the secret network as a danger to his government.[24] The French stay-behind army may have continued into the

1970s, however, code named CATENA, a group linked to the killing of five lawyers in Spain and a judge in Italy as well as to a major bank robbery carried out in Nice in 1976.[25]

U.S. and British military and intelligence agents set up hundreds of secret arms caches all across Europe, often under cover of U.S. military exercises; one cache was at the U.S. Army's Camp Derby.[26] The arms depots, like the stay-behind commandos themselves, were unknown to key government leaders. In fact, the Austrian government lodged an official protest in 1996 after learning that the CIA had placed arms caches there fifty years before without the knowledge of Austrian officials, thus violating its neutrality. The U.S. ambassador responded with a formal apology.[27] One member of Austria's stay-behind network was a former Nazi named Wilhelm Hottl, who was recruited in 1947 by the U.S. Army Counterintelligence Corps. He said that the United States had recruited, armed, trained, and supplied many former SS personnel and neo-Nazis to maintain the arms caches, and protected them from the Austrian police. Documents declassified in 2001 showed for the first time the full scope of the U.S. government's covert relationships with former Nazi war criminals during the Cold War.[28]

In Turkey, elements of the stay-behind network took part in military antileftist campaigns that used terrorist methods against social protest. A former prime minister, Bulent Ecevit, told journalist Lucy Komisar that in 1973 a high-ranking Turkish military commander asked him for funds for the Special Warfare Department, a secret unit funded previously by the CIA. The commander told Ecevit that the network was comprised of "volunteer patriots" who had "hidden arms caches in various parts of the country." Although fearful of the rightist nature of the secret apparatus, Ecevit did provide the military with the money. The secret unit, which was previously known as the Tactical Mobilization Group and worked out of the Joint U.S. Military Aid Team headquarters, was used against "internal subversion" after a military coup in 1971 and again in 1980. Military commanders admitted that the network was involved in the shooting of nine leftists in 1972 and may have been responsible for the sniper shootings of hundreds of unionists at a rally in 1977. Later the network was used to combat the Kurdish rebels. In 1990, the commander of Turkish Army Operations admitted that there was a secret NATO organization called the Special Warfare Department in Turkey that utilized civilian paramilitaries, but in 1997, Komisar was told by a Pentagon official that information about the stay-behind organization remained classified.[29]

In Portugal, a right-wing organization named Commandos for the Defence of Western Civilisation (CODECO) was accused in 1999 of a series of bombing attacks against well-known politicians, and the assassinations of former prime minister Francisco Sa Carneiro and his defense minister, Amaro da Costa. They died in a plane crash in 1980, blamed by the government at the time on technical failure. Experts who examined the crash site and victims, though, found evidence of explosives. Their report was suppressed by the government. A parliamentary commission interviewed several members of CODECO in the late '90s, who identified an active-duty general (in charge of border security) as a leading member of the secret group. Apparently, before his death, Da Costa had discovered a secret army fund, used for arms deals or perhaps for "countersubversive" purposes. The two CODECO members testified under oath that two bombers from the group had planted an explosive device on the plane. They also said that CODECO had infiltrated center-right political parties and had organized violence against leftist political leaders.[30] CODECO clearly fit the profile of the European stay-behind network. In December 1999, the government dropped the case, however, to general public outrage.

In Germany, former Waffen SS men were part of the stay-behind formation, as was the Gehlen Organization, a Nazi espionage network reorganized under U.S. auspices after the war by Hitler's former spy chief general Reinhard Gehlen.The Gehlen Organization was financed by the United States and used by NATO to spy on communists in Europe. Indeed, Henry Kissinger served in the U.S. Army Counterintelligence Corps (CIC) at the end of World War II, and after the war he was assigned to a unit that was involved in the recruitment of former Nazis. In 1950, he served as a consultant to another unit that carried out classified Defense Department studies on the use of Nazis for CIA covert operations and he continued to work on intelligence and covert operations in the 1950s through his links to the National Security Council.[31]

Gehlen, called the "spiritual father" of the stay-behind network in Germany, later became head of West Germany's state intelligence agency, the BND, created in 1956. The secret stay-behind army had a list of leftist politicians to assassinate, according to members, that included former prime minister Willy Brandt.[32] Another Nazi, Gestapo chief Klaus Barbie—the "butcher of Lyons"—was employed by the CIC after World War II and was also a stay-behind recruiter. Declassified U.S. documents proved that Barbie was a full-time CIC agent from 1946 to 1951, hired due to his professed expertise in French communism. Barbie impressed CIC officer Robert S. Taylor, who recruited him, as "strongly anti-Communist and a Nazi idealist." The CIC protected him from the French, who wanted Barbie for war crimes, and in 1951 the CIC helped him escape to South America through the infamous "ratline."[33] Barbie resettled in Bolivia and worked with right-wing military officers throughout South America, teaching torture and other repressive techniques in Bolivia, Paraguay, and elsewhere, thus providing another linkage between the stay-behind forces and

Condor. Like Condor, the stay-behind armies were secret parallel formations that targeted leftist, communist, and social democratic forces.

Italy's Gladio and Its Links to Condor

In 1990, an Italian judge first discovered evidence of Gladio as he studied the files of the military intelligence agency, SISMI, in the course of investigating a 1972 car bombing. Prime Minister Giulio Andreotti publicly confirmed, and defended, the stay-behind networks, saying that the CIA had first broached the idea to Italy in 1951.[34] Former CIA director Colby acknowledged that the CIA had funneled enormous funds to Italy's Christian Democrat Party as a counterweight to the left and that he himself had set up the stay-behind network in Scandinavia in 1951.[35] Andreotti's written deposition was quickly withdrawn from a parliamentary investigating commission at the request of NATO.[36] Soon, other European officials began to admit that the network had existed, under NATO auspices, in their countries as well. Discovery of the covert stay-behind projects caused a political firestorm in Europe. In 1990, the European Parliament passed a strongly worded denunciation of the transnational clandestine organization, its antidemocratic implications, and the terrorist acts associated with it.[37] A final meeting of the network took place in Belgium that year, when it reportedly was shut down.

Other intriguing links between the stay-behind armies and Operation Condor have emerged in recent years, indicating that they formed a secret part of a much larger anticommunist alliance under the leadership of the United States. Vincenzo Vinciguerra, an Italian fascist with connections to Gladio and to Operation Condor, was convicted in the 1990s of a 1972 terrorist bombing in Italy. He testified that the 1975 attack against Chilean leader Bernardo Leighton and his wife in Rome was arranged by "a secret structure of the Latin American intelligence services called Operation Condor." He said Condor was also responsible for the assassinations of Prats and Letelier.[38] At his trial for the 1972 bombing, Vinciguerra argued in his own defense that members of his paramilitary organization, Ordine Nuovo (closely linked to another neofascist organization, Avanguardia Nazionale), who were accused of responsibility, were actually tools of the secret services linked to Gladio, the Italian stay-behind network.[39] In fact, the explosives used in the 1972 bombing came from a Gladio weapons cache, set up by the CIA under the auspices of NATO.[40]

Vinciguerra said that Gladio had carried out bombings attributed to the left, that it was associated with NATO, and that it recruited among fascist circles. He added that the network had been used for domestic purposes "by national and international forces . . . principally the United States of America."[41]

Avanguardia Nazionale and Ordine Nuovo also collaborated in Condor operations. Assassins from Avanguardia Nazionale, the terrorist organization of Italian neofascist Stefano delle Chiaie, attempted the Leighton assassination in Rome. They left the couple for dead after gunning them down in the street. The couple was severely wounded, but survived.[42] Aldo Tisei, a leader of Ordine Nuovo and Avanguardia Nazionale, boasted that delle Chiaie and his Italian fascists coordinated with the Chilean DINA as well as the secret services of the Franco regime in Spain, and admitted that his forces carried out the Leighton attack at DINA's request.[43]

Pinochet himself met with delle Chiaie to discuss the Leighton assassination plot when he traveled to Madrid for Franco's funeral in November 1975. Condor assassin Michael Townley admitted that he met ten or fifteen times with delle Chiaie to organize the attack.[44] Testifying in an Italian court in 1995 about the Leighton crime, Townley confirmed that it was carried out via "a global anti-Marxist agreement." In 1995, an Italian court found DINA commanders Manuel Contreras and Eduardo Iturriaga Neumann guilty in absentia of the Leighton attack.[45]

Delle Chiaie was suspected of involvement in a major 1980 bombing in Bologna, Italy, blamed on the left at the time. He had many ties to Latin American military commanders and he participated in the 1980 coup in Bolivia, along with former Gestapo chief Klaus Barbie and Argentine military officers, an event that graphically illustrated the global nature of the anticommunist alliance.[46]

After World War II, some 1,000 military officers formed Gladio in Italy along with civilians in the Christian Democrat Party, and it was formalized in 1956 via a secret agreement between the CIA and SIFAR, Italy's intelligence apparatus. Significantly, Gladio was also called "the parallel SID" (Italy's renamed Defense Intelligence Service).[47] A former member of Gladio, Roberto Cavallaro, said in 1986 that Gladio's mission was "to engage in the covert training of groups who in the event the leftists in our country made a move, would take to the streets to create a situation so tense as to require military intervention. Our mission was to infiltrate these groups." When asked whether Gladio had infiltrated the Red Brigades, he replied, "I had specific knowledge that many of the terrorists—both red and black [e.g., left- and right-wing, respectively]—were acting on the basis of directives or suggestions from the secret services."[48] There were deep suspicions in the 1990s that Gladio was linked to infamous crimes officially attributed to left-wing guerrillas, such as the Red Brigades' 1978 assassination of Italian prime minister Aldo Moro, who had been moving to include the Communist Party in a coalition government. In 1974, Henry Kissinger and a U.S. intelligence official had met with Moro and warned him against a rapprochement with the communists, in a meeting that greatly upset Moro.[49]

An Italian parliamentary commission on terrorism concluded that the 1980 bombing of the Bologna rail station, which killed eighty-five people and wounded 200, used bomb materials from a Gladio arsenal.[50] One major neo-fascist figure, Licio Gelli, was found guilty by an Italian court in the Bologna case, but later the conviction was overturned, causing a national outcry. According to Arthur Rowse, Gelli also had joined the U.S. Army CIC after collaborating with the Nazis in World War II.[51] He was the founder (in 1964) of global Masonic lodge Propaganda-Due (P-2), an anticommunist organization with close links to military and intelligence organizations (notably the CIA) and powerful political figures worldwide.[52] P-2 was outlawed in Italy in 1981 after it was discovered to have infiltrated its members into strategic government, military, and intelligence positions, to influence government policy, prevent investigations, and prepare for a coup in the event of a communist electoral win. P-2 also wielded significant influence in Argentina and elsewhere in Latin America.[53] Italy's Ordine Nuovo was reportedly a paramilitary arm of P-2.[54] Gelli was a key figure linking U.S. officials, the CIA, and Argentine military commanders, among others,[55] and there was overlap between Gladio and P-2. U.S. colonel and former CIA officer Oswald LeWinter (also known as Ibrahim Razin) told the BBC in 1992 that during the Cold War, the CIA had penetrated or controlled right-wing terrorist organizations including P-2 and recruited members on the basis of anticommunism.[56]

U.S. forces trained Gladio operatives at a secret NATO base in 1968. According to a former NATO operative, Gladio received major U.S. funding with the approval of General Alexander Haig, future NATO commander, and Henry Kissinger, then head of the U.S. National Security Council.[57] During the investigation of Gladio, former Italian interior minister and founder of the Christian Democrat Party Paulo Taviani told a judge that CIA officers stationed in the U.S. Embassy directed and financed the Italian secret services.[58] Taviani, who was one of the organizers of the Gladio network, told a parliamentary committee on terrorism that before the 1969 Piazza Fontana bombing in Milan (which killed sixteen people), Italy's intelligence service was at the point of sending an officer to Milan to head off the bombing; after it occurred, another officer was sent to lay the blame on the left. Taviani added that while he did not believe the CIA had organized the bombing, "agents of the CIA were among those who supplied the materials and who muddied the waters of the investigation."[59]

In 2000, General Gianadello Maletti, chief of a division of the secret services of Italy in the 1970s, provided corroborating evidence to Taviani's account. He said the CIA had tacitly approved bombings carried out by right-wing forces and confirmed that the CIA worked closely with the Italian secret services in a strategy of terror to undermine the Communist Party and keep the Christian Democrats in power. Maletti also said that the Piazza Fontana bombing was carried out by Ordine Nuovo with materials sent from West Germany, where a large CIA base was located.[60] Such operations highlighted the CIA's close direction of, and collaboration with, parallel formations—right-wing terrorist groups such as Ordine Nuovo—to strengthen anticommunist forces and shape Italian politics, as it also did in Latin America at the same time. These actions were part of the so-called strategy of tension in Italy, to create havoc and fear in society, suppress civil liberties, empower the right, and ostracize the left, thus preventing a leftist electoral victory.[61]

General Giovanni de Lorenzo, head of SIFAR (1956), later head of the Carabinieri (1962) and then defense minister (1964), was the key Gladio contact with the U.S. government through General Vernon Walters (later deputy director of the CIA).[62] De Lorenzo admitted conducting secret counterterrorism planning with U.S. officials without informing his own government.[63] He formulated a plot called Operation Solo to take over media networks, arrest politicians, seize the offices of leftist parties, and even to assassinate Moro,[64] and SIFAR compiled surveillance information on tens of thousands of Italians. SIFAR was dissolved due to its role in an attempted coup in 1964. Another former member of Gladio, a civilian, said in 1990 that he left the organization after learning of a plot to kill two Italian communists, one male and one female.[65] Italy's reconstituted intelligence service, SISDI, was also suspected of links to Gladio; in 1993, it was accused of harboring a secret terrorist organization named the Armed Phalange that had claimed credit for the recent assassination of a judge and bombings in Florence and Milan.[66]

These sorts of connections and operations, linking right-wing forces in state security services with civilian paramilitaries, evoke Operation Condor. In Europe, U.S. military and intelligence forces set up a secret regional army to oppose the left and the Soviets. Organizers of the stay-behind formations met regularly in different capitals, exchanged visits, and trained civilian commandos, all within the framework of NATO. Condor, similarly, was organized within the inter-American military system, during the same approximate period. It seems plausible to surmise that U.S. forces transferred the stay-behind model to Latin America, and, indeed, the activities of several influential U.S. officials (such as Henry Kissinger, Vernon Walters, and Duane Clarridge) in Europe and Latin America lend additional weight to the thesis. Several Italian and German fascists in the stay-behind formations also developed close working relations with Condor figures such as Manuel Contreras and Michael Townley in Chile as well as Bolivian, Paraguayan, and Argentine officers. These links among Washington, the European stay-behind networks, and Condor suggested that the covert anticommunist infrastructure was integrated, and it was global.

The U.S. government transplanted the model of stay-behind armies to Vietnam in the 1950s. According to *The Pentagon Papers*, the First Observation Group, "a Special Forces type of unit" that was "highly classified," was organized in 1956 "with the initial mission of preparing stay-behind organizations in South Vietnam . . . for guerrilla warfare in the event of an overt invasion by North Vietnamese forces."[67] The First Observation Group was charged with operating in "denied" (enemy) areas in North Vietnam and made cross-border incursions into Laos as well. It was subject to joint control by the CIA and by the Military Assistance Advisory Group (MAAG), and its chain of command was separate from normal command structures.

In sum, the European parallel forces known as the stay-behinds functioned from within the state apparatus, but outside the democratic frameworks and legal systems of the European democracies. They were a manifestation of the parallel state and of a clandestine Western military-intelligence strategy to battle communism outside the rule of law. The stay-behind armies were sponsored by a supranational military organization (NATO) dominated by the United States. In similar fashion, Condor operated secretly within the structures of the inter-American military system, including the Rio Pact, the Inter-American Defense Board, the School of the Americas, and the Conference of American Armies. There is significant evidence that U.S. influence was, again, critical in the formation of Condor.

Security Structures and Doctrine in the Western Hemisphere

In the Americas, the United States acted in the 1940s to establish new inter-American security structures and agreements to interlink the Latin American militaries and solidify defenses against world communism.[68] Washington took the lead in unifying the militaries under one doctrine and mission, upgrading their capabilities, and facilitating coordinated counterinsurgency operations. After the 1959 Cuban revolution, the U.S. security establishment dramatically reoriented, reshaped, expanded, and mobilized the existing hemispheric system to combat the threat of communist-inspired subversion.[69] The Latin American military mission was redefined to combat "internal enemies" as the primary threat, as we have shown, and militaries were reorganized and trained to undertake aggressive counterinsurgency operations within their own societies.

U.S. strategists led the integration of the hemisphere's militaries within a dense network of continental defense organizations, including USARCARIB (1946), later called the U.S. Army School of the Americas (SOA), the Inter-American Defense Board (1948), and the Conference of American Armies

(1960). SOUTHCOM and Special Action Forces were "unilateral components" of the inter-American military system, to ensure U.S. dominance and control.[70] Essentially, U.S. policy centered on gaining strategic control of military and security forces in weaker states as a means to mold their internal security environments and, on a deeper level, shape political outcomes. As a spokesman for SOUTHCOM said in 2003, "If we can train and equip other people to act in what we consider to be U.S. national interests, then that, of course, is our job. And we have been successful in training other people to do that so far, particularly in the last few decades in Latin America."[71]

The Cold War came to Latin America in 1954 with the CIA covert operation code-named "PB Success" that ousted the nationalist government of Jacobo Arbenz in Guatemala.[72] Decades of political repression and human rights abuses followed under a series of military and military-dominated regimes. In the 1960s, U.S. colonel John Webber was in charge of introducing the counterterror system to Guatemalan forces. In 1968, he said openly that he had encouraged the formation of counterterror units, basically death squads.[73] "Disappearances" as a counterinsurgency strategy first appeared in Latin America in 1960s Guatemala. A declassified State Department memo of 1967 reported that "at the center of the Army's clandestine urban counterterror apparatus is the Special Commando Unit formed in January 1967. . . . Composed of both military and civilian personnel, the Special Unit has carried out abductions, bombings, street assassinations, and executions of real and alleged communists."[74] In 1968, U.S. Embassy official Viron Vaky expressed alarm about U.S. policy in Guatemala, which he said was encouraging and sanctioning savage and indiscriminate atrocities by the Guatemalan military.[75] Guatemala was a clear case in which U.S. counterinsurgency specialists led the effort to create parastatal forces, linked to the military, that used a strategy of terror, even as U.S. diplomats criticized that approach.

After the Cuban revolution, President John F. Kennedy (1961–63) created the Special Forces (Green Berets) and demanded that the U.S. Army reorganize to fight political-military wars. Kennedy ordered an ambitious new two-pronged security policy for Latin America: the Alliance for Progress, to foster social development in the region, and counterinsurgency programs, to prevent and contain revolution. The structural changes required for socioeconomic reform in Latin America were resisted, however, by the very elites and military forces strengthened by the counterinsurgency strategy. After Kennedy's assassination, under the Mann doctrine, the counterinsurgency half of the strategy came to dominate the U.S. approach to the region.

In 1960, the U.S. commander-in-chief of SOUTHCOM, Major T. F. Bogart, initiated the Conference of American Armies, a hemispheric security organization dominated by the United States and its organizational and ideological doctrines.[76] U.S. military officers played a prominent role in these conferences. SOUTHCOM hosted the first, at Fort Amador in the Panama Canal Zone, where commanders from seventeen armies discussed specific accords to guide and regulate future combined activities. The yearly conferences, secret sessions that excluded civilians, provided a means for the Latin American armies, under U.S. tutelege, to form coordinated strategies—with no civilian input or control—and solidify an anticommunist front in the Americas.[77] Partially through the vehicle of these conferences, the countersubversive security doctrine was developed and expanded, and the inter-American defense system reorganized to deal with the perceived subversive threat in the Americas.

The second of the secret articles forming the charter of the Conference of American Armies stated that the mission of the armies was "to protect the continent from the aggressive action of the International Communist Movement," a movement that instigated internal subversion. In the conferences planning, intelligence sharing, and strategizing overwhelmingly emphasized the subversive threat. According to a 1985 history of the conferences, early meetings in the 1960s focused on the creation of a continental doctrine to fight "communist aggression"; the interchange of intelligence about subversive groups and international communism; the establishment of a permanent inter-American intelligence committee, located in the Panama Canal Zone; the setting up of schools of intelligence in each country; the creation of a system of encoded telecommunications among the armies; and programs of training for all the armies in strategies of countersubversion, counterrevolution, and internal security.[78] Operation Condor, which was organized later, was clearly an outgrowth of these transnational structures and programs.

In the 1963 Conference of the American Armies, SOUTHCOM focused on international communism and emphasized the importance of hemispheric communications systems. U.S. personnel played a key role in setting up military and intelligence communications networks in order to integrate counterinsurgency command and control throughout the hemisphere. In the 1965 conference, the twin concepts of "security and development" in the continental doctrine were a central focus. In the 1969 conference, the armies shared information on communist subversion in the Americas and discussed the necessity of exchanging information on subversion, a topic that appeared repeatedly in subsequent conferences.

In June 1973, a meeting of the Conference of Chiefs of Communications of the American Armies was held in Brasilia, Brazil, in which discussion took place regarding how the military communications network should operate.[79] One document, "Permanent Instructions for Transmissions for the Network of Inter-American Military Communication [RECIM]," originating in Fort Clayton (Canal Zone) and dated October 1973, was sent confidentially to eighteen Latin American armies. The Permanent Commission of Inter-American Military Communication (Comisión Permanente de Comunicaciones Militares Inter-Americana, or COPECOMI), was set up during this period. The headquarters of COPECOMI was in the Canal Zone, and the system served as a means to upgrade the communications capabilities of the armies and link them together. Another document discussed how to integrate the overlapping communications systems of RECIM and COPECOMI; how COPECOMI should be financed (at the time, the U.S. Army mainly financed the system); and how very high frequency (VHF) signals could be used for military communications to give them greater security and speed.[80] This system may have later housed Condor's secure communications network, discussed in chapter 3.

School of the Americas training also changed dramatically after the Cuban revolution, specifically in 1961–62. The U.S. Army objective was to make U.S. strategies and doctrine dominant in Latin America. One army document stated that SOA courses were "designed to teach principles and techniques used by the United States as a result of experiences in World War II, Korea, and the ever present 'Cold War.'" As we have seen, French veterans of the dirty war in Algeria also taught courses to their U.S. and Latin American counterparts in the early 1960s. Greg Weeks shows that during that decade the mission of the Latin American military was geometrically expanded to include a role in virtually all aspects of national life. Courses on communism, intelligence, countersubversion, PSYWAR, and—for the first time—combating internal enemies appeared in SOA catalogues in 1961–62. In 1963–64, courses began to stress the central role of the militaries in economic development as well as strategies of guerrilla warfare. As Weeks notes, economic development was considered part of counterinsurgency, and courses in the 1960s urged military involvement in education, agriculture, mining, medicine, construction of infrastructure, postal service, and even entertainment. Officers "were learning how to run a country," Weeks observes. As the decade progressed, the concept of counterinsurgency continued to expand as Cold War national security doctrine redefined the military role. The new techniques and principles of counterinsurgency warfare and intelligence were considered extremely sensitive. By 1966–67, trainees required security clearances even to view the course descriptions of military intelligence courses.[81]

During those years, it is now known that SOA instructors taught torture techniques and other dirty war methods being used at the same time in Vietnam. In Vietnam in the late 1960s, the Phoenix Program—a CIA-led counterinsurgency operation using assassination, terror, and psychological warfare—was decimating civilian sympathizers of the Vietnamese insurgents.[82] Much of the "dirty work" was done by paramilitary hunter-killer squads and criminal thugs drawn from the ranks of South Vietnamese officers and civilians, while U.S. personnel provided lists of suspects, participated in interrogations, and supervised, controlled, and financed the program. There was no due process, and tens of thousands of civilians were tortured and killed. U.S. soldiers in the Phoenix Program were sworn to secrecy; they were warned that revealing the classified operation to unauthorized persons would result, at minimum, in a $10,000 fine and ten years in prison.[83]

Joseph Blair, a retired major and former Phoenix operative who taught at the SOA for three years, said that the author of the SOA and CIA "torture manuals," declassified in the mid-1990s, drew from intelligence materials used during the Vietnam War that advocated assassination, torture, extortion, and other "techniques."[84] The manuals were drawn from the U.S. Army's Project X.[85] Project X was part of the U.S. Army's Foreign Intelligence Assistance Program, first developed in 1965–66 at the U.S. Army Intelligence School at Fort Holabird, Maryland.[86] One U.S. counterintelligence officer said that Project X materials were based on lessons drawn from the Phoenix Program, and the U.S. Army Intelligence School taught a course on Phoenix at the same time as the Project X manuals were being written. An army intelligence officer involved in producing the manuals said Project X "was a program to develop an exportable foreign intelligence training package to provide counterinsurgency techniques learned in Vietnam to Latin American countries."[87] The manuals were used until 1976, when the Carter administration halted the training for fear that it contributed to human rights abuses. The training was reintroduced in 1982 under the Reagan administration.

The lessons based on the Phoenix Program clearly fostered and promoted the use of methods of terror in the countersubversive struggle. U.S. military officials who authored the School of the Americas training manuals believed that oversight regulations and prohibitions applied only to U.S. personnel, not to foreign officers. In other words, "U.S. instructors could teach abusive techniques to foreign militaries that they could not legally perform themselves."[88] At least one future Condor commander, Major Raúl Eduardo Iturriaga Neumann (who later led DINA's Foreign Department), attended a three-month senior officer intelligence course at Fort Holabird in 1970.[89]

In the 1975 Conference of American Armies, further discussions took place on the adoption of standards for the inter-American military communications system, COPECOMI. In the 1981 conference in Washington, D.C., an accord was signed among the armies to inhibit the activities of subversive organizations of any member country in another member country. Washington thus fostered the consolidation and integration of the region's military and intelligence forces and laid the groundwork for multinational, coordinated countersubversive policies, which spawned Operation Condor.

The conferences and the SOA, as well as other military training programs at Fort Holabird and elsewhere, were key vehicles for the U.S.-sponsored mobilization of the hemispheric security system in the anticommunist crusade. Each Latin American military blended the new security doctrine with its own historical traditions and perceptions of domestic threat. The form and extent of political repression differed in each country. But throughout the region, the armed and security forces adopted the messianic new mission: to remake their states and societies and eliminate "subversion," an expansive category that came to include large sectors of society.

Other U.S. Intelligence Programs

We have seen that tens of thousands of Latin American officers received instruction in such centers as the SOA and Fort Holabird in Maryland, and from MTTs of U.S. Special Forces. Significantly, during the 1960s Holabird was also the Intelligence Command Headquarters of a massive U.S. Army program to spy on U.S. citizens. Intelligence files on ten million U.S. citizens were stored there. In the context of riots, antiwar demonstrations, and other types of civil unrest in the United States, the army had produced extensive blacklists of U.S. citizens by 1967 and databases complete with photographs, personality, and organizational data. The army infiltrated civil rights and antiwar organizations and conducted illegal surveillance of virtually every political protest group in the country. It classified cities in terms of their riot potential and developed a "Compendium" of "subversives," an encyclopedia-sized book that included intelligence reports on every black leader in the country, among many other individuals.[90] The officer in charge of the database was an "architect of the Army's computerized intelligence center in Vietnam."[91] Thus, Latin American officers who used the manuals or took courses at Holabird learned U.S.-approved, extralegal "counterterror" methods like those used in the Phoenix Program, and possibly learned as well about the secret domestic intelligence operations being conducted within the United States at the time.

The U.S. Army's Office of Research and Development sponsored another counterinsurgency and intelligence-gathering project in 1964, called Project Camelot. The stated goals of the project were to "devise procedures for assessing the potential for internal war within national societies" and "to identify . . . those actions which a government might take to relieve [such] conditions."[92] Camouflaged as a university behavioral science project based in American University's Special Operations Research Office (funded by the army), Camelot was a covert intelligence enterprise with counterinsurgency objectives.[93] Camelot was originally conceived to have a vast sweep, encompassing countries throughout the Third World; one army general said it would "help us to predict potential use of the American army in any number of cases where the situation might break out."[94] Only in Chile was the project implemented, however, and not for long.

This U.S. effort was part of a much broader covert intervention in Chile's political affairs in the 1960s, costing millions of U.S. dollars, aimed at determining Chile's future political direction.[95] There, Camelot was presented as an academic survey, its relation to the U.S. Army concealed. Researchers surveyed Chileans from all walks of life to determine their political beliefs, their commitment to democracy, and other personal information. According to one Chilean who took part in the project, each person interviewed was then categorized according to level of danger or "subversive potential." When this individual later tried to get a U.S. visa, U.S. authorities had a complete file on her, with all the supposedly confidential information she had put in the form.[96]

Camelot's databases were used as well for psychological warfare: to influence political attitudes and thereby manipulate key elections. The CIA computerized and analyzed the data gathered by Camelot and used it to produce frightening anticommunist ads during the 1964 election campaign of Christian Democrat candidate Eduardo Frei against leftist Salvador Allende. For example, women were told that if Allende were elected, their children would be sent to Cuba and their husbands sent to concentration camps.[97] The counterinsurgency nature of Project Camelot was discovered by the Chilean government and the project was closed down in 1965 after hearings both in Chile and in the U.S. Congress.

In the 1960s, the militaries of Latin America began to categorize and computerize data on their own citizens and use the data to carry out targeted political repression. After Argentina's 1966 coup, for example, its state intelligence agency SIDE instituted an Advisory Committee for Ideological Classification that categorized persons as "communists," "probably communist, but with insufficient evidence to prosecute in court," and other groupings.[98] In the early 1970s, some of these people began to disappear. In Uruguay, the military regime of the 1970s assigned a category—A, B, or C—to each individual: A meant politically trustworthy, B ideologically suspect, and C enemies who were fired from jobs and subject to arrest.[99] As one Uruguayan put it, "The whole country was run like a prison. The actual prisons were merely the punishment cells."[100] U. S. personnel played a central role in setting up Latin American intelligence bodies that used computers to upgrade their lethal capabilities, agencies such as DINA in Chile, La Técnica in Paraguay,[101] the intelligence apparatus in Guatemala known as the Archivo,[102] Department 5 in El Salvador,[103] and, later, Battalion 3-16 in Honduras.[104] These intelligence organs soon became known for their savage violence.

Transnational Coordination of Repression Emerges in the Americas

The Latin American militaries began to put into practice the continental security doctrine in the tumultuous 1960s, and they increasingly collaborated in cross-border counterinsurgency operations. In their eyes, dangerously radical forces were gaining power. João Goulart became president of Brazil in 1961. Salvador Allende of Chile and Juan José Torres of Bolivia took office in 1970. Henry Kissinger explicitly linked Allende's election to the situation in Italy, where the left also stood to gain political power. "The example of a successful elected Marxist government in Chile would surely have an impact on—an even precedent value for—other parts of the world, especially in Italy," he wrote in 1970.[105] Washington supported coordinated action by the Latin American militaries to oppose the forces of social change. In Brazil, the fiery Goulart worried U.S. leaders and rightist sectors of the Brazilian military, who considered him a communist. To counteract the left, in 1962 the CIA subsidized some 600 candidates for state deputy, along with 250 for federal deputy, fifteen for federal senate, and eight for governor in Brazil.[106] U.S. ambassador Lincoln Gordon was at the center of a plot to overthrow Goulart, and military attaché Vernon Walters was close to insurrectionist officers such as Humberto Castelo Branco. The CIA was sponsoring numerous covert operations to undermine Goulart, including support for paramilitary units controlled by the Brazilian military.[107] The military putschists overthrew the government of Goulart in 1964. While U.S. forces did not directly participate, top-secret documents by the Joint Chiefs of Staff, later declassified, showed that a 110-ton package of arms and ammunition was held in reserve at McGuire Air Force base if needed by the Brazilian military. Also a U.S. carrier task force was in nearby waters, and an oil shipment was ready for delivery to the putschists. The Johnson administration was prepared to openly intervene if necessary.[108] After the coup, the military installed a long-term repressive regime.

Brazil became a major counterrevolutionary force and U.S. ally in South America. Brazil offered training in repressive methods, including torture, to other militaries in the 1960s. An officer of the Brazilian intelligence apparatus Serviço Nacional de Informações (National Information Service—SNI) confirmed in 2000 that in the 1960s, intelligence officers from other Latin American countries came to three Brazilian bases for training in counterguerrilla warfare, "interrogation techniques," and methods of repression. He divulged that beginning in 1969, combined teams "gathered data, later used in the political repression."[109] Cardinal Paulo Arns stated in 2004 that in the 1960s Brazilian forces "learned the new tortures of the United States, and taught torture in Argentina, Uruguay, even Chile, Bolivia, and Paraguay."[110] A document from the Paraguayan Archives, "Informe Confidencial No. 751," dated August

23, 1968, showed that the Brazilian political police unit, the Department of Social and Political Order (DOPS) of São Paulo, asked for the collaboration of the Paraguayan Police that year regarding a "network of guerrillas that acted between Asunción and São Paulo."[111] These examples highlighted the early roots of transnational collaboration in repression, which set the stage for Operation Condor.

The CIA played a key role in organizing this hemispheric collaboration and laying the groundwork for Operation Condor. During the late 1960s, the CIA facilitated the spread of repressive methods and death squad operations in the Southern Cone, always hiding the U.S. hand. CIA officers introduced Brazilian death squad operatives, including the notorious Sergio Fleury, to police officers in Montevideo and Buenos Aires, and arranged meetings between right-wing Brazilian officers and anti-Allende Chilean officers in the early 1970s. CIA men also put officers from these countries in touch with one another to obtain supplies of weapons and explosives and to share intelligence techniques. These contacts eventually led to combined efforts to overthrow leftist leaders and to monitor and persecute exiled political dissidents in the framework of Condor. A. J. Languuth described one incident:

> One Uruguayan police official, proudly nationalistic, resented the way in which U.S. intelligence operators seemed to be melding the intelligence services of the Southern Cone into one interlocking apparatus . . . [moreover] if this work was so valuable in stopping communism, he wondered, why did the CIA officers take such care that their role be secret?[112]

This Uruguayan policeman noticed that after a CIA officer set up a meeting between high-ranking Argentine and Brazilian officials to discuss a surveillance program in which each would monitor exiles in the other's territory—a key feature of the Condor system—the CIA man found an excuse not to attend. Clearly, this policeman was perceiving the crucial, if shadowy, role of the CIA in organizing the foundations of Operation Condor.

In another case, a Brazilian policeman who became an intelligence officer in DOPS, and then a death squad leader, spoke proudly of his CIA connections and his CIA training courses in the United States. "Sérgio" (a pseudonym) became an intelligence operative soon after the 1964 coup, and he touted his working relations with the CIA in Brazil. He was linked to a secret repressive organization based in São Paulo named OBAN, set up in 1969 at the urging of the United States. OBAN coordinated police and military counter-subversive forces and carried out offensive operations against suspected subversives. It has been compared to the Phoenix Program in Vietnam—set up just two years earlier by U.S. officers—because of its objective to liquidate civilian opposition networks. "Sérgio" said that during his training in the

United States he had learned how to conduct wiretapping and other surveillance techniques, how to infiltrate groups, and "how political police should operate." The most useful sessions, he said, were discussions with his CIA trainers on how to track subversives across national borders[113]—operations later subsumed under Condor. "Sérgio's" testimony revealed, again, the linkages between the CIA and Latin American death squads as well as the instrumental CIA role in laying the groundwork for Operation Condor.

Bolivia was another site of political conflict in the 1960s. In 1967, Che Guevara, the Argentine protagonist of the Cuban revolution, was captured and executed in Bolivia as he tried to spark an insurrection there. The Bolivian Ranger commando responsible was trained and directly assisted by U.S. forces, including Cuban exile and CIA agent Felix Rodríguez. (In fact, CIA station chief in Bolivia, John Tilton, said, "The operation to locate and capture if possible Che Guevara was a CIA operation run by the station with the cooperation in the field of Bolivians."[114]) In 1970, Juan José Torres, a populist military officer, was named president in Bolivia after a series of military rulers. He nationalized a tin mine owned by U.S. interests, expelled the Peace Corps, closed a U.S. military base, and opened lines of communication with Bolivian left and labor movements and with Cuba. U.S. ambassador Ernest Siracusa (who later became ambassador to Uruguay) pressured Torres to change his policies to no avail.

Then-colonel Hugo Banzer, graduate of the Army School of the Americas and former military attaché in Washington, staged a coup in 1971 (his second attempt). He was supported by land-owning elites in Santa Cruz, the Brazilian and Argentine militaries, and the CIA. In fact, according to Minister of the Interior Jorge Gallardo—later a victim of Condor—the plot was organized in Argentina, and one crucial meeting included Banzer, several CIA officers, the chief of the U.S. military mission in Buenos Aires, and a Pentagon commander who flew in from Washington. When Banzer's communications system failed during the coup, U.S. Air Force major Robert Lundin, who was based in Bolivia, put the U.S. Air Force radio system at his disposal. The multinational coup involved the direct participation of Brazilian officers and was partly funded by the Argentine military regime.[115] One U.S. Embassy report noted that "recent events in Bolivia, in which GOA [Government of Argentina] was involved, may well encourage those in GOA who look to this kind of [military] solution."[116] A 1971 *San Francisco Chronicle* article reported that the Bolivian coup was "part of a far-reaching movement, backed by the U.S. CIA, to seize power in a total of six South American republics."[117] These six countries, later, became the key members of Condor. Banzer reversed the policies of Torres and instituted iron rule in Bolivia on the Brazilian model, carrying out brutally repressive measures, with the use of assassination and torture, against the population.[118]

In Uruguay in 1971, the leftist Frente Amplio, a new political party, began attracting prominent members of the two traditional parties to its ranks. When it appeared that the Frente might win the presidency, the Brazilian military regime planned to invade Uruguay in a plan named Operation 30 Hours. Brazil also took covert steps to undermine the Uruguayan election, with the blessings of the Nixon administration.[119] Frente presidential candidate Liber Seregni was physically attacked more than once, for example, acts he linked to Brazilian and U.S. CIA agents.[120] Ballot boxes disappeared and a mysterious power outage occurred when the ballots were being counted. U.S. documents declassified in 2002 made clear that then-President Richard Nixon feared an Allende-style electoral victory in Uruguay and considered the Brazilian efforts "to rig the Uruguayan election" to be in the U.S. interest.[121] Declassified documents also showed that U.S. officials were encouraging the Argentine and Brazilian militaries to take an active role in undermining the Frente coalition, a democratic leftist force that was considered even more dangerous than the Tupamaro guerrillas. During a meeting with Brazilian dictator Médici, National Security Advisor Kissinger told him: "In areas of mutual concern such as the situations in Uruguay and Bolivia, close cooperation and parallel approaches can be very helpful for our common objectives."[122] Kissinger wrote to Nixon that the Brazilian dictatorship should be encouraged to "play a special role in the hemisphere in furthering our mutual interests,"[123] clearly as a U.S. proxy in the region.

The United States already had established intelligence operations in Uruguay to undermine the legal left. E. Howard Hunt, CIA station chief from 1956 to 1960, had recruited the chief of police and the chief of army intelligence and boasted that he and they formed "an operational triumvirate, and to the station's assets were added not only those of the federal police but of the Uruguayan Army as well."[124] Other covert operations were organized from the Office of Public Safety, set up in 1964. By 1970, social discontent was rising sharply in the country due to repressive government policies and economic restructuring. U.S. policeman Dan Mitrione was sent to Montevideo to train the police—reportedly in methods of torture (he had been stationed previously in Brazil).[125] Jeffrey Ryan has shown that in Uruguay, once known as "the Switzerland of South America," external influences transformed Uruguay's police from a neighborhood law enforcement force that served its citizens to one that terrorized them, and converted a constitutionalist military into hardened shock troops that imprisoned and tortured large numbers of Uruguayans.[126] Training at the International Police Academy in Washington and the Army School of the Americas in Panama succeeded in producing "a cadre of officials who would return to Uruguay as missionaries of American counter-insurgency methods and doctrine."[127] Gradually, the Uruguayan armed forces and police became brutal counterinsurgency forces, and torture became routine.

There were other examples of deepening repressive coordination. The 1973 Chilean coup itself was a multinational effort, as the 1971 Bolivian coup had been. Documents released in 2004 showed that Henry Kissinger acknowledged to Nixon that "we helped" the putschists and "created the conditions [for the coup] as great as possible [*sic*]." Richard Nixon responded that "our hand doesn't show" in the coup. Brazilian officers took part in the seizure of Brazilian exiles living in Santiago at the time of the coup and carried out interrogation and torture in the stadium where thousands of Chileans and exiles were rounded up.[128] In 1973, there were some one thousand Brazilians exiled in Chile. The SNI distributed in Rio a detailed report about the Brazilians who sought asylum in the Argentine Embassy in Santiago, evidence of the close cooperation between the SNI and the Chilean intelligence apparatus conducting surveillance in Santiago.[129] That same year, Brazilian police were also operating in Argentina. A death squad, possibly commanded by Sergio Fleury, abducted two Brazilians in Buenos Aires.[130] Other Brazilian exiles reported later that they were interrogated and tortured by Brazilians after the coups in Bolivia (1971), Chile (1973), and Argentina (1976).

Argentina was coming out of military rule in 1973, and populist leader Juan Perón was returning from an exile of eighteen years. Argentina's political juncture was crucial: it was an outpost of relative liberty surrounded by repressive military regimes. After Argentina returned to civilian rule (1973–1976) many thousands of dissidents and refugees from neighboring countries fled to that comparatively safe haven. The fearsome Alianza Anticomunista Argentina, or Triple A, death squads—a parallel force with direct links to the state security apparatus—surfaced in 1973, however, and operatives from these shadowy groups collaborated with some Condor assassinations, as did Argentine military and intelligence organizations.[131]

In Chile, DINA was created shortly after the September 1973 coup. Its first incarnation was as the secret DINA Commission, an ideologically extreme and committed group of colonels and majors of the army.[132] The junta publicly established DINA in June 1974 as an autonomous intelligence agency reporting directly to Pinochet. More powerful than the intelligence branches of the regular armed forces, DINA established a near-monopoly on countersubversive action and internal intelligence. One DINA operative explained DINA's strategy as follows: "First the aim was to stop terrorism, then possible extremists were targeted and later those who might be converted into extremists."[133] (Similar language was used in 1977 by Argentine general Ibérico St.-Jean when he said: "First we will kill all the subversives; then we will kill their collaborators; then their sympathizers; then those who remain indifferent.")

Such statements reflected the extremist concepts of the national security doctrine that formed the philosophical foundation of the national security states.

To conclude, this chapter has shown that Western leaders created and used parallel armies as part of a secret counterinsurgency strategy after World War II. The paramilitary formations incorporated right-wing individuals within and outside the state and included Nazi war criminals. U.S. leaders later transferred the concept to Asia and Latin America. The European parastatal formations presaged Operation Condor, and the evidence suggests that Condor was part of a broader clandestine organization of anticommunist and antidemocratic forces. Indeed, there were links among individuals within the stay-behind armies and Condor officers. In Western Europe, as in Latin America, the anticommunist crusade became a war against progressive and democratic sectors as well as communists and guerrillas. In short, there was an "underside" of the anticommunist crusade, as parallel state structures and clandestine operations escaped democratic control and violated basic human rights.

In the Americas, Washington and its regional allies moved to counter populist and revolutionary forces and secure the politico-economic status quo. The U.S. government led the restructuring of the inter-American system, particularly in the 1960s, in order to build a continental countersubversive movement of the region's militaries. The U.S. government strengthened military, intelligence, and police forces, trained them in counterinsurgency warfare and joint operations, urged the formation of clandestine counterterror squads, and encouraged anticommunist allies to actively interfere in neighboring countries. The Brazilian and Argentine militaries—the most powerful in the Southern Cone region—intervened in Uruguay, Bolivia, and Chile to assist counterrevolutionary forces and undermine democratic systems, aided indirectly by the U.S. national security apparatus. The CIA introduced members of Brazilian death squads to military and police officers in Uruguay, Chile, and Argentina, establishing links among them and diffusing the methods of terror, and encouraged them to track political opponents across borders. Brazil, acting in alliance with Washington, offered training in repressive methods to its neighbors. This was the environment in which Condor—a multinational, cross-border hunter-killer force—was organized.

Notes

1. I first made this argument in "Operation Condor: Clandestine Interamerican System," *Social Justice*, Vol. 26, no. 4 (Winter 1999): 144–174.

2. See, for example, Norman A. Graebner, ed., *The National Security: Its Theory and Practice 1945–1960* (New York: Oxford University Press, 1986); Walter LaFeber, *Inevitable Revolutions: The United States in Central America* (New York: W. W. Norton,

1983); Stephen Rabe, *Eisenhower and Latin America: The Foreign Policy of Anticommunism* (Chapel Hill: University of North Carolina Press, 1988); and Peter J. Schraeder, *United States Foreign Policy toward Africa: Incrementalism, Crisis and Change* (Cambridge, U.K.: Cambridge University Press, 1994).

3. Steven Metz, "A Flame Kept Burning: Counterinsurgency Support after the Cold War," *Parameters* (Autumn 1995).

4. Norman A. Graebner, "Introduction: The Sources of Postwar Insecurity," in Graebner, *National Security*, 20–21.

5. NSC-68 (1950) in Thomas G. Paterson, ed., *Major Problems in American Foreign Policy*. Volume II: *Since 1914*, 3rd ed. (Lexington, Ky.: D.C. Heath, 1989), 301, 304.

6. See, for example, LaFeber, *Inevitable Revolutions*; David Schmitz, *Thank God They're on Our Side* (Chapel Hill: University of North Carolina, 1999); and Rabe, *Eisenhower*.

7. U.S. Senate Select Committee, *Final Reports*, Book I, *Foreign and Military Intelligence*, 9, cited in Kathryn Olmsted, *Challenging the Secret Government: The Post-Watergate Investigations of the CIA and FBI* (Chapel Hill: University of North Carolina Press, 1996), 13.

8. See Cole Blasier, "Security: The Extracontinental Dimension," in Kevin J. Middlebrook and Carlos Rico, eds., *The United States and Latin America in the 1980s* (Pittsburgh, Pa.: University of Pittsburgh Press, 1988), 523–564; "The Soviet Union," in Morris J. Blachman, William M. Leogrande, and Kenneth Sharpe, *Confronting Revolution: Security through Diplomacy in Central America* (New York: Pantheon, 1986), 256–270.

9. This section builds on and expands my article "Operation Condor: Clandestine Interamerican System."

10. U.S. Senate, Church Committee Report, Book IV, 1976: 29–31, cited in Christopher Simpson, *Blowback: America's Recruitment of Nazis and Its Effects on the Cold War* (New York: Macmillan, Collier Books, 1988), 102.

11. Major D. H. Berger, U.S. Marine Corps, "The Use of Covert Paramilitary Activity as a Policy Tool: An Analysis of Operations Conducted by the United States Central Intelligence Agency, 1949–1951" (written in fulfillment of a requirement for the Marines Corps Command and Staff College), n.d., available on www.fas.org/irp/eprint/berger.htm.

12. Searchlight, "The Gladio Conspiracy," 1991, at www.searchlightmagazine.com/stories/gladio.htm (accessed in June 1999).

13. See Ed Vulliamy, *Guardian* (U.K.), December 10, 1990, in Statewatch compilation of European reporting on the stay-behind armies at www.statewatch.org (accessed June 1999). See also Stuart Christie, *Stefano Delle Chiaie: Portrait of a Black Terrorist* (London: Anarchy Magazine/Refract Publications, 1984), 141–143, for a secret NATO document from the 1960s detailing the clandestine underground structure.

14. "US Trained Secret NATO Group Resistance Network," *Boston Globe*, November 17, 1990.

15. Kati Marton, *The Polk Conspiracy: Murder and Cover-Up in the Case of CBS News Correspondent George Polk* (New York: Farrar, Straus & Giroux, 1990), 78–81, chapter 9, 109–112, 144–150; "'Staying Behind': NATO's Terror Network," *Arm the Spirit* (Canada), October 11, 1995 at www/misc.activism.progressive (accessed May 2003).

16. Yiannis Roubatis and Karen Wynn, "CIA Operations in Greece," in Philip Agee and Louis Wolf, eds., *Dirty Work: The CIA in Western Europe* (London: Zed Press, 1978), 148, 151.

17. Roubatis and Wynn, "CIA Operations in Greece," 154–155.

18. C. M. Woodhouse, *The Rise and Fall of the Greek Colonels* (New York: Franklin Watts, 1985), 7.

19. Woodhouse, *The Rise and Fall*, 12, 20, 25; Christie, *Stefano Delle Chiaie*, 39.

20. Daniel Singer, "The Gladiators," *The Nation*, Vol. 251, no. 20 (1990): 720–722.

21. For an account of later CIA operations in Italy and in Central America, see the memoir by former CIA officer Duane R. Clarridge (who later led the Latin American section of CIA operations in the 1980s and oversaw the Argentine army operation in Honduras). The book is a less-than-credible history, however. Duane Clarridge, with Digby Diehl, *A Spy for All Seasons: My Life in the CIA* (New York: Scribner, 1997).

22. George Black, "The Cold War's Devils Were on Both Sides," *Los Angeles Times*, November 29, 1990.

23. Simpson, *Blowback*, 100–102; Philip Willan, *Puppet Masters: The Political Use of Terrorism in Italy* (London: Constable, 1991), 27 and chapter 8; Arthur E. Rowse, "Gladio: The Secret U.S. War to Subvert Italian Democracy," *Covert Action Quarterly*, no. 49 (1994) at www.mediafilter.org/CAQ.

24. Willan, *Puppet Masters*, 27; Jonathan Kwitney, "The CIA's Secret Armies in Europe," *The Nation*, Vol. 254, no. 13 (April 6, 1992).

25. Personal e-mail from Pierre Abramovici, a French journalist researching this history, December 17, 2002. See also Christie, *Stefano*, 81.

26. Joe Lauria, "Italy's President Defends Secret Army," *Guardian* (New York), April 10, 1991, 15; Willan, *Puppet*, 170.

27. Paul Quinn-Judge, "US Caches in Austria Stir Diplomatic Concerns; Austria Unaware Supplies Were Stashed by CIA," *Boston Globe*, January 20, 1996; "Stay-behind Weapons Stash Catches up to CIA; U.S. Apologizes for Supplies Hidden in Austria 50 Years Ago," *Houston Chronicle*, January 22, 1996; Ian Traynor, "Britain Pressed to Reveal Arsenals; Austria Demands Truth on Allies' Cold War Tactics," *The Guardian* (U.K.), January 22, 1996.

28. "Britain Has Arms in Cold War Austria; Allies Relied on Former Waffen SS Personnel to Repel Potential Soviet Invasion," *The Guardian* (U.K.), January 27, 1996; Martin A. Lee, "CIA's Worst-Kept Secret," consortiumnews.com, May 16, 2001; Elizabeth Olson, "Documents Show U.S. Relationship with Nazis during Cold War," *New York Times*, May 14, 2004.

29. Lucy Komisar, "Turkey's Terrorists: A CIA Legacy Lives on," *The Progressive*, (April 1997), at www.progressive.org (accessed May 2003).

30. Eduardo Goncalves, "Right-Wing Terrorists Killed Portuguese PM in Faked Plane Crash," *The Guardian* (London), July 18, 1999; see also his "Portuguese Hero to Face Terror Charges," *The Guardian*, December 13, 1999.

31. David Johnston, "Prewar File Told of Hitler's Mental State," *New York Times*, April 28, 2001. For Kissinger history, see Seymour M. Hersh, *The Price of Power: Kissinger in the Nixon White House* (New York: Summit Books, 1983), 25–27. According to Christie and other sources, the Pentagon absorbed the entire Gehlen Organiza-

tion after World War II. Christie, *Stefano*, 69; Searchlight, "The Gladio Conspiracy,"1991; Federation of American Scientists, "Organization Gehlen," at www.fas.org/irp/world/germany/intro/gehlen.htm.

32. Black, "Cold War's Devils."

33. For Taylor quote see U.S. Justice Department, Office of Special Investigations, "Klaus Barbie and the United States Government: A Report to the Attorney General of the United States," August 1983, p. 39, at www.usdoj.gov/criminal/publicdocs/11-1prior/11-1prior.htm; see also Interagency Working Group, National Archives and Records Administration (NARA), "Analysis of Investigative Records Repository File of Klaus Barbie," September 19, 2001; Mark Weitzman, "Remarks before the Nazi War Criminals Interagency Working Group," NARA, 1999; George Lardner, Jr., "CIA Files Confirm U.S. Used Nazis after WWII," *Washington Post*, April 28, 2001; Searchlight, "The Gladio Conspiracy," 1991; and Martin A. Lee, "Torture Colony Raided in Chile: Nazi SS Veteran Still at Large," *Reality Bites*, October 30, 2000, at www.sfbg.com/reality/02.html.

34. Clare Pedrick, "CIA Organized Secret Army in Western Europe," *Washington Post*, November 14, 1990.

35. Pedrick, "CIA Organized."

36. Patrice Claude, "Strange Tale of Terrorism, Sabotage Shakes Italy," *San Francisco Chronicle*, November 14, 1990.

37. European Parliament Joint Resolution of November 22, 1990, in Statewatch report, May 1991.

38. Judgment of the Federal Court of Buenos Aires in the Prats Case, reproduced by politicaconosur@ gruposyahoo.com, no. 51, December 21, 2001, 20; Samuel Blixen, "Gunning for Pinochet," *Latinamerica Press*, June 8, 1995, 3; Horacio Verbitsky, "Gracias a la vida," *Página/12* (Argentina), May 16, 2001.

39. Court testimony cited by Willan, *Puppet*, 138, 141. See also Christie, *Stefano*, 19–21.

40. Pedrick, *Washington Post*, November 14, 1990; Edward Vulliamy, "Bomb Used at Bologna 'Came from NATO Unit,'" *Guardian* (U.K.), January 16, 1991.

41. Court testimony cited by Willan, *Puppet*, 141–142.

42. Esteban Cuya, "La 'Operación Cóndor': El terrorismo de estado de alcance transnacional" (December 1993), on Derechos website (www.derechos.org/koaga/vii/2/cuya.html); Christie, *Stefano*, 85–86.

43. "1975: Atentado en Roma," *Siglo XX en la Tercera* (Chile), n.d. (available at www.siglo20.tercera.cl/1970-79/1975/rep.htm); "Pinochet pudo encargar en Madrid el crimen de Leighton," *El País* (Spain), December 10, 1998; see also Christie, *Stefano*, 74–76.

44. See Townley letter in FBI report entitled "Dirección de Inteligencia Nacional," document ch02-01, National Security Archive website. For more on delle Chiaie, see Willan, *Puppet*, 1991; Tito Drago, "Spanish Judge Issues Indictment against Pinochet," *Interpress Service*, December 1998; "Un agente de la internacional negra," *Página/12* (Argentina), May 20, 1995; "Sugiere un ex agente chileno que Pinochet ordenó crímenes," *La Jornada* (Mexico), May 21, 1995.

45. See articles in *Clarín* (Argentina), June 24, 1995.

46. "Identifican en Bolivia a asesores de García Meza," *Tiempo Argentino*, June 27, 1985; see also Martin Edwin Andersen, *Dossier Secreto: Argentina's Desaparecidos and the Myth of the 'Dirty War'* (Boulder, Colo.: Westview, 1993) for various references to delle Chiaie.

47. Willan, *Puppet*, 26–27, 100–101, 113, 131–132, 146–147, 151, 292; David Guyatt, "Operation Gladio," www.copi.com/articles/guyatt/html.

48. Quoted in Andersen, *Dossier Secreto*, 317.

49. Willan, *Puppet*, 220.

50. Willan, *Puppet*; Rowse, "Gladio"; Edward Vulliamy, "Bomb Used at Bologna Came from NATO Unit," *The Guardian* (U.K.), January 16, 1991.

51. Rowse, "Gladio." For background on Gelli, see Andersen, *Dossier Secreto*, 87–94.

52. See Christie, *Stefano*, 162–63, for more on P-2.

53. Jimmy Burns, "Argentine Courts Impound Gelli Assets," *Financial Times* (London), August 17, 1983; Paul Burns, "The Right and Military Rule," in Sandra McGee Deutsch and Ronald H. Dolkart, eds., *The Argentine Right* (Wilmington, Del.: Scholarly Resources, 1993), 173–174. P-2 laundered enormous funds through its international network of businesses, the Catholic Church, and the underworld, according to Lewis; its political purpose was to serve as an anticommunist international. Many top military officers in Argentina were P-2 members.

54. George Black, "Delle Chiaie: From Bologna to Bolivia; A Terrorist Odyssey," *The Nation*, vol. 244 (April 26, 1987): 525–531.

55. See Andersen, *Dossier Secreto*, 87–94; Rowse, "Gladio"; Willan, *Puppet*, chapter 3; "Licio Gelli a la sombra: La conexión rioplatense," *El Periodista de Buenos Aires*, no. 159 (September 25 to October 1, 1987): 5–10; "Investigan la posible conexión entre Licio Gelli y la mafia," *Clarín*, August 18, 1992.

56. *Página/12* (Argentina), June 13, 1992. Razin also implicated Michael Townley, the CIA, and P-2 in the assassination of Olaf Palme, prime minister of Sweden, and implied that the crime was linked to the first Bush administration in the United States. This account has never been substantiated, or even investigated, to my knowledge.

57. Rowse, " Gladio," 5; Statewatch compilation: William Scobie, *Observer*, November 18, 1990; Richard Bassett, *Times of London*, July 24, 1990; see also Searchlight, "The Gladio Conspiracy," 1991.

58. Scobie, *Observer*, November 18, 1990.

59. Philip Willan, "Obituary: Paulo Emilio Taviani," *The Guardian* (U.K.), June 21, 2001; Christie, *Stefano*, 63.

60. "Italiano implica CIA em atentados," *Jornal do Brasil*, August 5, 2000.

61. See Willan, "Obituary."

62. Rowse, "Gladio," 3.

63. Wolfgang Achtner, *Sunday Independent*, November 11, 1990.

64. Achtner, *Sunday Independent*; Rowse, "Gladio," 4; Christie, *Stefano*, 23–24.

65. Pedrick, *Washington Post*.

66. Ed Vulliamy, "Italy's Secret Agents Accused of Terrorism," *The Guardian* (U.K.), October 1, 1993; see also Alan Cowell, "Italy in a Furor as 'Mata Hari" Talks of Military Plot," *New York Times*, October 19, 1993.

67. Neil Sheehan, Hendrick Smith, E. W. Kenworthy, and Fox Butterfield, *The Pentagon Papers* (New York: *New York Times*/Bantam Books, 1971), 131.

68. For an extended discussion, see my book *Incomplete Transition: Military Power and Democracy in Argentina* (New York: St. Martin's Press, 1997), especially chapters 2 and 3.

69. John Child, *Unequal Alliance: The Inter-American Military System, 1938–1978* (Boulder, Colo.: Westview, 1980), chapters 3 and 4.

70. Child, *Unequal Alliance*, 167.

71. Jeremy Bigwood, "U.S. Expands Military Presence in Latin America," *Interpress Service*, April 18, 2003, at globalinfo.org.

72. A rich bibliography exists on the case of Guatemala. Key texts include Susanne Jonas, *The Battle for Guatemala: Rebels, Death Squads, and U.S. Power* (Boulder, Colo.: Westview, 1991; Richard H. Immerman, *The CIA in Guatemala: The Foreign Policy of Intervention* (Austin: University of Texas Press, 1982, fifth printing 1990); Stephen Schlesinger and Stephen Kinzer, *Bitter Fruit: The Untold Story of the American Coup in Guatemala* (New York: Doubleday, 1983); Stephen Streeter, *Managing the Counterrevolution: The United States and Guatemala, 1954–1961* (Athens: Center for International Studies, Ohio University, 2000). See also State Department documents declassified in May 2003 at www.foia.state.gov.

73. This section draws from McSherry, "Tracking the Origins," 2002. See also Tom Barry, *Low-Intensity Conflict: The New Battlefield in Central America* (Albuquerque, N.M.: The Resource Center, 1986): 8; Susanne Jonas, "Contradictions of Revolution and Intervention in Central America in the Transnational Era: The Case of Guatemala," in Marlene Dixon and Susanne Jonas, eds., *Revolution and Intervention in Central America* (San Francisco: Synthesis Publications, 1983), 288–289.

74. U.S. Department of State, Director of Intelligence and Research, "Guatemala: A Counter-Insurgency Running Wild?" October 23, 1967: 2. See National Security Archive, "CIA and Assassinations: The Guatemala 1954 Documents," Electronic Briefing Book no. 4, and "U.S. Policy in Guatemala, 1966–1986," Electronic Briefing Book no. 11, 1997.

75. Vaky wrote: "Is it conceivable that we are so obsessed with insurgency that we are prepared to rationalize murder as an acceptable counter-insurgency weapon? Is it possible that a nation which so reveres the principle of due process of law has so easily acquiesced in this sort of terror tactic?" Vaky concluded that "counter-terror is wrong as a counter-insurgency tactic" and expressed the fear that "we will stand before history unable to answer the accusations that we encouraged the Guatemalan Army to do these things." Viron Vaky to ARA, "Guatemala and Counter-terror," March 29, 1968; at www.seas.gwu/nsarchive/ NSAEBB/NSAEBB11/docs/05-01.htm.

76. See Horacio P. Ballester, José Luis García, Carlos Mariano Gazcón, and Augusto B. Rattenbach, "El sistema interamericano de defensa como paradigma de la seguridad nacional," *Revista Cruz del Sur,* Instituto Latinoamericano de Estudios Geopolíticos 3 no. 7 (December 1985): 8. For other Latin American material on the Conference of American Armies, see República Argentina, Biblioteca del Congreso de la Nación, *Diario de las sesiones del congreso* (April 7, 1988, and April 13–14, 1988) 3005 and 3123; Samuel Blixen, "El estado policial que nos preparan los militares," *Brecha* (Uruguay),

3, no. 145 (August 26, 1988); Luis Garasino, "El 'narcoterorrismo,'" *Clarín*, November 9, 1987; articles in *Compañero* (Uruguay), 18, no. 139 (September 1, 1988); Fernando Nadra, "Los cerebros del terror," *Qué Pasa*, n.d. (c. 1988).

77. See interview with army chief Martín Balza, *Clarín*, March 24, 1996.

78. Henry Nevares (Lt.-Col.), "Antecedentes sobre las conferencias de ejércitos americanos: Trabajo y presentación efectuado por el delegado del ejército de los EEUU," Santiago: Secretaría Permanente, XVI Conferencia de Ejércitos Americanos, 1985. The author is grateful to Pierre Abramovici, French journalist, for sharing this document with her. See also Abramovici, "Latin America: The 30 Years' Dirty War," *Le Monde Diplomatique*, August 2001.

79. The author found documents on this meeting in the Paraguayan Archives in 1996.

80. Committee reports, Conference of Chiefs of Communications, June 1973, p. 4, reviewed by author at the Paraguayan Archives of Terror, 1996.

81. Greg Weeks, "Fighting the Enemy Within: Terrorism, the School of the Americas, and the Military in Latin America," *Human Rights Review* 5, 1 (October–December 2003): 12-27. For more on the SOA, see Lesley Gill, *The School of the Americas: Military Training and Political Violence in the Americas* (Durham, N.C.: Duke University Press, 2004).

82. Space constraints prevent an extended discussion of Phoenix here. See Douglas Valentine, *The Phoenix Program* (New York: William Morrow, 1990); John Doe, "Phoenix Program," in Harold V. Hall and Leighton C. Whitaker, eds., *Collective Violence: Effective Strategies for Assessing and Intervening in Fatal Group and Institutional Aggression* (New York: CRC Press, 1999), 633–642; and McSherry, "Tracking the Origins."

83. John Doe, "Phoenix Program," 634.

84. Barbara Jentzsch, "School of the Americas Critic," *The Progressive* (1997): 61.

85. Jentzsch, "School of the Americas Critic," 61; Mary A. Fischer, "Teaching Torture," *Gentlemen's Quarterly* (June 1997); Latin American Working Group, "Inspector General's Report on Army Manuals a Feeble Response: What the Recently Declassified Manuals Contain," ms, Washington, D.C., 1997; Dana Priest, "U.S. Instructed Latins on Executions, Torture," *Washington Post*, September 21, 1996; and "Army's Project X Had Wider Audience," *Washington Post*, March 6, 1997.

86. Office of House Representative Joseph Kennedy, "Report on the School of the Americas," March 6, 1997, 6–14.

87. Priest, "Army's Project X," *Washington Post*, March 6, 1997; Department of Defense, "USSOUTHCOM CI Training-Supplemental Information, Confidential," July 31, 1991, on National Security Archive website, Electronic Briefing Book 122, www.gwu.edu/~nsarchiv/ NSAEBB/NSAEBB122/index.htm.

88. Latin American Working Group (a project of the National Council of Churches), "Inspector General's Report on Army Manuals a Feeble Response; What the Recently Declassified Manuals Contain," Washington, D.C. (1997): 9. LAWG is quoting directly from an internal army report on the manuals.

89. Army bio of Iturriaga Neumann, from USDAO Santiago to RUEKJCS/DIA WASHDC, July 1987.

90. This information is drawn from a fascinating study by Christopher Pyle, a former army intelligence officer who denounced publicly the existence of this secret domestic intelligence apparatus in 1970. Pyle, *Military Surveillance of Civilian Politics, 1967–1970* (New York, Garland, 1986). See also Morton Halperin, Jerry Berman, Robert Borosage, and Christine Marwick, *The Lawless State: The Crimes of the U.S. Intelligence Agencies* (New York: Penguin Books, 1976); Pyle, "Irresponsible Journalists Are Jeopardizing Serious Investigations by the Press," *The Chronicle Review*, January 7, 2000.

91. Pyle, *Military Surveillance*, 311.

92. Irving Louis Horowitz, ed., *The Rise and Fall of Project Camelot* (Cambridge, Mass.: The MIT Press, 1967), 4, quoting from a description of Camelot dated December 4, 1964 and mailed to select scholars.

93. See Horowitz, *The Rise and Fall* and Robert A. Nisbet, "Project Camelot: An Autopsy," in Philip Rieff, ed., *On Intellectuals: Theoretical Studies, Case Studies* (Garden City, N.Y.: Doubleday, 1969), 283–313, for two contemporary accounts. These authors understandably missed much of the significance of the project because they were not yet aware of the large-scale secret CIA program in Chile between 1960 and 1973, featuring manipulation of the media, swaying of elections, sponsoring of terrorist groups such as *Patria y Libertad*, and promotion of a coup. The U.S. public learned more details of the CIA program in the mid-1970s via the Church Committee's meticulous report.

94. Nisbet, "Project Camelot," 284.

95. See, for example, the Church Committee report: U.S. Senate, Staff Report of the Select Committee to Study Governmental Operations with Respect to Intelligence Activities, "Covert Action in Chile 1963–1973," Washington, D.C.: Government Printing Office, 1976.

96. Interview with Chilean professional, Santiago de Chile, July 18, 1996.

97. Daniel Brandt, "U.S. Responsibility for the Coup in Chile," November 28, 1998, excerpt from "Leftist Christians in Chile and the Coup of 1973" (Berkeley, Graduate Theological Union, 1975), at www.namebase.org/condor.html.

98. McSherry, *Incomplete Transition*, 119.

99. Lawrence Weschler, *A Miracle, A Universe: Settling Accounts with Torturers* (New York: Penguin Books USA, 1990), 90–91.

100. Weschler, *A Miracle*, 92.

101. R. Andrew Nickson, "Paraguay's Archivo del Terror," *Latin America Research Review*, Vol. 30, no. 1 (1995): 127; see also lawsuit filed against the CIA by Marcial Riquelme, December 6, 2002.

102. Rachel Garst, "Military Intelligence and Human Rights in Guatemala: The Archivo and the Case for Intelligence Reform" (Washington, D.C.: WOLA, March 30, 1995): 4.

103. Valentine, *The Phoenix Program*, 422.

104. Cohn and Thompson, "Unearthed: Fatal Secrets," four-part series in the *Baltimore Sun*, June 11–18, 1995.

105. National Security Archive, "Update," February 3, 2003, Electronic Briefing Book no. 110.

106. A. J. Languuth, *Hidden Terrors: The Truth about U.S. Police Operations in Latin America* (New York: Pantheon, 1978), 91. Languuth was a former *New York Times* bureau chief in Saigon.

107. Languuth, *Hidden Terrors*, 107.

108. Languuth, *Hidden Terrors*, 111. Documents declassified in 2004 showed that President Johnson was deeply involved in the decision to back the coup and to ensure its success, and the files also revealed the CIA operations. See National Security Archive for documents at www.gwu.edu/~nsarchiv/NSAEBB/NSAEBB118/index.htm, accessed by author March 2004.

109. Eleonora Gosman, "Denuncian que Brasil colaboró activamente con Pinochet," *Clarín*, May 15, 2000 and "El desplume del Plan Cóndor," *Clarín*, May 28, 2000; see also *Clarín*, May 10, 2000; *Notisur*, July 7, 2000.

110. *Ambito Financiero*, May 15, 2000; Yana Marull, "Conmemoran 40 años de dictadura," *El Diario/La Prensa* (New York), April 1, 2004.

111. Paraguayan police document, "Informe Confidencial No. 731," August 23, 1968, obtained in Paraguayan Archives, 1996.

112. Languuth, *Hidden Terrors*, 244.

113. Martha K. Huggins, Mika Haritos-Fatouros, and Philip G. Zimbardo, *Violence Workers: Police Torturers and Murderers Reconstruct Brazilian Atrocities* (Berkeley: University of California Press, 2002), 71, 96–97, 170.

114. From the documentary "CIA–Executive Action," on the History Channel, 1996.

115. Martín Sivak, *El asesinato de Juan José Torres: Banzer y el mercosur de la muerte* (Buenos Aires: Ediciones de Pensamiento Nacional, 1998), 21, 52; see also Jerry Meldon, "Return of Bolivia's Drug-Stained Dictator," *The Consortium*, 1997 (at www.consortiumtnews.com/archive/story40.html).

116. U.S. Embassy, Buenos Aires, to Secretary of State, "Uruguayan Situation," August 27, 1971, in National Security Archives Electronic Briefing Book No. 71.

117. Cliff Pearson, "Texas Politician Linked to CIA/SOA Military Coup," *Dallas Peace Times*, May 1998.

118. For a concise, and fascinating, history of the era, see Herbert S. Klein, *Bolivia: The Evolution of a Multi-Ethnic Society*, 2nd ed. (New York: Oxford, 1992), 238–268.

119. Samuel Blixen, *Seregni: La mañana siguiente*, 2d ed. (Montevideo, Uruguay: Ediciones de Brecha, 1997): 70–74; National Security Archive Electronic Briefing Book No. 71 at www.gwu.edu/~nsarchiv/NSAEBB/NSAEBB71/.

120. U.S. Embassy, Montevideo, to Secretary of State, Joint State/Defense Message, "Seregni, pro-'Frente' press link U.S. to Attacks on 'Frente' Candidates," November 9, 1971, in National Security Archives Electronic Briefing Book No. 71.

121. "Nixon quis Médici à frente do continente," *Jornal do Brasil*, June 21, 2002; National Security Archive documents.

122. "Secret memorandum for Kissinger on his conversation with Brazilian President on December 8," December 10, 1971, in Electronic Briefing Book No. 71.

123. "Secret Memorandum from Kissinger to President Nixon," circa early December 1971, NSA Electronic Briefing Book No. 71.

124. E. Howard Hunt, *Undercover: Memoirs of an American Secret Agent* (London: W. H. Allen, 1975), 121.

125. See Langguth, *Hidden Terrors.* Mitrione was abducted and assassinated by the guerrilla group Tupamaros in 1971; a Costa-Gavras movie called "State of Siege" dramatized this case.

126. Jeffrey Ryan, "Turning on Their Masters: State Terrorism and Unlearning Democracy in Uruguay," in Néstor Rodríguez and Cecilia Menjívar, eds., *When States Kill: Latin America, the U.S., and Technologies of Terror* (Austin: University of Texas Press, 2005).

127. Ryan, "Turning on Their Masters," 2, 8.

128. For the conversation between Nixon and Kissinger, see TelCon 9/16/73 at the National Security Archive website.

129. "Encuentran en Brasil ficha que evidencia la Operación Cóndor," *La Tercera* (Chile), June 5, 2000.

130. Nilson Cezar Mariano, *Operación Cóndor: Terrorismo de estado en el Cono Sur* (Buenos Aires: Lohlé-Lumen, 1998), 42.

131. See McSherry, *Incomplete Transition,* chapter 3.

132. Comisión Nacional de Verdad y Reconciliación, *Informe Rettig.* Vols. 1 and 2. (Santiago: Chilean Government and Ediciones del Ornitorrinco, 1991), 43; Pamela Constable and Arturo Valenzuela, *A Nation of Enemies: Chile under Pinochet* (New York and London: W. W. Norton, 1991), chapter 4.

133. *Análisis* (Chile), March 7, 1988.

3

Operation Condor's Structures and Functioning: The Parallel State in Operation

THE CONDOR PROTOTYPE BEGAN TO OPERATE as a transnational state terror organization in late 1973 or early 1974. In previous work, I have suggested that Condor emerged from a 1973 surveillance arrangement between the Argentine and Chilean military intelligence organizations that culminated in the 1974 assassination of constitutionalist Chilean general Carlos Prats.[1] A declassified CIA cable of November 1973 reported that General Arellano Stark—the officer who led the Caravan of Death in Chile[2]—had "left Santiago on a special mission . . . [to] discuss with the [Argentine] military any [WORD DELETED] they have regarding the activities of General Carlos Prats. . . . Arellano will also attempt to gain an agreement whereby the Argentines maintain scrutiny over Prats and regularly inform the Chileans of his activities."[3] This sort of binational arrangement had been encouraged by CIA officers in Uruguay, as we have seen. It was similar to others set up later by Manuel Contreras, commander of DINA and a CIA asset, in other South American countries in 1974 and 1975.

Prats had been commander of the army under the Allende administration. He moved to Buenos Aires shortly after the 1973 coup in Chile, but despite living quietly he received death threats in Argentina. Prats and his wife planned to settle in Europe, but Chilean authorities denied them passports. Prats noted constant surveillance in Buenos Aires, and he believed that Chilean agents had traveled to the city to do him harm. He and his wife were assassinated in a car bombing on September 30, 1974, at a time when his official security protection (provided by the Argentine army and police) was absent. The assassinations were carried out by agents of DINA with the assistance of members of the fascist Argentine group Milicia (an outgrowth of the death squad Triple A) and the complicity of the Argentine army and police. They were the first major assassinations committed by the as-yet unnamed Condor prototype. One of the conspirators was Michael Townley, who later admitted his role. Another was a far-right Chilean operative named Enrique Arancibia Clavel, who was also implicated in the assassination of General René Schneider, the predecessor of Prats as chief of the Chilean army.[4] DINA chief Contreras himself had met with Arancibia Clavel in November 1973, when the latter was living in Argentina to escape legal queries related to his involvement in the Schneider murder.[5] Arancibia Clavel set up a Condor network in Buenos Aires, the first extraterritorial DINA base, by order of DINA Foreign Department commander Raúl Eduardo Iturriaga Neumann.[6] Arancibia carried out surveillance of Prats before the assassination and was also accused of torturing Chilean prisoners in secret Argentine detention centers.[7] In November 2000, an Argentine court found Arancibia guilty for his role in the Prats assassination, and an Argentine judge indicted in absentia five other DINA officers as well, including Iturriaga.

This chapter analyzes the origins of Operation Condor. It first examines the intelligence organs that comprised it nucleus. It then reviews how the Condor prototype began to take shape in 1973 and further coalesced in February 1974, in a pivotal meeting of security officers from five of the six Condor states. Thus, Condor, as a parastatal structure, was operational long before its "official" foundational meeting in November 1975. The chapter discusses both of these meetings and early Condor operations against Latin American exiles and two U.S. nationals living in Chile in 1973.

The Nucleus of Operation Condor

In each Condor country intelligence organizations that centralized countersubversive operations, outside normal military chains of command, formed the nucleus of Operation Condor. The Brazilian military junta that seized power in 1964, for example, created a secret intelligence apparatus, assisted by the CIA, called the Serviço Nacional de Informações (SNI). This powerful intelligence organ and its associated paramilitary groups were exceptional in the region because they became semiautonomous and occasionally acted to derail the political program of the military government itself through acts of terror. One analyst noted that this apparatus "had multipled in numbers and in power since 1964 such that by 1974 it had become a parallel power, or 'state within a state,' in direct contention with the [military] hierarchy for control over both the state and the military institution."[8] This section presents a brief comparative perspective of key intelligence organizations in the three most zealous Condor militaries, Chile, Argentina, and Uruguay.

Chile

In Chile, DINA became the central mechanism for both internal security and foreign Condor operations. It was created shortly after the September 1973 coup and began operations then, although the junta did not officially establish it, via Decree 521, until June 1974. A January 1974 CIA document confirmed the earlier, secret establishment of DINA and said the unit needed intelligence training.[9]

Chile, a long-standing democracy, had never before had a specific political intelligence apparatus. DINA commander Contreras stated in 2000 that shortly after the coup Pinochet had instructed him to ask the CIA for assistance in organizing DINA. Contreras said he met with General Vernon Walters, deputy director of the CIA, and in March 1974, the CIA sent eight officers to Chile to help set up DINA. According to Contreras, the CIA officers tried to assume permanent leadership positions within DINA, but Pinochet rebuffed the idea.[10] CIA Station Chief Ray Warren was instrumental in helping Contreras organize the secret police. One DINA agent observed, "At the beginning of 1974 [Contreras] had a full set of plans, and six months later he had built an empire. I thought he was a genius to have built up such a large, complicated apparatus in such a short time—then I found out how much help he got from the CIA in organizing it."[11]

The evidence also suggests that Warren was deeply involved in setting up the intelligence networks of Operation Condor. The CIA station chief used his contacts with the SNI to enlist Brazilian collaboration in the formation and training of DINA. Brazilian intelligence officers trained DINA personnel in communications, organization, interrogation, and torture at the express request of the CIA, and DINA used the SNI as an organizational model.[12] DINA operatives received training in Brazil and in U.S. centers, and Israel may also have trained DINA in intelligence.[13]

In a 2000 report to Congress, the CIA disclosed for the first time that Contreras, also known as Condor One, had been a CIA asset between 1974 and 1977 and that he had received an unspecified payment for his services. (Contreras later said that he maintained a DINA account at Riggs Bank in Washington.[14]) During these same years, Contreras was a leading organizer and proponent of Operation Condor. The CIA did not divulge this information in 1978, when a federal grand jury indicted Contreras for his role in the Letelier-Moffitt assassinations (Contreras eventually served a prison term in Chile for the crime). The fact that a central Condor figure was a CIA liaison is another strong indicator of the agency's covert role in Condor's formation and operations.

By February 1974, DINA was more powerful than the four branches of the armed forces: a Chilean junta source, quoted in a Defense Department intelligence document, said that there were only three sources of power in Chile: Pinochet, God, and DINA.[15] DINA played a major role in purging constitutionalist members of the armed forces from the active-duty ranks. The regular military intelligence agencies were instructed to turn over any soldiers responsible for "subversion" within the ranks to DINA.[16] DINA quickly became the main perpetrator of a pattern of terrorist practices such as disappearance and torture.[17] DINA's General Command, headed by Contreras, reported directly to Pinochet; various subdivisions reported to Contreras. One influential subdivision, covert operations, was under the charge of Colonel Pedro Espinoza. Covert operations targeted all aspects of Chile's society (Government Service, Internal, Economic, and Psychological Warfare) as well as exiles (the Foreign Department, created in early 1974).

Contreras placed Major Raúl Eduardo Iturriaga Neumann in charge of DINA's Foreign Department, the extraterritorial operations arm of Condor. Iturriaga Neumann, then second in command of the Black Berets battalion, had attended the U.S. Army School of the Americas (SOA), as did Contreras.[18] A declassified U.S. Army biography of Iturriaga Neumann, dated July 1987, reported that between February 1963 and March 1966, he was assigned to the 8th Special Forces Group (airborne) at Fort Gulick in the Canal Zone where "he excelled in all phases of formal training and later became instructor of several courses" at the SOA.[19] In 1970, he attended a three-month senior officer intelligence course at Fort Holabird, Maryland, as we have seen. The report noted that there was no official record of Iturriaga Neumann's activities between February 1974 and 1978—a period that included his command as head of DINA's Foreign Department, when he was involved in Condor operations. Iturriaga Neumann traveled to Buenos Aires regularly from Santiago, for example.

Michael Townley, who gave testimony to Argentine judge María Servini de Cubría in her investigation of the Prats case, named Iturriaga as a key actor in the Prats assassination.[20] Another former DINA agent, Ingrid Olderock, testified that she knew that Iturriaga was one of those in charge of the Prats assassination, and that he had traveled to Buenos Aires for that purpose. When he returned to Santiago, all the DINA officers congratulated him, including her.[21] In July 2000, the judge received an anonymous letter that stated that the major had supervised, controlled, and personally checked all the special operations of DINA in foreign countries—that is, Condor operations—by instruction of Contreras.[22] The anonymous author also said that Iturriaga had built a network of intelligence agents in Argentina who communicated via the "good offices" of the pilots of Lan Chile.

DINA forged close relations with Colonia Dignidad, a secretive German enclave in northern Chile that harbored former Nazis. DINA detainees were held and tortured there, and former German pilots at the colony maintained contact with General Gustavo Leigh, the air force member of the junta, according to one source. DINA sent agents to the enclave to be trained by the Nazis in interrogation and torture techniques. Colonia Dignidad leaders also served as a bridge between the German BND and DINA's foreign apparatus—that is, Condor units—and they apparently exchanged lists of "subversives" living in Europe, another link between the European and Latin American intelligence forces. One former DINA agent identified DINA torture centers in Villa Grimaldi and Colonia Dignidad, and added that at the latter location there was "a radio with which one can communicate in seconds with any part of the world; it is the central transceiver (*receptora*) of all the intelligence of DINA's foreign apparatus."[23] This powerful communications station, receiving reports from DINA teams in other countries, was evidently part of Condortel. A former prisoner at Colonia Dignidad said he heard a man with a Brazilian accent during his torture, and he and another prisoner heard two-way radio conversations in which interrogators were linked to their counterparts at Villa Grimaldi.[24] Interestingly, when queried in 1976 about reports linking DINA to this Nazi enclave, General Vernon Walters commented that they "sound(s) totally phony to me."[25] The colony's Nazi links and its role in Chile's repression were documented by former DINA agents and survivors, as well as the CIA, at the time, however.[26]

Argentina

In Argentina, the armed forces had ruled intermittently since 1930. After the 1955 ouster of populist president Juan Perón, French and U.S. counterinsurgency doctrines began to influence the military more deeply. The military imposed the first national security state in 1966. By 1970, officers trained in counterinsurgency gained dominance in the armed forces, and by 1972, the year before the return to civilian rule,the military began organizing the "task forces" or grupos de tareas (GTs) that became the dreaded death squads of the dirty war. One navy man, who was imprisoned for refusing to participate, testified later that the repression was part of "a plan that responded to the Doctrine of National Security that had as a base the School of the Americas, directed by the Pentagon in Panama."[27]

After the coup in neighboring Chile, the Argentine Anticommunist Alliance (Alianza Anticomunista Argentina, or Triple A), appeared. The Triple A was a parastatal confederation of death squads sponsored by the state and composed of police, military officers from the extreme right, nationalist sectors of the armed forces, and civilian gangsters. State officials José López Rega (minister of social welfare), José María Villone (head of the state intelligence service, Secretaría de Inteligencia del Estado, SIDE),[28] and Police Chief Alberto Villar, among other figures within the state, were directors of the Triple A, and there is evidence that it was penetrated by the CIA. Villar had been trained in counterrevolutionary warfare in France and later became one of the first police to receive training in "interrogation techniques" at the Army SOA in Panama.[29] DINA agent Enrique Arancibia Clavel, operating covertly in Buenos Aires, confirmed in a report to his superiors that the Triple A was a parastatal structure: "There are anticommunist groups of civilians who are working with the Armed Forces. The Triple A in fact is a paramilitary group of the government; political instructions are given to them through the third or fourth commander of SIDE."[30] The Triple A murdered some 2,000 persons between 1974 and 1976.[31]

In 1973, Argentina began a period of constitutional rule under Perón, who had returned from a lengthy exile to win the presidential election in that year. But during the constitutional interlude the Triple A attacked and murdered prominent figures from left-wing sectors of Peronism and other individuals (including parliamentarians, priests, university deans, lawyers, unionists, and guerrillas) who voiced opposition to right-wing Peronism. In November 1973 the Triple A detonated a bomb in the car of Senator Hipólito Yrigoyen of the Unión Cívica Radical (a moderate party), its first claimed terrorist act. The senator was severely wounded. Yrigoyen was the victim of another bomb attack in 1975 and was tortured and interrogated by army officers in that year. They told him: "You want to know all about the Triple A? Well, we're the Triple A. We put the bomb in your car."[32]

The Triple A collaborated with European fascists and terrorists, including the Franco regime in Spain and the Italian fascist lodge Propaganda-Due (P-2), revealing its links to the global anticommunist network discussed in the last chapter. López Rega was a member of P-2, as were high-ranking military officers and Perón himself.[33] There were also connections between the U.S. government and López Rega. Robert Hill met the Argentine when he was ambassador to Spain, and the two developed a friendship; Hill later became ambassador to Argentina.[34] In May 1974, the U.S. government awarded substantial funds to Argentina's police for narcotics interdiction and police training programs. López Rega and Ambassador Hill held a televised press conference in which the social welfare minister said openly, "the anti-drug campaign will automatically be an anti-guerrilla campaign as well."[35] A 1976 General Accounting Office report showed that U.S. narcotics funds to Latin American police forces increased by about 600 percent between 1973 and 1974. This was approximately the same amount that had been cut by Congress in 1974 from police training programs funded through AID's Public Safety Program, after Congress discovered that many graduates were engaged in torture and assassination.[36] The Triple A achieved its maximum power between late 1973 and 1974—the period in which Condor was organized—with sophisticated weaponry and modern vehicles.

The Triple A as an entity vanished after the March 1976 coup, and command of its operatives passed to army colonel Suárez Nelson, under General Albano Harguindeguy.[37] These two officers, hard-liners in the army's most extremist faction, had condoned Triple A death squad operations before the coup. Many operatives were absorbed by the federal police, by SIDE, and by army intelligence battalion 601, and they went on to function in "task forces" and death squads, some associated with Operation Condor. Battalion 601 was the cerebrum of the repression in Argentina in the 1970s and operated closely with SIDE, which was subsumed under army command during military rule. In short, the Triple A functioned as a parallel terrorist force before the armed forces took total power in Argentina, carrying out repressive acts while the armed forces were still partially restrained by the constitutional framework.

After the coup of 1976, the junta authorized savage countersubversive operations secretly, while seeking to project an image of moderation. SIDE commander Otto Paladino organized a parallel group based at Orletti Motors to carry out Condor operations, and incorporated Triple A operatives. He assigned Aníbal Gordon, a former Triple A torturer, to be chief at Orletti. Gordon supervised the torture and interrogation of Condor prisoners in conjunction with Uruguayan officers. Argentines Rubén Visuara, Rafael López Fader, and Eduardo Ruffo, SIDE operatives, were members of the death squad based in Orletti.

The three junta commanders decentralized control of the repression by granting substantial autonomy to burgeoning elements of the parallel state. The parastatal machinery operated from within the armed and security forces, but with a secret command structure. As the late Emilio Mignone explained in 1992,

> Everything was planned centrally . . . in each regiment, in each group, there was a nucleus that acted. We call it the parallel army. They had no connection with the regiment. They were directly linked to the chiefs, the commandantes of the zone, the chiefs of the divisions, for example Menéndez in Córdoba, Súarez Mason in the capital, Massera for the navy . . . they reported to these, and also they were linked to the intelligence service. They didn't report to the chief of the regiment.[38]

In 1983, Rodolfo Peregrino Fernández, a policeman linked to the Triple A, also referred to the task forces as "a parallel apparatus" that distorted the normal military hierarchy.[39]

Rodolfo Walsh, a well-known investigative journalist, learned by 1977 of the linkages among police officers, paramilitary death squads, the armed forces, the CIA station chief, and key Condor assassinations. Walsh wrote an open letter to the Argentine junta referring to the "confirmed participation in these crimes [the assassinations of Prats, Torres, Michelini, Gutiérrez Ruiz, and others] of the Department of Foreign Affairs of the Federal Police, directed by officers who received scholarships from the CIA via AID, such as commissioners Juan Gattei and Antonio Gettor, both of whom were under the authority of Gardener Hathaway, station chief of the CIA in Argentina." Walsh linked high-ranking officers of the army, such as General Menéndez, to the right-wing death squad Logia Libertadores de América, which was later incorporated into the armed forces.[40] The day after writing his letter, Walsh was "disappeared" and later, army troops ransacked his home and took away his research materials and personal journal.

Walsh had learned that Gattei was a nexus between the CIA and the Triple A, and the director of a Triple A death squad targeting Latin American exiles, part of a secret accord signed by Alberto Villar of Argentina and the police chiefs of Uruguay, Bolivia, Brazil, Chile, and Paraguay.[41] This agreement may have been signed at the pivotal February 1974 meeting previously mentioned (discussed in more depth presently). DINA and Condor agent Arancibia Clavel later admitted working with Gattei in 1974, when the latter was chief of the Department of Foreign Affairs of the federal police and a commander of the Triple A, confirming Walsh's information. Condor operations relied on the logistical assistance of parallel groups within the police and military forces.[42]

U.S. regional security officer James Blystone was briefed on the structure of Argentina's repressive apparatus in 1979. The Reunión Central, a unit within army intelligence battalion 601 set up in the beginning of the dictatorship, was assigned to integrate the intelligence and operations of army, navy, air force, and federal security elements. Beginning in 1971–72, according to Blystone's Argentine intelligence source, there were five GTs under the command of Intelligence Battalion 601, which in turn reported to the army's intelligence division (G-2), headed overall by the commander in chief, a general. The Argentine's description to Blystone of the objectives of each GT differed from that of Peregrino Fernández, however. Peregrino Fernández said in 1983 that GT1 was commanded by the First Army Corps and targeted the guerrilla group Ejército Revolucionario del Pueblo (ERP); the air force commanded GT2, which targeted several small leftist organizations; the navy commanded

GT3, which targeted the Peronist guerrillas, the Montoneros; and the federal police commanded GT4, which also targeted Montoneros. Each force had its own complex of clandestine concentration camps and torture centers.[43] In 1979, three more task forces were added, according to Blystone's Argentine source: GT6 focused on union, student, and religious activists; GT7 on political parties; and GT8 (or GTE), the Extraterritorial Task Force, on foreign activities.[44] GT8 operated in Central America, although the Argentine armed forces had participated in Condor operations in other countries long before 1979.

Uruguay

Uruguay's slow-motion coup took place over several years. In June 1973, the military dissolved Congress but permitted the civilian president to remain. In 1975, scheduled elections were cancelled and political parties were banned. Uruguay's intelligence organizations, reporting directly to the military high command, assumed control of extraterritorial operations against exiles. The Defense Intelligence Service (Servicio de Informaciones de Defensa, SID) controlled the Coordinating Organ of Antisubversive Operations (Organismo Coordinador de Operaciones Antisubversivas, OCOA), apparently formed around 1972. There was a unit of OCOA within each army division. General Amaurí Prantl, head of SID, supervised secret Condor operations, coordinating the actions of police, military, and intelligence operatives and units under OCOA. Prantl worked with Argentine General Otto Paladino—then head of SIDE—in coordinating cross-border operations. OCOA carried out numerous operations in Argentina from its base in Orletti Motors, which was under the operational control of the First Army Corps and SIDE in Argentina.[45] José Gavazzo was the Uruguayan chief of operations of OCOA, operating from Orletti. This intelligence structure also worked closely with the Uruguayan National Directorate of Information and Intelligence (Dirección Nacional de Informaciones e Inteligencia, DNII), originally set up in the 1960s with the assistance of the CIA.

In 1971, DNII had led a massive countersubversive campaign, a combined military and police operation, against the Tupamaro guerrillas. Former police officers stated that it also controlled death squads.[46] DNII housed a central computer database with voluminous personal information on "subversives," the type of computer that Condor linked through its system.[47] One former torturer who was part of the Technical Section of the Counterintelligence Company, Department II of the Uruguayan General Staff, said that OCOA also possessed full intelligence files, including photos, on suspected subversives.[48]

Two former navy intelligence officers gave extensive interviews in Uruguay in 1996. They confirmed that SID had collaborated closely with SIDE of Argentina and with security officials in Brazil during the 1970s and also said that the Uruguayan navy had developed close working relations with the Argentine navy, especially at its center of detention and torture, the notorious Escuela de Mecánica de la Armada (Navy Mechanics School, ESMA).[49] OCOA worked directly with GT3, the navy "task force" or death squad based in ESMA, they said. One operative outlined the key role of the Argentines: "The Argentines, pioneers in everything, were also pioneers in the establishment of an office of coordination of Intelligence of the Southern Cone, for which they organized a meeting in Argentina and invited the Colombians, the Brazilians, the Paraguayans, the Uruguayans, and the Chileans."[50] This was apparently the first multilateral meeting to coordinate repression across borders held by the nascent Condor network, and it took place in Buenos Aires.

Origins of the Condor System: The February 1974 Meeting

Several declassified U.S. documents report a crucial meeting of security officers from five of the six Condor countries in Buenos Aires in February 1974. There, the officers discussed ways to set up a system of coordinated cross-border hunter-killer operations. A top-secret CIA *National Intelligence Daily* of June 23, 1976, released in 2000, stated: "In early 1974, security officials from Argentina, Chile, Uruguay, Paraguay, and Bolivia met in Buenos Aires to prepare coordinated actions against subversive targets. [5 LINES EXCISED] Since then [3 LINES EXCISED] the Argentines have conducted joint countersubversive operations with the Chileans and with the Uruguayans."[51] This meeting assembled police chiefs (some of whom were military commanders) from Uruguay, Paraguay, Brazil, Bolivia, Chile, and Argentina, and it was called the First Police Seminar on the Antisubversive Struggle in the Southern Cone. General Miguel Angel Iñíguez, then commander of the Argentine federal police, chaired the meeting and called for new forms of transnational collaboration to confront the subversive threat.[52]

This meeting has received relatively little attention from analysts, who usually highlight the official founding meeting of Condor in Santiago in November 1975, for which documents have been recovered. Yet the evidence demonstrates that the Condor prototype was already functioning long before November 1975. Therefore, the 1974 meeting is of crucial importance. This CIA report showed that the Condor apparatus was already multinational and conducting coordinated operations in early 1974. Moreover, the February meeting confirmed that the system incorporated military, security (police), and intelligence officers, working together to carry out the combined countersubversive operations that became known as Condor.

Other sources have added details about the February 1974 meeting. In his intelligence reports, DINA agent Arancibia wrote that among his contacts in the Triple A and Argentine military intelligence forces in 1974 "the idea existed to form an anticommunist intelligence community at the continental level with Uruguayan military men and Argentines, who might be interested in making contact with the Chileans."[53] In November 2002, a Uruguayan military source said that the first contacts to arrange exchanges of detailed intelligence and plan joint operations against subversives took place in 1974.[54] A declassified State Department document added more data: in March 1974,

> Perón authorized the Argentine Federal Police and the Argentine intelligence to cooperate with Chilean intelligence in apprehending Chilean left-wing extremists in exile in Argentina. Similar arrangements had also been made with the security services of Bolivia, Uruguay, and Brazil. This cooperation among security forces apparently includes permission for foreign officials to operate within Argentina, against their exiled nationals. . . . This authority allegedly includes arrest of such exiles and transfer to the home country without recourse to legal procedures.[55]

Thus, Perón authorized the Condor prototype in Argentina before his death in July 1974. Moreover, he created an intelligence commission on left-wing terrorism within the state and "authorized the formation of paramilitary groups to act extralegally against the terrorists, including the utilization of abduction, interrogation, and execution."[56] In October 1974, after the death of Perón, the Argentine government "organized a clandestine security committee within the Defense Ministry. The AAA carries out its actions on the basis of recommendations from this Committee,"[57] the U.S. document stated. The document thus verified Arancibia's reports on the Triple A and its links to Operation Condor.

Another document corroborating the February 1974 meeting was a cable of July 20, 1976, signed by Henry Kissinger, secretary of state. Sent to all Latin American and some European diplomatic missions, it stated: "Over two years ago, security officials from all the Southern Cone countries except Brazil met in Buenos Aires and reportedly formalized arrangements to facilitate information exchanges and the movement of security officials on government business."[58] The bland language understated the terrorist nature of Condor and downplayed evidence of a transnational conspiracy. The cable rather posited that a "uniquely Argentine set of factors" explained the recent wave of Condor assassinations in that country. (Deputy Chief of Mission Maxwell Chaplin in Buenos Aires responded that the cable underestimated the level of transnational coordination.[59]) One revealing passage, excised from earlier declassified versions of the Kissinger cable, stated bluntly that "a reliable Brazilian source has described a Brazil-Argentina agreement under which the two countries hunt and eliminate terrorists attempting to flee Argentina for Brazil. Brazilian and Argentine military units reportedly have operated jointly and inside each other's border when necessary." This language clearly referred to the Condor prototype. The cable also stated that Brazil became a full-fledged member of Condor in June 1976.

A September 2000 CIA report, mandated by Congress, provided further confirmation of the operation of the transnational system before its official 1975 founding meeting. The report stated: "Within a year after the [Chilean] coup [that is, between September 1973 and August 1974], the CIA and other US government agencies were aware of bilateral cooperation among regional intelligence services to track the activities of and, in at least a few cases, kill political opponents. This was the precursor to Operation Condor, an intelligence-sharing arrangement among Chile, Argentina, Brazil, Paraguay, and Uruguay established in 1975."[60] This statement was misleading on several counts, however. First, the February 1974 meeting indicated that coordination of repression was already multilateral, not bilateral. Second, the statement omitted mention of Bolivia, one of the Condor countries. Finally, the use of the term "precursor" was questionable, although technically correct, since the code name "condor" was not yet in use. But the unnamed transnational system was already functioning as a cross-border repressive program—the essence of Condor—before 1975, on the basis of unwritten agreements, and before its computerized database and Condortel were added. The 2000 CIA report also revealed that the CIA knew of the Condor prototype earlier than admitted by the agency in 1978, when it reported that it had learned of Condor in 1976.[61]

Katie Zoglin, who conducted a four-month review of the Paraguayan Archives of Terror, also reached the conclusion that transnational coordination in the Southern Cone began in 1973 or 1974.[62] Bilateral and multilateral intelligence conferences were held regularly, some under the rubric of the inter-American military system and others through quasi-official anticommunist organizations. One conference in 1973, for example, was attended by Antonio Campos Alúm, director of Paraguay's Dirección Nacional de Asuntos Técnicos (National Directorate of Technical Matters, La Técnica, the office responsible for political intelligence and repression). He accepted, on behalf of the Stroessner regime, Brazil's offer to exchange intelligence with Paraguay through meetings and extraofficial conferences organized by the Latin American Anticommunist Confederation, part of the World Anticommunist League (WACL). Several WACL conferences were held in 1974, including one in Washington, D.C., that brought together Latin American military officers and anticommunist civilians who pledged to share intelligence on "subversion."[63]

Also in 1974, the CIA reported that DINA and its partners were seeking to establish a covert operations center in Miami, to link up with the anticommunist Cuban exile community. State Department officials proposed to Secretary of State Kissinger that the United States formally and directly protest to the governments involved, but Kissinger rejected that option. Instead, the CIA passed a secret message to DINA through intelligence channels, disapproving the idea but taking no other action to deter the nascent Condor system.[64] The Argentine GTE (Extraterritorial Task Force) did set up an intelligence and operations center in Florida later in the 1970s, however, apparently with the assistance of the CIA. It was used for Condor support operations including money laundering, arms shipments, and transfers of funds to Argentine officers training the contras in counterinsurgency in Central America (see chapter 7).

Early Operations of the Condor Prototype

The CIA reported in 1974 that navy captain Raúl López, chief of the Chilean Naval Mission to London, had called a meeting of all the Chilean navy officers living in Europe in order to organize surveillance of Chilean leftists exiled in Europe. López planned to assassinate high-level Chilean dissidents such as Carlos Altamirano, secretary general of the Socialist Party and a former senator, and Volodia Teitelboim, a Communist Party leader.[65] These planned Phase III assassinations were never successful. But numerous political exiles "disappeared" or were killed in 1973 and 1974 in Latin America in operations that bore the mark of Condor.

For example, a Bolivian named Jorge Ríos Dalenz was detained-disappeared in Santiago in 1973 in an operation coordinated by Bolivia and Chile. Ríos had been a leader of the Movimiento de la Izquierda Revolucionaria (Movement of the Revolutionary Left—MIR) in Bolivia (separate from the Chilean organization of the same name) until Banzer's 1971 coup prompted him to flee to Chile. He lived there quietly until the September 1973 coup, when he was kidnapped by a military commando.[66] In another case in November 1973, the former Bolivian interior minister under nationalist president general Juan José Torres, Jorge Gallardo Losada, was kidnapped by four armed men, two in military uniform, from his home in Santiago, where he had lived since the 1971 coup in his country. Gallardo had written a critical book detailing the multinational conspiracy that overthrew Torres. He was transported to Bolivia and then to Argentina, at a time when all aircraft traffic was tightly controlled by the Chilean junta.[67] In another 1973 case, Brazilian police abducted Joaquim Pires Cerveira and João Batista Rita, two Brazilian exiles living in Buenos Aires.[68]

The wave of disappearances escalated in 1974. In March, four Uruguayans, refugees in Argentina under UN protection, were detained, and in May they were illegally transferred to Uruguay. After energetic protests by the UN high commissioner for refugees, they were released and allowed to go into exile in other countries. On September 12, five other Uruguayans were abducted from their homes in Buenos Aires by men later identified as Uruguayan police. Their families were unable to locate them despite repeated requests to Argentine authorities. On October 14, two were released, and they took refuge in Sweden. The bodies of the other three, disfigured by torture, were discovered later that month. The two refugees in Sweden subsequently described the tortures used against them and said that they had been imprisoned among the bodies of those who had already died. They identified a Uruguayan policeman, Hugo Campos Hermida, as one of their torturers. Campos Hermida became notorious in Uruguay for his role in Condor operations, as he was identified by numerous survivors as one of the interrogators and torturers in Orletti Motors. In 1970, he had received a State Department scholarship to attend intelligence courses in Washington, D.C., at the International Police Academy (IPA),[69] and he was well known to the CIA.[70]

In April 1974, the chief of Argentine army intelligence traveled to Chile to advance the coordination of countersubversive operations with the Pinochet regime.[71] On November 8, 1974, five more Uruguayan exiles, two young couples and a single woman, were abducted from their homes in Argentina in separate, coordinated operations by heavily armed men in civilian clothes. Relatives made frantic inquiries of the Argentine government to no avail. On December 20, their bodies, mutilated by multiple stab wounds and burns, were found in Soca, Uruguay, near Montevideo. Apparently, Triple A members were involved in transferring the victims from Argentina to Uruguay.[72] The bodies were found at 7:30 in the morning—and that same morning, the Montevideo press already had, and published, the news of the grisly discovery. It appeared that the Uruguayans had been executed in retaliation for the assassination the day before of the Uruguayan military attaché in Paris, Colonel Ramón Trabal. This murder, however, was possibly a Phase III Condor operation (see chapter 4). The three-year-old son of one of the couples, "disappeared" with his parents, was recovered a year and a half later in Buenos Aires.[73]

In another case, Paraguayan educator Martín Almada was abducted in Paraguay in November 1974 by combined commando forces. He testified that there were officers from other Condor countries present at his interrogation and torture sessions, again showing that Condor was fully operative in 1974. By that year, increasingly visible cross-border terror operations carried out by shadowy squadrons—the parallel state—were causing dread and panic among exile communities. The accumulated evidence provides overwhelming confirmation that Condor's most essential feature—its cross-border "hunter-killer" operations against political enemies—began in 1973 and was fully operational by 1974, long before the program was officially baptized Operation Condor in 1975.

The Horman and Teruggi Cases

Understanding that the Condor prototype began to function in 1973–74 throws new light on the cases of U.S. citizens Charles Horman and Frank Teruggi. The disappearance and murder of both shortly after the 1973 coup in Chile (made famous in the Costa-Gavras movie "Missing") fit the profile of a Condor operation in key ways.[74] Moreover, a 1999 search for "Operation Condor" in the U.S. State Department website of declassified documents produced numerous files on the Horman case, indicating that the State Department itself had associated the case with Condor. Several of these documents reported accusations by a Chilean intelligence officer that a CIA officer was present when Horman's execution order was given. Others suggested that U.S. military officers might have "fingered" the two to the Chilean junta. Clearly, such involvement would indicate high-level cooperation between U.S. and Chilean intelligence in the abduction and murder of the two, and indeed, State Department investigators suspected as much at the time.[75] It stands to reason that the Chileans would not eliminate U.S. citizens without a green light, a fact noted by State Department officials in subsequent investigations. There were clearly close ties between U.S. and Chilean military and intelligence organizations, including the CIA and DINA. Coordination between two national intelligence services of extralegal abductions and executions was a central feature of Condor.

Horman and Teruggi were friends and disappeared at the same time in 1973, causing commotion in the United States. Horman was a leftist journalist who had been researching the assassination of René Schneider (the predecessor of Prats, whose "removal" had been authorized by the CIA).[76] A former Chilean government official said at the time that a Chilean military man had told him of seeing a large intelligence file on Horman's activities in the United States, which he presumed was from the CIA or State Department.[77] In fact, in 1976, Senator Edward Kennedy cited a *Washington Post* article of June 20 that also referred to the fact that Horman's captors had a dossier on him, including information on his antiwar and civil rights activity in the United States.[78] Kennedy complained to the assistant secretary of state for inter-American affairs in the Ford administration, Harry W. Schlaudeman, that information in the article had not been supplied to the Senate subcommittee investigating the murders.

The State Department did not conduct a serious inquiry into the cases until 1976, when two internal investigations were carried out. Both raised the issue of possible CIA involvement in Horman's death. Shlaudeman disregarded the recommendations in both reports to further investigate the activities of the CIA.[79] The Pinochet regime refused to turn over Horman's autopsy report despite several requests, and the two State Department inquiries failed to clarify the facts of the two deaths. The first report, dated August 1976, found that

> U.S. intelligence may have played an unfortunate part in Horman's death. At best, it was limited to providing or confirming information that helped motivate his murder. . . . At worst, U.S. intelligence was aware that the GOC [Government of Chile] saw Horman in a rather serious light and U.S. officials did nothing to discourage the logical outcome.[80]

Actually, there is an even worse scenario: that the CIA approved and collaborated with his abduction and murder by the Chileans.

Charles Horman and his friend Terry Simon had been stranded in Viña del Mar at the time of the coup, and there they met U.S. officers who spoke frankly of their involvement.[81] Lieutenant Colonel Patrick Ryan—second in command of the U.S. Military Group (Milgroup)—arranged for them to be taken back to Santiago by his superior, Captain Ray Davis, head of Milgroup. The U.S. Milgroup had an office in the Chilean Ministry of Defense. Both Ryan and Davis were fierce anticommunists and supporters of the military coup.

Charles and Joyce Horman had moved to a new house only a few days before the coup, yet a commando of Chilean security personnel knew where Charles was and abducted him from the house in what was clearly a planned, targeted disappearance. One of the U.S. military officers may have tipped off the Chileans about where Horman lived. A hotel clerk told a CBS journalist in 1973 that Ryan had taken a hotel card with Horman's new address. (In an interesting connection, General Prats told a reporter shortly before his murder that Ryan was the U.S. liaison with the Chilean coup plotters.[82]) The Horman family believed that the address was given to the Chilean military, and Horman disappeared soon afterward.

During the second review later in 1976, State Department lawyer Frederick Smith, Jr., reported to Shlaudeman that Rafael González Verdugo, a disgruntled Chilean intelligence officer, had said in an interview that he had seen a

U.S. intelligence officer present during a meeting with the Chilean intelligence commander, who said Horman "knew too much" and "had to disappear." Smith recommended "a high-level approach to the U.S. intelligence community, particularly the CIA, to try to determine whether any U.S. intelligence activities may have in any way contributed to Horman's death."[83] Smith acknowledged "the somewhat general denials by the Agency" but emphasized that "it is difficult to believe that the GOC would have felt sufficiently secure in taking such drastic action against two American citizens without some reason, however unjustifiably inferred or inadvertantly given, to believe that it could do so without substantial adverse consequences vis-à-vis the USG." Later in the report he made the point even more strongly, stating that "it appears strange that, given the obvious and important political considerations involved, the GOC would believe it could kill Horman and Teruggi without serious repercussions in its relations with the U.S. . . . If an explanation exists, it does not appear in the files and must be sought elsewhere."[84] It is important to note that these State Department officials were in the dark about CIA and military intelligence activities in Chile.

However, support for Pinochet was very clear at the top levels of government. The Nixon administration officially recognized the military regime soon after the coup. In February 1974, Assistant Secretary of State Jack Kubisch brought up the Horman and Teruggi murders with the Chilean foreign minister "in the context of the need to . . . keep relatively small issues in our relationship from making our cooperation more difficult."[85] Secretary of State Henry Kissinger assured the Chileans of U.S. support and made light of human rights concerns. In a September 29, 1975, meeting with Chilean military officials, for example, Kissinger said, "Well, I read the briefing paper for this meeting and it was nothing but human rights. The State Department is made up of people who have a vocation for the ministry. Because there were not enough churches for them, they went into the Department of State."[86] When Kissinger met personally with Pinochet in 1976, he said,

> In the United States, as you know, we are sympathetic with what you are trying to do here. I think that the previous government was headed toward Communism. We wish your government well. . . . My evaluation is that you are a victim of all left-wing groups around the world, and that your greatest sin was that you overthrew a government which was going Communist. . . . We are not out to weaken your position.[87]

Such messages from top U.S. officials made clear the U.S. support for Pinochet's destruction of democracy, and cruel repression, in the name of anticommunism.

There were also suspicions that the U.S. Embassy had provided a green light for Teruggi's abduction and murder. In 1977, Teruggi's father wrote to Secretary of State Cyrus Vance asking whether the CIA's arrest lists, made available to the junta, contained the name of his son. He complained that the CIA had told him that it possessed a document in its files pertaining to his son, but refused to release it to him.[88] U.S. documents declassified in 2000 revealed that Teruggi was, in fact, under U.S. Army and FBI surveillance in 1972 because of his leftist political activities.[89] One secret memorandum to the acting director of the FBI from the legal attaché of the U.S. Embassy in Bonn apparently drew on intelligence provided by the 66th Military Intelligence Group in Munich about Teruggi's antiwar work. This memo requested a search of FBI files on Teruggi, as well as on a group with which he was associated, the Chicago Area Group for the Liberation of the Americas.[90] Several other intelligence memos were declassified in 2000, and one, from the FBI, contained Teruggi's Chile address. The document implied that Teruggi was engaged in instigating and organizing military deserters.[91] Another memo, again from the Legal Attaché in Bonn, was headed "[LINE EXCISED]; SM - Subversive," and included information from someone who had infiltrated an antiwar group in Germany. This document also provided the name and address of Teruggi in Chile and identified him as a leftist journalist.[92] A final declassified document, a surveillance report on Teruggi by the FBI, reported on a conference in September 1971 on "Anti-Imperialist Strategy and Action," attended by some 200 persons, including Teruggi.[93]

On October 15, 1973, Chilean intelligence commander General Augusto Lutz verbally told the U.S. defense attaché that the junta had knowledge that Teruggi was in Chile to spread false rumors to the outside world about the situation in Chile, and he later wrote that he and Horman were leftist extremists.[94] The evidence raises serious questions as to whether U.S. officers passed Teruggi's address, along with derogatory intelligence information portraying Teruggi as a subversive, to the Chilean dictatorship. As one State Department report noted about the Horman and Teruggi cases, "Of 80 Americans who required the Embassy's attention, only these two appear to have been tortured and then shot. . . . In their October 30 memo . . . the Chileans lumped them together as radicals."[95]

Testimony of a Former Intelligence Officer

In September 1975, Rafael González went to the Italian Embassy in Santiago to request asylum. He had been an intelligence officer for many years but became disillusioned by the many abuses carried out by DINA. Moreover, he reported being threatened with death repeatedly by DINA after his criticisms became known. González was granted asylum by the Italians.[96] In March 1976, González was interviewed by the U.S. Embassy about his U.S. resident status. At that time, González said he had documented information that linked the CIA to covert DINA operations against "subversives" in Chile. A U.S. official (whose name is deleted, but the context leaves the impression that the person was CIA) "flatly denied such involvement" and implied that González was mentally unstable. Meanwhile, the Chilean military regime refused to grant the González family safe conduct out of the country.

In an interview with the *Washington Post* inside the Italian Embassy, González stated that he "knew that Charles Horman was killed because he knew too much. And this was done between the CIA and the local authorities."[97] He explained that some days after the coup he had been called to the office of General Lutz, Chilean army intelligence director, where he saw a bearded man in the custody of two Chilean officers. They identified the prisoner as Horman. In Lutz's office, he said, there were two other men present when Lutz gave the execution order: Lutz's deputy, a colonel, and an American. González, an experienced intelligence officer who knew CIA officers in Santiago, told the reporters he had concluded the American was CIA because of his demeanor and his clothing.

When he was interviewed by the U.S. Embassy, González said he had worked with U.S. intelligence in the past and mentioned several U.S. officials who had been in the Political Section of the embassy in the late 1950s.[98] Apparently, González also had carried out intelligence in the U.S. for Chile in the past. In 1973, the junta tasked González to accompany the vice consul of the U.S. Embassy, James Anderson, to retrieve the body of Horman. Anderson has since admitted that he was a CIA officer.[99]

The Chilean regime denied González's account, and Lutz died in 1974 (of an "accidental" injection in a clinic now suspected in Chile to be deliberate). A background check of González by U.S. officials confirmed much of his personal history, however, and officials reported that González seemed intelligent and lucid, if under stress.[100] González told embassy officials that he did not want to live in the United States "because the American Embassy are [*sic*] supporting this government."[101] By 1978, González had apparently left Chile. In October 1978, U.S. Embassy officials interviewed him once again. González adamantly refused to clarify the earlier interviews about the Horman case, saying that State Department records of the conversation were "replete with distortions of his words, deliberate omissions, and outright falsifications" and further stating that he had given his word to Chilean intelligence that once out of Chile he would never again discuss the Horman case.[102] González expressed fear of the CIA, which he said had followed him for years; had hypnotized, drugged, and programmed his wife to extract information, from which she was only now recovering; and had tried to drive him insane. When asked why the agency would try to drive him insane, he said that it was because he had profound and damaging knowledge about CIA operations in Chile during the Allende period.[103]

A 1987 cable from the U.S. Embassy in Santiago provided an intriguing link between the Horman case and Operation Condor. It reported on a Chilean informant seeking political asylum in the United States who told embassy officials that Pedro Espinoza, second in command of DINA and a Condor officer, had ordered the execution of Horman.[104] Michael Townley testified that Espinoza had ordered the assassination of Prats as well, and he was indicted in both the Letelier and Leighton cases by U.S. and Italian prosecutors.[105] The role of the CIA and U.S. military in the Horman and Teruggi cases remains unclarified. A trial on the Horman murder was in progress in Chile in 2003, and late that year, the case took an unexpected turn. The Chilean judge indicted González himself for complicity in the death of Horman, for participating in his interrogation. In an astounding retraction, González then denied his three-decade-old claim that a CIA man had been in the room when Horman was condemned to death.[106] He had sworn that to be the case in the 1970s, so either he was committing perjury then, or in 2003. The case was ongoing in 2004.

Condor Operations in 1975

The Condor system continued to develop geometrically in 1975. A Paraguayan intelligence report dated March 14, for example, revealed advanced intelligence coordination. Warning of a weeklong meeting of "Latin American extremists" in Palpala, Argentina, the report requested intelligence information through the military attachés of Argentina, Bolivia, Chile, Uruguay, Venezuela, and the United States.[107] In Chile, DINA carried out a major PSYWAR operation named Operation Colombo in conjunction with the Argentine Triple A in 1975. Mysterious newsletters reported that 119 Chileans who had disappeared, or had been arrested, in 1974 had been found dead in Argentina. These circulars listed the names of the victims and said that they had died in internecine battles within the Chilean Movimiento de la Izquierda Revolucionaria (Movement of the Revolutionary Left—MIR). Rightist media in Chile published lurid stories of mutilated corpses and warned of a guerrilla army massing outside of Chile and preparing to invade.[108] Operation Colombo was significant because it demonstrated that the Pinochet regime was manufacturing a guerrilla threat to justify its bloody repression at home. (In 1973, to justify the coup, the regime also had fabricated and publicized a supposed leftist plot of the Allende years, "Plan Z," supposedly aimed at murdering anti-Allende individuals.)

Years later, secret DINA files were discovered in the Buenos Aires office and home of Arancibia Clavel that included lists and identity documents of the 119 missing Chileans and reports that discussed the modus operandi of Operation Colombo. Arancibia Clavel's reports proved that the 119 actually had been "disappeared" by the regime and that DINA had coordinated with the Triple A to plant the false stories and false identifications. This example of a coordinated Condor operation was designed to terrorize Chileans and portray Pinochet as the protector of the nation. It also aimed to deflect international scrutiny regarding missing persons who had been reported as detained-disappeared. The UN, as well as Amnesty International, had been pressing the Pinochet regime to account for the missing. Through Operation Colombo, the Condor units "explained" the disappearances by using a familiar PSYWAR tactic: placing the blame for right-wing atrocities on the left. A Socialist Party activist who was "turned" into a DINA agent later testified that DINA commanders created the myth of a dangerous communist enemy to increase their power, justify extreme repressive measures, and build DINA's reputation as the most important security force.[109] Moreover, by portraying an extraterritorial enemy, Operation Colombo was also a justification for the expanding Condor system. In 2004, a Chilean judge charged sixteen top DINA-Condor officers with responsibility for these disappearances, including Contreras, Raúl Iturriaga Neumann, and Pedro Espinoza.

Arancibia's DINA files, seized in 1978, also included surveillance reports on Carlos Prats; documents on the assassinations of hundreds of other Chileans and Argentines; reports on combined actions in Europe with Avanguardia Nazionale operatives Stefano delle Chiaie, Pierluigi Pagliai (involved in the Leighton attack), and Vincenzo Vinciguerra; lists of detained-disappeared persons stamped by Argentine police commander Héctor García Rey; and reports on surveillance and actions undertaken with the Argentine paramilitary group Milicia of Martín Ciga Correa (an offshoot of the Triple A) and with Cuban exile terrorists, including the Novo brothers (who later participated in the assassination of Orlando Letelier in Washington, D.C.).[110] These files exposed the methods and operations of Condor and its worldwide reach.

A key 1975 case that illustrated U.S. involvement with Condor countersubversive operations was that of Chilean Jorge Isaac Fuentes Alarcón. A Chilean sociologist and member of the Chilean revolutionary group MIR, Fuentes was seized by Paraguayan police as he crossed the border from Argentina to Paraguay in May 1975. Several DINA officers, including Marcelo Moren Brito, traveled to Asunción to interrogate him and to transport him illegally to

Chile. Chile's Truth and Reconciliation Commission later learned that the capture of Fuentes was a collaborative effort by Argentine intelligence services, personnel of the U.S. Embassy in Buenos Aires, and Paraguayan police. Fuentes was brought to Villa Grimaldi, the secret DINA detention center in Santiago. He was last seen there by other prisoners, savagely tortured with beatings and electric shocks, his body covered with infections and scabies.[111]

The legal attaché in the U.S. Embassy in Buenos Aires informed the Chilean military in writing of the capture and interrogation of Fuentes and listed the names and addresses of three individuals living in the United States whose names had been in Fuentes's possession. The memo stated that the FBI was conducting investigations of the three in the United States.[112] This letter, among others, confirmed that U.S. officials and agencies were cooperating with the military dictatorships, sharing intelligence, and acting as a link in the Condor chain. Perhaps most striking was that this coordination was routine (if secret), standard operating procedure within U.S. policy. (In 2004, the Chilean Supreme Court revoked Pinochet's immunity from prosecution, opening the way to indict him for responsibility in the disappearances of Jorge Fuentes Alarcón and eight other leftist activists under Operation Condor.)

In August, three months after the seizure of Fuentes, DINA commander Contreras visited CIA deputy director Vernon Walters in Washington, D.C. The agenda of the meeting has never been revealed, but it is highly likely that cross-border collaboration was a subject. In the months afterward—leading up to the foundational meeting of Condor in November—Contreras traveled with a DINA team to Argentina, Bolivia, Uruguay, Paraguay, Brazil, and Venezuela to expand regional collaboration in counterinsurgency operations.[113] A Venezuelan officer later testified that Contreras had urged his Venezuelan counterparts to collaborate with DINA by keeping Chilean exiles under surveillance and reporting back to DINA on their activities (the Venezuelans declined). In September 1975, Contreras requested an extra $600,000 from Pinochet to finance DINA's foreign activities in Argentina, the U.S., Italy, and elsewhere, as well as counterguerrilla training in Manaus, Brazil.[114]

In August, Brazil and Chile made an agreement to operate jointly in Europe against their exiled nationals. A copy of the accord was discovered in the 1990s by Brazilian researchers in the archives of the Department of Social and Political Order (DOPS) of São Paulo. It showed that the Brazilian intelligence apparatus Serviço Nacional de Informações (National Information Service), or SNI, and DINA had agreed to cooperate in the transnational hunt for leftists.[115] The two forces pledged to target exiles in Portugal who opposed the regimes, to be the SNI's responsibility, and Spain, to be DINA's, and to "unify the activities of our intelligence services" on the Iberian peninsula. The document, written by a Pinochet official to SNI commander João Baptista Figueiredo, thus revealed an early Condor arrangement in Europe. The letter expressed the hope that coordinated operations in Europe between DINA and SNI "might extend to countries such as France, Italy, and Sweden, where the subversive activities of important groups are beginning to preoccupy our government."

Researchers discovered another letter from DINA chief Contreras to Figueiredo, dated August 28, 1975, in the DOPS files in Brazil in 1998. Although questions have been raised about its authenticity,[116] a 2001 study on the deaths of two presidents commissioned by Brazil's parliament concluded that the document was genuine. So did U.S. newsman Jack Anderson (who had published the document in 1975 in the *Washington Post*).[117] News articles stated that the family of former Brazilian president Juscelino Kubitschek had obtained the letter years earlier[118] and that Kubitschek's former aide had it in his possession.[119] In this letter, which was reproduced in the Venezuelan daily *El Nacional* on October 23, 1977, Contreras told Figueiredo that he had received the Brazilian's letter of August 21 (the date of the letter cited above). He wrote that he, like Figueiredo, feared the triumph of the Democrats in the next U.S. presidential elections because they might lend support to prominent exiles Orlando Letelier of Chile and Kubitschek, which "would seriously influence the stability of the Southern Cone." Contreras proposed that Chile and Brazil coordinate their actions against religious and political opponents.[120] The following year, 1976, Letelier was killed in a Condor assassination (see chapter 5), and the next month Kubitschek died in a car crash in Brazil.

Kubitschek's wife and aide suspected foul play, citing the death threats he had received, contradictory testimony by witnesses to the crash, incomplete forensic information, and missing official documents. Kubitschek had been president between 1956 and 1961, and then had become a senator. After the 1964 coup, the military cut short his term and suspended his political rights. In 1966, Kubitschek and former president João Goulart led a broad-based pro-democracy movement, but the military regime banned it. Goulart went into exile in Buenos Aires, where he received death threats in 1976, at the same time that his Uruguayan colleagues Zelmar Michelini and Héctor Gutiérrez Ruiz were abducted and killed.[121] Goulart also died in 1976 in Buenos Aires, victim of an apparent heart attack. His family found that death suspicious as well; even though he was taking medication for high blood pressure, Goulart had just been given a clean bill of health by his doctors. No autopsy was permitted by the Brazilian or Argentine militaries. After its investigation, the Brazilian parliament concluded in 2001 that Kubitschek's death was an accident, even though he had been a target of Condor. It resolved to continue studying the case of Goulart.

Chile and Brazil: Condor Collaboration in 1975

The DOPS files discovered in 1998 contained other extraordinary documents, including coded assassination orders from the director of the SNI to the Brazilian Embassy in Lisbon. Two Brazilians, Cândido da Costa Aragão and Carlos Sá, were exiled in Lisbon and were, according to a letter written on September 24, 1975, by Figueiredo, "considered a grave risk to national security."[122] Aragão was a navy officer who had remained loyal to Goulart during the 1964 coup and whose political rights were revoked by the dictatorship. Sá was a prominent lawyer and judge from São Paulo. In this letter, Figueiredo confirmed an earlier coded telex to the ambassador that had called for the initiation of an "operation code 12"—a contrived accident—against the two men. The coded telex (with an attached decoded copy), dated September 26, read in part:

> By decision of the Operational Command of the SNI, to be carried out by October 15, 1975: an operation code 12, an attack of "accident" type, against ex-admiral Cândido Aracão [*sic*] and Dr. Carlos Sá. Simultaneously we will take action to serve as a smokescreen in Paris or Rome, under DINA's charge. Signed, General João Figueiredo.[123]

It is interesting to note that the Condor assassination attempt against Christian Democrat Bernardo Leighton and his wife, Ana Fresno, occurred in Rome on October 6, 1975—within the SNI's time frame—organized and carried out by Italian neofascists on behalf of DINA. This letter raised new questions about whether the 1976 death of Goulart could have been a "code 12" operation. DINA had a stockpile of sarin, a nerve gas that induces heart attacks and leaves no traces (Goulart died of a heart attack). In fact, Townley had originally planned to use sarin to assassinate Letelier.[124]

A response to the above message, also found in the DOPS files and decoded, said:

> TO: Communications Center of Brazilian Army, with copy to the Army Ministry; FROM: Brazilian Embassy in Lisbon, Portugal. Distribution: G-2, secret service, and Chief of General Direction of the SNI in Brasilia, priority one. Message: To General João Figueiredo: Operation Code 12 against Admiral Aragão and Carlos Sá will only be completed when it is confirmed in writing and by operatives of the special team for this action transferred to Lisbon. Signed, General Carlos Alberto Fontoura, Ambassador.

These assassination plans were never carried out. While former SNI officers denied that the documents were genuine, Brazilian analysts suggested that sympathizers in the armed forces warned Aragão. In fact, in 1978 Aragão wrote an open letter to the head of a Venezuelan political party, Partido Acción Democrática, directly accusing Figueiredo of responsibility for the death of Kubitschek and asserting that he had proof of a conspiracy to assassinate him (Aragão) in Lisbon as well.[125]

A U.S. Defense Intelligence Agency (DIA) report from the same period (September 12, 1975) shed light on the fears of the Brazilian and Chilean militaries. Citing an analysis made by a "third country intelligence source," the U.S. defense attaché in Bolivia reported that a new leftist group, the Coordinating Board of Revolutionary Movements in Latin America (Junta Coordinadora de Movimientos Revolucionarios en América Latina, JCR) had been created in Portugal. The report said that some 5,000 Brazilian exiles lived in Portugal, as did other exiles from the Southern Cone, and surmised that the Brazilians were planning to return to the country to organize an antimilitary movement.[126] Fear of the emergent JCR, while exaggerated, no doubt provided additional motivation for the regimes to engage in Condor collaboration, although it was certainly not the only, or even the most important, factor. For example, in 1974 a Defense Department intelligence report stated that the Pinochet regime harbored strong fears about several international meetings in Europe that drew dissidents and political party representatives, including Allende's widow and François Mitterand of France, to protest the atrocities of the Pinochet regime.[127] More important, as I have shown, transnational military collaboration had been developing since the 1960s, to block leftist and nationalist political figures from coming to power in South America.

In September 1975, Argentine intelligence officer Osvaldo Ribeiro visited Santiago on Condor business. In October, the Conference of American Armies was held in Montevideo, as was the 8th Intelligence Conference of the armies. In a stark statement of the Argentine army's view, General Jorge Videla of Argentina said: "All those persons necessary will die in order to achieve the security of the country."[128] A secret Argentine army document of the same month outlined that army's extraterritorial operations.[129] The document contained orders for various commandos. One was ordered to "[i]solate the external support for subversive organizations with efforts according to the following priorities: Uruguay, Paraguay, and Brazil," and others targeted Bolivia and Chile.

Other documents found in the Paraguayan Archives detailed the increasingly fluid intelligence sharing of the Condor militaries in 1975. One secret document of October 20, from Colonel Benito Guanes Serrano of the Paraguayan armed forces,[130] reported on the surveillance of numerous Paraguayan opponents of General Stroessner, dictator of Paraguay, who were exiled in Argentina and Bolivia, and cited as sources the military attachés of Argentina and Brazil, the G-2 (intelligence) of Bolivia, and the Centro de Informaciones del Ejército (army intelligence) of Brazil. Another report, dated October 22, cited intelligence provided by the security advisor of the U.S. Embassy, "Mr. McWade," on a supposed subversive cell in Santa Cruz; the document also cited Bolivian and Argentine intelligence officers.[131] In the following month, November 1975, Condor was officially institutionalized and code named at the First Inter-American Working Meeting of Intelligence in Santiago.

Condor's Foundational Meeting

A letter from DINA chief Manuel Contreras found in the Paraguayan Archives, dated October 1975, established that the Condor prototype was to be institutionalized and upgraded in the November meeting. The letter was carried by DINA commander Mario Jahn to General Francisco Brites (or Britez), chief of the Paraguayan police, to invite him to "a Working Meeting of National Intelligence" to be held in Santiago under "strict secrecy." The purpose of the meeting was to formalize "an excellent coordination and improved action to benefit National Security."[132] In the proposal, Contreras noted that previous combined operations had taken place on the basis of "gentlemen's agreements" and that more sophisticated structures were needed to confront "the psychopolitical war" with subversion.[133]

The agenda for the meeting included a proposed plan of action and organizational structure, including a security system with three elements: an office of coordination and security, including a computerized central data bank of suspect persons, organizations, and activities, "something similar to Interpol, but dedicated to Subversion"; an information center with special communication channels, a cryptography capability, telephones with scrambling mechanisms, and message systems; and permanent working meetings. The Chileans offered Santiago as the headquarters of the system, specifying that the "technical personnel" of the system would be equally represented by participating countries. These technical personnel would have diplomatic immunity, and the Chileans proposed that they be from the intelligence services. The "technical personnel" were the agents who carried out Condor operations, including disappearances and assassinations.

The closing act of this meeting, dated November 28, 1975, was signed by officers representing Argentina, Bolivia, Chile, Paraguay, and Uruguay.[134] This document was essentially the secret charter of Operation Condor. The original proposals were adopted, and the participants agreed to establish a coordination office and a central directory "with the names and addresses of those persons who work in Intelligence so that they can directly solicit the antecedents of persons and organizations connected *directly or indirectly* with Marxism" (emphasis added). Point 5c recommended "rapid and immediate contact when an individual was expelled from a country or when a suspect traveled in order to alert the Intelligence Services" of Condor countries, and Point 5g recommended the installation of intelligence operatives in each country's embassy, where they would be fully accredited and thus have cover stories and identities. In fact, Condor officers were named as military attachés in many cases. The officers scheduled their next meeting to be one week before the upcoming meeting of the Conference of American Armies, in Santiago in June 1976, and at the suggestion of the Uruguayan delegation, they named the system "Condor" in honor of the host country, which used the condor as a national symbol. Colonel Contreras, "Condor One," signed the act, as did Colonel Benito Guanes Serrano of Paraguay, Captain José Casas of Argentina, Major Carlos Mena of Bolivia, and Colonel José A. Fons of Uruguay.

A declassified DIA document reported that Condor set up its telecommunications system (Condortel) in 1976 to upgrade its intelligence, planning, and operations against political opponents. An Argentine military officer divulged that the CIA played a key role in providing the computerized links among the intelligence and operations units of the six Condor states.[135] A declassified 1978 cable shed further light on Condor communications and pointed to direct U.S. military and intelligence collaboration.

The cable, from ambassador to Paraguay Robert White to Secretary of State Cyrus Vance, reported on a meeting requested by the commander of Paraguay's armed forces, General Alejandro Fretes Dávalos. Fretes informed White that Condor officers were using the U.S. telecommunications network, housed in a U.S. facility in the Panama Canal Zone, for Condor intelligence coordination throughout Latin America.[136] The general told White that intelligence chiefs from Brazil, Argentina, Chile, Bolivia, Paraguay, and Uruguay used "an encrypted system within the U.S. telecommunications net[work]," which covered all of Latin America, to "coordinate intelligence information." In his report, Ambassador White drew the connection to Operation Condor and advised the Carter administration to reconsider whether this linkage was in the U.S. interest. He stated in 2001 that he never received a response.

This direct involvement of U.S. military and/or intelligence forces in the Condor system is of weighty significance. Essentially, the U.S. government's official communications channel—its secure system for inter-American military and intelligence interchanges—was put at the disposal of Operation Condor. Such technological and operations support clearly was a crucial foundation for the coordination of Condor intelligence and covert operations, reflecting significant U.S. collusion. Access to classified U.S. communications systems requires official identification with secret or top-secret security clearances, knowledge of frequently changed passwords, detailed logs and record-keeping, and other rigorous security measures.[137] Thus, despite the carefully formulated half-denial in 2001 by the former DIA commander,[138] it is inconceivable that any foreign officer or military group could make use of the secure U.S. telecommunications system without the deep knowledge, collaboration, and engagement of top U.S. military and intelligence officials.

A senior U.S. intelligence officer I consulted, who also checked with a colleague in SOUTHCOM (U.S. Southern Command), thought that the communications system sounded like a CIA operation, run under military cover.[139] He said that such a system would operate without the widespread knowledge of SOUTHCOM officers, although SOUTHCOM's commander in chief was probably aware of it. If so, the communications system was also a parallel structure outside the normal chain of command. The Panama base—which housed the SOA, a large CIA station, the headquarters of SOUTHCOM, and the headquarters of the special forces and other military branches—was certainly the center of the hemispheric counterinsurgency effort. As one military graduate of the SOA put it, "the school was always a front for other special operations, covert operations."[140]

The sophisticated U.S. telecommunications network allowed Condor operations centers to communicate with one another and with the Panama Canal base and to direct covert actions in the region. Ambassador White subsequently underlined the importance of the Condor link to the Panama base, saying that his interchange with Fretes convinced him that the U.S. government was deeply involved in Operation Condor. He noted that such communications systems were generally set up for allied militaries so that U.S. personnel could monitor their communications and alert their superiors of planned operations.[141] High-ranking CIA officer David Atlee Phillips, in his 1977 book, wrote that CIA communications systems were used to support intelligence operations worldwide and to provide communications between CIA headquarters and its offices abroad and between headquarters and sensitive agents abroad "with whom regular contact was impracticable or a threat to their security."[142] The unavoidable conclusion is that select U.S. forces had complete knowledge of—and provided unambiguous operational support to—Condor intelligence and hunter-killer operations coordinated through the communications network.

In sum, the fledgling Condor system emerged in 1973, 1974, and 1975 as anticommunist Latin American military and police institutions, intelligence organizations, and parastatal groups such as the Triple A, and their

U.S. military and intelligence counterparts, decided to unify and make more lethal their offensive campaigns against political opponents in South America. In those years, as large numbers of exiles "disappeared" and tortured cadavers began to be found, Latin Americans perceived a terrible escalation of death squad operations. In February 1974—long before the well-documented Condor meeting of November 1975—a crucial gathering occurred in Buenos Aires, with security officials from five of the Condor states. This meeting raises the possibility that Argentine officers in the military and security forces, rather than Chileans, were the initial planners and organizers of the Condor prototype. Other official and quasi-official intelligence conferences, some in the United States and many under the aegis of the inter-American security system, cemented the transcontinental countersubversive network. U.S. military and intelligence officials, operating from the Canal Zone headquarters and U.S. embassies, provided vital resources and support to upgrade, modernize, and make more efficient the program of coordinated repression. Using parastatal structures and terrorist operations within the framework of Operation Condor, the militaries consolidated state power, crushed dissent, and extended their reach across the continent.

Notes

1. See my "Hidden Cold War History: Operation Condor's Structures and Operations," paper prepared for the 23rd International Congress of Latin American Studies Association (LASA), Washington, D.C., September 2001.

2. The Caravan of Death was an execution operation in which legally held political prisoners were killed by a military unit that traveled around the country. See Patricia Verdugo, *Chile, Pinochet, and the Caravan of Death* (Coral Gables, Fla.: University of Miami, North-South Center Press, 2001).

3. The date is illegible on the document itself and the State Department document index gives the date as November 1974; however, this is impossible since Prats was assassinated in September 1974. CIA Directorate of Operations, secret report of November 27, 1973, on State Department website. See also Lucy Komisar, "Documented Complicity," *The Progressive* (1999).

4. See J. Patrice McSherry, "Tracking the Origins of a State Terror Network: Operation Condor," *Latin American Perspectives*, Vol. 29, no. 1 (2002), for a discussion of the Schneider assassination.

5. Pablo Policzer, "Organizing Coercion in Authoritarian Chile," Ph.D. dissertation, MIT (2001), 98; see also "Arancibia Clavel, el único detenido," *La Tercera* (Chile), November 12, 2000.

6. Mónica González, "Confirman que el ejército de Pinochet mató a Prats," *Clarín* (Argentina), October 5, 2000.

7. He was accused of participating in the disappearances and torture of Chileans in Argentina under the Condor program. See "Procesan a Enrique Arancibia Clavel por caso de torturas en Argentina," *Primera Línea* (Chile), August 20, 2002.

8. João Resende-Santos, "The Origins of Security Cooperation in the Southern Cone," *Latin American Politics and Society*, Vol. 44, no. 4 (Winter 2002): 89–128. Cite appears on page 9 of Internet version, available from Expanded Academic Index. See also Alfred Stepan, *Rethinking Military Politics* (Princeton, N.J.: Princeton University Press, 1988).

9. CIA, Directorate of Operations, title blacked out, January 23, 1974.

10. Jonathan Franklin, "Ex-Spy Chief Says CIA Helped Him Set Up Pinochet's Secret Police," *The Guardian* (U.K.), September 23, 2000; see also *La Tercera* (Chile), September 21, 2000; *Jornal do Brasil*, September 22, 2000.

11. See John Dinges and Saul Landau, *Assassination on Embassy Row* (New York: Pantheon Books, 1980), chapter 5.

12. Stuart Christie states that Warren was involved with setting up Condor. He cites no specific source, but his book is well documented and much of his data has been borne out by other works. The fact that Warren was instrumental in forging ties between the Brazilian military regime and DINA does indicate that he had a key role in setting up Condor networks. Christie, *Stefano Delle Chiaie: Portrait of a Black Terrorist* (London: Anarchy Magazine/Refract Publications, 1984), 85. See also "Según CIA, Brasil organizó policía secreta de Pinochet," *Ambito Financiero* (Argentina), May 15, 2000; "Estructuran brasileños los Servicios Secretos de Pinochet," *Excelsior* (Mexico), May 15, 2000.

13. A former Israeli Mossad officer claimed that DINA received training from Mossad. The book is written in a sensational style, however, and the credibility of the source seems rather questionable. See Victor Ostrovsky and Claire Hoy, *By Way of Deception: The Making and Unmaking of a MOSSAD Officer* (New York: St. Martin's Press, 1990), chapter 11. Israel did provide arms to the Latin American militaries, however, especially after the Carter administration suspended aid due to human rights concerns, and this source briefly mentions Israeli assistance in training Pinochet's secret police: Benjamin Beit-Hallahmi, *The Israeli Connection: Who Israel Arms and Why* (New York: Pantheon, 1987), 98–107.

14. CIA, Report to Congress, September 18, 2000, 17; Televisión Nacional de Chile, "Contreras: Operación Cóndor nunca existió," August 27, 2004.

15. Department of Defense Intelligence Information Report (Secret), "DINA: Its Operations and Power," February 8, 1974.

16. See Department of Defense, Intelligence Information Report, "DINA Expands Operations and Facilities," April 15, 1975.

17. Comisión Nacional de Verdad y Reconciliación de Chile, *Informe Rettig* (Rettig Report), (Santiago: Chilean Government and Ediciones del Ornitorrinco, 1991), 449–452. For a graphic insider's view of DINA, see Luz Arce (trans. Alba Skar), *The Inferno: A Story of Terror and Survival in Chile* (Madison: University of Wisconsin Press, 2004).

18. Politczer, "Organizing Coercion," 98.

19. Army bio of Iturriaga Neumann, from USDAO Santiago to RUEKJCS/DIA WASHDC, July 1987.

20. Jorge Molina, "En declaraciones a jueza Servini de Cubría Townley asumió responsabilidad por asesinato de Prats," *El Mostrador* (Chile), May 9, 2000.

21. Marcos Salgado, "Caso Prats: Las pruebas contra la cúpula de la DINA," *El Mostrador* (Chile), July 3, 2001.

22. M. Valenzuela/J. Molina, "Exclusivo: La red de espías de Iturriaga Neumann para el caso Prats," *El Mostrador* (Chile), July 6, 2000.

23. "Declaración de un agente de la Dina," with cover letter by Raúl Vergara Meneses dated July 14, 1977, on State Department website. See also Pascale Bonnefoy, "El ocaso de Colonia Dignidad," *La Nación* (Chile), October 3, 2004, quoting John Dinges.

24. John Dinges, "Colonia Dignidad, Part II," *The Rebel* (February 13, 1984): 36, 40.

25. Director of Central Intelligence, "To George, from Karl," May 28, 1976.

26. CIA, "Latin American Trends: Staff Notes (secret)," August 16, 1976, stated that two wealthy Jewish brothers were "confined in a colony run by former German Nazis who enjoy the protection of the Chilean government" (page 5). See also Dinges, "Colonia Dignidad, Part I," *The Rebel* (February 8, 1984) and "Colonia Dignidad, Part II."

27. Victoria Ginsberg, "La represión fue un plan que manejó el Pentágono desde Panamá," *Página/12* (Argentina), June 12, 2000.

28. Santiago Pinetta, *López Rega: El final de un brujo* (Buenos Aires: Editorial Abril, documento de *Siete Días*, 1986), 57.

29. Rodolfo Peregrino Fernández, *Autocrítica policial* (Buenos Aires: El Cid Editor/Fundación para la Democracia en Argentina, 1983), 10, 72.

30. "Protagonista de la Operación Cóndor," *La Nación* (Argentina), April 29, 2001.

31. Ignacio González Janzen, *La Triple A* (Buenos Aires: Editorial Contrapunto, 1986), 19.

32. Penny Lernoux, *Cry of the People* (New York: Doubleday, 1980), 340–341.

33. Pinetta, *López Rega*, 99; *Buenos Aires Herald*, May 29, 1983, 11; *El Periodista*, no. 159 (25 September–1 October, 1987): 5–10; *Página/12*, June 13, 1992. Many other sources confirmed this, including retired military officers (interviews conducted by author in Buenos Aires, May 1992).

34. González Janzen, *La Triple A*, 93–100.

35. Lernoux, *Cry of the People*, 339.

36. Lernoux, *Cry of the People*, 339. Former CIA agent Philip Agee said that the federal police in Buenos Aires were the CIA's main liaison. One CIA officer told Lernoux in an interview, "If you think the Brazilian police's torture methods are bad, you should see what goes on in the Argentine prisons" (*Cry of the People*, 338).

37. Paino, *Historia*, 150, 162, 175.

38. Interview conducted by author with Emilio Mignone, then-head of *Centro de Estudios Legales y Sociales* (CELS), June 16, 1992, Buenos Aires.

39. Peregrino Fernández, *Autocrítica*, 36.

40. The full "Open Letter" was attached to a letter to Patricia Derian from a relative of Rodolfo Walsh, dated April 1977. Declassified State Department document on website.

41. Martín Sivak, "¿Quién mató a Juan José Torres?" *Brecha* (Uruguay), May 31, 1996, and Sivak, *El asesinato de Juan José Torres: Banzer y el mercosur de la muerte* (Buenos Aires: Ediciones del Pensamiento Nacional, 1998), 186.

42. "Protagonista de la Operación Cóndor," *La Nación* (Argentina), April 29, 2001.

43. Fernández did not identify GT5 in his testimony. Blystone's source said that there were five GTs under the command of Intelligence Battalion 601: GT1 and 2 targeted several small leftist organizations, GT3 targeted the Montoneros, GT4 the Ejército Revolucionario del Pueblo (ERP), and GT5 the Junta Coordinadora Revolucionaria (JCR). I place more stock in the account of Peregrino Fernández because it comports with those of other Argentine sources, including military officers, who told me in 1992 interviews that GT1, under army command, focused on the ERP. See Peregrino Fernández, *Autocrítica policial*, 35–48. CONADEP, in *Nunca más*, gave still another designation (quoting a former commando): that GT1 and 2 were run by army intelligence battalion 601; GT3 by the navy; GT4 by the air force; and GT5 by SIDE. Comisión Nacional sobre la Desaparicìon de Personas, *Nunca más* (Buenos Aires: Eudeba, 1984), 257.

44. See National Security Archive, Electronic Briefing Book no. 73, 2002, "Organigram del '601,'" and "Memorandum of Conversation: Nuts and Bolts of the Government's Repression of Terrorism-Subversion," August 7, 1979.

45. PIT-CNT [labor union confederation of Uruguay], *Desaparecidos: La coordinación represiva* (Montevideo: Editorial Espacio, 1998), 15–16.

46. National Security Archive, Electronic Briefing Book no. 71, "Introduction," ed. by Carlos Osorio, June 20, 2002 at www.gwu.edu/nsarchiv/NSAEBB/NSAEBB71/

47. "Secretos de la Dictadura," *Posdata* (Uruguay), no. 85 (April 26, 1996): 89.

48. J. Víctor García Rivas, *Confesiones de un torturador* (Barcelona: Editorial Laia, 1981), 51, 112.

49. "Secretos," *Posdata*, 14, 16.

50. "Secretos," *Posdata*, 16.

51. CIA, *The National Intelligence Daily* (Top Secret), June 23, 1976. Another CIA document mentioned in passing that "cooperation between the respective intelligence/security agencies had existed for some time—perhaps as early as February 1974," but then asserted that Condor was not formalized until May 1976. This document, which was intended as a briefing for the Letelier assassination prosecutor, contained several errors, including the statement that Condor was formalized in May 1976 (it was actually November 1975). See CIA, "Classified Reading Material re: 'Condor' for Ambassador Landau and Mr. Propper," August 22, 1978.

52. Mónica González and Edwin Harrington, *Bomba en una calle de Palermo* (Santiago, Chile: Editorial Emisión, 1987), 173–174, quoted in M. Gerardo Irusta, ed., *Espionaje y servicios secretos en Bolivia y el Cono Sur: Nazis en la Operación Cóndor*, 2nd ed. (La Paz, Bolivia, 1997), 523.

53. *La Nación*, April 29, 2001.

54. See interview in Osvaldo Burgos, "Manuel Contreras conocía asesinatos de opositores uruguayos," *Surmedia.com*, November 6, 2002.

55. C. M. Cerna, "Summary of Argentine Law and Practice on Terrorism," U.S. State Department, March 1976, cited in Martin Edwin Andersen, ed., *Dossier Secreto: Argentina's Desaparecidos and the Myth of the 'Dirty War'* (Boulder, Colo.: Westview, 1993), 108. See also Horacio Verbitsky, "El Vuelo del Cóndor," *Página/12*, January 28, 1996; and Miguel Bonasso, *El presidente que no fue: Los archivos ocultos del peronismo*, 2nd ed. (Buenos Aires: Planeta, 2002), 819.

56. State Department, "Summary of Argentine Law," cited in Andersen, *Dossier Secreto*, 109–110.

57. State Department, "Summary of Argentine Law," cited in Andersen, *Dossier Secreto*, 120.

58. Henry Kissinger cable, "South America: Southern Cone Security Practices," July 20, 1976, 4.

59. To SecState, From AMEmbassy, "Southern Cone Security Practices," July 23, 1976.

60. CIA, Report to Congress, "CIA Activities in Chile," September 18, 2000; www.odci.gov./cia/publication/chile.

61. CIA, "Classified Reading Material re: 'Condor' for Ambassador Landau and Mr. Propper," August 22, 1978.

62. Katie Zoglin, "Paraguay's Archive of Terror: International Cooperation and Operation Condor," *Inter-American Law Review*, Vol. 32, no. 1 (Winter–Spring 2001): 64.

63. Zoglin, "Paraguay's Archive of Terror," 66–67.

64. "Foreign Spy Activity Found Rampant in U.S.," *Washington Post*, August 9, 1979, A12. See also Peter Kornbluh, "Prisoner Pinochet: The Dictator and the Quest for Justice," *The Nation* (December 21, 1998): 15; and Lucy Komisar, "Kissinger Encouraged Chile's Brutal Repression, New Documents Show," *Albion Monitor*, March 8, 1999.

65. CIA Directorate of Operations, "To: File, From: CIA" (title blacked out), August 20, 1974.

66. Wilson García Mérida, "Un cochabambino en manos de Pinochet," *Los Tiempos* (Bolivia), November 1998.

67. "Two Mysterious Kidnappings," U.S. Embassy in Santiago to SecState, November 12, 1973; see also 1996 interview with Gallardo in Sivak, *El Asesinato*, 126–130.

68. Nilson Cezar Mariano, *Operación Cóndor: Terrorismo de Estado en el Cono Sur* (Buenos Aires: Lohlé-Lumen, 1998), 42.

69. "Campos Hermida y Castiglioni fueron entrenados en 'inteligencia' en EEUU," *La Hora* (Uruguay), December 30, 1986. Philip Agee, the former CIA officer who turned against the agency, stated that the IPA was run by the CIA using AID cover. For details confirming this CIA role in the IPA, see Michael McClintock, *The American Connection*, Volume I, *State Terror and Popular Resistance in El Salvador* (London: Zed Books, 1985), 57–63.

70. Interview with Carlos Osorio of the National Security Archive by Radio Espectador, Uruguay, August 4, 2001.

71. Rosendo Fraga, *Ejército: Del escarnio al poder (1973–1976)* (Buenos Aires: Grupo Editorial Planeta, 1988), 127.

72. See translation of Montoneros communique, April 2, 1975, p. 4, on State Department website; the writers of this document appear to be quite well informed about the murky doings of the Triple A at the time. See also Secretaría de Derechos Humanos y Políticas Sociales del PNT/CNT (Uruguay), "Dossier: El Capítulo Uruguayo de la Operación Cóndor," p. 37, at www.simonriquelo.org.uy/plancondor.pdf.

73. On the Soca case, see "Significado de la desaparición para la familia," xeroxed document found in archives of Servicio Paz y Justicia, SERPAJ [human rights organization]

in Uruguay by author in August 2001, n.d., no source; see also Secretaría de Derechos Humanos y Políticas Sociales del PIT/CNT, "Dossier: El Capítulo Uruguayo de la Operación Cóndor," n.d., at www.simonriquelo.org.uy/ plancondor.pdf, accessed by author June 2003.

74. I first suggested that these were actually Condor cases in 2000, in my "Analyzing Operation Condor: A Covert Inter-American Structure," paper prepared for the 22nd International Congress of Latin American Studies Association (LASA), Miami, March 2000.

75. The National Security Archive first reported new information on this case in October 1999. See *Pinochet Watch*, no. 9 (November 5, 1999) and www.gwu.edu/~nsarchiv/news/19991008/index.html; see also Diana Jean Schemo, "U.S. Victims of Chile's Coup: The Uncensored File," *New York Times*, February 13, 2000.

76. Thomas Hauser, *The Execution of Charles Horman* (New York: Harcourt, Brace, Jovanovich, 1978), 26.

77. Hauser, *The Execution*, 233, 244.

78. Letter from Senator Edward Kennedy to Harry W. Schlaudeman, assistant secretary and U.S. coordinator, Alliance for Progress, June 23, 1976.

79. Schemo, "U.S. Victims."

80. State Department memo from R. V. Fimbres/R. S. Driscoll/W. V. Robertson, through Ambassador Ryan to Harry W. Schlaudeman, "Charles Horman case," dated August 25, 1976, at National Security Archive website.

81. See, for example, statement by Terry Simon dated April 11, 1974, on State Department Chile Declassification Project website.

82. Hauser, *The Execution*, 231, citing an interview conducted by Marlise Simons that was published in the *Times of London* on October 27, 1974.

83. Department of State memo by Frederick Smith, subject "Further Steps in the Case of Charles Horman," 1976, 1. See also memo from Ambassador Popper to Kissinger, subject "Statement of Rafael Gonzales on Death of AMCIT Charles Horman," dated June 1976.

84. Smith memo to Shlaudeman, 2, 20.

85. Declassified State Department confidential memo, February 1974, on National Security Archive website.

86. Lucy Komisar, "Documented Duplicity," *The Progressive* website, 1999.

87. Lucy Komisar, "Kissinger Encouraged Chile's Brutal Repression, New Documents Show," *Albion Monitor*, March 8, 1999 (www.monitor.net/monitor).

88. Letter from Frank F. Teruggi to Cyrus Vance, secretary of state, dated February 7, 1977.

89. Teruggi documents, National Security Archive, at www.gwu.edu/nsarchiv/news/20001113; Diana Jean Schemo, "F.B.I. Watched an American Who Was Killed in Chile Coup," *New York Times*, July 1, 2000.

90. Letter (secret) to the acting director of the FBI from the legal officer of the U.S. Embassy in Bonn, October 25, 1972, in National Security Archive website, www.gwu.edu/~nsarchiv/news/20001113/.

91. Secret memo from U.S. Department of Justice, FBI, title blacked out, October 25, 1972.

92. Memorandum to acting director, FBI, from legal attaché, Bonn, November 28, 1972.

93. U.S. Department of Justice, FBI, "Frank Teruggi," December 14, 1972, at National Security Archive, Electronic Briefing Book No. 33, June 30, 2000.

94. Memo from Colonel W. M. Hon, October 16, 1973 (no. 207-SCS file), cited in report to Harry W. Schlaudeman from Frederick Smith, Jr., "Further Steps in the Case of Charles Horman," December 29, 1976, p. 5 of "Background and Chronology."

95. Report to ARA, Mr. Schlaudeman, from R. V. Fimbres/R. S. Driscoll/W. V. Robertson, re Charles Horman Case, August 25, 1976, at National Security Archive website.

96. State Department, Smith memo, 1976, 7. See also Hauser, chapter 22.

97. Smith memo, 1976, 8.

98. Smith memo, 1976, 9.

99. Vernon Loeb, "Spook Story," *Washington Post*, September 17, 2000.

100. Smith memo, 1976, 13–14; Larry Rohter, "New Evidence Surfaces in '73 Killing of an American in Chile," *New York Times*, March 12, 2004.

101. Smith memo, 1976, 15.

102. Confidential memo, subject "Rafael González Verdugo and Horman v. Kissinger," October 1978.

103. State Department memo, signed "Christopher," October 1978.

104. U.S. Embassy Santiago, "[Deleted] Reports on GOC Involvement in Death of Charles Horman, Asks Embassy for Asylum and Aid," April 28, 1987, in National Security Archive, Electronic Briefing Book No. 33, June 30, 2000.

105. Equipo Nizkor, "Testimonio secreto de Townley sobre el atentado al General Prats," November 14, 2000, at www.derechos.org/nizkor/index.html; accessed July 2003.

106. "Ex-Officer Indicted in '73 Slaying in Chile," *Washington Post*, December 12, 2003; "Rafael González: 'El juez miente al decir que interrogué a Horman,'" *La Tercera* (Chile), February 2, 2004. In this rather incoherent interview in *La Tercera*, González blames the CIA and the State Department for Horman's murder while retracting his statement about the CIA officer's presence in the room in 1973. See also Kevin G. Hall, "Spy: CIA Absent in 'Missing' Case," *Miami Herald*, February 17, 2004.

107. Colonel Benito Guanes Serrano, General Staff of the Armed Forces of Paraguay, March 14, 1975, distribution to attachés of ARG/BOL/CHI/URU/USA/VEN; obtained by author in Paraguayan Archives, 1996.

108. CODEPU, Equipo DIT-T, *La gran mentira: El caso de las listas de los 119* (Santiago: CODEPU, 1994), 27–30 and *Más allá de las fronteras: Estudios sobre las personas ejecutadas o desaparecidas fuera de Chile 1973–1990* (Santiago: LOM Ediciones, 1996); Rettig Report (Chile), 482–484.

109. Luz Arce (trans. Alba Skar), *The Inferno: A Story of Terror and Survival in Chile* (Madison: University of Wisconsin Press, 2004), 111, 260–263.

110. Interview conducted by author with Roberto Garretón, human rights lawyer, July 19, 1996, Santiago; CODEPU-DIT-T, *La gran mentira,* especially chapter 7; Mónica González, "Confirman que el ejército," *Clarín*, October 5, 2000; Horacio Verbitsky, "El vuelo del Cóndor," *Página/12*, January 28, 1996; Stella Calloni, *Los años del*

Lobo: Operación Cóndor, 2nd ed. (Buenos Aires: Peña Lillo, Ediciones Continente, 1999), 50.

111. Rettig Report, 595-96; CODEPU, Equipo DIT-T, *Más allá*, 78–83; Instituto Cono Sur, *Resumen nro. 385*, "Jorge Fuentes Alarcón, Víctima del Cóndor," August 12, 2001; "Las preguntas que el juez Guzmán tiene para Pinochet," *La Nación* (Chile), September 25, 2004.

112. National Security Archive, document 30-01 of 1975, at www.gwu.edu/nsarchive/NSAEBB/ NSAEBB8/ch30-01.htm.

113. Dinges and Landau, *Assassination on Embassy Row*, 155–157; Daniel Brandt, "Operation Condor: Ask the DEA," December 10, 1998, at www.pir.org/condor.html.Brandt.

114. There have been some doubts expressed as to whether this document is genuine. It has been in the public domain for almost thirty years. According to Lucy Komisar, the original was obtained in 1995 by an Italian court investigating the assassination attempt against Leighton and his wife. See "Into the Murky Depths of 'Operation Condor,'" *Los Angeles Times*, November 1, 1998. John Dinges questioned the document's veracity in "The Dubious Document," *Columbia Journalism Review*, Vol. 38, no. 5 (January 1, 2000): 10.

115. Enrique Montero Marx, Subsecretario del Interior, Chile, to Don João Batista de Oliveira Figueiredo, Jefe de Serviço Nacional de Informações, Brasil, "Unificación de las actividades de Inteligencia en la Peninsula Ibérica. Establece a continuación, comando territorial unificado, entre Chile y Brasil," August 21, 1975. I received a copy of this document, and others, in 2001 thanks to Professor João Roberto Martins Filho, of the Universidade Federal de São Carlos, Brazil, and Marco Aurélio Vannucchi Leme de Mattos, an investigator studying the DOPS files in a project entitled "Mapeamento e sistematização do Acervo Deops/SP: Série Dossiês," chaired by María Aparecida Aquino. See also "O acordo SNI/DINA," *Correio Popular*, November 4, 1998.

116. "Verbas para matar," *Correio Popular* (Brazil), November 4, 1998. John Dinges raised doubts about its authenticity to me, citing FBI sources, in a personal email communication on May 19, 2000.

117. Lúcio Reiner, consultor legislativo da area XIX, "Circunstâncias Políticas Quando da Morte do Ex-Presidente Juscelino Kubitschek," Estudio, Abril 2001, for Câmara dos Deputados, 3. Rafael González, the Chilean officer associated with the Horman case, also verified the document's authenticity. TO: SecState, FROM: AmEmbassy Santiago, "Rafael González Verdugo," May 18, 1977. Jack Anderson spoke with Brazilian legislators; see Helayne Boaventura, "Morte de JK sob suspeita," *Jornal do Brasil*, January 18, 2001.

118. "DINA Implicated in Death of Brazilian President," *Santiago Times*, May 28, 1996.

119. "Investigan en Brasil posible atentado contra Kubitschek," *Noticias* (Paraguay), July 11, 1996.

120. Letter from DINA chief Contreras to Figueiredo, dated August 28, 1975, copy in author's possession.

121. Dario Pignotti, "La extraña muerte de João Goulart," *La Jornada* (Mexico), May 25, 2000.

122. Letter (urgent, secret) dated September 24 1975, to General Carlos Alberto Fontoura, Brazilian ambassador in Lisbon, by Figueiredo, from DOPS files.

123. Free translation from Portuguese by the author. Letter from the director of the SNI to the Brazilian Embassy in Lisbon, September 26, 1975, copy in author's possession.

124. Townley actually smuggled sarin into the United States in a perfume bottle, but finally decided not to use it. Mónica González, "Un biólogo que fue una pieza clave en la máquina de matar," *Clarín* (Argentina) May 25, 1996; Samuel Blixen, "Berríos, the Bothersome Biochemist," *TNI's Drugs and Democracy Program*, December 1997, at www.tni.org/letelier. The United States conducted chemical warfare tests using sarin in Hawaii in 1967. See Thom Shanker, "U.S. Tested a Nerve Gas in Hawaii," *New York Times*, November 1, 2002.

125. Beatriz Elias, "A acusção pela morte de JK," *Correio Popular* (Brazil), November 5, 1998, 7. Elias conducted research for a year in the DOPS archives and wrote a series of articles on her findings. This article, and others, are part of the holdings of the Arquivo Ana Lagôa of the Universidade Federal de São Carlos.

126. U.S. Defense Attaché Office, La Paz (Bolivia), to U.S. SOUTHCOM, Department of Defense Intelligence Information Report, "Communist Coordinating Movement," 12 September 1975.

127. Department of Defense, National Military Command Center, cable to RUEKJCS/DIAWASHDC, from USDAO SANTIAGO CHILE, August 1974.

128. *Clarín*, October 24, 1975.

129. "Directiva del Comandante General del Ejército (secret), Nro. 404/75 (Lucha subversión)," October 1975. This and other documents were given to the author by the late José Luis D'Andrea Mohr, a former army captain, in Buenos Aires in 1998.

130. Colonel Benito Guanes Serrano, General Staff of the Paraguayan Armed Forces, "Informe No, 64, Acción Subversiva Combinada," October 20, 1975, obtained by the author in the Paraguayan Archives, 1996.

131. Colonel Benito Guanes Serrano, Estado Mayor General, Asunción, "Informe No. 65," October 22, 1975, obtained by author in Paraguayan Archives, 1996.

132. Manuel Contreras letter to General Francisco Britez, Item 151, 1975, in Paraguayan Archives.

133. "Primera Reunión de Trabajo de Inteligencia Nacional," October 29, 1975, prepared by DINA; obtained by author in the Paraguayan Archives, 1996.

134. The closing act was reprinted in *Posdata* (Uruguay), June 18, 1999: 19–20.

135. Saul Landau, *The Dangerous Doctrine: National Security and U.S. Foreign Policy* (A PACCA Book. Boulder, Colo.: Westview, 1988), 119; personal correspondence with author, February 13, 1999.

136. Robert White, cable to secretary of state, October 13, 1978, at foia.state.gov/documents/StateChile3/000058FD.pdf. See also Diana Jean Schemo, "New Files Tie U.S. to Deaths of Latin Leftists in 1970s," *New York Times*, March 6, 2001. This author unearthed the cable during her research.

137. See, for example, U.S. Department of State Foreign Affairs Manual, Vol. 12, "Diplomatic Security," 12 Fam 630, "Classified Automated Information Systems," 10–07–2002, at State Department website.

138. He said that "if such an arrangement existed on an institutional basis, I would have known about it, and I did not then and do not now," but added, "that such an arrangement could have been made locally on an ad hoc basis is not beyond the realm of probability." Schemo, "New Files," 2001.

139. Author telephone interview and e-mail exchange with senior U.S. intelligence officer, August 16, 2003, and September 2, 2003, respectively. The CIA did use military cover in other cases, as noted by CIA officer David Atlee Phillips in 1977. He said that the CIA covert operations training facility in Virginia known as "the farm" was protected for years by military cover; it appeared to be a military special operations training site. Phillips, *The Night Watch* (New York: Atheneum, 1977), 210.

140. Jack Nelson-Pallmeyer, *School of Assassins* (New York: Orbis Books, 1997), 31; see also Mary A. Fischer, "Teaching Torture," *Gentlemen's Quarterly* (June 1997), 189.

141. Author interview with Ambassador Robert White, conducted by telephone, April 8, 2003.

142. Phillips, *The Night Watch*, 228–229.

4

Condor's Killing Machine: Phase II Transnational Operations

THE LAST CLAUSE OF THE FOUNDATIONAL act of Operation Condor, signed November 28, 1975, stated that within sixty days the act required ratification by the military chiefs of each member country, and that the agreements entailed by the Condor system would enter into effect on January 30, 1976.[1] Long before this document was discovered in 1999, witnesses and victims of Condor in Latin American were well aware of the stunning increase in 1976 of disappearances and extrajudicial executions of exiles and political refugees. By that year, Operation Condor was functioning at a sophisticated and intense level of supranational coordination. A number of Phase III assassinations were carried out in 1976 as well as hundreds of covert abductions-disappearances and murders of lesser-known dissidents and rebels by combined Condor teams.

Condor's organizational advances, such as the centralization of intelligence information via the new office of coordination, and the technological modernization of the Condor system, made possible by sophisticated computers and communications equipment, greatly enhanced the lethal efficiency of the Condor apparatus. As suggested in previous chapters, there is substantial evidence that U.S. intelligence played an important secret role in these advances. For many years, U.S. officials in Latin America had worked to centralize military and police command structures and intelligence systems, modernize communications, and foster strategic and operational coordination in the countersubversive struggle. U.S. security agencies provided Condor with intelligence and cooperation, and the U.S. military and/or the CIA offered access to the U.S. continental communications system housed in the Panama

Canal Zone. Several sources reported that the CIA provided state-of-the-art computers to the Condor system. Moreover, the evidence suggests that in June 1976, Secretary of State Henry Kissinger signaled U.S. approval for Condor operations.

On March 24, 1976, the Argentine armed forces staged a coordinated nationwide coup, deposing President Isabel Perón and taking over the national government as well as all provincial and municipal governments throughout the country. Now the entire Southern Cone, and most of South America, was under military rule. The Argentine junta imposed the bloodiest dictatorship the country had ever known; according to human rights organizations, some 30,000 persons "disappeared," the highest number in South America. In the months after the coup, a new wave of Condor disappearances and assassinations took place in Buenos Aires, terrorizing the exile community.

This chapter presents some emblematic cases of Condor's covert abduction-disappearance-execution operations to convey a sense of the system's terrorist methods during its most violent years (1976–80). The next chapter focuses on Phase III assassinations. This chapter also documents the significant bureaucratic and organizational steps taken by Condor commanders to expand the deadly reach of the repressive system. Declassified U.S. materials and documents from the Paraguayan Archives and other Latin American sources are fitted in chronologically to provide an account of Condor intelligence conferences during this period. The record shows that Condor fused barbaric, lawless methods with twentieth-century science and technology.

Abduction and Assassination Operations in 1976

In April 1976, shortly after the coup in Argentina, Edgardo Enríquez of the Chilean Movimiento de la Izquierda Revolucionaria (MIR), who was under UN protection, was abducted in Buenos Aires, along with members of the Argentine Ejército Revolucionario del Pueblo (ERP) and a Brazilian. Enríquez was associated with the Junta Coordinadora Revolucionaria (Coordinating Board of Revolutionary Movements in Latin America, or JCR). The Pinochet government, in full psychological warfare mode, vociferously denied accounts that Enríquez had been illegally transferred to Chile, calling it part of a "Marxist anti-Chile" campaign.[2] But in 1992, Luz Arce, the former Socialist Party militant who was "turned" into a DINA collaborator, testified to the Rettig Commission that in 1976, when she was working in DINA headquarters, she saw a document on this case by mistake. The cable, marked "Communique via Condor," was from an Argentine intelligence service affiliated with Condor. It informed DINA of the capture of Enríquez and put him at DINA's disposal.[3]

The CIA soon knew of his fate. A secret July 2, 1976, CIA weekly summary cited "several reports that Chilean subversive leader Edgardo Enríquez, who was arrested by Argentine security forces on April 10, was subsequently turned over to the Chileans and is now dead."

"Meanwhile," the CIA report continued, "[LINE DELETED] the Argentine government has handed over to Chilean authorities a Brazilian political exile wanted by Santiago."[4] (The rest of this lengthy report on Condor operations was completely blacked out.) The CIA report commented that despite recent statements by the Argentine junta that it would not forcibly repatriate refugees, "[LINE EXCISED] suspect the acquiescence, and perhaps the direct involvement, of the Argentine security forces in many of these incidents."

The transfer of the Brazilian clearly could not have been carried out without the consent of Brazil's military government. On June 1, in fact, the U.S. Embassy in Brasilia had reported that Brazilian human rights activists had information on this case and had written a letter of protest to General Geisel, de facto president of Brazil, regarding the illegal transfer of the Brazilian.[5] On June 2, U.S. ambassador to Chile David Popper acknowledged prior information on the Brazilian, Regina Marcondes. She had requested political asylum at the Panamanian Embassy in Santiago after the September 1973 coup. Popper declined to take up her case. In a cryptic telegram he advised, "Embassy sees no grounds for approach to GOC [Government of Chile] on this matter."[6]

The Chilean Truth and Reconciliation Commission later verified that Enríquez was first taken to clandestine detention centers in Argentina, including El Olimpo, Campo de Mayo, and ESMA, and then illegally transferred to Villa Grimaldi in Santiago. Enríquez was never seen again. The commission also confirmed that Regina Marcondes was taken in a combined operation by the Argentine federal police and DINA agents at the same time.[7]

Another emblematic case, that of the Rutilo family, illustrated one of the routine practices of Operation Condor: the seizure of infants after the killing of their parents, and the transfer of the children to military or police families, to ensure a "nonsubversive" upbringing. Often children were illegally taken across borders with altered identities. The Grandmothers of the Plaza de Mayo in Argentina estimated that hundreds of children were victims of such trafficking; some of them have been recovered.

Graciela Rutilo Artes was an Argentine citizen married to a Uruguayan man, Enrique Lucas López, who belonged to the Tupamaro guerrillas. In 1976, Graciela Rutilo and their nine-month-old daughter Carla were living in a small Bolivian town. In April 1976, they were seized and transferred to La Paz, and Graciela was separated from her daughter. Graciela was subjected to brutal torture, with electric shocks, beatings, and cigarette burns, and sometimes the torturers brought in her daughter and hung her, naked and upside down, to torment her mother further. Bolivians and an Argentine team of federal police sent from that country carried out the torture. Carla was kept in an orphanage. After Graciela's mother, Matilde Artes Company, made repeated depositions to the Red Cross, her daughter and granddaughter were located and visited by a Red Cross representative.

After this visit, Carla was transferred to another orphanage in La Paz, where Matilde could visit her granddaughter. But on August 25, 1976, a Bolivian squadron again seized Carla. Graciela and Carla were handed over to Argentine security forces on August 29[8] and brought to the notorious Orletti Motors, the Condor torture center under the command of the Argentine Secretaría de Inteligencia del Estado, SIDE. Meanwhile, in September, Enrique Lucas was captured, tortured, and killed in Cochabamba. After the transfer to Argentina, Graciela Rutilo "disappeared," and Carla was given to Eduardo Ruffo, one of Orletti's most barbaric torturers and a former Triple A operative. Carla later told of vicious beatings she had received from her adoptive father. In 1983, immediately before the Argentine junta withdrew from government, the Grandmothers of the Plaza de Mayo found Carla living with Ruffo and instituted a legal proceeding to recover her. In 1985, she was reunited with her grandmother Matilde. It was one of the first cases of abducted children ever recovered by their biological families.[9] Ruffo served eight years in prison for illegally appropriating the child. In 2001, Carla filed a lawsuit and a request for extradition against former Bolivian dictator Hugo Banzer (then the elected president) and his wife before Spanish judge Baltasar Garzón, for their role in the illegal transfer of her mother and herself from Bolivian to Argentine security forces.[10] Banzer, who always denied the existence of Operation Condor, died in 2002.

In May 1976, the two Uruguayan legislators Michelini and Gutiérrez Ruiz were abducted and murdered, and in June Bolivian former president Torres was abducted and found dead, all Phase III operations of Condor (discussed in chapter 5). These assassinations revealed the interlocking system of repression among the Condor states of Argentina, Uruguay, and Bolivia and made clear the sharp escalation of murderous repression in 1976. The assassinations of such prominent dissidents sent political tremors throughout the region and the world.

Condor Coordination Accelerated

In the beginning of May 1976, the IV Bilateral Conference of Intelligence between the armies of Brazil and Paraguay was held, and General Alejandro

Fretes Dávalos, chief of the Paraguayan High Command, ordered Francisco Britez (sometimes spelled Brites), the general who commanded Paraguay's police, to prepare a report on "internal subversive activities and their connection with the exterior from November 1974 to the present."[11] In early June 1976, a key Condor meeting took place in Santiago, before the Sixth General Assembly of the Organization of American States and the Conference of American Armies. The fact that the OAS meeting was held in Santiago was a triumph for the Pinochet regime, which had been trying to improve its image on the world stage. Secretary of State Henry Kissinger traveled to the meeting, despite the advice of other State Department officials, specifically to enhance the prestige of the Pinochet regime. Senator Walter Mondale also wrote a letter to Kissinger asking the secretary not to "legitimize" the regime by traveling there. Kissinger responded by lecturing the senator that the visit would not signal endorsement since "relations do not signify approval" and arguing that "efforts to impress our own political and legal structures on other nations of the hemisphere is . . . paternalism." Yet Kissinger told Pinochet on his arrival: "We had the choice whether I should come or not. We thought it better for Chile if I came," and later added, "I encouraged the OAS to have its General Assembly here. I knew it would add prestige to Chile."[12]

The U.S. ambassador in Buenos Aires, Robert Hill, said in 1987 that, during the OAS meeting, Kissinger had specifically given the Argentine generals a green light for continued repression,[13] an accusation confirmed by recently declassified documents. The Argentines at the assembly had been worried that the United States would criticize the junta's dirty war. Prominent exiles Michelini, Gutiérrez Ruiz, and Torres had been assassinated in Buenos Aires in the previous several weeks, and "disappearances" and murders were occurring on a daily basis. But Kissinger stressed not state repression in Argentina but rather the importance of rapidly eliminating "subversion," before the next U.S. president took office and the new Congress convened.[14]

Kissinger met with Argentine admiral César Guzzetti, the foreign minister of the junta, on June 10, and later Guzzetti told Ambassador Hill that Kissinger had "understood" the junta's situation and offered U.S. support. Thereafter, Guzzetti flatly rejected the U.S. Embassy's protests regarding disappearances and massacres in Argentina, noting that executive branch officials in Washington sanctioned the junta's countersubversive policies.[15] In 2003 and 2004, newly declassified material provided documentary evidence that Guzzetti was interpreting Kissinger's message correctly. During the June 10 meeting, Kissinger made clear his support for the junta, telling Guzzetti that "we would like you to succeed." Guzzetti also specifically told Kissinger that all the Southern Cone militaries were collaborating to pursue "terrorists"—thus referring to Operation Condor and confirming the embassy's perceptions, recorded in declassified documents, of regional collusion in repression. Expressing no concern about the mounting human rights toll, Kissinger told Guzzetti that "the quicker you succeed, the better."[16]

The minutes of a private conversation between Kissinger and Pinochet on the day before the June OAS meeting show an identical pattern. Kissinger openly told the general to disregard his upcoming speech on human rights, which he said was "not aimed at Chile," since the U.S. government sympathized with Pinochet's countersubversive campaigns.[17] Kissinger told Pinochet that the U.S. government had "welcomed the overthrow" of Allende and added, "we are not out to weaken your position."[18] In 1999, a high-ranking Argentine military source familiar with junta secrets in 1976 confirmed that during the OAS meeting Kissinger had assured the Chilean and Argentine juntas of the support and cooperation of the Ford administration for counterinsurgency operations—and for Operation Condor.[19] Kissinger also met with the foreign ministers of Panama, Guatemala, Paraguay, and Chile on June 10.[20] The evidence demonstrates that, despite his speech on human rights, Kissinger privately gave carte blanche to the Condor states during his trip to the region.

By their June meeting, Condor officials had set up their computerized intelligence database and international communications system, Condortel, as decided at the founding meeting of 1975. The CIA, well informed of the June Condor meeting's substance, reported that the three most active Condor members (Argentina, Chile, and Uruguay) made a separate accord during the meeting to "operate covertly in Paris . . . against the Revolutionary Coordinating Junta and other leftist Latin American subversive groups."[21] That same month, a team of armed men broke into the office of an immigration agency in Buenos Aires, stealing records on thousands of refugees. Two days later, twenty-four Chilean and Uruguayan refugees whose names had been in the files (all of whom were under UN protection) were kidnapped, tortured with electric shocks and burnings, and then released with warnings to leave the country. The CIA was aware that the armed men were multinational Condor teams conducting combined hunter-killer operations against exiles in Argentina.[22] According to a declassified CIA document, Argentine, Uruguayan, and Chilean

> security services are already coordinating operations against targets in Argentina. In May armed men ransacked the offices of the Argentine Catholic Commission on Immigration and stole records containing information on thousands of refugees and immigrants. Argentine police did not investigate the crime and dismissed it as a simple robbery. Two days later, 24 Uruguayan and Chilean refugees, many of whom were the subjects of commission files, were kidnapped and tortured for several hours. Some of the refugees later said their interrogators were security officers from Chile and Uruguay.[23]

After this incident, U.S. Embassy deputy chief of mission Maxwell Chaplin reported to Secretary of State Kissinger: "conclusion almost inescapable that GOA [Government of Argentina] security forces either directly responsible or at least tolerating extra-official actions."[24] He noted that the interrogators had dossiers on each captive, including detailed histories and photographs, with information from the Catholic Commission but also from the home countries of the refugees. Chaplin observed that the Argentine junta's claims that such acts were perpetrated by the extreme left were "simply no longer sustainable." Ambassador Ernest Siracusa in Montevideo, who openly sympathized with the Uruguayan junta, denied increasing evidence of Condor coordination, however. He told Washington that he did "not believe the GOU was involved in the murders of Uruguayan exiles in Argentina" and even denied that the Uruguayan regime was a military dictatorship.[25] An exchange of cables between the U.S. ambassador in Buenos Aires, Robert Hill, and Siracusa suggested that the refugees' ability to identify their torturers raised concerns. In a June 16 memo to Hill, Siracusa wrote:

> Para three reftel states refugees reported they were interrogated by security officers from Chile and Uruguay. Not clear from tel how many Uruguayan security officers allegedly involved since cable as received here in some cases uses plural . . . and singular in other cases. In any event, important point to us is whether through UNHCR rep refugees(s) involved can identify by name Uruguayan supposedly involved. If not, would be useful have [*sic*] information from refugee(s) of previous encounter and where with alleged official(s) and any other information on which identification of Uruguayan national could be based or value of alleged recognition evaluated.[26]

Hill responded:

> Head of UNHCR office told Emboffs [Embassy officials] June 30 that he is aware that refugees told UNHCR subordinate that they recognized and could name Uruguayan security officials (plural) who are active in Buenos Aires in joint operations with Argentine officials against refugees. . . . One Uruguayan . . . stated that he was questioned during incident by same Uruguayan security official who had interrogated him two years ago in Montevideo.[27]

Hill continued that the embassy was unable to evaluate the refugees' claims but added, "Given weight of information accumulating through various channels concerning cooperation between regional security forces, we do not find it improbable that cooperation to degree claimed by refugees could be occurring. We have not expressed this view or discussed UNHCR allegations outside appropriate classified channels." The ambassador clearly perceived Condor, as did its victims.

Several documents from the Paraguayan Archives confirmed the increasingly interconnected nature of countersubversive operations by the region's intelligence organizations. In one document, Colonel Benito Guanes Serrano, intelligence chief of the Paraguayan high command, notified Pastor Coronel, chief of police investigations (and a notorious torturer), that a Paraguayan captive, his confession, and his personal effects were being transferred from military to police custody. The letter noted that the prisoner's antecedents had been requested from SIDE of Argentina and DINA of Chile.[28] In July 1976, a search request also signed by Guanes Serrano was distributed to "'A'-Condor 1-SIE (Arg.)-AGREMIL (P y A)"—that is, to Manuel Contreras of DINA (Condor 1), Army Intelligence of Argentina (Servicio de Inteligencia del Ejército, SIE), and, presumably, the military attachés of Peru and Argentina. This order, originating from Paraguayan army intelligence, warned of a supposed Paraguayan guerrilla camp led by an individual who was presently detained in Argentina, and requested more information.[29] In another document dated July 7, 1976, Fretes Dávalos invited Pastor Coronel to a presentation by Brazilian SNI chief João Baptista Figueiredo, titled "Fundamental Principles upon which to Base a National Intelligence Service."[30]

In July 1976, three priests and two seminarians of the Irish Pallotine order were murdered in San Patricio, Argentina, by parapolice or paramilitary operatives, and two other priests were abducted in La Rioja province several days later. In a July 23 memo, the U.S. Embassy expressed alarm about the murders of the priests and added that thousands of refugees, with no relation to guerrilla movements, were being targeted. Warning of the junta's anticommunist frenzy, the report continued, "Many officers, probably including Videla, are convinced the anti-terrorist fight here represents a major battle in 'World War III' and that Argentina has been chosen by 'international communism' as a testing ground in its campaign to conquer the world. This is an emotional reaction with little if any evidence to substantiate it . . . there is no evidence to suggest Cuba is involved." The report pointed out that the ERP guerrillas' ties to MIR and Tupamaro militants (in the JCR alliance) were "rather tenuous" and that the Argentine guerrillas were "essentially homegrown" and local.[31]

In another abduction in July 1976, Patricio Biedma, an Argentine who had moved to Chile after the Argentine coup of 1966, was seized in Buenos Aires. Biedma had married a Chilean named Luz Lagarrigua and had three children; he had become involved with MIR and with the fledgling JCR in Chile. After the 1973 coup in Chile, Biedma was threatened by the junta and the family moved back to Buenos Aires. There they lived quietly until Biedma was seized and disappeared in 1976, for his activities in Chile. He was held in Orletti Motors and interrogated repeatedly by a Chilean intelligence officer. Lagarrigua fled to Cuba and for years had no idea of what had happened to her husband.

In 1983, as the military government in Argentina prepared its exit, she returned there to search for Biedma. She learned nothing about his fate, however, and neither did CONADEP, the Argentine commission on the disappeared. Several years later, however, a young man came forward and said he had known her husband in Orletti. He told her that Biedma had been like a father to him in the torture center, teaching him how to survive and staying close to him. They were together forty-five days, but then the young man was released. His family sent him to Spain, where for years he was afraid to say anything about his experience.[32] Lagarrigua never learned what finally happened to her husband.

Another case shed light on the atrocities that occurred inside Orletti. Víctor Lubian was an Argentine who had moved to Uruguay at five years of age. He was one of some thirty Uruguayans who were abducted in Buenos Aires at around the same time in July 1976. Lubian had been active in the 1970s in the Federation of University Students of Uruguay, an organization declared illegal, by military decree, in December 1973. In January 1974, he returned to Argentina, but six months later he was abducted from his house by a parapolice commando of Argentines and Uruguayans. He was held in Orletti until July 24, when he was transferred to Montevideo with other Uruguayans in an unregistered Uruguayan Air Force plane.[33] On October 23, 1976, Lubian was charged there with "assisting a subversive association," and on November 29 transferred to Establecimiento Militar de Reclusión number 1, the notorious Libertad prison.

Lubian later described the methods of the torturers in Orletti. The torturers injected drugs into prisoners to disorient them and make them talk, and some enjoyed using sadistic sexual tortures against both men and women, he testified. Prisoners who collaborated were rewarded with drinks of water and beaten if they didn't, creating a sense of personal responsibility for torture. Lubian witnessed members of the Santucho family in Orletti. Mario Roberto Santucho, the leader of the Argentine guerrilla organization ERP, was killed in a military operation on July 18, 1976, effectively demobilizing the ERP. But afterward, other members of his family, who were not involved in politics, were tortured and killed out of pure sadism. In Orletti, brother Carlos Santucho was hung from a hook over a tub of filthy water and repeatedly lowered into it. He appeared to have lost his mind from torture, raving in a delirious manner. Lubian said the guards forced his sister, Manuela Santucho, to read aloud the newspaper story of Mario's death. Then they tortured and raped her, using methods that he called "the product of sick imaginations."

Lubian testified that the torturers all used the same name, Oscar: they called themselves Oscar 1, Oscar 2, and Oscar 3, and Oscar 5 was a doctor who kept victims alive. Other operatives in Orletti used the codes 301, 302, 303, 304, up to 309. Lubian perceived at the time that these were Uruguayan army officers, and his testimony has been confirmed by numerous other survivors and army defectors (although the Uruguayan officers subsequently denied ever being in Argentina). It has become known since that 302 was Major José Gavazzo of Organismo Coordinador de Operaciones Antisubversivas, OCOA; 303 was Lieutenant Colonel Manuel Cordero; 304 was Major Enrique Martínez; the others were lieutenants and captains, including Jorge Silveira, Pedro Mattos, José Arab, Hugo Campos Hermida, and Eduardo Ferro, names now infamous in Uruguay. Argentine judge Néstor Blondi, in a 1986 extradition request for Gavazzo, Cordero, Campos Hermida, and Silveira, identified them as "personnel assimilated into the Argentine army."[34] It was an appropriate characterization of Condor's secret, parallel, combined formations.

Discussions of Operation Condor

In late July 1976, U.S. officials discussed Operation Condor in the weekly meeting between the CIA and American Republic Affairs (ARA, later known as Inter-American Affairs in the State Department). According to a heavily redacted meeting summary, one official (whose name was deleted) spoke of "disturbing developments in its operational attitudes" and said of Condor: "the organization was emerging as one with a far more activist role, including specifically that of identifying, locating, and 'hitting' guerrilla leaders." Immediately following this description, however, the official justified those acts as "an understandable reaction" to the purported range of action of the JCR.[35] (Ironically, an earlier State Department intelligence report had characterized the JCR as an ineffectual coalition "that has not sponsored any major operations."[36])

During July and August, Condor operations continued to intensify. Condor agents Michael Townley and Armando Fernández Larios were preparing the Letelier assassination, under orders from DINA chief Contreras and his second in command, Pedro Espinoza. In late July, Conrado Pappalardo, chief of protocol and the right hand of Paraguayan dictator Stroessner, approached U.S. ambassador George Landau in Asunción, to obtain visas for the two Chilean agents to travel to the United States. They had already received Paraguayan passports falsely depicting them as Paraguayans.[37] Pappalardo told Landau that the two were engaged in a covert mission in the United States known to Vernon Walters and the CIA.[38] The provision of such documents to facilitate and camouflage the movements of Condor operatives was a key component of the Condor system. Landau approved the B-2 visas, but when the CIA denied that it knew of the mission he reported to Assistant

Secretary of State Schlaudeman, in an urgent Roger Channel [intelligence] cable, that the two were actually Chileans. Landau wrote that "the whole business was highly explosive" and told Schlaudeman that Pappalardo had told him that Pinochet himself had requested the passports from Stroessner, indicating the importance of the covert mission.[39] On August 7, Schlaudeman sent instructions for Landau: "If there is still time, and if there is a possibility of turning off this harebrained scheme, you are authorized to go back through Pappalardo to urge that the Chileans be persuaded not repeat not to travel."[40] Landau revoked the visas on August 9. This case is further discussed in chapter 5.

During that same week, on August 6, Paraguayan colonel and Condor officer Guanes Serrano addressed a memo to Pastor Coronel to accompany "photocopies of the list of names and photographs of the Brazilian subversives located in the Argentine Republic."[41] This memo documented the intelligence coordination occurring among Argentina, Brazil, and Paraguay. Several days later, on August 11, a secret CIA document on "Southern Cone Counterterrorism Plans" reported:

> Security officials of Chile, Argentina, and Uruguay are reportedly expanding their cooperative anti-subversive activities to include assassination of top-level terrorists in exile in Europe. The intelligence cooperation program of Argentina, Bolivia, Brazil, Chile, Paraguay, and Uruguay, known as "Condor," already includes development of a centralized data collection capability and the direction of joint operations. . . . The Chilean, Argentinian, and Uruguayan services now plan to train teams in Buenos Aires for the missions in Western Europe. The plans and targets of the teams will be withheld from at least some government leaders. The largest concentration of Latin American exiles in Europe is in Paris.[42]

This document was significant on several levels. First, the CIA's language—benignly characterizing Condor as a program of "cooperative antisubversive activities" and assassination operations as "missions"—reflected implicit acceptance of Condor as a legitimate and useful counterinsurgency program, despite its methods of disappearance, torture, and extrajudicial execution. This sort of language was also evident in U.S. military reports on Condor. (It is worth recalling that use of assassinations as a covert tool by U.S. forces themselves was not prohibited until 1976, after congressional hearings revealed CIA plots to assassinate Cuban Fidel Castro and other Third World leaders.) Second, the document showed that the CIA was fully aware of Condor's transcontinental assassination program long before the Letelier-Moffitt murders in Washington, D.C., and at the same time as the strange affair of the Paraguayan passports in Asunción, which indicated that Chilean intelligence agents were attempting to enter the United States for a covert operation, using false papers. Finally, the CIA, clearly well informed by sources inside the Condor apparatus, knew that some government leaders were unaware of Condor. This point was made clear in another report signed by Kissinger later in the month (discussed in more detail presently): Kissinger informed the U.S. ambassador to Uruguay that the acting president and the president-designate "apparently know nothing about Operation Condor and, in any event, would probably have little influence on situation."[43] General Julio Vadora, commander of the army—the real power in the country—directed the Condor structure, and Kissinger ordered the ambassador to approach Vadora regarding Condor. Kissinger obviously knew how the Condor apparatus functioned and how it was organized.

On August 12, another CIA report discussed the role of Brazil in Operation Condor, specifically its reticence regarding the assassination operations in Europe.[44] The CIA declassified only page 2 of this three-page document, but it demonstrated that the CIA had up-to-the-minute information about top-secret internal discussions within Condor. After reviewing Brazil's reluctance to participate, the document reported that the regime would provide communications equipment for Condortel and noted:

> [LINE DELETED] the Condor countries which would operate in Europe were Chile, Argentina, and Uruguay.) Condor countries have now decided to suspend their plans to operate in Europe and to hold a training course in Buenos Aires for those Condoreje officers who were to operate in Europe until Brazil decides whether it will participate with the others in Europe, to be centered in France.

The CIA's use of the term "Condoreje"—a first in the declassified documents—again demonstrated the CIA's inside knowledge of the system. The term apparently signified the "axis" or core group, the most fanatical members of Condor: the dictatorships of Argentina, Chile, and Uruguay.

Kissinger: Green Light for Operation Condor?

The orgy of violence continued unabated. In early August, the bishop of La Rioja, Argentina, Monseñor Enrique Angelelli, a critic of human rights abuses, was killed under suspicious conditions when his car exploded on the highway. On August 12, in Riobamba, Ecuador, security forces raided a retreat of religious and human rights advocates associated with Liberation Theology who had gathered from around Latin America. The conference included seventeen bishops, including four from the United States, and some twenty priests, and the party received the news of Argentine bishop Angelelli's death at the meeting; they had expected his presence. A few days later, some seventy heavily armed men in gas masks suddenly broke into the enclave and detained everyone there, accusing them of conspiracy and subversion. Security forces had information on the participants from their home countries, a sign of Condor coordination.[45] The CIA reported that the seizure "sparked sharp protest throughout Latin America."[46] On August 20, the dynamited, mutilated bodies of thirty persons were found in Pilar, a town north of the Argentine capital. A sign found beside them said they were "traitors" and Montoneros.

Throughout August, high-ranking officials in the office of the U.S. secretary of state worked on drafts of an important memorandum regarding Operation Condor. Several versions have been declassified, and, in fact, some words redacted in one version are visible in others, adding important elements to public knowledge. The final version, dated August 23, 1976, and signed by Kissinger, was sent to the U.S. embassies in the six Condor countries,[47] instructing ambassadors to convey to the military regimes the U.S. government's "concern" regarding "rumors" of assassination plans through Operation Condor (although the murders of Prats, Michelini and Gutiérrez Ruiz, and Torres, and the attempted assassination of Leighton, had already occurred). The memo instructed the ambassadors to stress U.S. government "appreciation of real host government concerns and threats to their security," and to convey U.S. understanding that official coordination of intelligence and countersubversive action by the Condor states was "useful." Thus, Kissinger indicated U.S. support for phases I and II of Condor. Plans for assassinations, though, had "most serious consequences," the memo stated.

Kissinger directed the ambassadors in Buenos Aires, Montevideo, and Santiago to approach the highest appropriate official and specifically told the ambassador in Uruguay to speak with Vadora. The ambassador in Bolivia was told, "While we are not repeat not instructing you to make the specific demarche on Condor, you may wish to take an appropriate occasion with [PHRASE DELETED] senior GOB official to propose periodic exchanges of information." In the August 18 version of this memo, the blank was filled in: "Banzer or other," thus suggesting that the military dictator of Bolivia was the top Condor officer. Kissinger's memo concluded with a warning to the ambassadors: "it is essential that we in no way finger individuals who might be candidates for assassination attempts."

Did Kissinger's demarche signify a genuine effort to deter Condor assassinations? A consideration of the cable's sequels, and Kissinger's own record, raises questions. First, Kissinger's discussions with Condor officials in Santiago two months before, in June 1976, were understood by both Latin American junta officers and U.S. Embassy personnel as signaling a green light for the repression and for the cross-border operations of Condor. Second, according to the available documents, it appears that not one ambassador actually acted on the secretary's August 23 instructions. On August 24, Ambassador David Popper in Santiago replied to the memo, telling Kissinger that Pinochet might be offended by a direct approach on Condor. Furthermore, he wrote, "cooperation among Southern Cone national intelligence agencies is handled by the DINA."[48] Ambassadors cannot ignore directives from the secretary of state, however, unless there is a back channel counterorder or some other communication. The former ambassador to Paraguay, Robert White, conjectured in 2003 that the original cable generated so much angry opposition from the Latin American intelligence organizations—and perhaps from the CIA and DIA themselves—that the State Department decided to withdraw it.[49] And, in fact, on September 20, 1976, the State Department did rescind the August 23 memo on assassinations—on the day before the Letelier-Moffitt murders.[50] The retraction of the demarche again conveyed the unwillingness of the Kissinger State Department to criticize or try to deter the military regimes' methods and operations, including Operation Condor.

Kissinger—who in 1943 had joined the U.S. Army Counterintelligence Corps and had become a captain in the Military Intelligence Reserve, as we have seen[51]—was the top U.S. foreign policy official, and he also approved all covert action operations during the Nixon and Ford administrations.[52] Kissinger is known to have distorted or obfuscated the historical record in his own interest in several cases. According to Kissinger's memoirs and his congressional testimony, for example, Cuban meddling in Angola in 1975 was the trigger for the U.S. intervention in that African country. But scholar Piero Gleijeses uncovered declassified documents showing that U.S. forces intervened in Angola, in an effort coordinated with the apartheid government of South Africa, weeks before the arrival of any Cuban forces and made no reference to countering Cuba at the time.[53] Gleijeses also found that Kissinger had the CIA rewrite a report to show an earlier Cuban presence, so that the written record would comport with the political aims of the administration.[54]

In another case, documents declassified in 2001 demonstrated that President Gerald Ford and Kissinger gave a green light to Indonesian dictator Suharto for his invasion of East Timor in 1975, which resulted in the deaths of some 200,000 people.[55] Kissinger had consistently and publicly denied doing so. Ford and Kissinger met with Suharto on December 6, the day before the invasion. In a secret State Department telegram to Suharto, Ford and Kissinger said that they would not object to "rapid or drastic action" in East Timor and added that they would "understand and will not press you on the issue." Presaging his message to the Argentines the next year, Kissinger told Suharto, "It is important that whatever you do succeeds quickly," and cautioned Suharto to wait until he and Ford had returned to the United States.[56]

In a third case, Kissinger claimed in his memoirs that he had "turned off" Track II, the U.S. covert operation to provoke a military coup in Chile, on October 15, 1970. However, declassified CIA documents (including one dated October 16, the next day) showed that Kissinger actually told the CIA to continue pressuring Allende "into the future until such time as new marching orders are given." The CIA deputy director of plans Thomas Karamessines also said that Track II never really ended.[57]

Kissinger also denied publicly that he and Defense Secretary James Schlesinger had directed the Joint Chiefs of Staff to ignore orders from President Nixon in the days of Watergate, when Nixon's behavior was increasingly erratic.[58] In a rebuttal, however, a former battle staff officer, Barry A. Toll, said he had received those orders himself in his position as a nuclear advisor. Toll stated that he had testified under oath on several occasions that Kissinger had signed or countersigned at least three such orders in the final years of the Nixon presidency. Toll wrote, "After the first such order in 1973 signed by Kissinger, the Joint Chiefs demanded that any subsequent ones be countersigned by at least one other Nixon cabinet officer. A second such order, again an instruction not to obey the president until further notice, was signed by Kissinger and . . . Eliot Richardson."[59] This stunning example demonstrated that Kissinger's enormous power had expanded to the point that he, an unelected official, could countermand the orders of the president.

During 1973 and 1974, Nixon was increasingly obsessed with and debilitated by the Watergate cover-up and his looming impeachment, and he resigned in August 1974. Meanwhile, revelations of CIA covert operations and assassination plots were roiling U.S. politics. Broad sectors of the U.S. public as well as many members of Congress were challenging Cold War anticommunist assumptions and the use of secret, amoral (some said immoral) U.S. foreign policies. Kissinger used his power to try to block congressional and public access to information about the secret U.S. role in Latin America and the world. In 1975, he convinced an executive commission investigating CIA operations to refrain from publicly releasing its chapter on CIA assassinations.[60] The Pike Committee in the House, also investigating CIA covert operations, went so far as to subpoena Kissinger to obtain pertinent documents.[61] Kissinger refused to appear before the Church Committee, the Senate body investigating CIA wrongdoing, and successfully suppressed open hearings on the CIA's covert action role in Chile. He also mounted a media campaign to paint the watchdog committees as McCarthyist witch hunters.

In 1975, David Atlee Phillips, former Western Hemisphere director of the CIA (who had been responsible for CIA covert action in Chile) formed a pro-intelligence lobbying organization to oppose the congressional investigations and shape media coverage. A few months later, President Ford organized a special high-level group—which included Kissinger and Chief of Staff Donald Rumsfeld—called the Intelligence Coordinating Group. The group met on a daily basis to manage the executive's rebuttal to Congress and mold public opinion.[62] In effect, during 1975 Kissinger and other Ford officials were engaged in a psychological warfare operation at home to preserve the secrecy of hidden U.S. foreign policies and covert operations. The Pike Committee's final report criticized Kissinger's "passion for secrecy" and said that his statements were "at variance with the facts."[63]

Kissinger was not only the national security advisor, secretary of state, and chair of the National Security Council, he also led the powerful 40 Committee, the secretive policy group that discussed and approved U.S. covert operations. Between 1972 and 1974, the Pike Committee discovered, the 40 Committee did not even meet; some forty covert operations were approved after telephonic consultation.[64] In effect, Kissinger and the CIA director dominated the control of U.S. covert operations in 1973 and 1974, the years in which Condor was incubating in Latin America. Many of Condor's victims, and several judges in Latin America and Europe, believe that Kissinger was deeply involved in Condor's genesis. Judges in France, Chile, Spain, and Argentina officially requested his testimony in cases related to Condor crimes, and in 2002 human rights lawyers in Chile filed a criminal case against Kissinger, accusing him of a role in organizing the Condor network.

Kissinger instructed U.S. ambassadors never to trust sensitive messages to cables.[65] The question that arises is whether the August 23 demarche on Condor may have been "for the record," especially because it was never implemented.

Seizure of Militants of Partido por la Victoria del Pueblo (PVP)

In July and September 1976, combined Argentine and Uruguayan intelligence commandos abducted some sixty Uruguayans in Buenos Aires and illegally transported them to Montevideo. Many were members of Partido por la Victoria del Pueblo (Party for the Victory of the People, PVP), a leftist, but not a guerrilla, organization, which worked to oppose the military regime. The Uruguayan military called it "OPR-33" and labeled it a terrorist group.[66] The illegal transfers were camouflaged within a larger Uruguayan military PSYWAR operation to portray the refugees as a terrorist invasion force threatening the state. The false montage echoed Operation Colombo, the black propaganda operation that fabricated a guerrilla invasion force to disguise the disappearances of 119 Chileans in 1974–75. Like Colombo, this PSYWAR operation was designed to conceal Condor abductions, discredit regime opponents, win continued aid and political support from the United States, and make the Uruguayan regime appear to be under threat, but law abiding. At the time, congressional representatives were strongly criticizing human rights abuses by the Uruguayan military as well as U.S. support for the Latin American military regimes. The PVP episode suggested that top Ford administration officials were, at minimum, cooperating with the Uruguayan regime to prevent human rights scrutiny by Congress; and that, possibly, they were cognizant of future Condor plans.

A first sweep was conducted against the PVP in late June and July. One person abducted was Sergio López Burgos, a Uruguayan unionist. He had been detained and maltreated after the June 1973 coup in Uruguay, so he moved to Argentina in April 1975 and became a legal resident, with permission to work. He, with a colleague, formed a commission-in-exile of the Convención Nacional de Trabajadores (CNT, National Convention of Workers) that was dedicated to solidarity activities with Uruguayan labor unions under repression. In July 1976, López and a colleague, León Duarte, were seized in a Buenos Aires café by a team of twelve men in civilian clothes that included Uruguayan army officers, among them Manuel Cordero. The two shouted to others in the café that they were Uruguayan unionists and that this was a disappearance. The kidnappers became infuriated; one flashed identification and shouted that this was an Argentine army operation and that people should remain calm. The Condor squad broke López's jaw as they dragged him out of the café. López testified that he was taken to Orletti Motors, where he saw Héctor Méndez, a Uruguayan leader of the Congreso Obrero Textil and the CNT.

A Uruguayan exile named Washington Pérez testified in Sweden in August 1976 about his experience with Orletti Motors and a Condor squadron. He had been living in Morón, near Buenos Aires. On June 13, a group of heavily armed Argentine and Uruguayan men burst into his house at 4:00 A.M. and demanded that he accompany them. They reassured him that they would do him no harm but said that there was someone he should see. Pérez was driven, blindfolded, to Orletti. There, he positively identified policeman Hugo Campos Hermida (whom he had known from a time he was arrested in Uruguay). An Argentine whom he deduced was a colonel (later identified as Aníbal Gordon) brought out Pérez's friend Gerardo Gatti, a union leader who had disappeared in June. Pérez saw that his arm was infected and he appeared badly tortured. His captors told Pérez that he was to approach Gatti's comrades and solidarity organizations to obtain a large sum of money for his ransom. Pérez later identified other Uruguayan and Argentine operatives, including José Gavazzo, chief of the Uruguayan unit, Manuel Cordero, Jorge Silveira, and Argentines Eduardo Ruffo and Osvaldo Forese. Both Pérez and Gatti were convinced that this was the same squad that had abducted and murdered

Uruguayan legislators Michelini and Gutiérrez Ruiz; they used the same expression that witnesses had heard in those cases: "your hour has come." (Also, witnesses to those abductions later identified Forese.) When he was forcibly taken to Orletti again, Pérez saw disappeared union leader Léon Duarte. Pérez did try to obtain the money, but he was unsuccessful. The Condor squad abruptly cut off negotiations, and Pérez fled Argentina shortly afterward.[67]

Others in the group of disappeared Uruguayans recognized each other in Orletti as well as Uruguayan officers such as Gavazzo. For twelve or fourteen days, the prisoners ate only three times. López later reported that he saw a guard raping a semiconscious woman prisoner. A second Condor sweep was carried out in September and October in Buenos Aires and more Uruguayans "disappeared."

After days or weeks of torture in Orletti, the Condor squad allowed the first group to bathe and put on clean clothes, and they were clandestinely transferred on around July 24 to Uruguay. Gavazzo said to some prisoners that the transfers were authorized by SID commander Amaurí Prantl and head of the Argentine SIDE Otto Paladino, key Condor commanders. In Montevideo, the prisoners were kept in a safe house, where they were again subjected to daily torture for several weeks. Toward the end of August, according to several testimonies, they were moved to another location, later established as the former headquarters of SID. There, Gavazzo presented the prisoners with an ultimatum: now that they were in the hands of the "special security services" of the Uruguayan army, which had "rescued" them from the Argentines, they had to "legalize" their presence in Uruguay. They would be forced to participate in a simulated terrorist attack. The military's plan was to publicly announce that the group had entered Uruguay with heavy armaments and false papers, in a terrorist invasion surprised by the military.[68] If the prisoners confessed, they would receive sentences of ten to thirty years in prison, Gavazzo continued; if they refused to cooperate, they would be sent back to "the Buenos Aires assassins."[69] In an impressive act of defiance, the entire group refused to cooperate in the charade. Gavazzo responded angrily that he would personally execute two of the prisoners, Margarita Michelini (daughter of the murdered legislator) and Raúl Altuna, in retaliation. He took them away, but did not kill them; however, they were severely tortured again.

For some days, Gavazzo did not return. When he did, the plan for the black operation was modified: the military offered prison sentences of two or three years. Gavazzo said that the prisoners would be "captured" in various Montevideo hotels, heavily armed, in mid-October 1976. They would be required to use military lawyers in a feigned legal process after their capture.[70] Again the group refused. Gavazzo, who was accompanied by soldiers with machine guns, warned that no one knew they were in Uruguay and his men could easily kill them all.[71] But the Uruguayan military—unlike the ruthless Argentines—did not normally murder their captives.

Finally, Gavazzo began taking the prisoners away one at a time. According to Enrique Rodríguez Larreta—a well-known Uruguayan journalist who had been seized because his son was a political activist—Gavazzo began to work out "agreements" with the prisoners individually. Finally, around October 20, the fictitious episode was carried out. Some prisoners were taken, blindfolded and bound, to a hotel. Later that day, the army surrounded the hotel and "captured" them. That evening, news reports broadcast a communique written by the military, charging the prisoners with "assisting a subversive association." Several days later, the military presented the prisoners in a press conference attended by some one hundred national and international journalists, and announced that they had legally arrested about sixty subversives in this operation.[72] In this way the military "explained" the disappearances of sixty Uruguayan refugees in Argentina. Rodríguez Larreta was soon freed, and others were sent to "legal" prisons. Many of the captives were never heard of again, however, and several children remained "disappeared."

The Role of the U.S. Congress

That summer, in Congress, Democratic representative Edward Koch proposed an amendment to stop $3 million in U.S. military aid to Uruguay.[73] Hearings were held in June, July, and August before the Subcommittee on International Organizations of the Committee on International Relations, House of Representatives, and representatives such as Donald Fraser and Koch raised sharply critical questions about U.S. aid to the regime.[74] On August 4, 1976, Deputy Assistant Secretary for Inter-American Affairs Hewson A. Ryan testified at the hearing that Uruguay was facing a terrorist threat. He admitted that "national security arrests" were rising in Uruguay, but blamed "the military apparatus of the Communist Party" and then added:

> Within the last several weeks the additional uncovering of an Argentine-based terrorist network, evidently code-named OPR-33 and having assassination plans directed against various officials of the Government of Uruguay, has also led to the detention of more suspected terrorists. . . . They have in custody some 200 persons . . . a group which they have no intentions of bringing to ordinary justice because they consider this a group of terrorists.[75]

With this remarkable declaration, the State Department essentially echoed the Uruguayan military's black propaganda story—the sudden discovery of a "terrorist network" in Argentina—that justified the disappearance and incommunicado detention of the exiles. More significant, the statement was made months before the fictitious "terrorist invasion" was staged in Uruguay. The incident thus raised the possibility that the Kissinger State Department was privy to Condor secrets. At minimum, the State Department was working in tandem with the military regime to impede the Koch amendment, rationalize the regime's illegal acts, and guarantee continued U.S. aid. Enrique Rodríguez Laretta, Jr., and other survivors testified that Gavazzo did not bring up the idea of a feigned "invasion" until late August—after Ryan's statements in Congress. Rodríguez Laretta, Jr., concluded that the transfer of the captives to Montevideo and the simulated terrorist invasion were motivated by and directly linked to the imperative of retaining U.S. aid.[76]

In the hearings, Congressman Fraser pointedly asked Ryan, "Is there torture in Uruguay, or is there not?" Ryan replied, "There has been apparently. The Government of Uruguay has admitted that there have been occasional cases of this but they tell us they have taken steps to prevent its recurrence." Congressman Koch, asked to sit in for part of the session, called for the State Department to send in an inspector general to investigate whether there was a consistent pattern of repression.[77] Fraser cited an Amnesty International report that detailed a dozen forms of torture used regularly by the Uruguayan military. Ryan commented, "We don't have any verification of any of those," and Fraser expressed incredulity: "You have not found a single person who has been tortured to talk to?"[78] Finally, Fraser asked a series of penetrating questions:

> Could you define U.S. national interests in helping arm the Uruguayan forces? . . . Uruguay was once a country which, like Chile, very much valued democratic values. This has largely disappeared. . . . Do you automatically continue to give countries military assistance without reference to what happens? . . . Why isn't it in the U.S. interest to disengage from that kind of [military] supply relationship as long as Uruguayans, rightly or wrongly, have suspended most of their political rights?[79]

A Defense Department intelligence report of October 1 also repeated the Uruguayan military's portrayal of the refugees—and displayed detailed knowledge of this Condor operation. In a memo entirely about Operation Condor entitled "Special Operations Forces," the U.S. defense attaché in Buenos Aires reported that between September 24 and 27, the Argentine SIDE, in coordination with Uruguayan military intelligence, "carried out operations against the Uruguayan Terrorist organization, the OPR-33. . . . SIDE officials claimed that the entire OPR-33 infrastructure in Argentina has been eliminated."[80] In contrast, the U.S. Embassy in Buenos Aires challenged the Uruguayan military's version of the "terrorist invasion" and the supposed capture of an invasion force of PVP members in Uruguay. In a November 2 cable, Robert Hill wrote:

> Embassy's sources dispute GOU's version of the disappearances. A UNHCR official told Emboff today (Nov. 2) that 12 of the 14 names were on its list of Uruguayan refugees kidnapped in July and September and that writs of habeas corpus had been filed in Argentina by the families of nine of them. . . . Our evaluation of the evidence and reports we have convinces us that the kidnappings of Uruguayan refugees in July and September were carried out by Argentine and Uruguayan security forces, acting clandestinely and in cooperation.[81]

In September, Congress suspended military aid to Uruguay. On September 21, Letelier and Moffitt were assassinated in a car bombing in Washington, D.C.

Condor Meetings and Training Courses

Several days after the Letelier assassination, a high-ranking State Department official wrote to Schlaudeman, in a memo titled "Operation Condor," that his CIA counterpart had provided all its reports to the FBI, which was investigating the crime. A previously excised sentence added, "My friend also told me that the security services in the Condor countries now know that we know about the proposed Paris operation."[82] (Apparently, SIDE chief Otto Paladino was responsible for the disclosure; the Argentine military removed him from the leadership of SIDE.) According to French lawyers investigating Condor cases, Kissinger himself had approved the idea of a Condor station in Paris.[83] On September 28, Robert Scherrer, the FBI liaison in Buenos Aires, wrote a memo describing in detail Operation Condor and raising the possibility that the Letelier-Moffitt assassinations had been a Phase III operation. He confirmed that Condor was targeting exiles in France and Portugal.[84] For over twenty years, until 1999, this cable was the only known U.S. document on Condor. Two days later, Scherrer wrote another cable requesting that the previous information not be passed to the Portuguese due to the sensitive nature of his source.[85]

A rapid series of Condor meetings occurred in the second half of 1976. On September 20, the Argentine army intelligence chief went to Santiago "to consult with his Chilean counterparts on Operation Condor."[86] According to U.S. army intelligence, a special Condor team was being organized in Argentina to carry out Phase III assassinations, consisting of members of SIDE and army intelligence (presumably Battalion 601). This army intelligence report said that Argentine officers were beginning to speak more openly about Condor to their

U.S. counterparts, even making jokes about "flying like a condor." In November, junta leader Videla traveled to Chile for five days and he discussed with Pinochet "the formation of an anti-terrorist mechanism which would function unofficially,"[87] an apparent reference to Condor coordination. Videla had traveled to Bolivia at the end of October, and after his trip to Chile he visited Uruguay and Paraguay. While the full agenda of this unusual series of trips remains unclear, one can surmise that Condor business, specifically the Letelier-Moffitt assassinations in September, was an urgent topic. The assassinations had caused an uproar in the United States and revealed the outlines of the Condor system. In fact, leadership of Condor may have passed from DINA to the Argentines at this time, given the spotlight of world attention focused on the Pinochet regime.

On November 23, the State Department's Bureau of Intelligence and Research discussed Condor:

> [PHRASE DELETED] reports that Uruguayan authorities have decided [TWO LINES DELETED] to limit the countersubversive organization's assassinations to known terrorists. A Condor training course now being conducted in Buenos Aires will conclude in early December when at least two Uruguayan operatives will be sent to Paris to perform unspecified duties. After reportedly learning the French knew of Condor's plans to operate in France, Argentine and/or Chilean security officials informed their French counterparts that they would function in Europe, but not in France.[88]

This document supports the view that the assassinations in Washington were a key focus of the Condor apparatus, since Condor commanders decided to "limit" Condor assassinations to "known terrorists" and not respected diplomats such as Letelier.

In November 1976, Bolivian dictator Banzer visited Buenos Aires. On December 6, former Brazilian president Goulart was found dead in Argentina. In mid-December, representatives from all six Condor states met in Buenos Aires to discuss future plans and evaluate their regional dirty war. The focus of this meeting, according to a CIA report, was the planning of coordinated psychological warfare operations against leftist and radical groups in their countries.[89] The CIA report also noted that there was a Condor operations center in Buenos Aires, and that Condor officers were deeply involved in organizing security for the Third Congress of the Latin American Anticommunist Federation, scheduled for March 1977, and Videla's trip to Paraguay in April.

Condor during the Carter Administration

Jimmy Carter took office in January 1977 on a platform of human rights and a new kind of foreign policy. During his tenure, Carter tried to tame CIA

TOP SECRET
NOFORN-ORCON

The National Intelligence
Daily

Published by the Director of Central Intelligence for Named Principals Only

Copy No.

WEDNESDAY JUNE 23, 1976

NR

APPROVED FOR RELEASE
DATE: SEP 1999

51

TOP SECRET

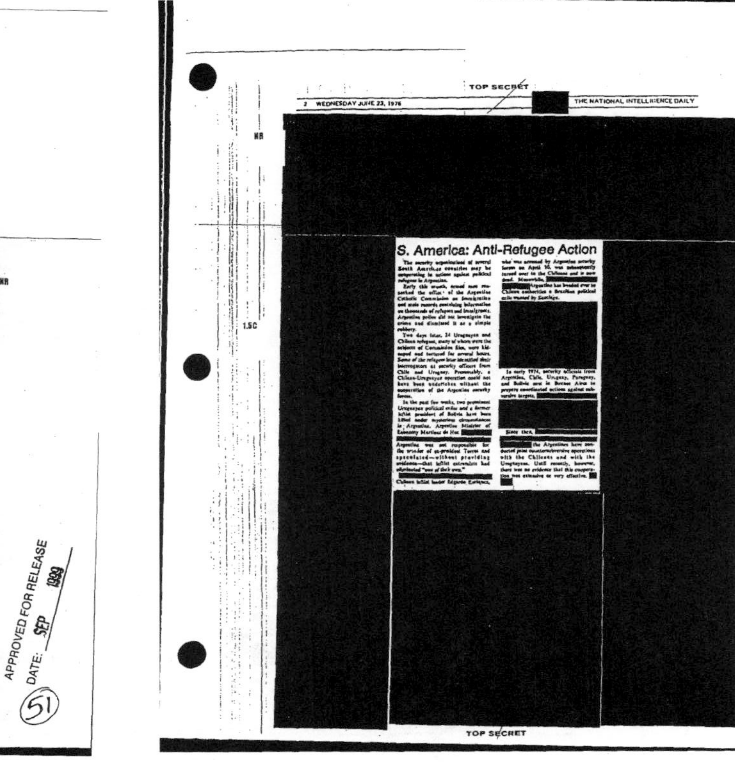

TOP SECRET

2 WEDNESDAY JUNE 23, 1976 — THE NATIONAL INTELLIGENCE DAILY

NR

1.5C

S. America: Anti-Refugee Action

The security organizations of several South American countries may be cooperating in actions against political refugees in Argentina.

Early this month, armed men ransacked the offices of the Argentine Catholic Commission on Immigration and stole records containing information on thousands of refugees and immigrants. Argentine police did not investigate the crime and dismissed it as a simple robbery.

Two days later, 24 Uruguayan and Chilean refugees, many of whom were the subjects of Commission files, were kidnaped and tortured for several hours. Some of the refugees later identified their interrogators as security officers from Chile and Uruguay. Presumably, a Chilean-Uruguayan operation could not have been undertaken without the cooperation of the Argentine security forces.

In the past few weeks, two prominent Uruguayan political exiles and a former leftist president of Bolivia have been killed under mysterious circumstances in Argentina. Argentine Minister of Economy Martinez de Hoz

Argentina was not responsible for the murder of ex-president Torres and speculated—without providing evidence—that leftist extremists had eliminated "one of their own."

Chilean leftist leader Edgardo Enriquez, who was arrested by Argentine security forces on April 10, was subsequently turned over to the Chileans and is now dead. Meanwhile, Argentina has handed over to Chilean authorities a Brazilian political exile wanted by Santiago.

In early 1974, security officials from Argentina, Chile, Uruguay, Paraguay, and Bolivia met in Buenos Aires to prepare coordinated actions against subversive targets.

Since then, the Argentines have conducted joint countersubversive operations with the Chileans and with the Uruguayans. Until recently, however, there was no evidence that this cooperation was extensive or very effective.

TOP SECRET

Sample of blacked-out CIA document, part of which refers to the February 1974 meeting in Buenos Aires. Available on State Department website, Chile Declassification Project.

UNCLASSIFIED

DEPARTMENT OF DEFENSE INTELLIGENCE INFORMATION REPORT

SECRET-NOFORN

(Classification and Control Markings)

1. COUNTRY: Argentina

2. SUBJECT: (U) Special Operations Forces (U)

3. IRC NUMBER: N/A

4. DATE OF INFORMATION: 1976, SEP 28

5. PLACE AND DATE OF ACQ: 1976, SEP 28, Buenos Aires

6. EVALUATION: SOURCE A INFORMATION 1

7. SOURCE: Legal Attache, AMEMB

8. REPORT NUMBER: 6 804 0334 76

9. DATE OF REPORT: 1976, OCT 1

10. NO. OF PAGES: 2

11. REFERENCES: PG1200 PG1100 ICR A-TAC-44396 PG2200 PG1300 PG2220 PG2240

12. ORIGINATOR: USDAO BUENOS AIRES

13. PREPARED BY: LTC JOHN [illegible], JR, USA, AARMA

14. APPROVING AUTHORITY: COL PAUL A. COUGHLIN, USA, ARMA, DATT

15. SUMMARY: This IR provides information on joint counterinsurgency operations by several countries in South America. Information was provided by US Embassy Legal Attache who has excellent contacts within the State Secretariat for Information and Federal Police Force.

This IR partially fulfills requirement of ICR A-TAC-44396.

RECD DS-4B 13 OCT76

WARNING NOTICE-SENSITIVE INTELLIGENCE SOURCES AND METHODS INVOLVED

1. "Operation Condor" is the code name given for intelligence collection on "leftists," Communists and Marxists in the Southern Cone Area. It was recently established between cooperating intelligence services in South America in order to eliminate Marxist terrorist activities in member countries with Chile reportedly being the center of operations. other participating members include: Argentina, Paraguay, Uruguay and Bolivia. In addition, Brazil has apparently tentatively agreed to provide intelligence input for Operation Condor. Members showing the most enthusiasm to date have been Argentina, Uruguay and Chile. These three countries have engaged in joint operations, primarily in Argentina, against terrorists targets. During the week of 20 September 1976, the Director of the Argentine Army Intelligence Service traveled to Santiago to consult with

DISTRIBUTION BY ORIGINATOR: USCINCSO; TAC/INOA, Langley AFB, Va 23665; 1st Special Operations Wing Eglin AFB Aux Field, Fl 1544; USDAO SANTIAGO; USDAO BOGOTA; USDAO MONTEVIDEO; USDAO ASUNCION; USDAO BRAZILIA

CLASSIFIED BY DATT EXEMPT FROM GENERAL DECLASSIFICATION SCHEDULE OF EXECUTIVE ORDER 11652. EXEMPTION CATEGORY TWO. DECLASSIFY ON 31 DEC 2006

ATTACHMENT DATA: NONE

Declassified by DIA in accordance with EO 12958

SECRET-NOFORN

DD FORM 1396

UNCLASSIFIED

DEPARTMENT OF DEFENSE INTELLIGENCE INFORMATION REPORT

CONTINUATION SHEET — SECRET-NOFORN — REPORT NO. 6 804 0334 76 PAGE 2 OF 2 PAGES — ORIGINATOR USDAO BUENOS AIRES

his Chilean counterparts on Operation Condor (This travel is similar to trip reported in IR 6 804 0309 76.)

2. During the period 24-27 September 1976, members of the Argentine State Secretariat for Information (SIDE), operating with officers of the Uruguayan Military Intelligence Service carried out operations against the Uruguayan Terrorist organization, the OPR-33 in Buenos Aires. As a result of this joint operation, SIDE officials claimed that the entire OPR-33 infrastructure in Argentina has been eliminated. A large volume of US currency was seized during the combined operation.

3. A third and reportedly very secret phase of "Operation Condor" involves the formation of special teams from member countries who are to carry out operations to include assassinations against terrorist or supporters of terrorist organizations. For example, should a terrorist or a supporter of a terrorist organization from a member country be identified, a special team would be dispatched to locate and surveil the target. When the location and surveillance operation has terminated, a second team would be dispatched to carry out an operation against the target. Special teams would be issued false documentation from member countries, could be composed either of individuals from one member nation or of persons from various member nations. Source stated that team members would not be commissioned or non-commissioned officers of the armed forces, but rather "special agents." Two European countries, specifically mentioned foe possible operations under the third phase were France and Portugal.

4. A special team has apparently been organized in Argentina for use in "Operation Condor." They are members of the Argentine Army Intelligence Service and the State Secretariat for Information. They are reportedly structured much like a US Special Forces Team with a medic (doctor), demolition expert, etc. They are apparently being prepared for action in phase three.

COMMENT: More and more is being heard about "Operation Condor" in the southern cone. Military officers who, heretofore, had been mum on the subject have begun to talk openly about it. A favorite remark is that, "one of their colleagues is out of country because he is flying like a condor."

SECRET-NOFORN

DD FORM 1396c

Key Defense Intelligence Agency report on Condor, "Special Operations Forces." Chile Declassification Project, State Department website.

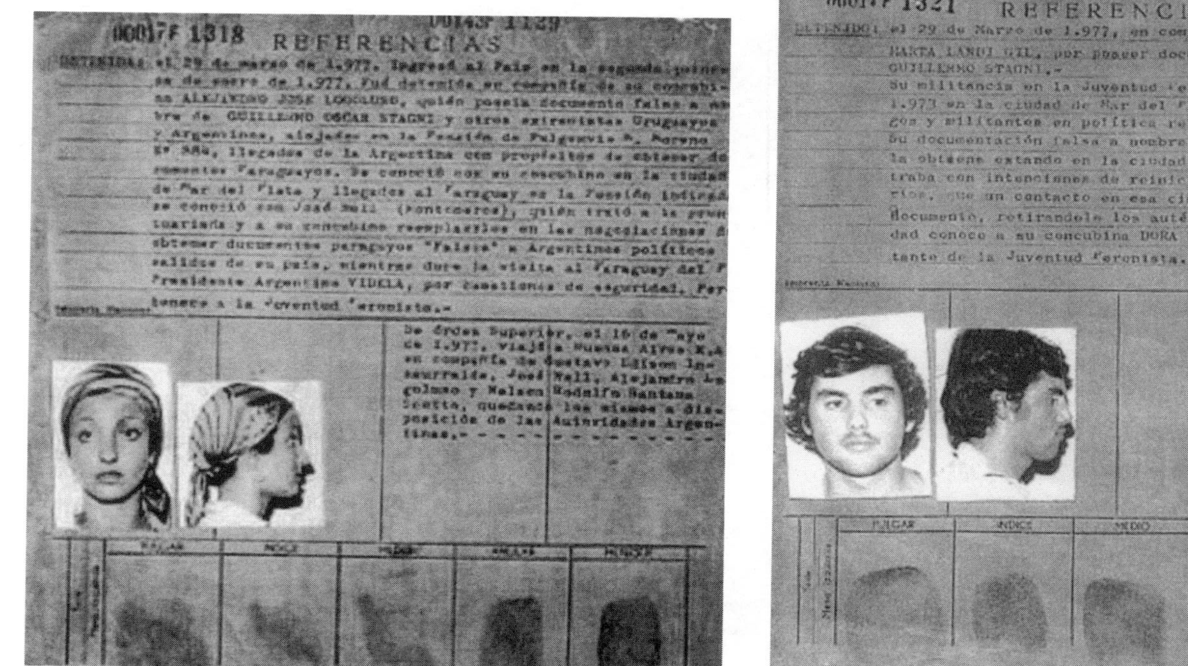

00017F 1318 REFERENCIAS 00143F 1129

DETENIDA: el 29 de marzo de 1.977. Ingresó al País en la segunda quincena de enero de 1.977. Fué detenida en compañía de su concubino ALEJANDRO JOSE LOGOLUSO, quién poseía documento falso a nombre de GUILLERMO OSCAR STAGNI y otros extremistas Uruguayos y Argentinos, alojados en la Pensión de [illegible], Moreno Nº [illegible], llegados de la Argentina con propósitos de obtener documentos Paraguayos. Se conoció con su concubino en la ciudad de Mar del Plata y llegados al Paraguay en la Pensión [illegible] se conoció con José Nell (Montoneros), quién trató a la [illegible] y a su concubino reemplazarlos en las negociaciones de obtener documentos paraguayos "Falsos" a Argentinos políticos salidos de su país, mientras dure la visita al Paraguay del Presidente Argentino VIDELA, por cuestiones de seguridad. Pertenece a la Juventud Peronista.-

De órden Superior, el 16 de Mayo de 1.977, viajó a Buenos Aires R.A. en compañía de Gustavo Edison Inzaurralde, José Nell, Alejandro Logoluso y Nelson Rodolfo Santana Scotto, quedando los mismos a disposición de las Autoridades Argentinas.- - - - - - - - - - - - - - -

00017F 1321 00143F 1123 REFERENCIAS

DETENIDO: el 29 de Marzo de 1.977, en compañía de su concubina DORA MARTA LANDI GIL, por poseer documento Falso a nombre de OSCAR GUILLERMO STAGNI.-

Su militancia en la Juventud Peronista, comienza en el año 1.973 en la ciudad de Mar del Plata, siendo captado por amigos y militantes en política relacionadas con el Peronismo. Su documentación falsa a nombre de OSCAR GUILLERMO STAGNI, la obtiene estando en la ciudad de La Plata, dónde se encontraba con intenciones de reiniciar sus estudios Universitarios, que un contacto en esa ciudad le hace entrega de dicho documento, retirandole los auténticos. Que en esa oportunidad conoce a su concubina DORA MARTA LANDI GIL también militante de la Juventud Peronista. Su domicilio de Mar del Plat

PULGAR | INDICE | MEDIO | ANULAR | MEÑIQUE

Dora Marta Landi Gil and Alejandro Logoluso, two young Argentines detained in Paraguay and subsequently "disappeared" in Argentina. Documents obtained by author in the Paraguayan Archives, 1996; reproduced courtesy of the Paraguayan Center for Documentation and Archives.

(top) Photo of Victoria Grisonas, a Uruguayan victim of Condor "disappeared" in Argentina and seen in Orletti Motors; her two children were found abandoned in Chile a year later. Photo reprinted with the permission of Uruguayan photographer Juan Angel Urruzola. ©Juan Angel Urruzola 2003.

(bottom) Monument in Villa Grimaldi engraved with the names of the disappeared, with a fragment from the renowned Uruguayan poet and novelist, Mario Benedetti: "What is forgotten is full of memory." © J. Patrice McSherry 1998.

covert operations and downsize the directorate of operations. The CIA's cold warriors never forgave him. Condor continued to operate throughout the Carter years, but administration officials seemed to accept CIA reports that portrayed the system in a benign light. In one cable to the embassies in the Condor states, for example, Secretary of State Cyrus Vance cited a CIA summary of the status of Operation Condor. The CIA reported that it had changed from its original purpose "to bring about an exchange of information" to "later . . . consideration of mounting assassination operations abroad." Again, actual assassinations was not discussed. Vance concluded that Condor might be "shifting more to non-violent activities." In another U.S. government review of Condor in March 1977:[90]

> Mr. Luers said that Ambassador Siracusa has asked for our current views on Condor. [PHRASE DELETED] said that it really exists, and that the CIA has [PHRASE DELETED] reporting on it. Mr. Luers said that it would be helpful to have an update on the subject of Condor, what we know about it, and how we should deal with the knowledge that we have. We might want to think again about whether we should raise the subject with the governments involved. *We haven't seen anything lately about Condor planning executions. Our attitude would be different if only exchanges of intelligence are involved.* [PARAGRAPH DELETED] (emphasis added)

However, Condor continued to target scores of lesser-known activists in violent extraterritorial actions in 1977 and up until 1980, which routinely resulted in torture and extrajudicial execution. Human rights organizations in the Condor countries have published lists of exiles disappeared in each of those years. Moreover, the CIA continued to cooperate with Condor. For example, one 1977 intelligence report on a suspected "terrorist" who belonged to a legal party in Venezuela, discovered in the Paraguayan Archives, was sent to Argentina and Brazil by Condor commander Col. Guanes Serrano. It listed the origin of the intelligence information as "C.I.A. (USA)."[91]

Well-documented case files, as well as numerous reports from declassified U.S. and Latin American archives, provide ample evidence of the ongoing cross-border disappearances, tortures, and murders in the framework of Condor during the Carter years. Space limits preclude discussion of more than a few more of these cases. In March 1977, five persons from Uruguay and Argentina were detained in Paraguay. José Nell, Alejandro José Logoluso, Dora Marta Landi Gil, Nelson Rodolfo Santana, and Gustavo Insaurralde were seized by Paraguayan police, interrogated and tortured by Paraguayan, Argentine, and Uruguayan intelligence personnel, transferred from Paraguay to Argentina, and "disappeared" there. Logoluso and Landi Gil were members of the Peronist Youth, Insaurralde a member of the PVP. Paraguayan authorities reported that they were freed, and the Argentine junta consistently denied any knowledge of their whereabouts. Official documents found in the Paraguayan Archives proved, however, that on May 16, 1977, the five were delivered to an Argentine SIDE unit (including an army intelligence officer and a navy officer from the infamous Navy Mechanics School). They were flown in an Argentine navy plane to Buenos Aires, where they disappeared. The Paraguayan police report included their photos and fingerprints and the names of the Argentine officers who took them.[92]

Condor continued to expand as an inter-American counterinsurgency program. In 1978, Ecuador agreed to join the secret apparatus. A CIA document revealed the Condor structure in that country:

> The overall responsibility for Ecuador's participation and activities in Condor lie with the Ecuadorean Joint Command of the Armed Forces; however, the Joint Command has assigned various individual responsibilities to the army, navy, and air force. . . . The National Intelligence Directorate (DNI) of Ecuador was incorporated into the Condor organization with the name of Condor 7.[93]

An Argentine lieutenant colonel, identified as the director of Condortel, was in Quito supervising the installation of the special telecommunications system in the Defense Ministry, and Chile offered scholarships for Ecuadoran intelligence personnel to attend the military intelligence school in Santiago. Clearly, Condor was an institutionalized component of the continental security system.

Peru apparently joined the Condor Group in 1978 as well. The renamed DINA (now Central Nacional de Inteligencia, CNI) assigned a Condor agent to Lima, Peru, to carry out Condor operations. A classified memo, uncovered in the Chilean Foreign Ministry archives in 1999, said that the Peruvian intelligence director was informed of this Condor posting at the Chilean Embassy in Lima. It noted that the document had passed "through the Condor system" via Buenos Aires, "the country that serves as Secretary of the Community." This sentence seemed to verify that Argentina was now in charge of the Condor system, as suggested earlier. Another secret memorandum discovered in Santiago at the same time, dated March 1979, informed Pinochet's foreign minister that the CNI had designated two new Condor officers to the Chilean Embassy in Brasilia and that "the SNI will be informed in accord with the stipulations of Plan Condor."[94] These documents confirmed, once again, that Condor's extralegal countersubversive program was authorized at the top levels of the military states.

One case that caused an uproar in 1978 was that of Lilián Celiberti and Universindo Rodríguez, Uruguayans who were abducted in Brazil by a combined Condor squad of Uruguayan military officers and operatives of the

Brazilian Division of Political and Social Order (DOPS), the political police. The commando beat the two and tortured them with electric shocks and near-drownings in cold water in the station house of DOPS. According to Rodríguez, the Brazilians tortured them while the Uruguayans interrogated them.[95] Celiberti's two children were also seized. Celiberti noted that the Uruguayans were in command during the abduction while the Brazilians co-operated in the torture and provided vehicles in Brazil (Uruguayan vehicles were left at the border). She and Rodríguez were held in a police station in Brazil, which she believed indicated that by 1978 there were no clandestine centers for torture of the disappeared in Brazil. When they were brought to Uruguay after that, she suspected transnational cooperation between the two intelligence services.[96]

After the media publicized the abduction and relatives denounced the disappearance, the children were freed. Celiberti was imprisoned in military facilities and eventually transferred to a legal prison. Because the Brazilian regime had lifted press censorship, the Celiberti-Rodríguez case was widely reported, and eventually, two officers of DOPS were convicted of the crime. However, they received sentences of only six months in prison, and two other accused DOPS officers were found innocent.[97]

A young military officer of the Technical Section of the Counterintelligence Company, Department II of the Uruguayan general staff, later deserted and related his involvement in the Celiberti case (and other tortures and abductions he had participated in), confirming the accounts of the victims.[98] He also testified that the Army Intelligence School in Montevideo held weeklong training sessions in torture, practicing electric shocks, near-drownings, and other sadistic methods on prisoners.[99] He said officers from Central America and Paraguay attended these "courses" and that Uruguayan officers also traveled to Panama—presumably to the U.S. Canal Zone base—for intelligence training.

An important 1977 case was that of Chilean Juan Muñoz Alarcón, who, in June, provided a declaration to lawyers from Vicariate of Solidarity in Santiago.[100] Muñoz was another former socialist who was "turned" by DINA into one of its agents. He confessed to identifying, torturing, and murdering Chilean leftists for DINA, and his statement provided many details that were not public at the time, including the names and methods of DINA operatives and multinational Condor squads. Muñoz identified major DINA torture centers in Villa Grimaldi and Colonia Dignidad, and said that at the latter location there was a DINA radio with transnational capabilities. Muñoz said that DINA agents were active in Colombia, France, Sweden, and Italy, and he described a death squad operating in Chilean territory that combined the intelligence services of Chile, Brazil, Argentina, and Uruguay. As he outlined the system of intelligence cooperation and exchange of disappeared prisoners among the Chilean, Brazilian, Argentine, and Uruguayan intelligence units, it is clear that Muñoz was describing Operation Condor, although he did not use the code name.

Muñoz also named several CIA officers and U.S. Embassy personnel, including one transcribed as "James John Blaayton," whom he identified as "very important" to the transnational network. Muñoz was murdered shortly thereafter, a fate he had foreseen in his confession. In several reports on this case, George Landau, the former ambassador to Paraguay who was by then U.S. ambassador to Chile, portrayed Muñoz as "unstable" ("a man who told weird tales").[101] The Vicariate lawyer who wrote the cover letter for Muñoz's declaration, however, found him a highly reliable source whose information had been corroborated by other sources. In his cables, Landau corrected the phonetic spelling of the American Muñoz had named as central to the Condor network: James John Blystone. Blystone later became the U.S. regional security officer, posted in Buenos Aires, and his role was indeed a significant one. As demonstrated in chapter 7, Blystone was privy to secret Condor operations, including one that involved Peru, Bolivia, Argentina, and Spain, and, in at least one case, he had advance knowledge that several abducted Argentines would be "permanently disappeared."

To conclude, evidence from numerous sources demonstrates that the Condor system extralegally captured, tortured, and murdered hundreds of Latin American activists, most of them very young, in its most violent period between 1976 and 1980. That same evidence clearly shows that the officials of several U.S. administrations were well informed of the criminal methods used by the Condor apparatus. Yet security officials in the Pentagon and the CIA continued to collaborate closely with the military regimes and considered Condor a legitimate counterterror or counterguerrilla program. In the Nixon and Ford administrations, the State Department provided the political support of the United States to the Condor militaries as well. While some embassy and other U.S. personnel, as well as many members of Congress, were troubled and alarmed by the unfolding carnage, Washington's overriding policy imperative, at least until the early Carter era, was the anticommunist crusade. Any method was apparently regarded as acceptable to destroy the "internal enemy" in Latin America.

Notes

1. "Acta fundacional del Plan Cóndor," in *Posdata* (June 18, 1999): 20.
2. Cable from American Embassy, Santiago, to Secretary of State, "Disappearance of Top Leader of Chilean MIR," May 19, 1976.

3. Luz Arce (trans. Alba Skar), *The Inferno: A Story of Terror and Survival in Chile* (Madison: University of Wisconsin Press, 2004), 238–239; CODEPU, Equipo DIT-T, *Más allá de las fronteras: Estudios sobre las personas ejecutadas o desaparecideas fuera de Chile, 1973–1990* (Santiago: LOM Ediciones, 1996), 98.

4. CIA, *National Intelligence Daily* (TOP SECRET), June 23, 1976 and CIA, *Weekly Summary* (SECRET), no. 1398, July 2, 1976. See also CIA, "Latin American Trends: Staff Notes (SECRET)," June 23, 1976, 3, and CIA "Disappearance of MIR Leader in Argentina," April 30, 1976.

5. To: SecState, From AMEmbassy Brasilia, "Argentina Allegedly Extradites Brazilian Leftist to Chile," June 1, 1976.

6. To State, From Santiago, "Alleged Argentine extradition to Chile of María Regina Pinto Marcondes," message no. 5275, June 2, 1976.

7. Comisión Nacional de Verdad y Reconciliación, "Informe Rettig," Vol. 2 (Santiago: Chilean Government and Ediciones del Ornitorrinco, 1991), 596.

8. The preceding account is from the testimony of Matilde Artes Company, mother of Graciela, before the Argentine Comisión Nacional sobre la Desaparición de Personas (CONADEP, National Commission on the Disappearance of Persons), Files no. 6333 and 7243, 1984.

9. Naomi Westland, "The Case against President Banzer," *Bolivian Times*, January 18, 2001; Tito Drago, "Argentine Activists Meet Spain's 'Pinochet Judge,'" *Inter Press Service*, April 16, 1999.

10. "Demanda de extradición contra ex-presidente Banzer," *Bolivia Press*, no. 1 (January 10, 2002); "Menores desaparecidos: Fallos y resoluciones judiciales (tomo 2)," Part 6, Casos Generales, "Ruffo, Eduardo," [fs. 2702 a 2725]," *Nunca más*, at www.nuncamas.org/investig/menores/fallos2_064.htm.

11. Memo to Francisco A. Britez B., from Alejandro Fretes Dávalos, Nota no. B/340 (secret), April 27, 1976, document obtained in the Paraguayan Archives by the author, 1996.

12. Henry Kissinger, letter to Mondale, April 9, 1975, no. 7506245, on State Department website. State Department, "Memorandum of Conversation [Secret/NODIS]," discussion between Kissinger and Pinochet on June 8, 1976, 6, 10.

13. Martin Edwin Andersen, "Kissinger and the 'Dirty War,'" *The Nation* (October 31, 1987): 477–480, and "Argentina 1976: Kissinger autorizó los crímenes militares," *Brecha*, Montevideo (Uruguay), October 23, 1987, 12–14.

14. Andersen, "Argentina 1976: Kissinger," 12, and "Kissinger and the 'Dirty War'"; see also J. Patrice McSherry, *Incomplete Transition: Military Power and Democracy in Argentina* (New York: St. Martin's Press, 1997), 81.

15. National Security Archive, "Argentine Military Believed U.S. Gave Go-Ahead for Dirty War," Electronic Briefing Book No. 73, Part II, ed. Carlos Osorio, 2003.

16. National Security Archive, "Kissinger to Argentines on Dirty War: 'The Quicker You Succeed the Better,'" Electronic Briefing Book 104, ed. Carlos Osorio, posted December 4, 2003, at www.gwu.edy/~nsarchiv/NSAEBB/ NSAEBB104/index.htm; National Security Archive, "Kissinger to the Argentine Generals in 1976: 'If there are things that have to be done, you should do them quickly,'" Electronic Briefing Book 133, ed. Carlos Osorio and Kathleen Costar, August 27, 2004.

17. State Department, declassified "Memorandum of Conversation," June 8, 1976, 3; see also Peter Kornbluh, "Kissinger and Pinochet," *The Nation* (March 29, 1999); Lucy Komisar, "Kissinger Declassified," *The Progressive* (May 1999).

18. "Memorandum of Conversation,"8.

19. Alberto Amato, "Anatomía de una dictadura," *Clarín* (Argentina), *Zona* section, March 21, 1999.

20. "Secretary's Calendar of Events—Thursday, June 10, 1976 (Santiago/Mexico City)," on National Security Archive website, Electronic Briefing Book no. 73 Part II, document 5.

21. CIA, *Weekly Summary*, no. 1398 [SECRET], July 2, 1976.

22. CIA, *Weekly Summary*, no. 1398 [SECRET], July 2, 1976; see also U.S. Embassy, Buenos Aires, "Aftermath of Kidnapping of Refugees," June 15, 1976.

23. See also State Department Action memorandum of July 17, 1976, from Harry W. Shlaudeman (ARA), J. M. Wilson, Jr. (d/HA), and Leonard F. Walentynowicz (SCA) to the secretary of state, entitled "Expanded Parole Authority for Chilean and Other Refugees." The memo noted that congressional and public pressure to protect political exiles in Argentina was intensifying, and included a reference to UNHCR's report that "on June 9 lists and files concerning 2000 refugees were stolen from one of the voluntary agencies and on July 11, 24 refugees were abducted from their hotel by forty armed men and subjected to severe torture before being subsequently released."

24. To: SECSTATE, From: AMEMBASSY Buenos Aires, "Aftermath of Kidnapping of Refugees in Buenos Aires," June 15, 1976.

25. To RUEHC/SECSTATE, From AMEMBASSY Montevideo, "Refugees in Argentina," June 7, 1976.

26. TO AMEmbassy Buenos Aires, From AMEmbassy Montevideo, "Kidnapping of Refugees in Buenos Aires," June 16, 1976.

27. To: AMEMBASSY Montevideo, From AMEMBASSY Buenos Aires, "Kidnapping of Refugees in Buenos Aires," July 2, 1976.

28. Memo from Colonel Benito Guanes Serrano, intelligence chief of the Paraguayan high command, to Pastor Coronel, chief of police investigations, Nota. no. 494, June 26, 1976, obtained by author in Paraguayan Archives, Asunción, 1996.

29. Paraguayan Armed Forces, "Pedido de Búsqueda no. 23/76," July 6, 1976, obtained by author in Paraguayan Archives, 1996.

30. Invitation from Alejandro Fretes Dávalos to Pastor Coronel, Note no. B/555, July 7, 1976, obtained by author in Paraguayan Archives, 1996.

31. TO: SECSTATE, From AMEMBASSY Buenos Aires, "The Military Government after Four Months in Power," signed by Chaplin, July 23, 1976, 4–5.

32. Author interview with Luz Lagarrigua, Santiago, July 19, 1996; see also "Informe Rettig," 596–597.

33. Testimonies provided to Centro de Estudios Sociales y Legales (CELS), Buenos Aires, 1978–79; CELS microfiches 30 and 31, studied by author in Buenos Aires in 1996.

34. Testimony of Alicia Raquel Cadenas Ravela, Uruguayan prisoner at Orletti, August 3, 1979, in archives of CELS, Argentina, microfiche no. 30, obtained by author in Buenos Aires in 1996; testimony of Julio César Barboza Pla, Uruguayan officer who

defected from SID, n.d., obtained by author in SERPAJ archives, Montevideo, 2001; Samuel Blixen, "Cordero torturaba en Argentina," *Brecha*, no. 827 (2001), at www.brecha.com.uy.

35. "Memorandum for the Record: ARA-CIA Weekly Meeting—30 July, 1976," August 3, 1976.

36. TO the Secretary, From INR-Harold H. Saunders, "Murders in Argentina—No Intergovernmental Conspiracy," June 4, 1976, p. 2.

37. See Taylor Branch and Eugene M. Propper, *Labyrinth* (New York: Viking Press, 1982), 2.

38. Untitled CIA memorandum, September 1976; "'Favor urgente de Stroessner para Pinochet," *El Mostrador* (Chile), November 14, 2000; To: File, From State Department, "Resume of USG Evidence and Defense Position in the Contreras, et al., Extradition," December 31, 1979.

39. State Department telegram to Schlaudeman from Amb. Landau, "Travel by Chileans," August 6, 1976.

40. Secret memo (Special Handling) to AMEMBASSY from SecState, immediate, "Travel by Chileans," August 7, 1976.

41. Paraguayan High Command, Note no. B/650, "Remitir fotocopia de Lista Nominal y fotografías," August 6, 1976, obtained by author in Paraguayan Archives, 1996.

42. CIA, "Latin American Trends. Staff Notes [secret]," August 11, 1976.

43. Department of State, Roger Channel (top security channel), Memo from Secretary of State, Washington, to U.S. Embassies in Buenos Aires Immediate, Montevideo Immediate, Santiago Immediate, La Paz Immediate, Brasilia Immediate, Asunción Immediate, "Subject: Operation Condor," August 23, 1976.

44. CIA cable (secret), "Brazil's Role in Operation Condor," August 12, 1976, at www.gwu.edu/ ~nsarchiv/news/20010306/.

45. Adolfo Pérez Esquivel, "Prólogo," in Stella Calloni, *Los años del lobo: Operación Condor*, 2nd ed. (Buenos Aires: Ediciones Continente, 1999), 9. Pérez Esquivel, who won the Nobel Peace Prize in 1980, was subject to several Condor detentions in various countries.

46. CIA, "Latin American Trends. Staff Notes [SECRET]," August 23, 1976, 4.

47. U.S. Secretary of State, Immediate, Roger Channel memorandum to Buenos Aires, Montevideo, Santiago, La Paz, Brasilia, Asunción, "Operation Condor," August 23, 1976.

48. To SECSTATE, From U.S. Embassy Santiago, August 24, 1976.

49. Author interview with Robert While, conducted by telephone, April 8, 2003.

50. John Dinges and Peter Kornbluh, "An Assassination, a Failure to Act, a Painful Parallel," *Washington Post*, September 22, 2002, B01; Diana Jean Schemo, "Latin Death Squads and the U.S.: A New Disclosure," *New York Times*, October 23, 2002.

51. National Public Radio, "Timeline of Henry Kissinger's Career," August 8, 2001, at www.npr.org/programs/ atc/features2001/aug/kissinger/010808.kissinger.html.

52. See, for example, Christopher Andrew, *For the President's Eyes Only: Secret Intelligence and the American Presidency from Washington to Bush* (New York: Harper Collins, 1995), 389–400.

53. Howard W. French, "From Old Files, a New Story of U.S. Role in Angolan War," *New York Times*, March 31, 2002. The article was based on research conducted by Piero Gleijeses for his book *Conflicting Missions: Havana, Washington, and Africa, 1959–1976* (Chapel Hill: University of North Carolina Press, 2003). Nathaniel Davis, Kissinger's assistant secretary of state for Africa (and in 1973, U.S. ambassador to Chile), resigned in July 1975 over the U.S. intervention in Angola.

54. Anthony Boadle, "U.S. Lied about Cuban Role in Angola," Reuters, April 1, 2002, reprinted in *Kissinger Watch*, no. 3, April 10, 2002, at www.icai-online.org/kissingerwatch.

55. Dana Milbank, "1975 East Timor Invasion Got U.S. Go-Ahead," *Washington Post*, December 7, 2001, A38; David Corn, "Kissinger's Back . . . As 9/11 Truth Seeker," *The Nation* (November 27, 2002); Christopher Hitchens, "Kissinger's Green Light to Suharto," *The Nation* (February 18, 2002).

56. See National Security Archives, documents on Indonesian invasion of East Timor at www.gwu.edu/~nsarchiv/NSAEBB/NSAEBB62/press.html; Christopher Hitchens, *The Trial of Henry Kissinger* (London: Verso, 2002); Anthony Lewis, "No Blind Eye," *New York Times*, November 25, 1996. Lewis stated that Kissinger had suggested that aides justify the invasion as self-defense against communism.

57. Andrews, *For the President's Eyes*, 374.

58. See letter from Kissinger and Brent Scowcroft, *New York Times Book Review*, November 5, 2000.

59. Letter to editor from Barry A. Toll, *New York Times Book Review*, December 3, 2000.

60. Kathryn Olmsted, *Challenging the Secret Government: The Post-Watergate Investigations of the CIA and FBI* (Chapel Hill: University of North Carolina Press, 1996), 82–83.

61. Pat Holt, *Secret Intelligence and Public Policy: A Dilemma of Democracy* (Washington, D.C.: Congressional Quarterly Press, 1995), 222.

62. Olmsted, *Challenging*, 148.

63. U.S. House Select Committee on Intelligence, *CIA: The Pike Report* (Nottingham, U.K.: Spokesman Books, 1977), 249, 251, cited in Olmsted, *Challenging*, 155.

64. Holt, *Secret Intelligence and Public Policy*, 158; Olmsted, *Challenging*, 142.

65. Scott Shane, "In Calls to Kissinger, Reporters Show that Even They Fell under Super-K's Spell," *New York Times*, October 22, 2004.

66. See DIA, "Special Operations Forces," October 1, 1976. A member of the PVP explained to me that PVP was a political organization that worked in the union and student sectors to resist the military dictatorship. One of the smaller groups that made up what later became the PVP was OPR-33. It had carried out armed actions, but the PVP, while not theoretically opposed to armed struggle against the regime, was not a guerrilla group. E-mail exchanges with PVP member, June 2004.

67. See Amnesty International, "Abridged Version of Taped Testimony of Washington Pérez," August 1976, in Argentine Project archive of State Department; Samuel Blixen, "En nombre de la patria y con ánimo de lucro," *Brecha*, no. 823, September 2001.

68. Testimony of Sergio López Burgos, in CELS files, microfiche no. 31, April 1984; obtained by author in Buenos Aires, 1996; see also Enrique Rodríguez Larreta testimony, Legado no. 2539, CONADEP, *Nunca más* (Buenos Aires: Eudeba, 1998), 269–270.

69. Testimony of Alicia Raquel Cadenas Ravela, CELS microfiche no. 30, obtained by author in Buenos Aires, 1996.

70. Cadenas Ravela testimony; Rodríguez Larreta testimony.

71. López Burgos testimony; Rodríguez Larreta testimony.

72. López Burgos testimony; Rodríguez Larreta testimony.

73. Author interview with Edward Koch, New York, July 3, 2003.

74. To see portions of the transcripts, which were obtained by Carlos Osorio of the National Security Archive, see Emiliano Cotelo, "EE.UU: desclasificación de documentos secretos revela los ataques a exiliados uruguayos," *Espectador* (Uruguay), August 4, 2001, at www.espectador.com/principal/ documentos/doc0109041.htm, accessed by author June 2003.

75. Hearings before the Subcommittee on International Organizations of the Committee on International Relations, House of Representatives, August 4, 1976, 112, 117. This incident was discussed in "Coordinación represiva en el Río de la Plata," *Las Bases* (Uruguay), April 28, 1985; copy obtained by author in Montevideo, 2001.

76. Statement of Rodríguez Larreta before Comisión Investigadora sobre Personas Desaparecideas (Uruguay), 1985, obtained by author in SERPAJ files, Montevideo, August 2001.

77. Hearings, 1976, 117, 121.

78. Hearings, 1976, 126–127.

79. Hearings, 1976, 132.

80. Department of Defense Intelligence Information Report, "(U) Special Operations Forces (U)," October 1, 1976.

81. To: SECSTATE, From AMEMBASSY Montevideo, "GOA Silent on Uruguay Revelation of Terrorist Plot," November 2, 1976, at National Security Archive Briefing Book no. 73, www.gwu.edu/~nsarchiv/ NSAEBB/NSAEBB73/.

82. TO: ARA Harry Schlaudeman, From Philip Habib, "Operation Condor," September 25, 1976; see also Lucy Komisar, "New Document: CIA Knew about Latin Terror Plan for Paris," June 24, 2002.

83. Regarding Paladino's security breach, see CIA, "Comments on Operation Condor [SECRET]," April 18, 1977. According to French researcher Pierre Abramovici, French attaché colonel Robert Servent told Judge LeLoire, who was investigating Condor, that he learned of Condor from an Argentine officer. Author e-mail exchange with Pierre Abramovici, December 17, 2002. On the Condor base in Paris, see "The trials of Henry Kissinger," *The Independent* (U.K.), April 23, 2002, which quotes one of the lawyers. My efforts in 2003 to confirm this information with one of the lawyers were unsuccessful.

84. TO: Director of FBI, From: Buenos Aires, "Condor [SECRET]," September 28, 1987. This was known as the CHILBOM cable.

85. TO: Director, From: Buenos Aires, "Operation Condor [SECRET]," September 30, 1976.

86. Defense Department Intelligence Information Report, "(U) Special Operations Forces (U)," October 1, 1976.

87. CIA Directorate of Operations, title blacked out, November 11, 1976.

88. State Department, "INR Afternoon Summary," November 23, 1976.

89. CIA, "Comments on Operation Condor [SECRET]," April 18, 1977.

90. To: Embassies in Asunción, Brasilia, Buenos Aires, La Paz, Montevideo, Santiago, From SecState, "Operation Condor," message #65403, March 24, 1977. A similar argument was made in a report by the State Department's Bureau of Intelligence and Research, "South America's Southern Cone—Bloc in Formation?" Report No. 864, October 6, 1977, 2. See also "Memorandum for the Record," ARA/CIA Weekly Meeting, 4 March 1977, 3.

91. Colonel Benito Guanes Serrano, "Informe no. 033/77," obtained by author in Paraguayan Archives, 1996.

92. CELS, "Querella contra militares argentinos por el asesinato de un desaparecido" (on the Logoluso case) Buenos Aires, December 27, 1993, obtained by author in Buenos Aires, 1996; arrest documents and photos in Paraguayan Archives on Landi Gil and Logoluso, obtained by author in Asunción, 1996. See also Alfredo Boccia Paz, Myriam Angélica González and Rosa Palau Aguilar, *Es mi informe: Los archivos secretos de la policía de Stroessner* (Asunción: CDE), 321–332.

93. CIA, Report (title blacked out), Secret, February 14, 1978.

94. These documents were reproduced and described in detail in Jorge Molina, "Expedientes secretos," *Qué Pasa* (Chile), 1999 (the article notes that the documents were first made public by *La Nación* in Chile on June 16, 1999); see also Gustavo Gonzalez, "Fresh Proof of Operation Condor Surfaces," *Inter Press Service*, June 16, 1999. For confirmation that Peru joined Condor around 1978, see CIA, "Classified Reading Material re: 'Condor' for Ambassador Landau and Mr. Propper," August 22, 1978.

95. BBC Brasil, "Vítima da Operação Condor ainda teme relatar tortura," May 14, 2000.

96. Interview with Lilián Celiberti conducted by author, Montevideo, August 3, 2001.

97. J. Víctor García Rivas, *Confesiones de un torturador* (Barcelona: Editorial Laia, 1981), 161.

98. García Rivas, *Confesiones*, 50.

99. García Rivas, *Confesiones*, 67 and chapter 4.

100. "Declaración de un agente de la Dina," cover letter from Raúl Vergara Meneses dated July 14, 1977, on State Department website. See also Diana Jean Schemo, "There's Still a Lot to Learn about the Pinochet Years," *New York Times*, March 5, 2000.

101. See Landau's report, From AmEmbassy Santiago, to Secstate WashDC, December 1977, "The Strange Case of Juan Muñoz," on State Department website.

5

Phase III: Condor's Assassination Capability

IRREGULAR PARAMILITARY SQUADS responding to the Condor command structure carried out the assassinations of Carlos Prats and Sofía Cuthbert in 1974 and attempted the assassinations of Bernardo Leighton and Ana Fresno in 1975, as I have shown. Leandro Sánchez Reisse, a civilian agent of the Argentine intelligence service Battalion 601 and a Condor operative, hinted in veiled language to a journalist how the Condor apparatus targeted individuals for disappearance and assassination. "All I can tell you is that inside the intelligence community of the different Latin American intelligence services, something like an 'Intelligence Advisory Committee,' Mr. Harold Conti [a well-known Argentine writer who disappeared in 1976] was known as the man of Fidel Castro in Argentina," he said in 1985. The 601 operative thus implied that intelligence commanders from all the Condor countries drew up a combined list of persons to eliminate. In 1987, Sánchez Reisse confirmed to a U.S. Senate subcommittee that the "intelligence advisory committee" was linked to other military intelligence organizations in the region as well as to the U.S. DIA and CIA, providing another testimony of U.S. involvement in Condor.[1]

Another assassination took place in December 1974. Uruguayan military attaché Ramón Trabal was assigned to Paris. His murder was never clarified, and opinion is mixed in Uruguay about whether this assassination was the work of Condor or the result of a deadly internal dispute between factions of the military (few believed that it was a leftist group).[2] Trabal, former head of military intelligence, had opposed the hard-line faction of the Uruguayan armed forces led by Julio Vadora, and had opposed President Bordaberry's decision to declare illegal the major labor union, Convención Nacional de Trabajadores, in 1973. Trabal had also overseen secret peace negotiations with members of the Tupamaros.[3] A mysterious group calling itself the Raúl Sendic International Brigade (after the leader of the Tupamaros) claimed credit for Trabal's assassination.[4] The Uruguayan regime immediately presented the killing of five young Uruguayan exiles, who had disappeared in Argentina and reappeared, murdered, in Soca, Uruguay, as retaliation for the Trabal assassination. But with Trabal's murder, an officer who had represented an alternative vision for the Uruguayan army—as had Schneider and Prats of Chile—was eliminated, and a pretext created for more repression against the left.

In Bolivia questions linger, too, about the death of General Joaquín Zenteno, who died in Paris two years later, in May 1976. Bolivian dictator Hugo Banzer feared Zenteno as a potential rival. Zenteno had participated in the capture of Che Guevara and in the 1971 coup against Juan José Torres in Bolivia; his anticommunist credentials were impeccable. Nevertheless, Zenteno was troubled by the assassination of the interior minister, a fellow military man, in April 1973, by Banzer's forces.[5] Banzer ousted Zenteno as commander of the armed forces shortly thereafter and took over the position himself. He named Zenteno ambassador to France, and Zenteno moved to Paris in October 1973. Zenteno was in contact with political figures in Bolivia, including former president Víctor Paz Estenssoro, who were beginning to coalesce in opposition to Banzer.

Zenteno was assassinated by a gunman on a Paris street, and a shadowy group called the Che Guevara International Brigade assumed responsibility. French authorities rounded up and questioned some 2,000 South American refugees and exiles, and police suspected the infamous Carlos the Jackal of the assassination. Like the Raúl Sendic Brigade, the Che Guevara Brigade had never been heard of before, and never acted again, raising suspicions that they were phantoms created as part of a rightist black propaganda operation.[6] Many observers, including Juan José Torres, believed the Zenteno assassination was the work of Banzer.[7] Again, it remains unclear whether this murder was a Condor Phase III operation or a purely Bolivian venture. But according to a still-classified 1979 U.S. Senate report, the Condor states planned to use the 1974 murder of Trabal and two other officials to justify several assassinations of left-wing figures in Europe.

Two known Condor targets living in Europe in 1976 were Carlos Altamirano, head of the Chilean Socialist Party and a former senator, and Volodia Teitelboim, a key figure in the Chilean Communist Party. Chilean military men organized a transcontinental surveillance operation against both in August 1974,[8] and Pinochet discussed eliminating Altamirano with Italian terrorist Stefano delle Chiaie during a meeting at Franco's funeral.[9] Michael Townley, the DINA assassin, was part of a team assigned to assassinate two journalists in Paris in the fall of 1976, but the attack was called off because the French learned of the plan and refused to tolerate it.[10] According to the 1979 Senate report, the CIA had warned France and Portugal about impending Condor assassinations and those governments warned the targeted individuals.[11] DINA commander Pedro Espinoza then ordered Townley to assassinate Altamirano in Madrid, but that attack failed.

Given the CIA's role in warning the Europeans, why was it unable (or unwilling) to warn Orlando Letelier of Condor plans targeting him in the United States, especially since officials in the U.S. government were aware that DINA operatives were attempting to enter the United States surreptitiously? Then-CIA chief George Bush (senior) personally warned then-U.S. representative Edward Koch in October 1976 about a death threat by the Condor apparatus, although he did so long after the fact.[12]

This chapter explores several Condor assassinations: in Buenos Aires of Zelmar Michelini and Héctor Gutiérrez Ruiz in May 1976, and in Washington, D.C., of Orlando Letelier and Ronni Moffitt in September 1976. These crimes revealed the outlines of Condor's shadow command structure and the ways in which Condor operatives recruited and organized parastatal "special groups," or death squads, for Phase III operations. The chapter also examines several assassination plots that were foiled.

The Michelini-Gutiérrez Ruiz Case

The May 1976 Condor operation that resulted in the murders of Zelmar Michelini and Héctor Gutiérrez Ruiz targeted another prominent Uruguayan living in Buenos Aires as well: Wilson Ferreira, a third exiled political leader. Uruguayan authorities had revoked the passports of all three in April 1975, thus preventing planned visits to safer countries. Michelini and Ferreira perceived that they were under surveillance in Buenos Aires.

Michelini had been a student leader and later a union leader associated with the Colorado Party, one of the two traditional political parties in Uruguay. He was one of the founders of the center-left coalition Frente Amplio, formed in 1970 to seek progressive change through the electoral system. Michelini became a senator representing the Frente. In the Senate, he was a fierce critic of the slow-motion coup and the use of torture by security forces. After dissolving Congress in 1973, the military declared him a seditious subversive. Michelini and Gutiérrez Ruiz, a member of the National (or Blanco) Party who had been president of the House of Representatives, left for Buenos Aires with their families in 1973. Ferreira, leader of the Blanco Party, senator, and former presidential candidate, left at the same time. Several days before his abduction, Michelini wrote to the publisher of the Buenos Aires newspaper *La Opinión* that he had received warnings that he was in danger of being attacked and forcibly repatriated to Uruguay.[13] He declared for the record that he had no intention of returning to Uruguay and that no one should believe such a story if he should disappear.[14]

The abductions of Michelini and Gutiérrez Ruiz reflected the modus operandi of Operation Condor: the use of parallel squadrons with the complicity of official security forces. A large commando of armed men, with police and military credentials, arrived at the home of Gutiérrez Ruiz in the early morning, carrying radios with which they communicated with and received instructions from their commanders. The men acted with military demeanor and discipline. Those who entered the building shouted down to those in the street, without fear of attracting police attention. They took objects of value from the apartment and finally took Gutiérrez Ruiz out, half dressed and with a pillowcase over his head. U.S. ambassador Hill wrote in a June 7, 1976 telegram,

> Those who kidnapped Gutiérrez Ruiz . . . remained at his home for something like an hour, made no effort to hide their presence, and obviously did not fear intervention on part of police. Left-wing terrorists unlikely to have behaved with such impunity. Further, Federal Police at first refused to even accept *denuncia* of Mrs. Michelini . . . and they made no effort to investigate until several days later.[15]

While Hill continued to cling to the belief that Videla and the upper levels of the junta were "moderate" and not involved in the intensifying carnage in Argentina, he concluded that "elements of security services are involved, that they have approval of at least their immediate superiors and count with tolerance (or more) of levels even higher." Moreover, Hill had been cognizant of the operation of Chilean, Uruguayan, and Brazilian commandos in Argentina for some time.[16]

The abduction of Michelini, shortly thereafter, was similar. Several Ford Falcons (the model used by the Triple A previously), without license plates, pulled up outside the Hotel Liberty, where the Michelini family lived. A squad of heavily armed men entered the hotel and occupied the lobby, demanding the key to the Michelini residence. There, they took Michelini into custody and blindfolded him in the presence of two of his young sons. The commando did not leave immediately, but sacked the apartment of valuables, including identity documents, files, and the watches of the two boys. (Michelini's daughter Margarita, abducted soon afterward and held in Orletti Motors, testified later that she had seen her father's distinctive typewriter in the headquarters of SID (Servicio de Informaciones de Defensa, military intelligence—in Montevideo). As they left, hotel personnel demanded identification, but the men threatened them with their guns and said, "We're at war."[17] Military guards at a major state-owned telephone facility nearby did not intervene, nor did anyone from the U.S. Embassy, also close by.[18] Over the next days, the wives of both men tried repeatedly to contact Argentine authorities, including junta leader Videla, Interior Minister Harguindeguy, and the chief of police, to ask them to investigate the abductions, but they were ignored. The captors had worn no gloves and left fingerprint evidence everywhere, which would have facilitated their identification, since in Argentina every resident's fingerprints were stored in a central file. But no investigators came to either location for five days.

The bodies of the two legislators were found in a car on May 21, along with those of a Uruguayan couple, William Whitelaw Blanco and Rosario del Carmen Barredo de Schroeder, who had disappeared earlier. No government authority informed the families officially of the discovery; the police announced it on the radio. All four bodies bore signs of torture and multiple bullet wounds, in the style of the Triple A, and pamphlets from a supposed subversive organization, claiming responsibility for the crimes, were found in the car. A few days later, Ferreira learned that while he was attending the wake for his two colleagues, men who identified themselves as police had come to his residence to ask questions about his whereabouts. He requested asylum at the Austrian Embassy and soon left for Paris.[19] Before leaving, he addressed a letter to Videla in which he gave a detailed account of the abductions and their aftermath, and strongly criticized the regime's violation of long-standing traditions of political sanctuary. It concluded, "When the hour of your own exile comes—as you can be sure it will, General Videla—if you seek refuge in Uruguay, a Uruguay whose destiny will once again be in the hands of its people, we will receive you without warmth and without affection; but we will guarantee you the protection which you denied to those whose death we mourn today."[20]

Ferreira's Testimony to Congress

On May 27, Representative Wolff of New York accused the Argentine regime of failure to protect Michelini and Gutiérrez Ruiz, criticized the Uruguayan regime's "terrorist tactics," and stated that new legislation under consideration, which would deny U.S. aid to states that violated human rights, would be used in such cases. In a sharp reaction to such congressional criticism, Ambassador Siracusa defended the Uruguayan regime, insisting that "not a shred of evidence has appeared to indicate GOU involvement in these killings." Later he wrote that he strongly opposed "a blanket program for paroling foreign refugees from Argentina to the United States." Many of the Uruguayan refugees in Argentina, he argued, were Tupamaros who "for years, terrorized their nation, murdering, burning, robbing, bombing, and otherwise wreaking havoc among a peaceful people."[21] The memo reflected Siracusa's visceral hatred of the left and his pro-military bias. His blatant misrepresentation of the tens of thousands of Uruguayan refugees in Argentina doubtless contributed to the Uruguayan regime's hostility and paranoia toward those who had gone there. The memo also exaggerated the violence of the Tupamaros, who had been basically destroyed organizationally by 1972.[22]

On June 17, 1976, Ferreira testified before the congressional subcommittee chaired by Donald Fraser.[23] In a passionate speech, Ferreira argued that no terrorism of the left had occurred in four years and that "the only people who kidnap, torture, and kill today in Uruguay are the government [*sic*] . . . terror was aimed at the whole population . . . it turned against any citizen who had ever had any link with workers' syndicates or trade unions and eventually against the entire population, anyone, 'just in case.'"[24] Ferreira was blunt about the U.S. role in his country as well. He declared,

> The Uruguayan repressive apparatus was built up with the assistance of abundant material and technical aid from the United States. Uruguayan military personnel had and still have prolonged periods of instruction in several places in your country, especially in the Canal Zone in Panama. . . . The U.S. Embassy in Montevideo gives direction, counsel, and opinion about the course of Uruguayan politics, and goes so far as giving its seal of approval to specific institutional formulas which would bring about the abolition of the right of the Uruguayan people to a self-elected government. The U.S. Embassy in Montevideo acts as a public relations agent for the Uruguayan government in that it publicizes throughout the world false information about the situation of the country . . . it supports and claims that subversion cannot be curbed without the suppression of liberties and it gives currency to the lie that in Uruguay "only a handful of communists" have been arrested.[25]

Ambassador Siracusa reacted with fury to Ferreira's testimony, only part of which is presented here. He particularly focused on Ferreira's assertion that Michelini and Gutiérrez Ruiz had applied for visas from the U.S. Embassy in Buenos Aires, but that Siracusa had notified the Uruguayan regime, which then cancelled their passports. Siracusa adamantly disputed this, arguing, "The obvious implication of this totally unfounded and irresponsible charge is that the U.S. ambassador to Uruguay had participated in what he chose to call 'a death sentence.'"[26] Siracusa insisted that embassy records showed no application from the two for U.S. visas nor any visa clearance inquiry from Buenos Aires. Siracusa also denounced Ferreira for labeling him a CIA agent and wrote a lengthy, detailed defense of his record.[27]

A month later, Siracusa wrote a somewhat unclear follow-up memo to clarify a "discrepancy" regarding the issue of visas for Michelini and Gutiérrez Ruiz. The embassy had found records showing that Siracusa had, in fact, spoken to officials of the Uruguayan regime in April 1975 about Michelini in the context of an invitation from Senator Edward Kennedy to Michelini to visit the United States. Several Uruguayan officials had asked Siracusa for "information about the trip," but the ambassador's responses to the officials, or any statements he made about Michelini, were not disclosed in the cable. Siracusa downplayed the importance of the conflicting information and again made the case that Ferreira's original charge had been untrue.[28] The passports of all three Uruguayans were cancelled after Kennedy's invitation, however, in April 1975, and respected Uruguayan sources reported much later that Siracusa had "unofficially" told Uruguayan officials that Michelini was trying to obtain a U.S. visa in Buenos Aires in order to travel to the United States.[29]

Investigations of the assassinations of the legislators were not pursued until after the transitions from military rule in Argentina and Uruguay in the mid-1980s. In 1986, during the landmark trial of the juntas in Argentina, Judge Néstor Blondi requested the extradition from Uruguay of four men in relation to this case and others in Argentina: Major José Gavazzo of Organismo Coordinador de Operaciones Antisubversivas, OCOA, Lieutenant Colonel Manuel Cordero of SID, Captain Jorge Silveira, and police officer Hugo Campos Hermida, other Orletti operatives.[30] The Uruguayan government "lost" the extradition order and, reacting to military threats, pushed through Congress an "impunity law" (Ley de Caducidad) that protected human rights violators from legal action. Then, in 1989, in an unusual and questionable act, Argentine civilian president Carlos Menem pardoned the four Uruguayan officers along with hundreds of Argentine military and security personnel who had been indicted for sedition or human rights abuses during the dirty war.

Later Testimonies about the Assassinations

After Uruguay's transition from military rule, several persons came forward with information about the Michelini-Gutiérrez Ruiz assassinations. Enrique Rodríguez Larreta, Jr., testified before the Uruguayan Investigative Commission on Disappeared Persons in 1985 that while he was imprisoned in Orletti Motors, an Argentine torturer called "Paqui" told him that the two legislators had been held there. Matilde Rodríguez, the wife of Gutiérrez Ruiz, positively identified the Argentine operative as one of the abductors. Margarita Michelini, the daughter of Zelmar, also identified Paqui at Orletti and at SID headquarters in Uruguay. His real name was Osvaldo Forese, and he represented a key link between the Orletti death squad and the twin abductions of the legislators.[31]

Another witness, Haydeé Trías, a nurse, told a major Montevideo newspaper in 1996 that she had met several military men, including Pedro Mattos and Manuel Cordero, in 1973. They told her they were part of a "movement against subversion," she said, and began to tell about their operations and foreign missions. Trías said that one evening in 1976 she was called to her friend's house to help calm Mattos, who was having a crisis of nerves, threatening to shoot himself. He confessed that he had gone to Buenos Aires with Cordero and had killed Michelini in Orletti Motors, she said. Mattos told her that he had been promised U.S. $50,000 for the murder. He said that he had been following orders and that Cordero had been ordered to execute Gutiérrez Ruiz at the same time, but that the legislator had already died under torture. After the transition from military rule, Trías decided to testify (with her identity hidden) before the congressional commission of inquiry in 1986. Her testimony leaked to the media. The parliamentary inquiry ended without resolution, and afterward Trías received several death threats and suffered several suspicious accidents.[32]

In 2002, the Uruguayan press reported that the former organ of the dictatorship, the military-dominated National Security Council, had, in a secret session in May 1976, decided to eliminate Michelini, Gutiérrez Ruiz, and Ferreira. Former president Bordaberry, Condor chief Julio Vadora, the heads of the armed forces, and one Argentine colonel, among others, were said to be at the session. (The military ousted Bordaberry as the figurehead civilian president soon afterward, in June 1976.) Reputable Uruguayan sources gave an anonymous document to the parliamentary investigative commission in 1985, describing the deliberations of the council.[33]

In 2002, Bordaberry denied the story and said that the Argentines were responsible for the assassinations of Michelini and Gutiérrez Ruiz.[34] Citing Wilson Ferreira's testimony before the U.S. Congress, he asserted that those who had abducted the two had Argentine accents. He also argued that the Argentines had been determined to exterminate the left and that they had considered Uruguayan exiles to be subversive. However, in 1996 former Argentine army chief Martín Balza had told Senator Rafael Michelini, one of the legislator's sons, that the Uruguayans had carried out the crime and that the legislators were not a target of the Argentine security forces. In Rafael Michelini's own investigation—during which he spoke to most active-duty Uruguayan generals—three credible sources (including one general) verified that the authors of the crime were Uruguayan officers. Another inside source, Eduardo Ruffo, a former Argentine operative at Orletti, also said the assassins were Uruguayan officers. His testimony was credible because he had previously given accurate information to Sara Méndez, one of the Uruguayan Partido por la Victoria del Pueblo members "disappeared" in Buenos Aires with her baby in 1976 (she gained her freedom years later). Ruffo's information allowed her to finally locate her missing son in 2002; he had been adopted by an Argentine military couple twenty-six years before.[35] Despite Bordaberry's denial, the modus operandi of Condor was to obscure responsibility. As we have seen, the evidence suggests that Argentine operatives carried out the disappearances and delivered the two to Uruguayan Condor operatives, precisely to enhance deniability.

A 1978 document regarding this case surfaced in 2001 and caused a stir when it was made public by two newspapers in Buenos Aires and Montevideo.[36] It was a typed confession signed by a man who claimed to be "Agustín Efraín Silvera" and an officer of the Argentine federal police. He stated that he had been charged with the surveillance of Michelini in Buenos Aires in 1976. Journalists expressed some doubts as to whether the document was a sophisticated exercise in black propaganda by shadowy intelligence services. Senator Rafael Michelini noted, however, that the document's abundant details corresponded to other testimonies and to little-known information about his father's routines, which only someone who knew him well, or had him under surveillance, would have known.[37] He thought the account seemed "very real," but harbored doubts about the true identity of the document's signatory. Michelini explained that the original typewritten document had come into his possession through Uruguayans who had been in exile in Europe. In 1978, a Uruguayan exile living in Paris had obtained the document—the senator was not sure who had originally received it—but it had been largely forgotten until rediscovered in a trunk in 2001.[38]

In the confession, Silvera wrote that he was afraid of repercussions and possibly of being set up after taking part in the preparations for the assassination and therefore had decided to record his testimony. The police officer identified the Uruguayans "Sosa" and Hugo Campos Hermida, key Orletti operatives, as central figures in the assassination of Michelini. According to the document, Campos commanded a paramilitary squadron of fifteen Uruguayan men in Buenos Aires. A Brazilian, who frequently traveled to Brazil and who had much information, worked with the group, as well as a Paraguayan and a Chilean from DINA who took part in interrogations, Silvera wrote. The squad worked closely with SIDE and the Argentine Federal Police. Campos Hermida hired Silvera to carry out surveillance of various targets, and finally assigned him to shadow Michelini. The abductions of Michelini and Gutiérrez-Ruiz were planned so that some forty Argentines would carry them out, with only a few Uruguayans, Silvera wrote—clearly to camouflage Uruguay's role.

Silvera's account was an insider's view, filled with names of those with whom he worked and detailed information about the methods and infrastructure of the squadron: the numbers and types of autos they had, the surveillance methods used on Uruguayan exiles, the commanders who gave orders, and the personnel who carried them out. For example, Silvera said that Campos Hermida and the Uruguayans received commands from Montevideo, while an Argentine colonel named Ojeda was in charge of the operational level in Buenos Aires.[39] The document showed the interaction among Brazilian, Argentine, Chilean, and Uruguayan Condor operatives, which, at the time, was not public knowledge. In perhaps the most explosive part of the testimony, Silvera named an official attached to the U.S. Embassy, Jaime del Castillo, whom he believed was a CIA officer, as a key player. Del Castillo (a false name), according to the confession, was a Puerto Rican who traveled with an entourage (including a French arms instructor who was a veteran of the war in Algeria) and always carried large sums of money. Del Castillo was closely associated with the Condor squadron's leaders and attended meetings, the document stated—and he provided funds to carry out the Michelini assassination. After the assassination, Silvera wrote, he was sent by Campos Hermida to the U.S. Embassy with a package of cassette tapes for del Castillo, and del Castillo gave him a package for Campos Hermida that Silvera believed contained a large amount of money.

Miguel Bonasso of *Página/12* checked the document against the account of former policeman Rodolfo Peregrino Fernández, who gave testimony to the Argentine Commission of Human Rights in Madrid in 1983 regarding the repressive methods of the junta and of the Triple A, and against writings of Rodolfo Walsh, the Argentine journalist who had disappeared in 1977 after writing a letter to the junta. He also researched military and police personnel named in the account. Fernández Peregrino's testimony verified key aspects of Silvera's, according to Bonasso. Fernández had named General Edmundo R. Ojeda as second in command of the Tandil headquarters in Buenos Aires province, where a clandestine detention center was located when the abductions occurred. Silvera mentioned Tandil several times; it seemed to be the site where instructions for the team of Argentines originated, according to Silvera, and Fernández said the two legislators had been taken to Tandil after Orletti. Shortly after the assassinations, Ojeda was made head of the federal police, replacing an officer who had attempted to stop illegal methods, a suggestive fact.[40] Such rotations indicated that the most violent and extreme sectors of the military, linked to Condor, were gaining ascendency and predominance within the military and the regime.

Both Fernández Peregrino's later testimony and the Silvera document also mentioned a Uruguayan colonel named Ramírez who played an important role in the Condor command structure. He was possibly the top Condor commander in Buenos Aires. Fernández Peregrino named him, along with Argentine interior minister Albano Harguindeguy and General Edmundo Ojeda, as involved in the Michelini-Gutiérrez-Ruiz assassinations. Fernández Peregrino said in 1983 that Harguindeguy met Guillermo Ramírez when the former had served as military attaché in Uruguay. According to one Uruguayan journalist, who conducted an exhaustive study to identify "Ramírez," there were several officers with that surname in the Uruguayan armed forces. One was a close collaborator of the CIA (as was Amaurí Prantl, the senior Uruguayan Condor commander named by former CIA officer Philip Agee as the liaison to the CIA station in Montevideo, another link between Condor and the CIA). This journalist was not able to identify which Ramírez was linked to the assassination, however, or whether Ramírez was used as a code name like "Oscar" to disguise the identity of its user.[41]

The Silvera confession noted that the abductions of the two legislators were carried out by some forty men, mainly Argentines; this information matched Ferreira's testimony, and Bordaberry's. Finally, Rodolfo Walsh—whose sources inside the security forces were legendary—had linked these assassinations to the federal police, operating under the supervision of the CIA station chief, another piece of data that meshed with the Silvera account.

Assessing the Silvera Document

Clearly, it is necessary to closely scrutinize the Silvera document. After several years of investigation, the overall judgment of Senator Rafael Michelini was that it was produced by shadowy agents who wove together much factual information with some that was questionable.[42] Senator Michelini suspected that the montage was aimed to conceal the real perpetrators of the assassination. He questioned the testimony of Trías for similar reasons. Curiously, he noted, both testimonies named as responsible for the crime enemies of the key Condor officer in Buenos Aires: Gavazzo (despite the fact that the operatives named in the document worked with him). Colonel Gavazzo had led the repressive operations against Uruguayans in Argentina in those years.[43] The senator emphasized that, nevertheless, both testimonies laid the blame for the crimes squarely on the Uruguayan dictatorship, which had conducted repression beyond its borders and was the ultimate responsible party for the assassinations of Gutiérrez Ruiz and Michelini. The assassinations could only have been carried out under the accords of Operation Condor, something never denied by the Uruguayan military, Michelini concluded.[44]

The federal police told Miguel Bonasso of *Página/12* in August 2001 that Silvera had never been with the force. Adding to the intrigue, in the midst of that newspaper's investigation, journalists received several mysterious calls, and one message said that the journalists had been looking for the wrong man in the federal police. This man left a phone number, but, on calling the number, the journalists found that a password was needed to complete the call.[45]

In Uruguay, journalists pursued the story as well. *La República* told its readers that while it could not authenticate the story or the existence of Silvera, it could confirm that the original document dated from 1978. The paper consulted military sources, including one who had operated in Orletti (with the condition that his identity not be revealed), who said that Gavazzo and Cordero had used several aliases when in Buenos Aires, and "Sosa," named in the document as commander of the Uruguayan unit, could have been Gavazzo.[46] Other sources told the newspaper that del Castillo was still attached to a U.S. embassy in another country. In a 2004 article on the case, journalist Jorge Elías stated that a former CIA man was in Argentina investigating the Silvera document and its leads.[47]

In my own investigation, a State Department officer who had served in Buenos Aires expressed doubts as to whether a CIA officer would associate with a Condor squadron, as portrayed in the document.[48] In contrast, a senior U.S. intelligence officer did not find the testimony about the role of del Castillo to be unbelievable. Before the 1980s, when stricter oversight was established, he said, CIA officers had broad latitude in foreign operations. The involvement of a U.S. intelligence figure with a Condor assassination team would not surprise him, he said, although he was unfamiliar with the officer in question.[49] Rafael Michelini, son of the assassinated senator, was convinced that del Castillo really did exist, probably with another name. His sources never denied that, he said, but they did refuse to give more information. During his investigation the Uruguayan senator was unable to identify del Castillo, but his conclusion was that he was someone associated "informally" with the CIA or some intelligence branch of the U.S. government, perhaps a contract agent, "one of the many individuals who are recruited in Latin America, who are trained, who ostentatiously flaunt their connection [with the CIA] while rushing from here to there, until one day when they are finally retired, certainly with a good pension," he commented drily.[50]

It is known that Campos Hermida operated in Orletti and that he was close to the CIA. In 1970, he had received a State Department scholarship to attend intelligence courses in Washington, D.C., at the International Police Academy (IPA). Philip Agee, the former CIA officer, stated that the IPA was run by the

CIA using AID cover, and this relationship has been confirmed by scholars.[51] In 1974, the U.S. Congress abolished police training funded through AID's Public Safety Program after discovering that many of its graduates were carrying out torture and assassination in their countries.[52] Campos also attended training courses in Brazil in "squadron operations"—actually death squad operations, according to a fellow participant.[53] Other documents obtained more recently by the National Security Archive confirmed Campos Hermida's links to U.S. intelligence. U.S. lists of Uruguayan officers trained in the Office of Public Safety (OPS) program included Campos Hermida; many were trained in "investigation of terrorist activities." Finally, an August 1972 letter written by Campos Hermida, then-chief of Department 5 of the DNII (Dirección Nacional de Informaciones e Inteligencia, Uruguayan National Directorate of Information and Intelligence) to Byron Engle, director of the U.S. Office of Public Safety (and a CIA officer), decried the assassination by the Tupamaros of Dan Mitrione. Campos Hermida wrote that he had known and worked with Mitrione, the OPS director in Montevideo accused of teaching torture techniques to Uruguayan police.[54] According to a former agent, CIA officer William Cantrell supervised and controlled DNII, and DNII controlled a death squad and served as its cover.[55]

Michael McClintock has demonstrated that in Southeast Asia, Latin America, and elsewhere, "the organization of secret paramilitary groups and their deployment in assassination operations was in accord with mainstream [U.S] military doctrine in the 1960s."[56] Certainly in other cases up through the 1980s, CIA officers and contract agents acted as collaborators or paymasters of anticommunist paramilitary groups that carried out human rights crimes, such as the Chileans who assassinated General Schneider and, later, the Nicaraguan contras and Honduran Battalion 3-16 (see chapter 7). The CIA prepared lists of persons to assassinate as far back as the early 1950s in Guatemala,[57] and a CIA assassination study from the 1950s advised that "no assassination instructions should ever be written or recorded."[58] The agency routinely worked to penetrate and control foreign police and military forces.[59] In the 1960s, the CIA planned and attempted to assassinate several Third World leaders, and declassified documents placed a CIA officer in the room when Guatemalan intelligence officers planned death squad killings in 1965.[60] It is also clear from declassified documents that CIA officers and U.S. military men knew details of key Condor operations, worked closely with the intelligence units that carried them out, and were accepted within the inner circles of Condor. In short, it is not unthinkable that a CIA officer was involved.

Is the Silvera confession genuine, and if so, how accurate is it? To clarify the facts, a high-level, well-funded investigation is required, something that no government has been willing to do thus far. The Uruguayan government never conducted an official investigation of the assassinations. At this point, the Silvera document remains a rich but unproven set of clues that should be further pursued. Reputable investigative journalists in Argentina and Uruguay have taken the document seriously, as has Senator Rafael Michelini. The senator is a highly respected and credible figure who has carried out a comprehensive investigation, utilizing the access to high-ranking military officers permitted by his position and stature. Many hope that new criminal inquiries (one was launched in Argentina by the Michelini and Gutiérrez Ruiz families in 2004) will uncover the full facts of this case.

Ojeda was pardoned for human rights crimes under the Punto Final Law in Argentina and has since died. In 2001, Argentine judge Rodolfo Canicoba Corral indicted Vadora and Orletti operatives Gavazzo, Cordero, Silveira, and Campos Hermida for crimes committed in Buenos Aires under Operation Condor, and in 2003 he indicted Forese (who had been pardoned under the Due Obedience Law) for responsibility in these two assassinations. The Uruguayan government refused to detain or extradite any of the Uruguayans, and later that year the army gave an honorary decoration to Silveira. Campos Hermida died in November 2001.

The Letelier-Moffitt Assassinations: The Operatives

The Letelier-Moffitt case reflected key aspects of Condor as a supranational parallel structure. Condor united not only anticommunist states but also extremist and fascist organizations in a global anticommunist crusade; moreover, this case, like others, also revealed a web of murky links between Condor and the CIA. Orlando Letelier, former foreign minister under Allende, had been imprisoned by the Chilean military shortly after the 1973 coup, but eventually was released. He came to Washington, D.C., where he worked with the leftist Institute for Policy Studies and became an important international voice for the recovery of democracy in Chile. According to a declassified CIA document, the agency was quite concerned about Letelier's activities in Washington: "Letelier, who is a lecturer at American University, has been quite vocal in his criticism of United States, and especially Agency, involvement in events leading up to the coup . . . [he has] charged that Secretary Kissinger lied to him concerning the role the U.S. was playing in Chile at that time."[61] This CIA memo decried Letelier's appearance on a television panel in which he accused the Chilean military of instituting a reign of terror, and noted that "the results of this criticism has [*sic*] been widespread negative publicity for the U.S. government which resulted in further anti-Agency propaganda" in the United States and abroad. The language implied that the CIA considered Letelier a threat to

U.S. national security interests—and to the CIA itself—and that it feared the impact of his activities in mobilizing opposition to the Chilean regime.

The assassinations of Orlando Letelier and his coworker Ronni Moffitt, which took place on September 21, 1976, occurred in an environment of public skepticism about the foreign and domestic policies of the U.S. government. Young people in the United States had been galvanized by the war in Vietnam to protest U.S. intervention in Asia, Latin America, and Africa. Watergate had recently occurred, with its revelations of the unconstitutional measures used by Nixon and his men. The Church and Pike commissions had uncovered international CIA assassination plots targeting foreign leaders, including René Schneider of Chile and Fidel Castro of Cuba.[62] The Senate committee had recently released its report on CIA attempts to prevent the assumption of, and then destabilize, the Allende government in Chile.

Michael Townley eventually gave a detailed account of the planning and execution of the Letelier-Moffitt assassinations in a U.S. court.[63] It was a striking act of international terrorism, yet the official U.S. reaction seemed strangely ambivalent. The CIA and State Department failed to share key information with prosecutors, delaying the investigation, and the CIA promoted the thesis that the left was responsible for the assassinations. Two U.S. administrations (Nixon and Ford) were reluctant to challenge the Chilean junta's refusal to cooperate with the investigation. Washington requested the extradition of the DINA officers indicted (Manuel Contreras, Pedro Espinoza, and Armando Fernández Larios) in 1978, two years later.

The Chilean dictatorship never agreed to the extraditions and continued to protest its innocence, blaming the CIA for the crime. Contreras was promoted to general and remained a powerful figure (although he was removed from DINA, which changed its name to Centro Nacional de Inteligencia, CNI). Espinoza and Fernández Larios remained on active duty in the army. In 1995, after the transition from military rule, the Chilean courts finally tried Contreras and Espinoza, found them guilty of masterminding the crime, and sentenced them to prison terms. Thousands of Chileans gathered outside the courthouse to demonstrate support for the verdicts.[64]

Townley was a U.S. citizen raised in Chile, where his father headed Ford Motor Company in Santiago. The younger Townley was a U.S. Embassy informant with close relations to embassy officials such as Fred Purdy, the consul involved in the Horman case in 1973.[65] Townley was also a militant in Patria y Libertad, the right-wing terrorist group funded by the CIA.[66] Embassy officials had extensive information about his deep involvement with the fascist group, including his role in the murder of a caretaker, in bombings, and in designing wiretapping devices. In fact, Patria y Libertad gave the U.S. Embassy tapes of some of Allende's intercepted conversations, made by equipment designed by Townley. Townley also gave U.S. officials intelligence information, such as the fact that Allende's death was not a suicide (as claimed by the junta) and that extreme-right Chileans had formed an assassination squad in 1973.[67]

Townley claimed in Chile that he was a CIA operative, and so did the defense attorney of the accused Cuban exiles in the Letelier/Moffitt assassination trial in the United States. In fact, Townley was interviewed by CIA recruiters in November 1970[68] and was judged to be "of operational interest as a possible [PHRASE EXCISED] of the Directorate of Operations in 1971."[69] The memo carefully stated, however, that the "Office of Security file does not reflect that Mr. Townley was ever actually used by the Agency." A separate affidavit stated that "in February 1971, the Directorate of Operations requested preliminary security approval to use Mr. Townley in an operational capacity."[70] A State Department report gave a later date, however: "Michael Townley approached the agency in 1973 [PHRASE EXCISED] but they told us the contact was never pursued."[71] It remains unclear whether Townley was a CIA agent, although most Latin American analysts assume that he was. Townley turned state's evidence in the assassination trial, informing on his erstwile co-conspirators; he served a short sentence, and entered the Witness Protection Program.

Chilean Armando Fernández Larios, who was also suspected of a role in the 1974 Prats murder, conducted surveillance of Letelier in Washington in preparation for the assassination. He had attended the U.S. Army School of the Americas (class of 1970). In Chile, Fernández was a member of the Caravan of Death, a military unit that, in October 1973, traveled through the northern countryside to brutally torture and execute political prisoners. Fernández Larios, in his mid-twenties at the time, was remembered by a number of witnesses as a particularly savage and sadistic torturer.[72] A Chilean army corporal also recalled him at Chile's National Stadium immediately after the coup. He said that Fernández Larios was one of the prominent executioners of political prisoners at the stadium and "a psychopath and the biggest murderer in Chile. In my regiment he took a soldier from my section and disfigured his face. He tortured him for a week."[73] Fernández Larios gave himself up to U.S. prosecutors in 1987.

The newly formed DINA recruited Townley in 1974 for his expertise in electronics, his record of violence in Patria y Libertad, his U.S. citizenship, and his links with extremist anti-Castro Cuban organizations in the United States; he played an important liaison function. DINA wanted to unite forces with right-wing Cubans, and several Cuban exile organizations sought to set up a government in exile in Santiago, supported and recognized by the Pinochet regime.[74] The Cuban exile organizations had grown out of a subversive network created by the CIA after the 1959 Cuban revolution, based in Miami (where a large CIA station called JM/Wave was set up at the University of Miami). The CIA-directed exiles carried out a secret war against Cuba, including an invasion by a parallel army at the Bay of Pigs in 1961 and, subsequently, an ongoing campaign of economic sabotage and terrorism on Cuban soil called Operation Mongoose. Many exile leaders had long records of service to the CIA.[75]

Townley made contact with right-wing Cuban organizations between 1970 and 1973. He met Guillermo Novo, founder of the extremist New Jersey–based Cuban Nationalist Movement (CNM), and José Dionisio Suárez, author of numerous terrorist acts, in 1974. Townley organized one meeting in Santiago that brought together Virgilio Paz, an anti-Castro Cuban from the CNM, and Martín Ciga Correa of the Argentine paramilitary Milicia, which reportedly had collaborated in the Prats assassination.[76] In 1975, Townley made contact with Italian fascist Stefano delle Chiaie in Santiago to discuss the assassination of Leighton in Rome, and DINA provided the Italians with an office and telex machine in Santiago.[77] In 1975, DINA ordered Townley to murder several Chilean exiles—including Altamirano and Teitelboim—during a human rights conference in Mexico. Townley traveled there from the United States with an assassination team that included his wife, also a DINA agent, and Virgilio Paz. They arrived too late.[78] He and Paz then traveled to Europe to develop the Condor network there and arrange the Leighton assassination.[79]

In Santiago, Townley had full-time use of a DINA car, use of DINA medical facilities, DINA-made false documents, and three full-time employees provided by DINA, a secretary, an aide, and a driver.[80] Townley made more than a dozen trips to Miami to buy electronics equipment for DINA. He utilized a U.S. enterprise linked to the CIA, Audio Intelligence Devices, that required security clearances for purchasing; Townley possessed authorization to buy equipment for the government of Chile.[81] Yet, later, Contreras insisted that Townley was not a DINA operative. Townley used many aliases to conduct his covert missions, including Kenneth Enyart, Andrés Wilson, Hans Petersen Silva, and Juan Williams Rose.

In July 1976, Pedro Espinoza, DINA operations chief and Condor commander, assigned Townley to coordinate the Letelier assassination and instructed him to recruit anti-Castro terrorists to carry out the actual murder. Espinoza also told Townley that DINA preferred that the assassination appear as a suicide or an accident.[82] He ordered Townley and Fernández Larios to go to Asunción to obtain false Paraguayan passports and then to seek U.S. visas at the U.S. Embassy in Paraguay. DINA chief Contreras sent a message through the Condor channel to Conrado Pappalardo, the right-hand man of dictator Stroessner, saying that the two had CIA approval for a secret mission in the United States and that they had an appointment with General Vernon Walters, deputy director of the CIA. This was the explanation that Pappalardo gave Ambassador George Landau. The plan fit the profile of a Condor operation, as outlined in the founding document of the system, providing plausible deniability to the perpetrators of the covert operation.

On arrival in Asunción in July, Townley and Fernández communicated with Colonel Benito Guanes,[83] chief of Paraguayan Military Intelligence, now known to be a Condor officer. U.S. ambassador Landau supplied the visas, but then became suspicious. He cabled Walters to obtain confirmation of the mission. Landau also made copies of the passports and photos as a precaution. Walters cabled back that he was retiring and that he knew of no such mission.[84] (Walters had traveled to Paraguay just two weeks before; he also had visited Asunción in 1975.[85]) Walters had discussed Landau's secret cable with CIA director George Bush; the cable also crossed the desk of Secretary of State Henry Kissinger.[86] After the response from Washington, Landau revoked the two visas and demanded the return of the passports. Contreras recalled Townley and Fernández Larios to Santiago, but sent two other agents to Washington to act as decoys, using the same false names that the first two agents had used. These two decoy agents spent time at the Chilean Embassy, where General Nilo Floody—another Condor officer—was military attaché. In fact, Floody called Vernon Walters to obtain an appointment for the two with the CIA, thereby alerting the CIA that the two officers were in the United States.[87]

Thus, the CIA received two signals that DINA agents were involved in a covert mission in Washington, D.C.: from Landau in Paraguay, and from the Chilean Embassy in Washington. It stands to reason that given the friendly relations between the two intelligence services, it would have been standard practice for the CIA to check with DINA about its claim to have a meeting scheduled with Vernon Walters. The CIA also knew very well that Operation Condor was functional and that it had already exercised its assassination capability. Yet the CIA did not take any steps to warn Letelier of the presence of DINA agents in Washington nor interfere with the operation. Nor did it inform law enforcement about its prior knowledge after the double assassination took place.

Soon afterward, Fernández Larios and Townley traveled on false Chilean passports, with valid U.S. visas obtained in Santiago, to Washington. Fernández Larios arrived in August 1976 and conducted surveillance of Letelier to develop intelligence on his normal routines. He left as Townley arrived on September 9, passing him the surveillance reports in Kennedy Airport. Townley contacted Virgilio Paz and asked him to set up a meeting with CNM chief Guillermo Novo in New Jersey. Through Novo, Townley recruited other operatives from the CNM to assist him in the assassination. Three of the five had

CIA training and had been involved in the Bay of Pigs operation.[88] They monitored Letelier, bought explosives, built a bomb, and placed it under his car. Townley left Washington before the crime took place, a cautionary measure. He flew to Miami, where he held discussions with CNM leaders about deepening relations with DINA. These relationships again illustrated the nature of Condor as a transnational parastatal apparatus incorporating anticommunist states and radical right-wing organizations.

The car bombing destroyed Letelier's legs, killing him rapidly; Ronni Moffitt drowned in her own blood. After the murders, the CIA promoted the theory that leftist forces had committed the crime to embarrass the Pinochet regime and that the Chilean junta was not involved.[89] The CIA did not inform federal prosecutors of the copies of the passport photos that Landau had made or of Landau's warning cable. As one of the prosecutors said in 1988, "Nothing the agency gave us helped us break this case."[90] The CIA did not inform the Justice Department or the FBI that Manuel Contreras was a CIA asset at the time (1974–1977) and that he had received an unspecified payment for his services. (In fact, Townley said in 1979 that Contreras had set up U.S. bank accounts years earlier to receive CIA payments.[91]) The explosive disclosure that Contreras had been a CIA asset was released by the CIA in a report to Congress in 2000,[92] raising more questions about why the agency had been unable to prevent an assassination that involved DINA, its Chilean partner. As experts on the case have suggested, the assassinations revealed either gross negligence by the CIA or the darker scenario of complicity.[93] The primary federal prosecutor in the case also pointed to "incompetence or willful concealment in the State Department," which delayed critical evidence about the DINA agents' activities in Washington for a year.[94] The result was that in September 1976, under the tenure of Secretary of State Kissinger and CIA director Bush, Operation Condor's transcontinental assassination program extended its reach to the United States.

The Cuban Connection

Shortly after the assassinations, a CIA agent in Caracas, Venezuela, reported that Orlando Bosch, a ferociously anti-Castro Cuban who was imprisoned there, had said that the Novo brothers had a hand in the crime.[95] Bosch had fled the United States in 1974, in violation of his parole for a terrorist attack against a Cuban target in the United States, and settled in Santiago, Chile. He was there as DINA, and Condor, were in their formative stages. In 1976, he was held in Caracas for the terrorist bombing of a Cubana passenger jet on October 6 (all seventy-three on board died). Bosch said in a 1977 interview that he had planned numerous terrorist acts from safe havens in Chile and, later, Venezuela.[96] Bosch was the leader of a coalition of violent anti-Castro organizations named CORU, Coordination of United Revolutionary Organizations. CORU was formed during a 1976 meeting in Bonao, Dominican Republic, that brought together all the paramilitary and terrorist anti-Castro organizations. There, leaders decided to unify their forces under one umbrella. Interestingly, that meeting took place in June, at the same time as the Condor meeting in Santiago. According to several sources, the CIA had actively approved of the Bonao meeting—and perhaps even instigated it—and encouraged CORU to "punish" Castro for Cuban intervention in Angola.[97] The FBI was fully aware of CORU's terrorist acts.[98] CORU carried out dozens of bombings in the Western hemisphere (including the United States) in 1976. All five of the Cuban terrorists involved in the Letelier-Moffitt assassinations were CORU members.

DINA chief Contreras, who insisted that the CIA was responsible for the assassination of Letelier, argued that the CIA had organized the Bonao meeting and that Townley, as a CIA agent, had participated. Contreras also said that the decision was made there to assassinate Letelier.[99] While Contreras's word is clearly suspect, other sources gave conflicting accounts to federal prosecutor Eugene Propper about whether a "death sentence" against Letelier had been discussed at the terrorist summit. But one high-ranking officer in DISIP, Dirección de Servicios de Inteligencia y Prevención (Directorate of Intelligence and Prevention Services), the Venezuelan secret intelligence service (a Cuban who was also a CIA agent and FBI informant), did confirm it.[100] (DISIP's top levels were filled by Cuban exiles with links to the CIA at that time.[101]) Clearly, the Bonao meeting is a crucial piece of evidence since the CIA had informants in the meeting. FBI agents told reporters in 1989 that Letelier was, in fact, targeted for assassination at this meeting[102]—which implies that the CIA knew of the assassination plans months in advance.

It was never proven that Townley was at the terrorist summit, though, and the Chilean court rejected Contreras's argument during his trial (with Espinoza) for the Letelier-Moffitt assassinations in the 1990s.[103] In 1991, Contreras sought to obtain testimony from George Bush, Sr., and former Venezuelan president Carlos Andrés Pérez to corroborate his claim that Letelier's death had been planned in June 1976, but the Chilean judge refused to grant his request.[104]

Significant links existed between Cuban exile organizations and Condor. In 1974, DINA had sought to open a Condor headquarters in Miami in order to combine forces with Cuban anti-Castro organizations, as shown previously. In March 1975, a group of Cuban exiles traveled to Santiago and met with Pinochet himself, seeking recognition as a government in exile. Pinochet demurred but promised to assist the Cubans with arms and funds if they combined forces. Pinochet also said he would approach his military counterparts in Uruguay and Paraguay to encourage their support for the Cuban exiles.[105] The Bonao meeting did unify the Cuban terrorist organizations, as Pinochet had directed. Cuban exiles also carried out assassination operations for DINA. Virgilio Paz collaborated with Townley, as we have seen, and CORU leader Bosch was held for two months in Costa Rica (and then deported) for conspiracy to murder Pascal Allende, nephew of the slain president of Chile and a Condor Phase III target.[106] Some sources reported that Bosch had planned to murder Henry Kissinger at that time (1976), but authorities in Costa Rica said that Allende was Bosch's real target.

Bosch and another anti-Castro Cuban, Luis Posada Carriles, were detained in Venezuela for suspected involvement in the 1976 Cubana airliner bombing. A group identifying itself as "El Cóndor" had claimed responsibility.[107] Posada Carriles, also known as "Basilio" or "Bambi," had long been affilated with the CIA. He and Bosch had been trained by the CIA for the Bay of Pigs operation, and Posada reportedly had functioned in a top-secret CIA assassination unit, code named ZR/RIFLE, in the early 1960s.[108] He later became operations chief of Venezuelan intelligency agency DISIP. Fidel Castro blamed the CIA for the Cubana bombing and renounced an antihijacking agreement he had forged with Washington. The U.S. government was forced to deny that the CIA was involved in the bombing.[109] Posada Carriles served prison time in Venezuela for the Cubana bombing. Later, in the 1980s, he worked again on behalf of the CIA in Central America, helping to coordinate the contra supply network.[110] The extremist anti-Castro Cuban networks served at various times as key resources for CIA-sponsored covert operations and parallel armies, as well as for Condor operations.

The Cuban exile community was also involved in drug trafficking. Space precludes an extensive review of this evidence, but several exiles spoke openly of this involvement during congressional investigations in the mid-1980s. Ramón Milian Rodríguez, a drug money launderer closely associated with Bay of Pigs veteran Manuel Artime, told a subcommittee that his first assignment was to deliver money to the Cuban exiles who had carried out the Watergate burglary.[111] He testified that by the 1970s many former and current covert warriors in the exile community had turned to drug smuggling.[112] Proceeds from the drug trade were used to shore up various anti-Castro covert operations and, later, the contra counterrevolution in Nicaragua.[113] CORU was deeply involved in drug trafficking in the 1970s, and forged close ties not only with DINA and the Argentine death squads but also with the "cocaine lords" who staged a coup, with Bolivian and Argentine military backing, in Bolivia in 1980.[114] The Cuban Nationalist Movement obtained much of its income from extortion and drug trafficking, and Virgilio Paz and José Suárez were linked to Colombian drug cartels. When Alvin Ross was arrested in 1978 in connection with the Letelier case, he was carrying a large bag of cocaine.[115] Such operations by the exile community were often protected by the CIA for "national security" reasons.[116] Drug trafficking may have played a role in financing covert Condor operations.

Evolution of the Assassination Case

In 1978, Chilean officers identified a photo of Townley, leading to a breakthrough in the case. In that year, Chile agreed to expel Townley to stand trial in the United States. Townley told federal prosecutors that issuance of the Paraguayan passports to Chilean agents occurred within the rubric of Operation Condor, as did Paraguayan colonel Guanes.[117] Worried that Contreras would "attempt to drag the Agency into the case," CIA officials met with prosecutors in August 1978 to agree on what information could be made public. Prosecutor Eugene Propper said he had three areas of concern: "Contreras' relationship with [EXCISED], the issuance of U.S. visas for Paraguayan passports . . . and the relationship of 'Condor' to the case."[118] The prosecutors wanted to question the Cuban terrorist Bosch, but the State Department declined to pursue him. In 1976, Kissinger had requested his deportation, not extradition, from Venezuela (on grounds of Bosch's violation of U.S. parole for previous crimes).[119] In 1978, the secretary of state under Carter, Cyrus Vance, decided again not to extradite Bosch.[120] In fact, Washington had refused to take back Bosch on several previous occasions despite the fact that he was still, technically, a wanted man.[121]

In 1978, the grand jury in the Letelier-Moffitt case indicted Chileans Contreras, Espinoza, and Fernández Larios, and Cubans Guillermo Novo, Ignacio Novo, Alvin Ross, Virgilio Paz, and José Dionisio Suárez, with murder and conspiracy to murder. Townley was an unindicted coconspirator. As part of the plea bargain worked out with prosecutors, Townley was required to testify only on matters narrowly related to the Letelier assassination. His knowledge of the Condor apparatus—its structures and operations, its links with global anticommunist movements and governments (including the U.S. government), and its ongoing crimes, committed in the name of anticommunism—was off limits, protected from public scrutiny and criminal investigation.

In 1978, a jury found the assassination team guilty. Michael Townley pleaded guilty to one count of conspiracy to murder and was given a sentence of three to ten years for his role. He served the minimum, three years and four months. Alvin Ross and Guillermo Novo received two consecutive life sentences for conspiracy and murder, and Ignacio Novo received eight years in prison for perjury and covering up the crime. Their sentences were overturned on appeal, however, on technical grounds. U.S. prosecutors retried both Guillermo Novo and Alvin Ross in early 1981 and they were acquitted of the murder charges. The Letelier and Moffitt families brought a civil suit against the assassination squad members, which they won by default (the defendants refused to appear in court). The Chilean junta claimed sovereign immunity.[122] In 1980, the court entered a judgment in favor of the families and awarded them damages of $5 million, holding the Cubans and the government of Chile liable. No award was ever paid.

In 1987, Fernández Larios left Chilean army intelligence and came to the United States to make a deal with the Justice Department. He provided corroborating information to implicate Contreras and Espinoza in the Letelier/Moffitt assassinations and arranged to plead guilty as an accessory to murder. He served seven months in prison for his role in the Condor assassination. After he was freed, Fernández Larios received permission to live and work in the United States, a special Immigration and Naturalization Service (INS) status, although he denied that he entered the Witness Protection Program.[123] In 1999, he was sued by the family of a victim of the Caravan of Death, who charged that Fernández had inflicted tortures, cruel and inhuman punishments, and wrongful death on Winston Cabello, a Chilean economist, in 1973.[124] In a civil trial in a Miami courtroom in October 2003, a jury found him liable for crimes against humanity, extrajudicial killing, torture, and cruel, inhumane, and degrading treatment of Cabello.[125]

In 1990, both Ross and Novo were associated with the Cuban-American National Foundation, the powerful anti-Castro lobbying group in Miami.[126] Suárez and Paz were fugitives for years, managing to elude authorities until 1990 and 1991, respectively. Paz served seven years in prison and then remained in the custody of the INS. He was released in August 2001. Suárez served eight years for his role and four additional years in INS custody. Released a day after Paz in 2001, Suárez said he might write a book because "[t]here have been many lies."[127] Guillermo Novo and Luis Posada Carriles were arrested in Panama in 2000 for a plot to assassinate Fidel Castro during his presence at the Ibero-American Summit. They were found guilty for crimes against public security in 2004—and were promptly pardoned by the outgoing Panamanian president.

Analyzing the Assassinations of Letelier and Moffitt

The assassinations were an enormous intelligence-counterintelligence failure, at the very least, for the U.S. government. Despite warnings and clues that a

Condor operation was planned for Washington, D.C., and knowledge of the Condor network's previous operations, the CIA and the State Department did not react to the DINA presence in Washington. Part of the explanation, clearly, is that DINA was considered a CIA partner in the anticommunist crusade. After the assassinations, the CIA leaked information to the news media that the assassinations were the work of the left, not the Chilean junta. The CIA and State Department did not give the photos of the DINA agents to FBI investigators or federal prosecutors, nor tell them of the Paraguayan connection. Additionally, Dinges and Landau documented five cases of withholding, destruction, or concealment of key evidence. For example, INS forms documenting entry into the United States of three members of the assassination squad were removed from INS computers, and "someone with access to United States citizen registration files in the U.S. Consulate in Santiago removed the photograph of Michael Townley on file there."[128] In fact, according to federal prosecutor Propper, Townley removed it himself.[129] How could Townley have access to such sensitive files in the U.S. Consulate? Townley's close relationship with Fred Purdy, the consul, may have played a role. The difficulty in identifying the perpetrators threw the investigation off track for at least a year.

As the Letelier case made headlines in 1978, revealing the outlines of Operation Condor, the Chilean ambassador to Washington made a significant comment to a reporter from the *Washington Star*. A CIA memorandum of the conversation the same day noted that the reporter had just interviewed the Chilean ambassador on the Letelier case and, to draw him out, had listed the states that were members of Condor. The ambassador corrected the reporter, declaring that there was another member of Condor: the United States. When pressed for evidence, the ambassador cited CIA deputy director Vernon Walters's recent trip to Asunción, Paraguay, but refused to say more.

Within the CIA the interchange clearly caused concern, as did the prosecutor's confirmation to the journalist that Walters had, in fact, visited Asunción two weeks before the passports episode.[130] Just two days later, Paraguayan Condor commander Alejandro Fretes Dávalos approached Ambassador Robert White in Asunción to tell him about Condor's link to the U.S. telecommunications system in Panama. The timing of the message suggests that it was meant to send a warning: that Washington should keep Condor hidden from view, and protect its members, or risk having U.S. involvement in the terrorist system exposed. Manuel Contreras had sent a similar threat via an emissary the previous August, as prosecutors prepared to charge him in the assassinations case. Contreras's emissary requested appointments with the departments of Justice, State, and the CIA in order to "negotiate" a settlement of the case. A declassified document noted that the message contained "a blackmail hint": Contreras had implied that "in defending himself, [Contreras] would have to reveal details [TWO LINES EXCISED]. It would not be in his, Chile's, the USG's, or the other countries' interest to have this information become public knowledge, but he regretfully would have no choice."[131] It seems clear that Contreras was threatening to expose Condor and U.S. involvement in the system if his prosecution proceeded.

What was the CIA's role in this assassination case? The evidence might be interpreted in several ways. First, the crime might have succeeded due to gross incompetence by U.S. agencies charged with counterintelligence and terrorist lookouts. This view seems quite unlikely, given CIA knowledge of Operation Condor and the information provided by Landau in Paraguay. A second possibility, put forward by Dinges and Landau, is that DINA tried to implicate the CIA in the operation and then waited for a sign that the CIA wanted it called off. The sign never came.[132] This version offers one explanation for the withholding of evidence and the release of information to the media blaming the left for the crime. A third possibility is that U.S. policymakers and intelligence officials protected and covered up the Condor operation rather than have U.S. involvement in Condor revealed by their Latin American counterparts. The darkest hypothesis is that top officials knew of the assassination plans but expressed no opposition. The evidence that the Cubans targeted Letelier for death at the Bonao meeting—which was penetrated by the CIA—supports this view.

Dinges and Landau showed that during the trial the United States protected the Pinochet regime from culpability. The crime was portrayed as originating with Contreras and not as an act of state ordered by Pinochet, head of the Chilean dictatorship.[133] That admission would have called into question U.S. support for its anticommunist ally and for the secret police of other Latin American national security states. Additionally, the role of Operation Condor, and its assassination capability, were protected from scrutiny. These elements substantiate the argument that U.S. national security and intelligence interests—including the U.S. relationship to the Condor system—ranked higher than concerns for human rights or justice in the upper policymaking levels of the government. Without further investigation, or the testimonies of knowledgeable participants, key questions about this case may remain unresolved.

Phase III Plots that Were Foiled

There were several cases in which U.S. officials warned individuals that they were in danger from Condor, although at times they were not aware of the code name. In 1975, for example, the FBI warned two prominent Chileans of death threats: Radomiro Tomic, a former ambassador to the United States, and Gabriel Valdés, a high-ranking UN official. Both left the United States and experienced no attacks.[134]

In 1977, the political counselor in the U.S. Embassy in Uruguay, John Youle, protected Brazilian Labor Party leader Leonel Brizola, then in exile in Uruguay. The Carter administration (1977–81) had rotated the top embassy personnel in Montevideo. Lawrence Pezzullo had replaced Siracusa as ambassador, and the CIA station chief, deputy chief of mission, and political counselor were also replaced. The embassy began to play a completely different role, protecting leaders of the three major political parties, unionists, and others under threat. When the Brazilian military president scheduled a visit to Uruguay, the military told its Uruguayan counterparts to hand Brizola over to them. It was a Condor operation, although at the time Youle did not know the code name; he believed it was a Brazilian intelligence operation.[135] Brizola was ordered to report to Uruguayan military authorities, but two foreign embassies warned him that there was a coordinated plot to kill progressive leaders in the region. He began to search for an embassy that would provide him asylum. Many were surrounded by Uruguayan troops; others avoided lending protection to the fiery Brazilian leader.

Brizola finally went to the U.S. Embassy and Youle held a lengthy conversation with him. The diplomat agreed to provide a transit visa so that Brizola could leave Uruguay and go to Portugal through the United States. Although the State Department's ARA (American Republics Area), led by Terence Todman, was not happy about assisting Brizola (or about Carter's human rights policy in general), Youle did eventually obtain the visa. The State Department did not approve Youle's request to accompany Brizola to the airport, however. To protect Brizola, Youle organized a press caravan of five or six cars carrying journalists, which followed Brizola to the airport. Senator Edward Kennedy met with Brizola during his stopover in New York, and the State Department's attitude changed due to Kennedy's support. Brizola was allowed to stay in the United States for six months. Relations between the embassy in Montevideo and the Uruguayan military authorities were tense. Embassy personnel received death threats and their phone conversations were interrupted by voices threatening them, clearly from the intelligence apparatus.

Youle experienced brutal retribution for his role in preventing a probable Phase III assassination. As he walked to the embassy shortly after Brizola left Uruguay, following his normal routine, he was forced into a car full of men wearing ski masks. These men, whom he and his colleagues later presumed to be a military intelligence unit, took him to a secluded spot and beat him, smashing all the vertebrae in his neck and upper back. Youle's injuries—aimed to "send a message," according to the diplomat—took four years of treatment to heal and resulted in permanent nerve and muscle damage. Youle, too generously, did not believe the men meant to do him serious harm, saying that "they got carried away." The U.S. Embassy protested, but the Uruguayan regime denied a role, blaming criminals for the incident.[136] In 2000, Brizola said that he believed that two former Brazilian presidents, João Goulart, his brother-in-law, and Jucelino Kubitschek, had been Condor victims and that he had narrowly escaped Condor's clutches.[137]

Edward Koch, former congressman and mayor of New York, was also the target of a Condor threat. Koch's 1976 amendment to suspend military aid to the Uruguayan regime infuriated the military. The minister of defense warned U.S. officials that if it became law it "would intensify cooperation of political, economic, and anti-subversive matters among countries of the Southern Cone," and another high-ranking official called it "gross intervention in Uruguayan internal affairs."[138] Shortly after the amendment passed, Koch received a call from George Bush, director of the CIA. The two knew each other and had served together in Congress. After an exchange of pleasantries, Bush told Koch that his agents had learned that the Chilean DINA had a contract out on his life. Koch was alarmed and asked for protection. Bush replied that the CIA could not provide protection in the United States. Koch argued that as a member of Congress he was entitled to protection. Bush again said he could not provide it and added, "Just be very careful."[139] The Letelier-Moffitt assassinations had just occurred, but at the time Koch was unaware of Operation Condor.

At around the same time, Koch received an invitation from Ernest Siracusa, U.S. ambassador in Uruguay, to visit the country. Koch decided to decline the invitation after consulting with his staff; it seemed too dangerous. Siracusa later said that he was unaware of the death threat, a claim that Koch thought was hard to believe.[140]

According to several investigators, the two military men who made the threat were Uruguayans José Fons—who had signed Condor's founding act—and José Gavazzo, OCOA commander. DINA was apparently working with the Uruguayans, using the methods of Condor to conceal and deceive. These two officers were named at that time to become delegate to the Inter-American Defense Board in Washington and military attaché in the United States, respectively. These postings suggested, again, that Condor operated within the structures of the inter-American system, using such positions as a vehicle for Condor coordination. The U.S. government vetoed the naming of these two operatives.[141]

In the 1990s, new questions arose about whether DINA was involved in other deaths, including that of former Chilean president Eduardo Frei (1964–70). He had died of a stomach infection and heart failure while in a clinic after minor surgery in 1981. The Christian Democrat had opposed Allende and supported the coup initially, but he gradually became an opponent of Pinochet's national security state. Family members feared that a biological agent was covertly injected into Frei while he was in the clinic.[142] In 1989, when the transition to democracy was beginning in Chile, former DINA members (then in the CNI) planned to assassinate Patricio Aylwin, a presidential candidate in the upcoming election. The chief of the CNI, who headed the plot, planned to blame the left and derail the transition. The assassins considered chemical means to kill Aylwin as well as firearms, the CIA learned. Apparently, the CIA never informed Aylwin of the plot; it was discovered in the State Department's document declassification of 2000. The CIA also had information that the murders of several other prominent Chileans in the early 1990s, including right-wing senator Jaime Guzmán, may have been carried out not by a leftist guerrilla group as charged at the time, but by former DINA agents who had infiltrated the group and were acting under orders from Contreras.[143] Guzmán's murder occurred just as the report of the Truth and Reconciliation Commission was released, diminishing its impact and reawakening fear in Chilean society.

In 1976, a perceptive British journalist wrote: "The assassinations of leading Latin American officers and politicians in the last three years have become so numerous that there is a growing feeling amongst observers of the continent's politics that something akin to Operation Phoenix is now underway."[144] Within the framework of Operation Condor, a right-wing offensive was launched to destroy all perceived threats to the military regimes and their counterrevolutionary project, targeting communists, socialists, Christian Democrats, and members of other political parties. Condor's Phase III operations showed that the anticommunist crusade was an onslaught against the principles and institutions of democracy, and against progressive and liberal as well as revolutionary figures in Latin America and elsewhere.

The assassinations discussed in this chapter revealed the modus operandi of Condor: the deadly determination of the Condor militaries to eliminate their political opponents; the recruitment of parallel groups of "special agents" led by military commanders in a shadow Condor command structure; the impunity with which the squadrons operated; the methods used to obscure the identities of Condor operatives beneath multiple layers of disinformation, deception, and deceit. These cases also uncovered murky links with the CIA, although, typically, direct involvement was difficult to substantiate. The tradecraft of the CIA, under the doctrine of plausible deniability, is to deliberately stay in the shadows, using "assets" and agents from third countries to convey messages and undertake action; sometimes those assets are not even aware that they are acting on behalf, or in the interest, of the CIA.[145]

The Condor militaries combined forces with fascist networks, Cuban exile terrorists, and other extremist groups worldwide to carry out their objectives, disguise their role, and forge a global counterrevolutionary movement. In many cases, successive U.S. administrations lent political, military, and technological support to these forces in the name of anticommunism. The cost was a whole generation of socially conscious Latin American political leaders.

Notes

1. Juan Gasparini, *La pista suiza* (Buenos Aires: Editorial Legasa, 1986), 258; U.S. Congress, Sánchez Reisse testimony to Subcommittee on Terrorism, Narcotics and International Operations, under Senate Committee on Foreign Relations, July 23, 1987, 8–9, 106, cited in Ariel Armony, *Argentina, the United States, and the Anti-Communist Crusade in Central America, 1977–1984* (Athens: Center for International Studies, Ohio University, 1997), 150.
2. Author interviews, Montevideo, August 2001.
3. Samuel Blixen, *Seregni: La mañana siguiente* (Montevideo: Ediciones de Brecha, 1997), 58, 93, 100, 102, 108, 115.
4. Martín Sivak, *El asesinato de Juan José Torres: Banzer y el mercosur de la muerte* (Buenos Aires: Ediciones del Pensamiento Nacional, 1998), 154.
5. Sivak, *El asesinato*, 135–140.
6. Sivak, *El asesinato*, 150.
7. Sivak, *El asesinato*, 148–149, 151.
8. CIA report, To File, From CIA, title blacked out, dated August 20, 1974.
9. Sergio Sorin, "Conspiración para matar," February 4, 1999, Equipo Nizkor site at www.derechos.org/sorin/ doc/p2.html.
10. Taylor Branch and Eugene M. Propper, *Labyrinth* (New York: Viking Press, 1982), 323–325.
11. Senate Foreign Relations Committee Report cited in Stella Calloni, "The Horror Archives of Operation Condor," *Covert Action Bulletin*, no. 50 (Fall 1994): 57; see also Sorin, "Conspiración para matar." Sorin says Altamirano was warned by an unnamed intelligence service.
12. Author interview with Edward Koch, New York, July 3, 2003; see also Ana Laura Lissardy, "El Plan Cóndor en la mira," *El Observador* (Uruguay), September 29, 2001. Koch wrote about this incident in his 1992 book *Citizen Koch*.
13. To SECSTATE, From AMEMBASSY Buenos Aires, "Abduction and murder of Uruguayan refugees Michelini and Gutiérrez; Status of Ferreira," May 25, 1976.
14. The letter was published in *La Opinión* on May 25, 1976.
15. To SecState, From AMEMBASSY Buenos Aires, "Possible International Implications of Violent Deaths of Political Figures Abroad [IMMEDIATE]," June 7, 1976, 1.
16. "Possible International Implications," 2–5; documents from 1975 also showed that the embassy (and Kissinger) were fully aware of joint Chile-Argentine operations in the matter of the missing 119 Chileans.

17. Judicial Proceeding, "Denuncia hechos. Promueve la reapertura del proceso," n.d. on my copy (probably 1976); see also *La Opinión* (Argentina), May 25, 1976, 8; both obtained by author in SERPAJ files, Montevideo, August 2001. Regarding the typewriter, see Samuel Blixen, "Zelmar y el," *Brecha* (Uruguay), April 16, 2004.

18. Letter from Wilson Ferreira to Jorge Rafael Videla, n.d. (but June 1976), 2, from State Department declassification; my account draws largely from this source. See also "Documentos para entender qué pasó," *Posdata* (Uruguay), May 17, 1996, 92–93.

19. Judicial Proceeding, 7; Telegram To SECSTATE, from AMEMBASSY Buenos Aires, "Ferreira Leaves Argentina for Paris," June 2, 1976.

20. Letter from Wilson Ferreira to Jorge Rafael Videla, n.d. (but June 1976), 9, from State Department declassification.

21. To RUEHC/SECSTATE, From AMEMBASSY Montevideo, "Murders of Michelini et al.," June 1, 1976; and To RUEHC/SECSTATE, From AMEMBASSY Montevideo, "Refugees in Argentina," June 7, 1976.

22. The Tupamaros were known in their early years for spectacular prison escapes, propaganda feats, bank robberies, and exposure of corruption in high places, all of which gave them a Robin Hood image and generated considerable sympathy among Uruguayans. After their kidnapping and execution of Dan Mitrione, whom they accused of training the Uruguayan police in torture techniques, public sympathy began to decline. Their use of violence was not wanton or indiscriminate, however, nor directed against ordinary civilians. Some murders and bombings attributed to the Tupamaros were actually carried out by military and police personnel. James Cockcroft, *Latin America*, 2nd ed. (Chicago: Nelson-Hall, 1996), 617; Martin Weinstein, *Uruguay: Democracy at the Crossroads* (Boulder, Colo.: Westview, 1988), 38–42. For a sympathetic early portrait by an Argentine journalist, see María Esther Gilio, *The Tupamaro Guerrillas: The Structure and Strategy of the Urban Guerrilla Movement* (New York: Saturday Review Press, 1972).

23. To AMEMBASSY, Montevideo, from SECSTATE, "Ferreira Testimony before House Subcommittee on International Organizations," June 22, 1976.

24. "Ferreira testimony," 1.

25. "Ferreira testimony," 2.

26. To RUEHC/SECSTATE, From AMEMBASSY Montevideo, "Irresponsible charges by Wilson Ferreira," June 19, 1976, 1.

27. Cable from Siracusa, 2. Actually, several Latin American sources assume that he was a CIA officer with diplomatic credentials, a conclusion I was not able to confirm or deny. See, for example, Gerardo Irusta Medrano, *Espionaje y servicios secretos en Bolivia y el Cono Sur: Nazis en la Operación Cóndor*, 2nd ed. (La Paz, 1997), 542–544; Stella Calloni, *Los años del lobo: Operación Cóndor*, 2nd ed. (Buenos Aires: Peña Lillo, Ediciones Continente, 1999), 93. The populist Velasco regime in Peru had declared Siracusa and another U.S. diplomat, Frank Ortiz, "personas non grata" in 1970 for secretly wiretapping government officials, and expelled them from that country. Siracusa was then named ambassador to Bolivia, and, during his tenure there, Torres was overthrown.

28. To RUEHC/SECSTATE, From AMEMBASSY Montevideo, "Clarification of Statement regarding Zelmar Michelini," July 21, 1976.

29. Samuel Blixen, "Una votación dividida en la cúpula de la dictadura," *Brecha*, no. 859, May 2002.

30. Samuel Blixen, "Cordero torturaba en Argentina," *Brecha*, no. 827, June 2001.

31. Rodríguez Larreta testimony before the Comisión Investigadora sobre Personas Desaparecidas (Uruguay), 1985, 7, obtained by author in SERPAJ files, Montevideo, August 2001; "Documentos para entender qué pasó," *Posdata* (Uruguay), May 17, 1996, 92–93.

32. Edison Lanza, "Testigo clave decidió romper el silencio," *El Observador* (Uruguay), May 21, 1996; see also Samuel Blixen, "Dealing with past impunity," *Latinamerica Press* (Peru), Vol. 28, no. 21 (June 6, 1996); "Documentos," *Posdata*, 93–95.

33. Author e-mail exchange with Senator Rafael Michelini, a son of Zelmar, August 16, 2003. See also Samuel Blixen, *Brecha* (Uruguay), May 17, 2002, 6–7; "El magnicidio de Zelmar y el Toba se decidió en el Cosena, por 4 votos a 2," *La República* (Uruguay), May 20, 2002.

34. Titina Núñez, "Nunca hubo reuniones para decidir la muerte de nadie," *Brecha*, no. 859, May 2002.

35. Samuel Blixen, "Una votación dividida en la cúpula de la dictadura," *Brecha*, no. 859, May 2002, and Samuel Blixen, "20 de Mayo: Los asesinatos de Michelini y Gutiérrez Ruiz," reproduced from *Brecha* at www.medh.org.ar/osv31.html; Eduardo Delgado and Roger Rodríguez, "Fué desarchivada la causa judicial por los asesinatos de Michelini y Gutiérrez Ruiz," *La República* (Uruguay), November 7, 2002. For the citation of Ruffo's testimony, see Samuel Blixen, "Colorados con los pelos de punta," *Brecha*, January 30, 2004.

36. Miguel Bonasso, "La sombra del cóndor," *Página/12* (Argentina), August 5, 2001; "Documento de hace 20 años revela cómo prepararon el crimen de Zelmar y el Toba," *La República*, August 5, 2001. Manuel Flores Silva, director of *Posdata* (Uruguay), also had obtained the document in early 2001. He asked in March of that year for the collaboration of this author in ascertaining the authenticity of the facts of the document.

37. "Michelini: 'Me sorprende la cantidad de detalles sobre la rutina de mi padre,'" *La República*, August 6, 2001; see also Miguel Bonasso, "La sombra del cóndor." The senator also expressed this view to me in an interview on August 2, 2001, in Montevideo, and in e-mail exchanges with the author in August 2003.

38. Author e-mail exchange with Senator Rafael Michelini, August 5, 2003.

39. Silvera testimony, 1, obtained by author from Manuel Flores Silva, March 2001.

40. Miguel Bonasso, "La sombra del cóndor;" Rodolfo Peregrino Fernández, *Autocrítica policial* (Buenos Aires: El Cid Editor, 1983), 47, 50–51, 66–67; see also report by Deputy Chief of Mission Maxwell Chaplin to Secretary of State, "Human Rights Situation in Argentina," August 27, 1976, 9.

41. Roger Rodríquez, "Ramírez es, pero no," manuscript e-mailed to me by Manuel Flores Silva of *Posdata* (Uruguay) in March 2002.

42. Author e-mail exchange with Rafael Michelini, August 6, 2003.

43. Author e-mail exchanges with Senator Rafael Michelini, August 4–6, 2003.

44. Author e-mail exchange with Rafael Michelini, August 6, 2003.

45. Miguel Bonasso, "La sombra del cóndor."

46. "Documento de hace 20 años revela cómo prepararon el crimen de Zelmar y el Toba," *La República*, August 5, 2001.

47. Jorge Elías, "Caso Zelmar Michelini: Montevideo esquina Buenos Aires Julio 2004," July 2004, at www.impunidad.com/cases/zelmar_michelini.htm.

48. Author interview with former State Department diplomat, Washington, D.C., July 20, 2003.

49. Author telephone interview with U.S. senior intelligence officer, August 16, 2003.

50. Author e-mail exchanges with Rafael Michelini, August 11 and 18, 2003.

51. "Campos Hermida y Castiglioni fueron entrenados en 'inteligencia' en EEUU," *La Hora* (Uruguay), December 30, 1986. For details confirming this CIA role in the IPA, see McClintock, *The American Connection*, 63.

52. Penny Lernoux, *Cry of the People* (New York: Doubleday, 1980), 339.

53. Testimony of former agent Nelson Bardesio in Belgium, cited in José Luis Baumgartner et al., "Desaparecidos" (Centro de Estudios de América Latina, n.d. on my copy), 205. Obtained by author in SERPAJ archives, Montevideo, August 2001. See also Peter Gribbin, "Brazil and CIA," *Counterspy* (April–May 1979): 8.

54. See documents at www.espectador.com/principal/graficos/documentos/aid2/aid2.htm. See also A. J. Languuth, *Hidden Terrors: The Truth about U.S. Police Operations in Latin America* (New York: Pantheon, 1978).

55. Testimony of Nelson Bardesio, in Baumgartner, "Desaparecidos," 205; Gribbin, "Brazil and CIA," 8.

56. Michael McClintock, *The American Connection*, Volume I, *State Terror and Popular Resistance in El Salvador* (London: Zed Books, 1985), 24.

57. Walter Pincus, "CIA Had Hit List of 58 Guatemalans in the 1950s," *Washington Post*, May 24, 1997; for a look at truly chilling declassified CIA documents, see National Security Archive, "The CIA and Assassinations: The 1954 Documents," Electronic Briefing Book no. 4.

58. The manual then provided detailed, unemotional instructions in how to plan assassinations and use various assassination techniques and weapons (it concluded with a diagram showing how to rapidly kill everyone in a room). CIA, "A Study of Assassination," at www.gwu.edu/~nsarchiv/NSAEBB/NSAEBB4/ciaguat2.html.

59. According to Philip Agee, "In most of Latin America, indeed in much of the Third World, the local security forces were penetrated and manipulated by the CIA—in some cases they were the very creatures of the Agency." When Agee was assigned to the Quito CIA station between 1960 and 1963, the chief of police intelligence and a number of government officials were on the CIA payroll. After helping foment a military coup in Ecuador, Agee was transferred to Uruguay in 1964. There, he said, "We pretty much ran the military and the police intelligence services." The involvement of the CIA remained deniable. Philip Agee, "Exposing the CIA," in Agee and Louis Wolf, eds., *Dirty Work: The CIA in Western Europe* (London: Zed Press, 1978), 40. Agee began to question his role after overhearing someone being tortured by the police. That person, it turned out, was an activist whom Agee had told the police to pick up. This example showed that Uruguayans were detained by order of the CIA. Interview with

Philip Agee in *Playboy*, August 1975, at www.connix.com/~harry/agee.htm (accessed by author June 2003).

60. Clifford Krause, "The Spies Who Never Came in from the Cold War," *New York Times*, March 7, 1999.

61. Heavily redacted CIA memo, To: Chief [excised], From: Chief [excised], "Subject: [excised] Letelier," March 6, 1975.

62. See, for example, Thomas Powers, "Inside the Department of Dirty Tricks," *Atlantic Monthly*, Vol. 244, no. 2 (August 1979): 33–64.

63. For detailed histories of this complex case, see Branch and Propper, *Labyrinth*; John Dinges and Saul Landau, *Assassination on Embassy Row* (New York: Pantheon Books, 1980); Donald Freed with Fred Landis, *Death in Washington: The Murder of Orlando Letelier* (Westport, Conn.: Lawrence Hill, 1980). This last book argues that Townley was a deep cover CIA operative. The book's limited use of sources is problematic, however.

64. See, for example, Calvin Sims, "Two in Chile Get Jail Terms in U.S. Killing," *New York Times*, May 31, 1995. The military had issued dark warnings of renewed violence and repression if the two were sentenced, but it never materialized.

65. Letter from David H. Stebbing, Second Secretary, U.S. Embassy in Quito, Ecuador, to Arnold Isaacs, Chief, Chilean Political Affairs, State Department, October 17, 1973, 3. Purdy was suspected to be a CIA officer in Thomas Hauser, *The Execution of Charles Horman* (New York: Harcourt, Brace, Jovanovich, 1978), 225.

66. Dinges and Landau, *Assassination*, 349, 382–389; Pamela Constable and Arturo Valenzuela, *A Nation of Enemies: Chile under Pinochet* (New York: W. W. Norton, 1991), 104; Saul Landau, "They Educated the Crows: An Institute Report on the Letelier-Moffitt Murders" (Washington, D.C.: Transnational Institute, 1978), 21.

67. Letter from Stebbing, 2, 3; see also To: SECSTATE, From: AMEMBASSY Santiago, "Letelier-Moffitt Case: Embassy File on Michael Vernon Townley," March 8, 1978.

68. CIA, memo dated March 1978, heading excised.

69. CIA, Security Analysis Group to C/SAF, March 6, 1978.

70. CIA General Counsel, affidavit by Robert W. Gambino, November 9, 1978.

71. State Department, Briefing Memorandum from ARA/Viron Vaky to Deputy Secretary, "Letelier/Moffitt Investigation,"August 15, 1978.

72. Patricia Verdugo, *Chile, Pinochet, and the Caravan of Death* (Coral Gables, Fla.: University of Miami, North-South Center Press, 2001), 134.

73. Douglas Grant Mine, "The Assassin Next Door, Part II," *Miami New Times* (October 12, 2000): 6.

74. Dinges and Landau, *Assassination*, 147–148, 264–265; Jesús Arboleya, *The Cuban Counterrevolution* (Athens: Ohio University Center for International Studies, 2000), 150, chapter 5; María Soledad de la Cerda and Beatriz Burgos, "Los nexos entre Pinochet y el exilio cubano," *La Tercera* (Chile), November 26, 2000.

75. For an excellent summary, see Arboleya, *The Cuban Counterrevolution*, chapter 4.

76. Extradition request for Chileans wanted in the Prats case in Argentina, Lawsuit brought by Argentine Judge María Servini de Cubría, March 21, 2001, 8, 10.

77. Dinges and Landau, *Assassination*, 159–160, 177.

78. Branch and Propper, *Labyrinth*, 241–247; Dinges and Landau, *Assassination*, 149–155, 352.

79. Servini extradition lawsuit, March 21, 2001, 7; Federal Bureau of Investigation, To: FBI, From: Washington D.C., "Attempted Assassination of Bernardo Leighton," April 9, 1980.

80. From State, To File, "Resumé of USG Evidence & Defense Position in the Contreras, et al, Extradition," December 31, 1979, 8.

81. "Resumé," 9; see also Dinges and Landau, *Assassination*, 143–144; Freed, *Death*, 140–141.

82. Summary of criminal case, "To: Files, From: Chile (Embassy)," January 1, 1988, first page unreadable, on State Department website, 3; Dinges and Landau, *Assassination*, 182.

83. See Landau, "They Educated the Crows," 29.

84. Dinges and Landau, *Assassination*, 383; see also Viron Vaky memo of August 15, 1978 to the Deputy Secretary, "Subject: Letelier/Moffitt Investigation."

85. Vaky memo, August 15, 1978. Walters denied any knowledge of Condor operations. Headings blacked out, Vernon Walters interview, June 21, 1978, on State Department website.

86. Dinges and Landau, *Assassination*, 242, 311, 383.

87. Dinges and Landau, *Assassination*, 201.

88. Landau, "They Educated the Crows,"12; Dinges and Landau, *Assassination*, 393.

89. See Landau, "They Educated the Crows," 33–35; Dinges and Landau, *Assassination*, 243–244, 382–398.

90. Robert Parry, "Bush and the Condor Mystery," October 5, 1999, at www.consortiumnews.com/100599b.html; and "George H. W. Bush, the CIA, and a Case of State Terrorism," September 23, 2000, at www.consortiumnews. com/092300a.html.

91. Branch and Propper, *Labyrinth*, 596.

92. The information that Contreras was a CIA asset had already been uncovered by *Newsweek* journalist Robert Parry in 1988 and published in his 1992 book. *Newsweek* refused to publish the revelation, and one editor even accused Parry of a vendetta against George Bush. Parry noted the information in a 1999 article as well, before the CIA report was issued. See Robert Parry, "Clouds over George Bush," April 1999 at www.consortiumnews.com; also Parry, "George H. W. Bush, the CIA, and a Case of State Terrorism," September 23, 2000, at www.consortiumnews.com/092300a.html. See also CIA, Report to Congress, "CIA Activities in Chile," September 18, 2000 at www.odci.gov./cia/publication/chile.

93. See Parry, "Clouds over George Bush"; Peter Kornbluh, "CIA Outrages in Chile," *The Nation* (October 16, 2000); Dinges and Landau, *Assassination*, especially 382–397, where they raise a series of disturbing aspects and questions about the case.

94. Branch and Propper, *Labyrinth*, 403; see also chapter 14 and 352–357.

95. Secret FBI cable, "Coordinación de Organizaciones Revolucionarias Unidas (CORU)," September 30, 1976; Blake Fleetwood article in *The New Times*, 1977, cited in CIA, title excised, May 5, 1977.

96. Blake Fleetwood article in *The New Times*, 1977, cited in CIA, title excised, May 5, 1977. See also State Department cable, from U.S. Embassy in Santiago to Secretary

of State, "Letelier Assassination—Orlando Bosch and the GOC," message no. 11197, November 22, 1976.

97. Dinges and Landau, *Assassination*, 250–252; Branch and Propper, *Labyrinth*, 260–261; Arboleya, *The Cuban Counterrevolution*, 154–156.

98. Report by Miami FBI office (secret) to Director, FBI, "Coordination of United Revolutionary Organizations (CORU)," August 16, 1978. This declassified document contained an intriguing annex: a memo about the assassinations of Prats and Cuthbert written by Legal Attaché Robert Scherrer, based in Buenos Aires, indicating that the FBI had linked CORU to Condor.

99. Miguel Bonasso, "La Triple Alianza," *Página/12*, October 15, 2000; "Los documentos secretos de Contreras," *Qué Pasa* (Chile), April 29, 2000.

100. Secret FBI cable, "Coordinación de Organizaciones Revolucionarias Unidas (CORU)," September 30, 1976; Branch and Propper, *Labyrinth*, 204, 293. In an example of a clerical error, the passage in the FBI document naming its informant was not blacked out, despite handwritten notations that identifying him would put his life in danger. See also "New Light on Old Crime," *Boston Globe*, January 31, 1989.

101. Branch and Propper, *Labyrinth*, 99–101.

102. "New Light on an Old Crime," *Boston Globe*, January 31, 1989.

103. "Los documentos secretos de Contreras," *Qué Pasa* (Chile), April 29, 2000.

104. TO: SECSTATE, FROM: SANTIAGO, "Letelier-Moffitt: Indictment appeal set for October 24; Contreras seeks testimony from President Bush; Townley reportedly interrogated," no. 8540, October 19, 1991.

105. To: Director/CIA, From: Director FBI, "Request for Information on President Pinochet of Chile and his Family," April 29, 1986.

106. Cable from U.S. Embassy, San José to Secretary of State, "Orlando Bosch: Parole Revocation Hearing," March 23, 1988; Branch and Propper, *Labyrinth*, 319–320.

107. Memo to SECSTATE, FROM AMEMBASSY CARACAS, "Gov Seizes Orlando Bosch and Others in Connection with Cuban Air Crash," no. 12253, October 15, 1976.

108. Leslie Cockburn, *Out of Control: The Story of the Reagan Administration's Secret War in Nicaragua, the Illegal Arms Pipeline, and the Contra Drug Connection* (New York: Atlantic Monthly Press, 1987), 98–99.

109. Memo from AMEMBASSY PORT OF SPAIN, to SECSTATE, "Cubana Crash—October 16 Press Coverage," no. 2724, October 16, 1976.

110. Arboleya, *The Cuban Counterrevolution*, 156–157.

111. See U.S. Senate, Committee on Foreign Relations, "Drugs, Law Enforcement, and Foreign Policy: Panama: Hearings before the Subcommittee on Terrorism, Narcotics, and International Communications," Part 2, February 8, 9, 10, and 11, 1988, 222.

112. "Hearings," 1988, 223–225.

113. "Hearings," 1988, 260–262; author interview with Jack Blum, former Special Counsel, Committee on Foreign Relations, U.S. Senate, in Washington, D.C., July 30, 1993. See also Peter Dale Scott and Jonathan Marshall, *Cocaine Politics: Drugs, Armies, and the CIA in Central America* (Berkeley: University of California Press, 1991); Jack Blum testimony to Senate Select Committee on Intelligence, October 23, 1996.

114. Scott and Marshall, *Cocaine Politics*, 23–25, 28–31.

115. Scott and Marshall, *Cocaine Politics*, 28–31.

116. Numerous sources confirm this finding. See, for example, U.S. Senate, Committee on Foreign Relations, "Drugs, Law Enforcement and Foreign Policy, A Report," prepared by the Subcommittee on Terrorism, Narcotics and International Operations, December 1988, 120–124, 133–144; Scott and Marshall, *Cocaine Politics*, especially chapter 2.

117. Memorandum for the Record (secret), "Meeting with State Department and Justice Department Officials regarding Letelier Case, 1100–1200 hours, 21 August 1978," August 23, 1978; see also document To: Files (State Department), From: Chile, first page and title illegible, January 1, 1988, 3.

118. "Meeting with State Department and Justice Department," 1.

119. Cable from Kissinger to U.S. Embassies in Georgetown, Bridgetown, Caracas, Kingston, "U.S. Position on Investigation of Cubana Airlines Crash," no. 252295, October 9, 1976.

120. Memo from SECSTATE, to AMEMBASSY Santiago, "Orlando Bosch," no. 30881, February 6, 1978; To: SECSTATE, From: AMEMBASSY Buenos Aires, "Orlando Bosch Avila—Fugitive," no. 754, January 31, 1978.

121. "Anti-Castro Extremists Tolerated, If Not Encouraged, by Some Latin Nations," *New York Times*, November 15, 1976.

122. Summary of case, first page illegible, To: File, From: Chile (State Department), January 1, 1988.

123. Douglas Grant Mine, "The Assassin Next Door," *Miami New Times* (November 18, 1999): 3.

124. Vicky Imerman, "Notorious Chilean School of the Americas Graduates," on SOA Watch website (www.soaw/grads/chile-not.html); David Kidwell, "Chilean's Survivors Sue Miami Businessman," *Miami Herald*, March 23, 1999.

125. The jury ordered Fernández Laríos to pay $4 million in damages to the family of Winston Cabello. See Center for Justice & Accountability website, at www.cja.org.

126. Saul Landau and Sara Anderson, "Autumn of the Autocrat," *Covert Action Quarterly* (Spring 1998); "The Ghost of Letelier," *New York Times* editorial, November 27, 1990.

127. "Conspirator in '76 Letelier Assassination Released," *Miami Herald*, August 16, 2001.

128. Dinges and Landau, *Assassination*, 388–389.

129. Branch and Propper, *Labyrinth*, 431.

130. CIA, Memorandum of Conversation, "Press Inquiry Concerning Travel of General Walters to Asunción," October 11, 1978.

131. To: SECSTATE, From AMEMBASSY SANTIAGO, "Letelier/Moffitt Assassination Case: Manuel Contreras," August 24, 1978.

132. Dinges and Landau, *Assassination*, 394–395.

133. Dinges and Landau, *Assassination*, 391–393.

134. United States Government Memorandum, To: Director, FBI, From: SAC, WFO (185-301) (C), "Threat to Assassinate Gabriel Valdés, Chief of United Nations Development and Former Foreign Minister of Chile, and Radomiro Tomic, Former Chilean Ambassador to the United States," October 10, 1975. This document attached as an

annex the FBI's first cable on Operation Condor, written by Robert Scherrer in September 1976. See also Lewis H. Diuguid, "Chilean Violence Increasingly Spreads beyond Its Borders," *Washington Post*, September 22, 1976.

135. Author telephone interview with John Youle, former political counselor at U.S. Embassy in Montevideo (1977–81), July 24, 2003.

136. Youle interview, July 24, 2003; see also EFE, "EEUU comunicó a familiares muerte de desaparecidos en los años 70," *El Diario/La Prensa* (New York), May 11, 2001.

137. See J. Patrice McSherry, "Breaking News: Operation Condor," *Report on the Americas*, Vol. 34, no. 1 (July–August 2000):1; *Notisur*, Vol. 10, no. 24 (July 7, 2000); Dario Pignotti, "La Extraña Muerte de João Goulart," *La Jornada* (Mexico), May 25, 2000.

138. To: USDEL SECRETARY PRIORITY, From: SECSTATE, "Initial Reaction to Conference Committee Action on So-Called Koch Amendment," September 24, 1976, 1.

139. Author interview with Edward Koch, New York City, July 3, 2003.

140. Koch interview, July 3, 2003.

141. Martin Edwin Andersen, *Dossier Secreto: Argentina's Desaparecidos and the Myth of the 'Dirty War'* (Boulder, Colo.: Westview, 1993), 228; Samuel Blixen, *El Vientre del Cóndor: Del archivo del terror al Caso Berríos*, 2nd ed. (Montevideo: Ediciones de Brecha, 1995), 189; Sivak, *El asesinato*, 108; Ana Laura Lissardy, interview with John Dinges in "El Plan Cóndor en la mira," *El Observador* (Uruguay), September 29, 2001; see also Dinges, *The Condor Years* (New York: New Press, 2004).

142. Gustavo González, "New Clues in Ex-President's Mysterious Death," *Inter-Press Service*, April 16, 2002. He cites a book by Chilean journalist Jorge Molina, *Crimen imperfecto* (Santiago, Chile: Lom Ediciones, 2002).

143. Mónica González, "Revelan que planeaban matar a Aylwin en 1989," *Clarín* (Argentina), November 15, 2000; CIA intelligence report with heading blacked out, TO: DIRNSA, DEPT OF STATE, April 29, 1991; Gustavo González, "CIA Revelations Fatten Pinochet Case File," November 14, 2000, at www.globalinfo.org.

144. Richard Gott, "Shots and plots," *The Guardian* (U.K.), June 4, 1976.

145. Author interview with Jack A. Blum, attorney and former special counsel for the Senate Committee on Foreign Relations (1987–89), conducted in Washington, D.C., July 30, 1993.

6

Commanders and Operatives of Condor

A STUDY OF THE PROFILES OF CONDOR commanders and operatives provides an individual-level view of the essence of Condor and a means of understanding the sorts of criminal behavior it embodied. Previous chapters have briefly sketched the histories of Michael Townley (U.S.), Raúl Eduardo Iturriaga Neumann (Chile), Armando Fernández Larios (Chile), Eduardo Ruffo (Argentina), and Hugo Campos Hermida (Uruguay). Numerous other individuals have been named in recent legal cases as Condor commanders and operatives, including such high-ranking Argentine officers as Jorge Videla, Albano Harguindeguy, and Guillermo Suárez Mason; Uruguayan generals Amaurí Prantl (deceased) and Julio Vadora; Chileans Augusto Pinochet, Manuel Contreras, and Pedro Espinoza; and Paraguayans Alfredo Stroessner, Francisco Britez, and Pastor Coronel. Most of the preceding were named in Argentine judge Rodolfo Canicoba's 2001 indictment.[1] Others named in court documents include José Gavazzo, Jorge Silveira Quesada, Manuel Juan Cordero, Pedro Mattos, Enrique Martínez (all members of the Uruguayan military intelligence organizations Servicio de Informaciones de Defensa, SID, or Organismo Coordinadora de Operaciones Antisubversivas, OCOA), Juan Martín Ciga Correa (former Triple A, Milicia, SIDE, Argentina) and Aníbal Gordon (Argentine, Triple A and Orletti torturer), among many others.

This chapter recounts the partially known histories of several other Condor commanders and operatives, and, when possible, traces their trajectories up to the present time. This exercise sheds additional light on the inner workings of Condor as a parallel structure during the 1970s, and allows us to observe the vestiges of Condor networks and structures in recent times, long after the end of the Cold War. Such personal profiles also highlight the types of individuals who carried out Condor's crimes against humanity. While some of them may well have been psychopaths, many functioned with an icy, calculated rationality. Why, and how, are such men able to inflict the most savage, inhuman atrocities upon other human beings? Analyses vary across disciplines, from psychological to institutional theories. But clearly, the institutional context is central: soldiers and policemen were trained to torture and kill, and they were indoctrinated with the view that such torture and killing were patriotic acts. Their commanders and instructors conditioned them to believe that their prisoners were dangerous subversives rather than defenseless victims. Officers learned techniques of torture and murder through a bureaucratic process.

Torture is a crime of the state, a tool used to maintain and augment the power of the state. Professional training is required to shape individuals into torturers and to teach them to torture "effectively." A key causal factor of torture and killing is a military or police culture that condones or promotes such methods as legitimate and justified means of counterterrorism or counterinsurgency. The ideology to which Condor operatives were committed—extremist versions of national security doctrine—was crucial, allowing them to dehumanize their victims and imagine themselves as holy warriors in an exalted cause. Additionally, torturers and abductors functioned within an extensive clandestine apparatus, including secret operations and detention centers, with unregistered vehicles, helicopters, and the like. A large, secret repressive infrastructure is necessary for the organized, mass use of disappearance and torture, what I have termed "industrial repression."

A number of Condor commanders were officers trained in counterinsurgency and counterterrorism at the School of the Americas (SOA) and other U.S. training centers, while some Condor torturers were criminals and fascists who had carried out torture, theft, murder, and other crimes in the past. As such men became part of Condor's shadow parastatal structure, the line between military and criminal activity blurred.

How Are Men Molded into Torturers?

Several studies of torturers have shown that ordinary individuals, regardless of their specific psychological traits, can be made to torture others. Dr. Robert Jay Lifton noted that ordinary individuals "can all too readily be socialized to atrocity. . . . These killing projects are never described as such. They are put in terms of the necessity of improving the world, of political and spiritual renewal. You cannot kill large numbers of people without a claim to virtue."[2]

The well-known experiments by Stanley Milgram demonstrated that obedience to authority is an important social determinant of human behavior.[3] In the experiments, participants were told by a white-coated instructor that they were involved in a study of memory. A subject behind the glass in another room, who was strapped in a chair, was to be given shocks by the participant if the subject gave an incorrect answer. The machine in front of the participant showed a range of voltage (from 15 to 450, slight to dangerous shocks, and finally XXX, severe shock, the highest level). In the experiment, the subject strapped in the chair was an actor and the machine had no effect, unbeknownst to the participant. When told to increase the voltage by the instructor, most participants increased the level to XXX, even if the actor in the other room feigned intense pain. The experiment showed that ordinary persons were reluctant to challenge authority, transgress social norms (by being impolite), or face their own role in inflicting pain on another person.[4]

Despite this human tendency to obey authority, other studies have shown that specific personality types are more likely to become torturers, through a process of self-selection and institutional selection. One Chilean former torturer said that his superiors looked carefully for men known for "their ferocity and their reliability."[5] Many torturers demonstrate a need for power and are inclined to violence, choosing to associate with paramilitary groups, for example.[6] But since most humans recoil from the deliberate infliction of pain and torment on others, the creation of a cadre of torturers and assassins requires specific training within an institutional context. Future torturers in military and police forces go through a process of desensitization and dehumanization, in some cases suffering torture themselves. They are told that using torture proves their manhood or their professionalism and that they are weak if they feel empathy for the victim.[7] They are shown films that include torture and they practice torture on actual prisoners. They are conditioned to believe that their enemies are less than human, dangerous killers who would murder the soldier if he or she could.[8] The soldiers/police are taught to devalue the enemy and his or her group and told that the enemy is to blame for society's problems.[9] Many soldiers and police develop a hatred for those they repress and abuse; they consider themselves part of a heroic elite fraternity that will "cleanse" society.

Sarcasm, laughter, and cruelty are fused to facilitate the process of dehumanization. Torturers are encouraged to mock and make fun of their victims as they inflict pain. "This way a monster is born within these soldiers," one former torturer said.[10] In short, recruits are gradually led through a process that allows them to abandon individual conscience and human empathy and adopt barbaric forms of behavior. Torture and cruelty are learned through social interaction. One study of Greek torturers found that only 1.5

percent of total recruits in a military police camp were chosen yearly to become torturers.[11]

The larger institutional context and authority structure are crucial. Torturers do not act alone; their institutions provide the framework for their behavior. In effect, professional torturers are produced by institutions. The formal training required for torture, aimed to get results without killing the victim, includes anatomical instruction and other quasi-medical learning. As one expert summarizes, "for torture, as opposed to simple ill-treatment, you need some knowledge as to techniques, dangers, and the like."[12] Moreover, "scientific" torture techniques were exported and transferred among security professionals during the Cold War. According to the Catholic Church's meticulous report on torture in Brazil, for example, U.S. policeman Dan Mitrione pioneered the practice of taking beggars off the street to torture in classrooms.[13] Later, Mitrione was stationed in Uruguay, where he was accused of carrying out the same functions. (Mitrione was kidnapped and eventually assassinated by the Tupamaros in 1970.)

Permanent internal security apparatuses and security teams that operate in secrecy often specialize in extralegal, "unconventional" methods. Intelligence and commando-type units that act against suspect civilians, "internal enemies," and ideological foes are particularly prone to the use of torture.[14] Human rights abuses are also more likely to be committed against prisoners who are held for long periods of time in incommunicado detention.[15]

Finally, in vertical organizations such as military and police institutions, the role of commanders is key. They set the norms and define the culture of the institution.[16] Commanders establish the tone and the limits of action;[17] torture and assassination units operate within a chain of command. According to one former torturer,

> not a sheet of paper is moved there without the army command knowing about it, or without the police command knowing. . . . In the army, for you to take a person in, you can't do it because you wanted to, because you felt like it. You have to rely on the infrastructure to do it. You need cars; you need radios . . . the army informs the police that it's working in such and such a place, so they won't interfere . . . everything's in a chain, no unit can operate independently.[18]

In the Southern Cone, specific units were assigned to abduct and torture political opponents within DINA in Chile, DOPS (Department of Social and Political Order) in Brazil, Battalion 601 and the task forces in Argentina, and OCOA in Uruguay, among others. In the "war against subversion," military and police officers held values and standards that condoned and even glorified torture and other crimes against humanity in the service of the state.

Osvaldo Romo Mena, Chile

Osvaldo Romo was a notorious DINA operative, trained in torture methods by Brazilian officers who came to Chile after the 1973 coup. In the early 1970s, he posed as a supporter of Movimiento de la Izqueirda Revolucionaria (Movement of the Revolutionary Left, MIR) and moved among the poor neighborhoods that were loyal to Allende. After the coup, he appeared in military uniform to identify leftist leaders and militants, and he became known as one of DINA's cruelest torturers. Luz Arce, the Socialist Party militant, was raped and tortured by Romo, and remembered him as "massive and greasy, a ferocious dog . . . the indisputably ruthless torturer and implacable rapist."[19] Romo was responsible for dozens of abductions and disappearances of MIR members, and he participated in the DINA raid of October 1974 that killed the historic leader of MIR, Miguel Enríquez (Romo kept his watch as a trophy). An infamous figure in Chile, Romo left Chile assisted by DINA in 1976 to escape judicial scrutiny and worked with death squads in Brazil. That fact alone shows that he was a Condor operative. Romo lived in Brazil for sixteen years. He was finally detained in 1992 and deported to face trial in Chile for his participation in some eighty-one murders, disappearances, and other violations of human rights committed between 1974 and 1976. One case, which the Pinochet regime and DINA officers had insisted at the time was not their responsibility, concerned the detention-disappearance of MIR members Viviana Uribe Tamblay and Edwin Van Yurick. Despite the denials of the state, witnesses saw Romo abduct the couple, and later Romo's own admissions were used by the judge in making the decision to prosecute.[20] But the Supreme Court applied the Pinochet-era amnesty law to Romo and dismissed charges in this case.

In 1995, from a prison cell, Romo gave a stunning interview to journalists from the U.S. Spanish-language television channel *Univisión*, in which he "gave his audience a lesson in torture methods and said he was sorry that the DINA allowed some of its victims to live."[21] Romo expressed a grotesque, sadistic relish while talking about the brutality he had carried out, especially sexual tortures against female prisoners.[22] As he described the tortures he had inflicted, Romo said he would gladly do it again. Asked about the testimony of several Argentine officers, who had admitted throwing live prisoners to their deaths in the sea, Romo said sarcastically, "But you have to feed the fish." It was clear that he had no remorse about his crimes nor about the pain he had inflicted.

Romo confirmed to a judge that Colonia Dignidad was a clandestine detention center during the Pinochet regime and that prisoners were transferred there to "disappear." He also confirmed that the Germans of Colonia Dignidad collaborated actively with the human rights atrocities committed during the dictatorship.[23] After his extradition from Brazil, Romo was charged in many other cases of disappearance and torture. In one, a case of a young MIR activist who was tortured and killed in 1974, the charges were dismissed in 1994 under a statute of limitations technicality. Eventually, this case was also dismissed on the basis of the amnesty law. In another case of a MIR activist who also disappeared in 1974, the Chilean Supreme Court in 1992 granted the military courts jurisdiction, and the military tribunal closed the case. The tribunal later reopened it to apply amnesty to Romo. In May 2004, a Santiago judge finally sentenced Romo to ten years imprisonment for the disappearance of another young journalist and MIR activist.[24]

Enrique Arancibia Clavel, Chile

Formerly a member of the paramilitary group Patria y Libertad in Chile, Arancibia Clavel operated covertly in Buenos Aires as a DINA officer between 1974 and 1978, as we have seen. He posed as an employee of Banco de Chile, using the name Luis Felipe Alemparte Díaz. In 1974–75, Arancibia formed close ties with Argentine military and intelligence officers and with ultra-right paramilitary groups, namely the Triple A and Milicia, to develop a web of Condor connections. Triple A and Milicia (headed by Ciga Correa) provided operational and logistical support for several Condor operations, as did the chief of the Federal Police Department of Foreign Affairs, Juan Carlos Gattei.[25] (Several testimonies given in the Prats trial implicated Gattei as a key actor in the Prats assassination; he was responsible for Prats's security and apparently cleared the area to allow the DINA team to carry out the bombing.)

As this counterinsurgency collaboration deepened, Arancibia met Lieutenant Colonel Jorge Osvaldo Ribeiro Rawson, a high-ranking Argentine army intelligence officer, who had the idea "of forming an intelligence center coordinated among Chile, Argentina, Uruguay, and Paraguay," Arancibia reported to DINA at the time. Ribeiro supplied intelligence about Chilean exiles in Argentina to DINA and also sent a Condor team to Chile, Arancibia wrote. Ribeiro reappeared in Central America in the 1980s as an organizer of the anti-Sandinista contras and the death squads in Honduras, Guatemala, and El Salvador (see chapter 7).

In 1975, DINA officer Raúl Eduardo Iturriaga came to Buenos Aires, Arancibia later testified, with the mission to "make appear in Argentina a dead Chilean subversive," indicating his involvement in Operation Colombo, the PSYWAR operation to disinform about the fates of 119 missing Chileans.[26] By that year, Arancibia had formed close links with Argentine officers associated with SIDE and Jefatura II de Inteligencia of the army, with whom he made an agreement to "collaborate in an extraofficial manner, without embassies."[27]

In 1976, Arancibia collaborated with a military intelligence officer in Córdoba, who secretly commanded a local Triple A group called Libertadores de América.[28] This death squad abducted some thirteen persons in Córdoba on January 8, 1976, according to U.S. ambassador Robert Hill, using unmarked cars and in some cases claiming to be police. Libertadores also claimed responsibility for the murders of nine students in late 1975.[29] When the Beagle Channel conflict erupted between Chile and Argentina in 1978, bringing the two military regimes almost to the point of war, Arancibia Clavel was taken prisoner and accused of spying, but he revealed his secret role and was later set free.

During the Prats trial in Argentina, Judge María Servini de Cubría gained access to four boxes of DINA intelligence documents that had been stored in Arancibia's Buenos Aires office.[30] These files revealed the operations in which Arancibia had been involved and documented the extensive contacts among DINA, Milicia and the Triple A, and Argentine military intelligence within the framework of Condor. One 1978 intelligence report written by Arancibia made clear DINA's detailed knowledge of Argentine black operations and mass murder:

> Attached is a list of all the deaths during the year 1975. The list is classified by month. It includes the "official" deaths as well as the "unofficial." This work [e.g., the listing] was done by Battalion 601 of Army Intelligence located at Callao and Viamonte, that depends on *Jefatura II de Inteligencia* of the General Command of the Army. The lists correspond to annex 74888.75/A1.EA. and annex 74889.75/id. Those that appear NN are those whose bodies were impossible to identify, almost 100% of which correspond to extremist elements eliminated by the security forces extralegally. There are computed 22,000 between dead and disappeared from 1975 to the present.[31]

Arancibia Clavel's reports suggested that the figures estimated by human rights groups of the dead and disappeared in Argentina—30,000—were probably accurate. This agent's history illuminated the functioning of Operation Condor as an extraterritorial parastatal structure. Arancibia was convicted in an Argentine court for his role in the Prats assassination.

Carlos Mena Burgos, Bolivia

During the 1970s, Carlos Mena Burgos was commander of the intelligence unit of the Bolivian Interior Ministry, later minister of the interior, and then commander of the state intelligence apparatus. He was a key Condor figure in Bolivia, and, significantly, he was identified as one of the principal officers of the Bolivian armed forces with command power over paramilitary forces in that country.[32] Mena received training in Argentina in interrogation and torture techniques.[33] He signed the foundational act of the Condor system, on behalf of the Bolivian military, in November 1975.

Working with Colonel Rafael Loayza, commander of the State Intelligence Service under the Banzer dictatorship, Mena organized the intelligence apparatus of Bolivia and geared it to combat real and imagined subversion. He and Loayza were central architects of the countersurbversive mission in Bolivia. A Condor communications system was installed in the Interior Ministry under his supervision.[34] Mena eventually became chief of intelligence.

Mena traveled frequently to Argentina, where he participated in interrogations of foreign political prisoners. Human rights advocate Roberto Calasich reported that a few days before the assassination of former Bolivian president Juan José Torres in Buenos Aires, Mena interrogated a Peruvian prisoner, and then arranged the illegal transfer of the Peruvian and a Chilean prisoner to Bolivia.[35] Thus, Mena was in Buenos Aires when Torres was killed by Condor. According to a Peruvian investigation, Mena also was involved in drug trafficking.

In 1978, Bolivia entered a period of intense political conflict. In 1979, during a brief period of civilian rule, parliamentarian Marcelo Quiroga Santa Cruz initiated a congressional investigation to study and hold responsible dictator Banzer, Colonel Alberto Natusch, Colonel Mena, and others of human rights crimes and involvement in a transnational system of repression. (After Banzer's coup, Quiroga Santa Cruz had fled into exile in Argentina; there, he was threatened by the Triple A.) Quiroga Santa Cruz had gathered documentation of the role of Operation Condor—although he was not aware of its code name—in the assassinations of Bolivians Juan José Torres, Jorge Ríos Dalenz, and Joaquin Zenteno in foreign countries, and of the disappearances of Argentines in Bolivia, including Graciela Rutilo.[36] A month later, in November, Natusch led a coup and directed a repressive sweep that resulted in some 100 killings, 140 disappearances, and 204 wounded, a bloodbath that became known as the massacre of Todos Santos.[37] Mena was identified by human rights groups as "a professional torturer" and as "a principle responsible for the massacre of Todos Santos."[38]

That military regime was short-lived. After reasonably fair elections in 1980 in which a plurality voted for the left, the even fiercer "cocaine coup" occurred, led by military officer Luis García Meza and assisted by Argentine operatives and European neofascists (García Meza confirmed in 2000 that military attachés from the Argentine Embassy in La Paz were among those involved). According to one source, the coup was planned in 1979 during the XIII Conference of American Armies in Colombia, with the Argentine junta playing a leading role.[39] Italian terrorist Stefano delle Chiaie participated in the coup, as did Klaus Barbie, the former Gestapo commander. The coup blocked the ascension of the democratically elected government of Dr. Siles Zuazo, from a leftist party. One of the first targets of the *golpistas* was the Bolivian Workers Center (Central Obrera Boliviana), where Quiroga Santa Cruz was meeting with unionists. Quiroga Santa Cruz was seized by the military, interrogated, tortured, and murdered. His documentation of the Condor system disappeared.[40] Survivors of this operation reported that they were tortured by paramilitaries with Argentine accents. Later, a member of Quiroga's political party (the Socialists) said that during his own torture, both Argentine and Bolivian interrogators were present. They repeatedly asked him which military officers had secretly collaborated with Quiroga to prepare the documentation on Condor, and assumed that Quiroga had obtained copies of Banzer's secret decrees authorizing Condor operations.[41] Banzer was a key supporter of both coups.

Mario Jahn Barrera, Chile

Mario Jahn, Chilean air force colonel and deputy director of DINA's foreign operations (1973–75), was a high-ranking commander within the Condor apparatus and a torturer. In 1973, as an air force intelligence officer, he participated in the torture and interrogation of other members of the air force who had opposed the coup against Allende. He also had a role in the formation of a death squad in the air force that later became known as Comando Conjunto.[42] Jahn ordered the manufacture of false passports for DINA agents—reportedly including the passports used by Townley, Fernández Larios, and one other DINA agent in preparation for the Letelier assassination—and was reportedly involved in an aborted assassination attempt against Allende before the 1973 coup.[43]

Jahn had a direct role in developing the Condor network, acting as a Condor organizer and emissary. In testimony before a judge, he said that he had traveled to Argentina, Brazil, Panama, Spain, Bolivia, Uruguay, Paraguay, and Guatemala on DINA business, activities undoubtedly linked to the Condor agenda.[44] In November 1975, he visited Paraguayan general Francisco Britez (sometimes spelled Brites) in Asunción, accompanied by the Chilean military attaché in Paraguay, to personally deliver DINA's invitation to attend the foundational Condor meeting in Santiago later that month. Jahn briefed Colonel Benito Guanes Serrano, intelligence chief of the high command of the

Paraguayan army, on the concept of Condor as a transnational parastatal network and showed him the proposed structure of the central Condor organization (later discovered in the Paraguayan Archives of Terror).[45]

In 1976, disgruntled officer Rafael González Verdugo (indicted in 2003 in the Horman case) accused Jahn of ordering the savage torture of the former head of CORFO, Chile's agency for economic development, in 1974.[46] When González reported the torture, he asserted, he was harassed and personally threatened with death by Jahn, through intermediaries. Jahn also played a role in relocating and concealing several DINA and Condor operatives and torturers: Carlos Herrera Jiménez in Argentina, Osvaldo Romo in Brazil, and Miguel Estay in Paraguay.[47] (Herrera Jiménez was extradited from Argentina in 1994 in connection with human rights crimes, including the 1982 murder of union leader Tucapel Jiménez and the disappearance of DINA chemist Eugenio Berríos [discussed below]; he confessed to the murder of Tucapel Jiménez and was imprisoned.[48]) In 1975, the air force command, seeking to check the expanding power of DINA, ordered Jahn to resign as deputy director. The navy was actively lobbying to place one of its officers in DINA to replace Jahn and gain more power within the intelligence organization. Jahn refused to leave DINA, however, sparking a tense confrontation with the commander of the air force.[49] As a result of Jahn's intransigence, DINA functioned with two deputy directors.

According to one Chilean source, Jahn was seen in Europe shortly after the 1975 attack on Bernardo and Ana Leighton.[50] He was also in the United States at the time of the Letelier-Moffitt assassinations. In January 1976, Jahn took up a post in Washington, D.C., as a Chilean delegate to the Inter-American Defense Board.[51] This was another indication that Condor operated within the structures of the inter-American system.[52] In September 1976, U.S. ambassador to Chile David Popper pointed out the significance of the DINA commander's position on the board, and advised that, given the recent Letelier-Moffitt assassinations, his superiors at the State Department consider the "implications for the investigation of Letelier's death" of Jahn's presence in Washington and the "question of the role of the Inter-American Defense Board with respect to activities of Southern Cone governments." Popper added that Jahn might be trying "to drum up support with his Southern Cone colleagues for joint intelligence and security operations."[53] In fact, it was far more likely that advanced Condor planning and coordination were occurring within inter-American security structures, since "support" for transnational collaboration was already well established. Popper certainly seemed to be implying that Condor officers were utilizing the board to advance Condor's extralegal program, including Phase III assassinations.

In 1984, Jahn was named director of the National Aeronautical Museum in Santiago. In 2001, Argentine judge Canicoba Corral charged him with crimes committed in the framework of Operation Condor. In 2002, Jahn resigned from the museum amid a public outcry.

Claudio Vallejos, Argentina

Claudio Vallejos told his story to Brazilian journalists in 1986. As an Argentine navy intelligence officer, he had participated in the torture and murder of Brazilian prisoners in Argentina in the 1970s, working in the infamous Grupo de Tarea 3/3-2 with navy operative Alfredo Astiz and others. Vallejos was born into a working-class Peronist family. He had always wanted to be a military man, he said. He joined the navy imbued with the desire to be a hero for his nation. As the countersubversive crusade took shape, he joined the naval intelligence service, recommended by his commanding officer. In those days, Vallejos said, he was a faithful officer who obeyed orders without questioning them. He worked alongside criminals who were recruited into the intelligence apparatus in order to torture and murder.[54] Vallejos said that his instructors were Argentines, U.S. intelligence officers, and former Nazis who lived in Argentina.[55] The U.S. officers taught intelligence methods and ways to fight communism, and the Nazis taught "practical" elements such as methods of torture, he said.

Vallejos was so dedicated to the countersubversive struggle that he decided never to marry, and he spent most of the dirty war within the walls of La Escuela de Mecánica de la Armada (Navy Mechanics School, ESMA). He said that he had killed his first victim at the age of eighteen, and that in the secret Argentine task force he killed another forty.[56] In a cold, emotionless voice, he told journalists about victims he had abducted and tortured. The navy man still refused to see himself as an assassin, however, and corrected his interviewer's use of the word "crime" when referring to murders he had committed.[57] Unlike other Condor operatives, though, Vallejos apparently switched his loyalties. He moved to Brazil and began to work with human rights organizations to document the fates of various disappeared persons. He also sold his testimony to European media as a way of raising personal funds.

Vallejos clarified the disappearance of a Brazilian musician who had vanished in Argentina in March 1976, Francisco Tenório Junior, or Tenorinho. An accomplished pianist, Tenorinho was abducted in a countersubversive operation headed by Alfredo Astiz in the center of Buenos Aires, Vallejos said.[58] It was a few days before the coup of March 24, and the navy had sent two hunter-killer squads to the neighborhood of the Hotel Normandie, where the musician was staying with other Brazilians during a tour.[59] The squadrons were searching for Montoneros in the vicinity.[60] Vallejos explained that men with beards were regarded as suspicious and that when his squad saw the pianist on a street corner, they thought he might be a subversive. They stopped and questioned Tenorinho and found that he had a membership card showing that he belonged to a musicians' union. Regarding that as even more damning, the task force hooded Tenorinho and forced him into the car.

The squadron first brought the Brazilian to a nearby police station, where they ran a check through a minicomputer owned by the Brazilian regime's Serviço Nacional de Informações (SNI), "provided by the CIA," Vallejos said.[61] When questioned, Tenorinho said he played piano in the orchestra of famous Brazilian composer Vinícius de Moraes. Unfortunately, the navy considered de Moraes to be a communist and a subversive.[62] The squadron brought Tenorinho to ESMA, the navy's fearsome torture center. "In this case the only way to know [if Tenorinho was a subversive] was to interrogate him. Then to investigate together with the Brazilian intelligence service that operated in Argentina," Vallejos said, exposing the modus operandi of Condor.[63]

Vallejos said that while the Argentines interrogated Tenorinho ("at first, without violence") they were joined by officers of the SNI, specifically by an officer named Souza Batista. The navy officers also informed the Brazilian Embassy, Vallejos said. Vallejos named other Brazilian SNI officers operating in Argentina in that era as well as ESMA commander rear admiral Rubén Chamorro and Captain Jorge "El Tigre" Acosta, chief of the navy intelligence unit GT3/3-2. He described how Tenorinho was subjected to cruel tortures after proclaiming his innocence:

> he denied everything. Then they started to strike him. He was then brought to the *parrilla*, [the grill]. The *parrilla* was where we applied electric torture. It has this name because, in Argentina, the *parrilla* is where you grill beef. Tenorinho was beaten, tied up, and thrown onto it. Water was thrown on him to facilitate the effect of the shocks and to give him a last opportunity to talk.[64]

Vallejos, asked whether he was bothered by the torture, replied, "No, no. We were prepared, trained. Unfortunately this desensitized me. He screamed, screamed." The next day Tintorinho was tortured with the *submarino*, his head immersed in water. Eventually, the squadron decided the musician was not a subversive.

While the pianist was "disappeared," his colleagues in Brazil initiated an urgent effort to locate him. Musicians who worked with him visited the Brazilian foreign ministry to demand action. None of these efforts was successful.[65] After two months, Tenorinho was still missing. Unbeknownst to his friends and family, Tenorinho was already dead. In a meeting in ESMA between Brazilian Embassy officer Marcos Cortes, other Brazilian officers, and the Argentines, Vallejos said, it was decided that Tenorinho had to die—because he knew too much about the role of Brazilian intelligence in Argentina.[66] The musician had seen Brazilian Embassy personnel in ESMA, where embassy official Marcos Cortes—a hard-liner who, in 1986, was Brazil's ambassador to Australia—actually questioned the musician himself in his prison cell.[67] Tenorinho thus learned of official countersubversive collaboration between the governments of Argentina and Brazil; he could compromise covert Condor connections and operations. Vallejos said that Astiz assassinated the hooded Tenorinho with a shot to the head several days after he was captured.

The decision to kill Tenorinho was made jointly between the Argentina ESMA officers and the Brazilian officials, Vallejos reiterated. A Brazilian colonel told journalists that Marcos Cortes had close ties to the Brazilian military attaché in the Brazilian Embassy in Buenos Aires.[68] The military attaché (and Condor operative) was Souza Batista.[69]

Vallejos said that the Argentine Navy had access to the lists of refugees in Buenos Aires that belonged to the UN High Commission for Refugees. He said that the Argentine intelligence apparatus knew the detailed histories of every refugee in the country, including their political activity. "In Latin America we worked in combined operations with other services of intelligence," he explained in one interview, "sharing information and receiving it."[70] Vallejos also admitted that he traveled to Brazil three times with a paramilitary squad in pursuit of Argentine "terrorists." He explained that during interrogations, some officers specialized in questioning the prisoner and others specialized in torture. Souza Batista was an expert in torture, he said, especially use of electric shocks.[71]

Vallejos said he had information on the case of María Regina Marcondes, the Brazilian woman abducted in Argentina in 1976, saying that she was brought to ESMA, where she was tortured to death and her body thrown into the sea.[72] According to other sources, however, Marcondes was illegally transferred to Chilean military personnel, suggesting that the memory, or credibility, of Vallejos could not be assumed.[73]

Vallejos testified before the Argentine National Commission on the Disappeared (the Sábato Commission) in 1984. Afterward, he suffered several assassination attempts.[74] He related his role in other operations to the Argentine newspaper *La Semana*, including the abduction of former Argentine ambassador to Venezuela, Héctor Hidalgo Sola. He also gave information in Europe about the role of ESMA and the Argentine Navy in the torture and murder of French nuns Alice Domon and Leonie Duquet, and Swedish teenager Dagmar Ingred Hagelin, although it appears that he gave false information in the latter case.[75] Astiz was convicted in the case of the two nuns, in absentia, in France in 1990. In 2003, France asked Argentina again for Astiz's extradition. Vallejos said that he felt hatred for the military and that he had never meant to become a killer. "I am destroyed morally and mentally," he said.[76]

Eugenio Berríos, Chile

Eugenio Berríos, code-named "Hermes," was an extreme-right and brilliant DINA chemist who worked with Michael Townley in the early 1970s. He met Cuban exile Orlando Bosch in Santiago then and met Virgilio Paz when he stayed with Townley in his DINA-provided villa in the Lo Curro neighborhood of Santiago. Berríos also met Italian terrorists such as Stefano delle Chiaie in the early 1970s.[77] In 1975 Berríos worked with a firm called Ibercom founded by delle Chiaie to finance Condor operations.[78] In that year, Berríos also was in contact with SIDE, a signal of Condor coordination, and he traveled to Argentina to meet Ciga Correa of Milicia, supposedly on Ibercom business. He may have played a role in Operation Colombo, the joint Chilean-Argentine PSYWAR campaign.[79]

In a DINA laboratory in the basement of Townley's villa, Berríos perfected ways of using the deadly nerve gas sarin for assassinations and mass murder. DINA's top-secret chemical and biological warfare experiments were code named Project Andrea. Berríos and Townley were experimenting with ways to produce a delivery system for sarin and other toxins to give DINA the capacity to kill masses of people.[80] Berríos was also developing an antidote to the lethal poison, an effort equally important to DINA, given the terrifying power it would provide the agency. Townley's father—who may have worked for the CIA in the 1960s—sent his son and Berríos materials from Great Britain that were needed to manufacture the sarin gas.[81] Townley had originally planned to use sarin to murder Orlando Letelier and actually brought some of the nerve agent in a perfume bottle into the United States. Therefore, Berríos was linked to the Letelier assassination.

In July 1976, Berríos may have been involved in the torture and murder of Carmelo Soria, a Spanish diplomat serving in a UN post in Santiago. Soria, a supporter of Allende, was abducted by DINA's Mulchén Brigade, a unit involved in Condor operations. Townley later asserted in a 1993 interview that Soria had been interrogated, tortured, and killed in the basement of Townley's house. An autopsy showed that Soria died after his neck was broken during torture. Soria's body was dumped in a canal, in a contrived accident.[82] The Pinochet regime immediately launched a disinformation campaign, spreading rumors that Soria had committed suicide because his wife had been unfaithful.

After Townley was expelled from Chile to U.S. custody in 1978, a DINA agent moved vats of sarin and chemical equipment from Townley's villa to an army facility in the south of Chile. Berríos, now marginalized from his previous work, made a living by making amphetamines and an odorless form of cocaine. According to a Chilean intelligence source who spoke with Uruguayan newsmagazine *Posdata*, Berríos was recruited at around this time by the U.S. Drug Enforcement Administration in Santiago as an agent.[83] Later, he was associated with a Peruvian drug-trafficking ring that also involved Chilean officials in a global criminal network.[84]

In 1991, shortly after the transition to democracy in Chile and long after Condor operations had faded from view, a judge subpoenaed Berríos for questioning in the Letelier case. Berríos, and other former DINA agents summoned by the judge, disappeared. In a covert operation named Control de Bajas, military intelligence officers arranged the clandestine escapes of several former dirty warriors linked to Condor who were wanted in Chile for questioning.[85] The DINA agent who had cleaned out Townley's villa was found dead in January 1992, his body floating in the Maipú River.[86] Since then, much evidence regarding Berríos has come to light, indicating that a secret system of intelligence coordination, using Condor networks, still existed in the 1990s.

Berríos was taken into hiding by a Chilean intelligence unit, in cooperation with Argentine and Uruguayan officers, and he traveled with a false passport secretly through these three countries. The operation was an indication that parallel military networks were still functional even after the transitions to democracy in the region. Berríos traveled through Argentina and arrived in Uruguay with his Chilean handlers in late 1991. There, he first stayed in a house that was rented by a Uruguayan intelligence commander, Lieutenant Colonel Tomás Casella.[87]

At some point, Berríos realized that he was no longer under protection but rather a prisoner of the intelligence services. Somehow, he managed to call the Chilean consulate in Montevideo on November 12, 1992, to ask for safe conduct back to Santiago. Several days later, he escaped his captors and made his way to a police station. He told startled police that he was being held by Chilean and Uruguayan officers and that Pinochet wanted him killed. A Uruguayan lieutenant colonel named Eduardo Radaelli arrived and ordered police to turn Berríos over to him; the police refused. Radaelli made a call and soon the station was surrounded by troops from Army Counterintelligence Operations. The commanding officer, Tomás Casella, took custody of Berríos.[88] The regional police chief, a retired colonel, ordered the destruction of all police records on Berríos. Chilean military intelligence men made sure that all traces of Berríos were eradicated, including the police log, hotel records, and personal belongings in the apartment where Berríos had lived in

Uruguay.[89] In February 1993, Pinochet himself (then army commander) came to Uruguay, ostensibly for a vacation; he was always accompanied by Uruguayan counterintelligence commander Casella.[90]

In June 1993, several Uruguayan police officers who were troubled by the case wrote a report about it and sent it anonymously to Uruguayan legislators, including Matilde Rodríguez, the widow of Héctor Gutiérrez Ruiz.[91] Civilian president Luis Alberto Lacalle was apparently unaware of the operation, which caused a political firestorm in Uruguay. The episode indicated that the intelligence services of the militaries continued to operate beyond civilian control. Lacalle cut short a visit to Europe and returned to Uruguay.[92] Army generals made clear to the president that they would not tolerate an investigation of the case.[93] In June 1993, a letter supposedly written by Berríos was sent to the Uruguayan consulate in Milan, saying that he was well and living in Italy.[94] The letter also accused Townley of being a traitor due to his confessions to U.S. authorities in the Letelier case.[95] Actually, the letter—an exercise in PSYWAR—was written after Berríos had already been murdered. In April 1995, fishermen found a skeleton on a beach in Uruguay. Forensic and DNA tests determined that it was Berríos and that he had been executed in March 1993. In August 1996, legal documents and secret files on the Berríos case gathered by a Uruguayan parliamentary commission were stolen from a locked strongbox in the Uruguayan Senate.[96]

Chilean legislator Jaime Naranjo said of this case, "There is no doubt in my mind that a network of ex-state terrorists is protecting each other from the law. This is Condor II."[97] Like the infamous "rat line" after World War II—when Nazis escaped justice in Europe—Condor torturers and killers from the dirty war era had access to finances and resources to escape trials in the 1990s and find refuge in other parts of the world. In 2001, the Berríos case was reopened, and in 2002 a Chilean judge indicted six Chilean army officers—including two generals and one of Pinochet's former bodyguards—for their roles in the murder of Berríos. In 2004, a Chilean judge asked for the extradition of Casella, Radaelli, and several other Uruguayan officers in connection with this case.[98]

Juan (or John) Battaglia Ponte, Uruguay

Juan Battaglia Ponte was a Uruguayan policeman who became a naturalized U.S. citizen. According to Argentine press sources, cited in a 1980 State Department report, he traveled between Argentina and the United States during the 1970s to practice an illegal ploy to defame and defraud exiled Argentines. In Argentina he accused individuals of being terrorists and informed security officers of their whereabouts. Then, in New York, Battaglia impersonated the Argentine ambassador or an Argentine admiral in order to warn Argentine relatives living in the United States that their family members were under detention in Argentina. If they paid him a sum of money, he told the relatives, their family members in Argentina would be released. In one such case, one of the accused reportedly died of a heart attack after his arrest. Battaglia Ponte was eventually arrested and imprisoned in New York.[99] Argentine and Uruguayan sources believed that Battaglia Ponte was in New York for other reasons as well: to detect and persecute Uruguayan and Argentine exiles and report on them to the Argentine and Uruguayan militaries. These functions indicated that Battaglia was a Condor agent operating in the United States. Battaglia also traveled frequently to Argentina, Uruguay, and Paraguay.[100]

Battaglia said that he was a former Navy Seal, that he had served in Vietnam, and that he was a Condor operative. He said openly that he had worked in Argentina with ESMA and the Uruguayan OCOA in Condor operations and, additionally, said that the CIA not only knew of Condor, but supervised it.[101] The latter quotation was cited by legislators of the Genevan parliament in a 1999 legal request for the extradition of Augusto Pinochet. A Swiss-Chilean student, Alexei Jaccard, had been "disappeared" in 1977 in a Condor operation.[102]

Later, during the 1980s, Battaglia worked with the CIA in Central America, where Argentine counterinsurgency specialists linked to Condor and the CIA organized and trained the counterrevolutionary Nicaraguan contras (see chapter 7). In Central America, Battaglia reportedly worked with Jorge Osvaldo Ribeiro ("Balita") and Martín Ciga Correa ("Major Santamaría"), key Condor figures. He also may have helped the dictator Anastasio Somoza flee the country as the Sandinista revolutionaries drew near Managua.[103] In the 1980s, when Battaglia's house in Uruguay was searched pursuant to an Interpol order, police found numerous classified documents, including some from the CIA, which confirmed his links to the U.S. agency. (Battaglia claimed that he was preparing a book on his career as a secret agent.) One letter from the CIA, reproduced in *Posdata*, was dated July 18, 1986, and signed by Lee S. Strickland, a high-ranking CIA officer who served as the CIA's assistant counsel in the 1980s (he became, in the 1990s, chief of the information review group for the CIA, managing declassifications). According to *Brecha*, Battaglia was in Paris at the time of the Trabal assassination; he also boasted that he had played a role in preparations for the Letelier assassination, which he called a "sanction,"[104] although this last claim has never been verified. Manuel Flores Silva, director of *Posdata*, considered Battaglia Ponte a professional disinformation specialist.[105]

It is indisputable, however, that Battaglia Ponte was well connected in military and intelligence circles. He had close relations with former Condor personnel and with Oliver North, the right-wing U.S. military officer infamous for organizing the counterrevolution in Central America and for his role in the Iran-contra scandal. In 2000, Battaglia reappeared in Buenos Aires as the representative of a private security enterprise named Trident Investigative Services. The enterprise was linked to North and several former CIA officers and covert operators, including anti-Castro Cuban paramilitary Félix Rodríguez. Battaglia had worked with North, managing contra operations and covert actions, in Central America in the 1980s.[106] Security firms like Trident represented a nexus between intelligence operations and profit-making ventures. Trident's U.S.-based website advertised corporate special services, intelligence advice, contraband detection, canine services, explosives detection, security consulting, and other services.[107] After Battaglia established a Trident office in Buenos Aires in 2000, North's own security supply firm, Guardian Technologies, provided it with armored cars, bulletproof vests, logistical and intelligence equipment—and contacts with U.S. intelligence agencies in the United States.[108]

The Argentine news media reported that Battaglia was negotiating with Argentine army officers to sell a system of "intelligent cameras" designed to be attached to the underside of aircraft, equipment obtained from North.[109] Battaglia stood to become wealthy through the extensive personal networks he retained within the Argentine military, security, and intelligence forces. He knew such former Condor operatives and dirty warriors as Raúl Guglielminetti and Leandro Sánchez Reisse (who handled covert financing and drug money laundering for Argentine intelligence operations in Central America during the 1970s), and former members of the *grupos de tareas* of ESMA, some of whom had also become involved in various profit-making businesses.[110]

In a 2004 conversation with an Argentine journalist, Battaglia and two fellow Uruguayan intelligence operatives, Ricardo Domínguez and Julio Poblete Cortez, defended their service in the "war against subversion" and lauded their friend and comrade José Gavazzo, with whom they had worked in intelligence operations. Domínguez and Poblete Cortez were now officers in a private security agency in Montevideo. In response to a question about Operation Condor, Domínguez remarked:

> This Plan functioned within the framework of Latin American integration, something like Mercosur, and served to defend us from Marxist aggression. But then the United States reversed itself and, to protect itself, left us on our own. The same way they betrayed Oliver North and Osama Bin Laden. From the

United States you can't expect anything. What we did was professional work in the service of the state.[111]

The operative clearly implied that the United States had been a crucial member or sponsor of Condor. The men also acknowledged that Gavazzo had transported Uruguayan prisoners from the Orletti detention center to Montevideo, something Gavazzo himself had never admitted. After these statements were made public, two Argentine lawyers denounced them and asked a judge to formally question the men in regard to their knowledge of Condor operations.

José Osvaldo Ribeiro, Argentina

José Osvaldo Ribeiro or Riveiro, code-named "Balita," was a high-ranking Argentine army intelligence officer and a key Condor commander. Ribeiro was detained in Argentina in 2001 at the request of French judge Roger LeLoire (who also sought, unsuccessfully, to question Henry Kissinger about Condor operations when he was in Paris in 2001). In 2003, France requested Ribeiro's extradition again, for the disappearance of fifteen French nationals in the early 1970s under Operation Condor.[112] One of them was French-Chilean Jean Yves Claudet Fernández, who disappeared in 1975 in Buenos Aires in a Condor operation. Claudet had been detained twice by the Pinochet regime after the 1973 coup, and indicted by a military prosecutor. He was repatriated to France, but he went to Buenos Aires in 1975. On November 1, 1975, he was abducted from the Hotel Liberty by a combined Condor commando of Argentine and Chilean operatives.[113] DINA commanders, including Manuel Contreras and Pedro Espinoza, were also indicted in Paris in the Claudet case.[114]

In December 1974, Ribeiro was a high-ranking officer in Battalion 601, part of the high command of the army. Ribeiro organized the clandestine detention and torture center in the army's Campo de Mayo garrison. He later became army intelligence chief in Mendoza and Bahía Blanca provinces. Ribeiro's name was listed in the address book of covert DINA officer Enrique Arancibia Clavel, convicted for his role in the assassination of Chilean general Prats and his wife. Ribeiro was a key intelligence link between Argentine army intelligence and DINA.[115] In the archives of DINA agent Arancibia Clavel, which were examined by the judge in the Prats case, there were many reports by the Chilean that reflected his frequent interaction with Ribeiro in the early 1970s.[116]

In September 1975, Ribeiro traveled to Asunción and then to Santiago, with all expenses paid by DINA, to prepare conditions for the first formal Condor meeting in November of that year in Santiago.[117] He installed a telex machine in the central headquarters of DINA in Santiago, allowing DINA to communicate securely and directly with Argentine army intelligence.[118] Ribeiro also passed intelligence information to DINA on Chilean exiles living in Argentina and shared secret information on other covert operations carried out by the Argentine military, such as the capture and killing of guerrilla Mario Roberto Santucho in 1976 and the abduction and murder of Jean Yves Claudet.[119] Ribeiro also worked closely with Uruguayan and Paraguayan intelligence officers and helped to reorganize and modernize the Paraguayan intelligence apparatus.[120]

Later, in Central America, Ribeiro supervised the contra war from the Hotel Honduras Maya, working closely, if with some discord, with the CIA. Ribeiro was "distributing American money and dispensing what CIA officials viewed as unsound military advice . . . since his own experience was in urban rather than rural combat, he advised the Contras to mount a program of urban terrorism. The CIA wanted to cultivate a popular insurgency in the countryside."[121] Ribeiro headed Battalion 601's Extraterritorial Task Force (GTE) in Honduras, organizing and training Honduran intelligence officers and Nicaraguan contras in counterterrorism and dirty war operations. The GTE also operated clandestine offices in Florida, according to Leandro Sánchez-Reisse, with the approval of the CIA.[122] The Honduran National Commission of Human Rights accused Ribeiro of involvement in the disappearance of some 184 persons in Central America.[123] Eventually, the CIA took over the leadership of the contra counterrevolution.

In 1999, *Página/12* discovered that Ribeiro had been contracted by the minister of defense of President Carlos Menem to direct the Instituto de Ayuda Financiera para Pagos de Retiros y Pensiones Militares (Institute of Financial Assistance for Payments of Military Retirements and Pensions).[124] He was arrested for human rights violations afterward.

James Blystone, U.S. Regional Security Officer

U.S. Regional Security Officer (RSO) James John Blystone was cited by a DINA operative in 1977 as playing a very important role in the Condor network in Chile (see chapter 4). While it is not clear whether he was specifically a Condor intelligence liaison, or simply an official trusted by the Condor apparatus, Blystone had intimate knowledge of the inner workings of the transnational repressive system. In one case, Blystone was informed in advance of the "permanent disappearance" of several Argentines who were abducted and disappeared in Lima, Peru in 1980. This case, well known in Argentina, demonstrated that Condor members Argentina and Bolivia acted with the collaboration of Peru and Spain. Argentine Noemí Gianetti de Molfino, a Mother of the Plaza de Mayo, and three other persons were detained-disappeared in Lima on June 14, 1980, by a combined Condor team of Argentine and Peruvian intelligence officers. Gianetti de Molfino had been working with human rights groups in Peru. She had denounced the 1979 disappearances of her daughter and son-in-law before the UN. Gianetti de Molfino's body was discovered a month after her abduction, on July 21, in Madrid. Spanish judge Baltasar Garzón reopened the case in 1996 at the request of Gustavo Molfino, the slain woman's son and a former Montonero. In December 1999, Gustavo was awarded an indemnity from the Argentine government for the death of his mother. It was the first time the Argentine state had officially recognized its responsibility in the death of an Argentine citizen in a Condor operation.

In a June 19, 1980, report to U.S. ambassador to Argentina Raúl Castro,[125] Blystone summarized his meeting with an unnamed Argentine military intelligence officer from Battalion 601, army intelligence. The Argentine officer informed him that the four disappeared persons seized in Lima would be "held in Peru and then expelled to Bolivia where they will be expelled to Argentina. Once in Argentina they will be interrogated and then permanently disappeared. Source stated that 601 had had a good record on apprehending terrorists who had fled the country and were preparing to reenter." Clearly, the RSO had been briefed on a top-secret Condor operation involving the intelligence services of three separate countries; he was accepted as a trusted member of Condor's inner circle.

This memo reported other top-secret information. Blystone wrote that the main topic of the meeting with the Argentine intelligence officer was "the RSO's stay in Bolivia and how the political situation there was developing." The Argentine-assisted "cocaine coup" in Bolivia occurred one month later, on July 17. On June 19, the date of Blystone's memo, coup preparations in that country were well advanced. According to one study, on June 17 six of Bolivia's major drug traffickers had met with military *golpistas* to arrange protection for their narcotics trade in exchange for financing military operations after the planned coup.[126]

The main conspirator was Colonel Luis Arce Gómez, a cousin of Bolivia's main drug trafficker, Roberto Suárez. The Argentines, under the doctrine of "ideological frontiers" that was so conducive to Condor operations, sent at least 200 military and intelligence officers to Bolivia to help launch the coup, including Colonel Osvaldo Ribeiro. Stefano delle Chiaie, the Italian terrorist, was there, training an assassination squad called the Phoenix Commando, and Klaus Barbie, the Nazi war criminal and one-time U.S. intelligence asset, was also involved in coup preparations.[127]

An Argentine officer, a former counterintelligence director of SIDE who had taken courses at the SOA, spoke to me openly in 1992 of his participation in Bolivia as an advisor during this time. Another SIDE officer and Condor figure, Leandro Sánchez Reisse, told a U.S. Senate subcommittee in 1987 testimony that drug trafficker Roberto Suárez had used some $30 million to finance the Bolivian coup—and that the coup had CIA support. He also said that Suárez used drug money, funneled through Sánchez Reisse's money laundering base in Miami, to finance the Nicaraguan contras.[128] After the coup, Arce Gómez embarked on a campaign of brutal repression in Bolivia and also released numerous drug traffickers from prison. Barbie and delle Chiaie organized paramilitary squads to protect the traffickers and their drug trade.[129]

Two obvious questions arise from Blystone's report: what he told his Argentine counterpart about "how the political situation was developing" in Bolivia and whether he played a liaison role between the Argentine and Bolivian putschists. The memo certainly leaves the impression that he did play a role in the Condor intelligence network, something suggested by repentant DINA agent Juan Rene Muñoz Alarcón in 1977, three years earlier. Blystone's June report was significant for one other piece of information it revealed. His Argentine contact, the intelligence officer, was preparing a trip to Panama, Costa Rica, Guatemala, and San Salvador "to analyze the situations there and report back to 601." This data confirmed that the Argentine contact was a central Condor figure and someone who helped to extend the Condor counterrevolutionary apparatus to Central America (see chapter 7). Blystone's contact could very well have been Ribeiro himself, who commanded Argentine covert forces in Central America.

In another memo dated April 7, 1980,[130] Blystone reported that he had "jokingly" asked his Argentine intelligence contact what had happened to two Montoneros who had disappeared during a trip from Mexico to Rio de Janeiro. The Argentine again told the RSO top-secret information: that the Argentine military had previously captured a Montonero who, under interrogation, had revealed the time and place of a meeting in Rio. The report continued:

> The Argentine military intelligence (601) contacted their Brazilian military intelligence counterparts for permission to conduct an operation in Rio to capture two *Montoneros* arriving from Mexico. Brazilians granted their permission and a special team of Argentines were flown [*sic*] under the operational command of Lt. Col. Roman, to Rio aboard an Argentine airforce C130. Both of the *Montoneros* from Mexico were captured alive and returned to Argentina aboard the C130. The Argentines, not wanting to alert the *Montoneros* that they had conducted an operation in Rio, utilized an Argentine woman and man to register at

> a hotel using the false documents obtained from the two captured *Montoneros*, thereby leaving a trail that the two *Montoneros* from Mexico had arrived in Rio. . . . These two *Montoneros* are presently being held at the army's secret jail, Campo de Mayo.

These two Argentines were seized in the airport near Rio by twenty armed men. They were never seen again. In 2000, the Brazilian government granted an indemnity to their families (and to the family of one other Argentine who was detained-disappeared in Brazil). In 2001, an Argentine judge opened a criminal case regarding the disappearances of some twenty Montoneros in late 1979 and early 1980, including these two, and in 2002 he indicted thirty-two Argentine officers.

Blystone's declassified reports are unusual because they provide evidence of a U.S. official's advance knowledge of top secret and extralegal Condor operations. Clearly, this U.S. official was accepted within the highest levels of the Argentine Condor structure, at minimum. Several State Department officers who spoke with me said that since the RSO's role was to collect intelligence, his behavior in these cases could not be faulted. This argument neglects the fact that while such U.S. officers were developing intimate and friendly relations with their Latin American counterparts, the latter were directing campaigns of state terror and presiding over unspeakable torture and mass murder at the same time. Indeed, in many cases U.S. officials received detailed briefings from the Latin American officers on the disappearance, torture, and murder of hundreds if not thousands of persons while, to their own citizens, the military regimes denied responsibility. To take no action in such cases—even if in accord with standard operating procedures—crossed the line into complicity, thus becoming morally indefensible. For foreign officers, U.S. officials represent the policy of the United States. As one military chaplain wrote, "The only operational U.S. foreign policy a foreign human rights violator sees is embodied in the responses of Americans with whom he has to do."[131] U.S. officers who expressed no objection to, or explicitly sanctioned, Condor human rights crimes thus provided a green light. Overall, however, the heaviest weight of responsibility and the burden of complicity with these terrorist regimes lay primarily with U.S. political leaders and U.S. national security policy, which excused all manner of atrocity in the name of the anticommunist cause.

This chapter has sketched the structures and operations of Condor through an examination of Condor commanders, kidnappers, and torturers. Their histories suggest that Condor's men were trained, indoctrinated, and otherwise socialized through professional institutions to become torturers and killers, and that they were convinced that such torture and killing were acceptable, even laudable, in the service of the anticommunist crusade. The ideological framework of the dirty warriors in their holy war against subversion was central: the ends justified the means, and any means were legitimate to eliminate the perceived internal threat. The counterinsurgents rejected principles of democracy and the rule of law, and concepts of rights, as impediments to the anticommunist cause. National security doctrines and anticommunist ideologies were an important determinant of state terrorism, as they dehumanized whole categories of people and provided a quasi-religious rationale for their torture and destruction. Moreover, U.S. officials shared, condoned, and actively promoted such ideologies and practices.

Notes

1. "Fallos: Videla," *Lexpenal.com*, July 10, 2001.
2. Chris Hedges, "A Skeptic about Wars Intended to Stamp Out Evil," *New York Times*, January 14, 2003.
3. Stanley Milgram, *Obedience to Authority: An Experimental View* (New York: Harper and Row, 1974).
4. Mick Underwood, "Social Influence: Obedience to Authority," at www.cultsock.ndirect.co.uk/ MUHome/cshtml/socinf/obed.html; Mika Haritos-Fatouros, "The Official Torturer: A Learning Model for Obedience to the Authority of Violence," in Ronald D. Crelinsten and Alex P. Schmid, eds., *The Politics of Pain: Torturers and Their Masters* (Boulder, Colo.: Westview, 1995), 130.
5. Ronald D. Crelinsten, "In Their Own Words: The World of the Torturer," in Crelinsten and Schmid, *The Politics of Pain*, 45.
6. Ervin Staub, "Torture: Psychological and Cultural Origins," in Crelinsten and Schmid, *The Politics of Pain*, 106.
7. Martha K. Huggins, Mika Haritos-Fatouros, and Philip G. Zimbardo, *Violence Workers: Police Torturers and Murderers Reconstruct Brazilian Atrocities* (Berkeley: University of California Press, 2002), chapters 6–8. These experts found, though, that torturers embodied various forms of masculinity, and not necessarily the simplistic stereotype of macho men.
8. Crelinsten, "In Their Own Words," 46–51.
9. Staub, "Torture," 101–102, 104.
10. Crelinsten, "In Their Own Words," 48.
11. Haritos-Fatouros, "The Official Torturer," 137.
12. Wolfgang S. Heinz, "The Military, Torture and Human Rights: Experiences from Argentina, Brazil, Chile and Uruguay," in Crelinsten and Schmid, *The Politics of Pain*, 69; see also Federico Allodi, "Somoza's National Guard: A Study of Human Rights Abuses, Psychological Health and Moral Development," 118–123 in Crelinsten and Schmid, *The Politics of Pain*, for a useful heuristic research model of how torturers are created.

13. Catholic Church, Archdiocese of São Paulo, *Torture in Brazil*, trans. Jaime Wright (Austin: University of Texas Press, 1998), 14.

14. Heinz, "The Military," 69, 76.

15. Stanley Cohen and Daphan Golan, *The Interrogation of Palestinians during the Intifada: Ill-Treatment, 'Moderate Physical Pressure' or Torture?* (Jerusalem: B'TSELEM, Israeli Information Center for Human Rights in the Occupied Territories, 1991), cited in Ronald D. Crelinsten, "The Discourse and Practice of Counter-Terrorism in Liberal Democracies," *Australian Journal of Politics and History*, Vol. 44, no. 3 (September 1998): 110. Version found on website of Expanded Academic Index.

16. See Crelinsten, "The Discourse and Practice," 389.

17. Colonel Charles Garroway, British Ministry of Defense, in panel entitled "The Training of the Military: National Law and the Teaching of the Geneva Conventions," in a conference sponsored by the New School University, "International Justice, War Crimes, and Terrorism: The U.S. Record," New York, April 25–27, 2002.

18. Crelinsten, "In Their Own Words," 43–44.

19. "Osvaldo 'Guatón' Romo Mena—DINA," compilation at www.memoriaviva.com/cupables/criminales%20r/romo.htm; Luz Arce, *The Inferno: A Story of Terror and Survival in Chile* (Madison: University of Wisconsin Press, 2004), 125.

20. Chile Information Project, *Santiago Times*, March 30, 1994.

21. Pascale Bonnefoy, *Latinamerica Press* (Peru), Vol. 27, no. 20 (June 1, 1995): 4.

22. Nancy Guzmán, *Romo: Confesiones de un torturador* (Santiago: Planeta, 2000), 165–169; "Estupor y repudio por confesiones de torturador," *El Diario/La Prensa* (New York), May 3, 1995.

23. Radio Espectador (Uruguay), August 7, 2001.

24. Inter-American Commission on Human Rights, Report on cases 11.657, 11.705, and 11.505, at www1.umn.edu/humanrts/cases/1997; U.S. State Department, "Chile Human Rights Practices, 1993," January 31, 1994, at State Department website; "Carta abierta a los gobernantes chilenos: No a la libertad del criminal, asesino y torturador y ex-agente de la DINA, Osvaldo Romo Mena," issued by various Chilean human rights groups on October 8, 2000; "Pinochet Stripped of Immunity," at www.americas.org/item_15055.

25. *Página/12* (Argentina), October 12, 2000; "Protagonista de la Operación Cóndor," *La Nación* (Argentina), Enfoques section, April 29, 2001. This latter article was based on Arancibia's DINA files of the 1970s.

26. The Arancibia testimony formed part of Judge María Servini de Cubría's extradition request for Augusto Pinochet, March 21, 2001, 9, 13. See www.snillebild.com/pinochet/argentina/extradition2.html.

27. *La Nación* (Argentina), April 29, 2001.

28. *La Nación* (Argentina), April 29, 2001.

29. Limited Official Use cable from U.S. Embassy, Buenos Aires to Secretary of State, "Wave of Kidnapping in Argentina," message no. 133, January 9, 1976.

30. "Canicoba Corral procesó a Videla por organizar el plan Cóndor," *La Nación* (Argentina), July 11, 2001.

31. *La Nación* (Argentina), April 29, 2001; Victoria Ginzberg, "Videla, procesado por el Plan Cóndor," *Página/12* (Argentina), July 10, 2001.

32. Derechos, "Narcotráfico y Política," at www.derechos.org/nizkor/bolivia/libros/cocacoup/oficiales.html.

33. Martín Sivak, *El asesinato de Juan José Torres: Banzer y el Mercosur de la muerte* (Buenos Aires: Ediciones del Pensamiento Nacional, 1998), 105.

34. Gerardo Irusta Medrano, *Espionaje y servicios secretos en Bolivia y el Cono Sur*, 2nd ed. (La Paz: 1997), 548–549.

35. Martín Sivak interviewed Calasich in 1996. See Sivak, *El asesinato*, 105.

36. Wálter Vásquez Michel, "Juicio al general Banzer," *La Razón* (Bolivia), January 25, 2002.

37. Yuri Aguilar Dávalos, "El coronel Alberto Natusch Busch no perdona ni a los muertos," *Bolpress*, November 1, 2002.

38. "Responsables de la Masacre de Todos Santos y de la dictadura de Natush," at 222.bolpress.com.index. php?Cod=2002222057648 accessed by author in July 2003.

39. Stuart Christie, *Stefano Delle Chiaie: Portrait of a Black Terrorist* (London: Anarchy Magazine/Refract Publications, 1984), 97.

40. Vásquez Michel, "Juicio"; "Confesiones de un dictador: Presencia de militares argentinos en el narcogolpe," *Página/12* (Argentina), May 27, 2000. According to Christie, an Italian neofascist—one of delle Chiaie's men—was responsible for the torture and murder of Quiroga Santa Cruz. See Christie, *Stefano*, 107.

41. Vásquez Michel, "Juicio"; "Confesiones de un dictador."

42. Amaldo Pérez Guerra, "Un torturador en el museo," *Punto Final/La Insignia* (Chile), May 21, 2002, 1.

43. Pérez Guerra, "Un torturador," 2, citing Osvaldo Puccio, *Un cuarto de siglo con Salvador Allende.* See also "Jahn Barrera Mario," www.memoriaviva.com/culpables/criminales%20/jahn_ barrera_ mario.htm.

44. Pérez Guerra, "Un torturador," 2; Pascale Bonnefoy Miralles, "Actual director de Museo Aeronáutico fue clave en Operación Cóndor," *El Mostrador* (Chile), July 5, 2001.

45. Jefe de Policía, "Informe," November 6, 1975, document obtained by author in the Paraguayan Archives, 1996; Samuel Blixen, *El Vientre del Cóndor: Del archivo del terror al caso Berríos* (Montevideo: Ediciones de Brecha, second ed., 1995), 82–83.

46. Rafael Agustín González Verdugo, letter to the president of the Commission of Human Rights of the Organization of American States, June 16, 1976, 1.

47. Amaldo Pérez Guerra, "Un torturador," 1.

48. Chile Information Project, *Santiago Times*, April 25, 1994.

49. Defense Intelligence Agency (DIA), "(U) Directorate of National Intelligence (DINA) Expands Operations and Facilities," April 10, 1975.

50. Pérez Guerra, "Un torturador," 2.

51. González Verdugo letter, 2.

52. See McSherry, "Operation Condor as a Hemispheric 'Counterterror' Organization," in Cecilia Menjívar and Néstor Rodríguez, eds., *When States Kill: Latin America, the U.S., and Technologies of Terror* (Austin: University of Texas Press, 2005).

53. U.S. Embassy, Santiago, "Chile: Report re Ex-DINA Official in Washington," September 27, 1976.

54. Maurício Dias, "Eu, Cláudio, me arrependo do que fiz," *Senhor* (Brazil), May 20, 1986, 50. See also Juan Gasparini, *La pista suiza* (Buenos Aires: Editorial Legasa, 1986), 183–190.

55. Dias, "Eu, Cláudio," 50.

56. Rio Agencia Estado (Brazil), "O ex-militar: Argentino revela como torturou e matou políticos," xerox copy missing name of newspaper and date; probably May 1986. Article obtained by author at Arquivo Ana Lagôa at the Universidade Federal de São Carlos in Brazil, 2001.

57. Rio Agencia Estado, "O ex-militar."

58. Rio Agencia Estado, "O ex-militar."

59. Maurício Dias, "A história oficial," *Senhor* (Brazil), no. 270, May 20, 1986, 44.

60. Dias, interview with Vallejos, 48.

61. Dias, interview with Vallejos, 48.

62. Dias, interview with Vallejos, 49.

63. Agencia Estado, "O ex-militar."

64. Dias, interview with Vallejos, 49.

65. Dias, "A história," 45.

66. Agencia Estado, "O ex-militar"; Dias, interview with Vallejos, 49.

67. Dias, "A história," 45.

68. Dias, "A história," 46.

69. Dias, interview with Vallejos, 47.

70. Dias, interview with Vallejos, 47.

71. Dias, "A história," 47.

72. Dias, interview with Vallejos, 50.

73. See, for example, CIA, "Weekly Summary [secret]," July 2, 1976.

74. Dias, "Eu, Cláudio," 51.

75. Dias, "A história," 46; Gasparini, *La pista suiza*, 185.

76. Dias, "Eu, Cláudio," 51.

77. "La historia encubierta de Eugenio Berríos," *Posdata* (Uruguay) no. 82 (April 4, 1996): 13, 15; see also Samuel Blixen, "Berríos, The Bothersome Biochemist," Transnational Institute, December 1997, at www.tni.org/drugs/folder3/blixen.htm; and Blixen, *El Vientre del Cóndor*, 25.

78. Horacio Verbitsky, "El diablo que mata," *Página/12* (Argentina), October 18, 2002. See also *Posdata*, "Berríos trabajó con los neofascistas italianos que pusieron bomba en la estación de Bologna," April 4, 1996, 15. This source gives the dates of Berríos's work with the Italians as 1976–77, however.

79. Verbitsky, "El diablo"; "Por qué mataron a Berríos," *Brecha* (Uruguay), Vol. 881, no. 18, October 2002.

80. Taylor Branch and Eugene M. Propper, *Labyrinth* (New York: Viking Press, 1982), 309, 313, 317–318, 540; Verbitsky, "El diablo."

81. Verbitsky, "El diablo."

82. See, for example, Ernesto Ekaizer, "El caso 'Soria' ya es internacional," *El País Digital* (Spain), January 10, 2000; Amnesty International, "The Case of Carmelo Soria, A United Nations Official," January 1995; *Posdata*, "La historia," 13–14.

83. *Posdata*, "La historia," 16–18; Verbitsky, "El diablo."

84. Blixen, "Berríos, The Bothersome Biochemist."

85. Mónica González, "Pacto de sangre: Los asesinos de Berríos," article from *Siete + 7* (Chile), reproduced in *Brecha* (Uruguay), no. 882, October 25, 2002.

86. Verbitsky, "El diablo."

87. Verbitsky, "El diablo."

88. Blixen, "Berríos, The Bothersome Biochemist"; Verbitsky, "El diablo."

89. Verbitsky, "El diablo."

90. Blixen, "Berríos, The Bothersome Biochemist."

91. Blixen, *El Vientre del Cóndor*, and "Operation Condor apparently alive and well," *Latinamerica Press*, Vol. 25, no. 22 (June 17, 1993): 1, and "Berríos, The Bothersome Biochemist," Transnational Institute, December 1997; see also William R. Long, "Missing Chilean Scientist Raises Ghost of Military Rule," *Los Angeles Times*, June 19, 1993.

92. Raúl Ronzoni, "Political Tension Mounts over Secret Army Operation," *Inter-Press Service*, June 9, 1993.

93. Long, "Missing Chilean Scientist."

94. Patricio Vargas, "Régimen de Pinochet había fabricado gas sarín en 1975," *Prensa Libre* (Guatemala), May 23, 1995.

95. Raúl Ronzoni, "Supuesta aparición en Italia de ex agente chileno," *InterPress Service*, June 21, 1993.

96. "La muerte del agente chileno," *Clarín* (Argentina), August 9, 1996.

97. "South American Suspects Disappearing before Trials," *St. Louis Post-Dispatch*, August 1, 1993.

98. "Chile/Berríos: Procesan a militares," *BBC Mundo.com*, October 18, 2002; Verbitsky, "El diablo"; see also Jorge Molina Sanhueza, "Oficiales activos del Ejército vinculados a muerte de Berríos," *El Mostrador* (Chile), May 10, 2001; "Un juez chileno pidió la detención y extradición de 4 militares uruguayos,"*La República* (Uruguay), April 6, 2004.

99. TO: SECSTATE, FROM: AMEMBASSY Buenos Aires, "Human Rights Summary—March 1–7, 1980," March 7, 1980.

100. Gerardo Young, "Enigmas de una visita secreta del coronel Oliver North a la Argentina," *Clarín* (Argentina), July 15, 2002; Alejandro Guerrero, "Inteligencia privada: Una historia criminal," October 20, 2001, at www.paginadigital.com.ar/articulos/2001seg/denuncias/oculta20-10-01.html.

101. Raúl Zibechi and Marcelo Pereira, "El insólito agente Battaglia: ¿Otra punta de la madeja?" *Brecha* (Uruguay), May 9, 1997.

102. This document, presented by Geneva legislators, also requested an investigation of the possible penal liability of Henry Kissinger. Secrétariat du Grand Conseil, "Proposition présentée par les députés," November 18, 1999; see Kissinger Watch, March 7, 2002, at www.icia-online.org/kissingerwatch/resolutiongeneve.pdf. On the Jaccard case, see Juan Gasparini, *La pista suiza* (Buenos Aires: Editorial Legasa, 1986), chapter 9.

103. Alberto Amato, "Los muchachos de North," *Clarín* (Argentina), August 13, 2000.

104. *Brecha*, May 9, 1997.

105. Personal e-mail communication to author from Manuel Flores Silva, July 22, 2001.

106. Gerardo Young, "Enigmas," *Clarín*, July 15, 2002.

107. See Trident's website at www.tridentseattle.com/; site accessed by author in August 2003.

108. Amato, "Los muchachos," August 13, 2000.

109. Gerardo Young, "El Estado utiliza a los espías privados pero no los controla," *Clarín*, August 14, 2000.

110. Young, "El Estado utiliza." See also McSherry, *Incomplete Transition: Military Power and Democracy in Argentina* (New York: St. Martin's Press, 1997), 182–186; Gasparini, *La pista suiza.*

111. Felipe Yapur, "El otro amigo uruguayo de Oliver North que defiende el Plan Cóndor," *Página/12* (Argentina), January 16, 2004; Roger Rodríguez, "Un juez argentino indagará a Domínguez, a Battaglia, y a Poblete por el Plan Cóndor," *La República*, January 16, 2004; see also Felipe Yapur, "Buenos Aires es la meca de los servicios," *Página/12* (Argentina), January 12, 2004.

112. *La Tercera* (Chile), December 19, 2001; Grupo Reforma Servicio Informativo, "Piden castigo para represores argentinas," July 16, 2003.

113. Equipo Nizkor, "Ciudadanos franceses asesinados o desaparecidos durante la dictadura de Pinochet," November 23, 1998.

114. Victoria Ginzberg, "Dos más buscados por represores," *Página/12* (Argentina), November 30, 2001.

115. *Juicios Orales*, at www.juiciosorales.com/TripleA.htm; *Página/12* (Argentina), "Balita Riveiro fue detenido," December 20, 2001, Human Rights Watch, "The Role of the United States," December 2001, at www.nuncamas.org/ investig/hrw_121201_13 .htm.

116. Ginzberg, "Dos más."

117. Mónica González, "Un Cóndor al fin desgarrado," *Clarín* (Argentina), May 14, 2000.

118. "Protagonista de la Operación Cóndor," *La Nación* (Argentina), April 29, 2001.

119. "Protagonista," *La Nación* (Argentina), April 29, 2001.

120. Samuel Blixen, "Narcotráfico de Estado," at www.geocities.com/rpallais/ narco.htm.

121. *Wall Street Journal*, March 5, 1985, cited in Ariel C. Armony, *Argentina, the United States, and the Anti-Communist Crusade in Central America, 1977–1984* (Athens: Center for International Studies, Ohio University, 1997), 133.

122. Human Rights Watch, "The Role of the United States," December 2001, at www.nuncamas.org/ investig/hrw_121201_13.htm.

123. Comisionado Nacional de los Derechos Humanos, *Los hechos hablan por si mismos, informe preliminar sobre los desaparecidos en Honduras 1980–1993* (Tegucigalpa, Editoriales Guaymuras, 2002), 429; Fernando Rodríguez, "Escenas y rostros repetidos," *La Nación* (Argentina), April 29, 2001.

124. Sergio Moreno, "Defense echó la culpa al Ejército por contratar al 'Balita' Riveiro," *Página/12* (Argentina), May 5, 1999.

125. James J. Blystone memo, "Meeting with Argentine Intelligence Service," June 19, 1980; see also Joseph Contreras, "Latin America: Knowing Too Much" in Periscope, *Newsweek*, International Editions, October 27, 2002. This author uncovered this Blystone memo in 2002.

126. Peter Dale Scott and Jonathan Marshall, *Cocaine Politics: Drugs, Armies, and the CIA in Central America* (Berkeley: University of California Press, 1991), 45.

127. Scott and Marshall, *Cocaine Politics*, 44–46; Sivak, *El asesinato*, 98.

128. Author interview with retired Argentine lieutenant colonel, Buenos Aires, August 26, 1992; "Confesiones de un dictador," *Página/12* (Argentina), May 27, 2000.

129. Scott and Marshall, *Cocaine Politics*, 46.

130. James J. Blystone, "RSO Conversation with Argentine Intelligence Source, to Ambassador via Chaplin," April 7, 1980.

131. Kermit D. Johnson, *Ethics and Counterrevolution* (Lanham, Md.: University Press of America, 1998), 252.

7

The Central American Connection

In 1979 and 1980, a new Condor system was established in Central America. Working closely with U.S. intelligence personnel, Argentine army officers fresh from their own dirty war—with its tens of thousands of disappeared, tortured, and murdered victims—began to jointly train Honduran and Guatemalan military men and anticommunist Nicaraguan paramilitaries (the contras) in strategies of counterrevolution and methods of repression. At first, Hondurans and Nicaraguans traveled to Buenos Aires for the training, but soon a decision was made to have Argentine instructors provide training "in country" instead, based in Honduras. Some of the Argentine officers involved, such as Colonel Osvaldo Ribeiro (or Riveiro) and operative Juan Martín Ciga Correa, were key Condor figures. Essentially, Condor was extended to Central America.

New methods used against exiles and refugees in Central America in the early 1980s reflected defining features of Operation Condor: targeted abductions and murders by multinational "hunter-killer" squadrons, often made up of contras and Honduran commandos in civilian clothes; clandestine "transfers" of prisoners across borders; methods of disappearance, torture, and assassination of victims, including the use of electric shock, the "*capucha*" (asphyxiation), and the throwing of live persons from helicopters; interrogations of prisoners by officers from several countries; and detention centers for foreign disappeared prisoners. The Honduran government officially recognized 184 disappearances from that era, and of these, there were thirty-nine Nicaraguans, twenty-eight Salvadorans, five Costa Ricans, four Guatemalans, one American, one Ecuadoran, and one Venezuelan, along with 105 Hondurans.[1]

Hondurans had experienced many military regimes before but never the forms of terror that appeared in the 1980s. The sudden disappearances and ferocious torture and murder of well-known student leaders, unionists, peasant leaders, leftist activists, and exiles in a concentrated setting produced a stunning psychological impact on society.[2] In El Salvador, Nicaragua, and Guatemala, the number of tortured, disappeared, and massacred reached levels never seen before. In Guatemala alone, more than 150,000 disappeared or died in genocidal military counterinsurgency campaigns; in El Salvador, some 100,000; and in Nicaragua, at least 50,000 more. The case of Central America is crucial in terms of illuminating not only the long arm of Operation Condor but also the deep involvement of the U.S. government in Latin American repression.

In Central America, U.S. involvement is well documented, more so than in the Southern Cone. In Tegucigalpa, the Argentines taught military officers and contra paramilitary commandos how to torture and disappear suspects. They worked hand in hand with U.S. military and intelligence personnel who taught methods of surveillance and interrogation.[3] Essentially, U.S. officers trained and financed the death squads that emerged in Honduras. According to a former Honduran Special Forces officer, "The Argentines came in first, and they taught how to disappear people. The United States made them more efficient." General José Bueso, former Honduran army chief of staff, said that U.S. advisors offered to help them organize a special countersubversive unit and stipulated that it report directly to the chief of the armed forces.[4] This unit—a key parallel state structure—became Battalion 3-16, which incorporated several earlier death squads to become a centralized apparatus of terror. The CIA continued to train and finance the unit with full awareness of its role in human rights atrocities. Some 3-16 members were flown to a secret base in Texas, which appeared on no map, for counterinsurgency instruction. A CIA official confirmed in later hearings that 3-16 personnel participated in a CIA interrogation course, although he claimed that the CIA discouraged physical torture.[5]

This chapter sketches the establishment of a Condor terror system in Central America in the 1980s. It focuses mainly on Honduras, about which less is known in general, because the case of Honduras graphically illustrates the reproduction of Condor methods and operations in Central America.[6] Honduras is geopolitically strategic in Central America due to its central location, bordered by Nicaragua, El Salvador, and Guatemala. The multinational counterrevolutionary strategy called for Honduras to supply the base of operations, the United States the funding and direction, and Argentina the instructors for dirty war.

Social, Economic, and Political Context

The conflicts of the 1960s–1980s in Central America were rooted in the exclusionary, unequal, antidemocratic, and repressive structures that dominated the region, supported by the oligarchy, the military, and almost always, by U.S. policy. Long-standing U.S. economic interests were obscured during the Cold War, especially during the Reagan administration, as social unrest in Central America was portrayed in terms of the East-West struggle. Throughout most of the Cold War, U.S. policymakers argued that revolutionary and reformist forces in the Third World were Soviet agents rather than indigenous movements fighting to transform unjust conditions.

In the 1980s, however, four of the five Central America countries reflected the legacies of the colonial era in terms of their economic and social structures: small, powerful land-owning classes, praetorian militaries, and large, poor peasant populations.[7] Central America had been integrated into the U.S. political economy since the nineteenth century, supplying primary products such as coffee, bananas, sugar, and cotton to U.S. companies and markets. The first challenge to the old oligarchic order in the region was the 1944 revolution in Guatemala; next, a revolution occurred in Costa Rica in 1948 that culminated with the abolition of the armed forces. In Nicaragua, dictator Anastasio Somoza, originally installed as head of the National Guard in the 1930s by the United States, created a family dynasty that endured until 1979. The Somozas practiced cruel repression and appropriated vast tracts of land and other national assets to enrich themselves. In 1979, after many years of social conflict, a popular revolution united an armed movement (the Sandinistas) with peasants, workers, and the small middle class to oust Somoza from power.

In El Salvador, reform movements based on the Christian Democratic (CD) and Social Democratic (SD) parties arose during the 1960s, and political protest grew among popular sectors. The government responded by creating paramilitary forces including ORDEN, formed to counter the political organizing of the CD Party in the rural areas. ORDEN, with direct organizational assistance from the U.S. Green Berets, the State Department, and the CIA,[8] used bloody methods of repression against any opposition. In 1980, El Salvador erupted into open warfare between government security forces, backed by wealthy landowners, and a strong revolutionary movement.

Guatemala's reformist president, Jacobo Arbenz, carried out social and economic reforms in the early 1950s. After the CIA-organized ouster of Arbenz in 1954, a pro-U.S. officer was installed as president. He overturned all the reforms of the democratic era. The Guatemalan guerrilla movement first emerged from rebellious and nationalist factions of the army who were angered by U.S. use of Guatemala as a training area for the Bay of Pigs invasion. They were joined by elements from the small Communist Party, students, unionists, and peasants. Later, other sectors of the population joined the revolutionary movement. Guatemala's internal armed conflict (which began in the 1960s) intensified in the early 1980s.

In the 1960s in Central America, the U.S. government encouraged the formation of CONDECA, a military alliance among the countries established in 1963. The U.S. military set up a secure Central American telecommunications network in 1964 under cover of the U.S. Public Safety Program. The Central American interior ministers met and established formal links among the secret services of all five regimes in 1965.[9] They agreed to share intelligence and operations in a secret arrangement presaging Operation Condor.

U.S. Policy in the 1980s

After the Carter interlude (1977–81), the Reagan administration reintroduced Cold War categories to U.S. foreign policy and adopted a hostile and coercive attitude toward the struggles for change in Central America. The administration sent a delegation, led by hard-liner Jeanne Kirkpatrick, to Latin American capitals to meet with military leaders and essentially apologize for Carter's human rights policy. U.S. diplomats who had favored the policy were replaced or exiled from the State Department.[10] The Reagan administration devoted millions of dollars in resources to finance the counterinsurgency armies in El Salvador and Guatemala and the contras in Nicaragua, utilizing a "low-intensity conflict" strategy that maximized destruction while avoiding extensive use of U.S. troops. In diplomatic arenas, the Reagan administration rejected strategies of negotiation or compromise with revolutionary and progressive forces in Central America and viewed the conflicts in strictly zero-sum terms. Washington actively worked to prevent or weaken United Nations resolutions that denounced human rights atrocities by its client armies.

The triumph of the Sandinista revolution over the Somoza dictatorship in July 1979 was a major event in Latin America, the first successful popular revolution in the region since the 1959 Cuban revolution. The Carter administration had tried to promote an eleventh-hour "moderate" and nonrevolutionary interim government to replace Somoza, but it was unsuccessful. After taking office in 1981, the Reagan administration initiated an undeclared war against the Sandinista government, militarized Honduras, and pressured Costa Rica to rebuild an army to wage the anticommunist struggle. In its first years, the Reagan administration denied that its goal was the overthrow of the leftist Nicaraguan government. However, Reagan signed two secret "findings" in 1981 (in March and November) that authorized secret paramilitary operations against Nicaragua.[11] Honduras became a virtual U.S. military center for the counterinsurgency war against the Sandinista government and the major base of operations for the contras. The United States upgraded its base at Palmerola to create a sophisticated military command and control center that became the headquarters of the covert war, and built the El Aguacate base, near the Nicaraguan border, for use of the contras and the CIA. The CIA directed, financed, and organized the contra war, to the point of deciding the strategies of the contras. In 1997, former CIA station chief Donald Winters boasted, "I ran a war . . . I started with 500 rather ragtag people, and turned that into 10,000 fairly disciplined troops [who] challenged the Sandinista government."[12]

U.S. advisors were instrumental in setting up Proyectos Militares Técnicos (PROMITEC, Military Technical Projects) in Honduras, a psychological warfare unit that used deception and propaganda as methods of counterinsurgency. CIA manuals used in Central America, the "Human Resource Exploitation Manual" and the contra assassination manual, drew directly from army manuals of the 1960s and advocated harsh tactics of dirty war. In 1983 in Honduras, the United States set up the Centro Regional de Entrenamiento Militar (CREM, Regional Military Training Center) to upgrade the capabilities of all the Central American armed forces and encourage them to work together in combined counterinsurgency operations. Under the aegis of military exercises such as Big Pine II, U.S. forces installed advanced radar tracking stations and an air defense system in Honduras, and modernized airports and runways. Finally, substantial documentation has emerged of the covert ways in which U.S. military and intelligence officers encouraged, or turned a blind eye toward, extralegal and atrocious methods used to combat revolution in Central America.

The Argentines Export Dirty War Methods

Ariel Armony has consolidated much evidence that Argentine dirty warriors began to work with Somoza's brutal National Guard long before 1979, as part of an autonomous foreign policy aimed at expanding the military regime's regional influence and leading an international "war against subversion."[13] The Argentine military was deeply involved in the 1980 coup in Bolivia as well, as we have seen. Armony argues that the Argentine military, not the CIA, formed and trained the first contra army after the 1979 triumph of the Sandinista revolution. In fact, during the 1977 meeting of the Conference of American

Armies in Managua, the Argentine junta had promised Somoza military and financial assistance to defeat the popular insurrection.[14] Armony shows that the juntas' anticommunist foreign policy in Central America was driven by national security ideology: they were convinced that President Jimmy Carter had relinquished the holy war against communism. Armony also suggests that in the late 1970s, the CIA collaborated with and helped to finance counterrevolutionary operations by Argentine intelligence in Central America, contrary to the stated policy of the Carter administration. His key primary source here is Leandro Sánchez Reisse, the Argentine intelligence operative who testified before a Senate subcommittee in 1987.[15] If the CIA secretly sponsored the Argentine regime's Central American campaigns during the late 1970s, however, then the Argentines' foreign policy was not as independent as it appeared. It stands to reason that the Argentines would not operate in the U.S. "backyard" without a green light.

In a 1987 monograph, a former contra leader, Edgar Chamorro, confirmed that during the Carter administration "there was secret contact between present and former CIA operatives and early *contra* organizers."[16] He stated that the CIA secretly consulted with the Argentine junta and other right-wing forces in Latin America before Reagan's election and that U.S. military intelligence veteran Vernon Walters went to Argentina in 1980 to discuss the formation of a counterrevolutionary army in Central America.[17] In that year, Chamorro wrote, at a meeting of the Latin American affiliate of the World Anticommunist League (WACL) in Buenos Aires, Salvadoran neofascist Roberto D'Aubuisson also arranged for the Argentines to train paramilitaries in his country to combat "subversion," and Argentine officers worked with the Salvadorans to form death squads that would carry out their dirty war.[18]

The early Argentine presence was confirmed by another Argentine intelligence commando, Carlos Alberto Lobo, who admitted publicly that he was contracted by Somoza's National Guard to fight the Sandinistas in 1979.[19] Lobo said he carried out the same dirty war operations in Nicaragua that he had in Argentina: disappearances and other illegal acts. Additionally, in 1982 testimony Héctor Francés, member of Argentine intelligence Battalion 601, said that he had operated in Central America as well. Francés added that Argentine training of the contras and the Hondurans occurred "under the permanent oversight and direction of the CIA."[20]

According to Sánchez Reisse, Argentine intelligence set up a Condor base in Miami in the mid-1970s, staffed by Battalion 601 officers. He told the Senate subcommittee in 1987 that he had directed drug money laundering and counterinsurgency operations in Latin America from the clandestine military headquarters in Florida, and that it was set up with the sanction of the CIA. Sánchez Reisse explained that his Florida businesses were fronts for weapons shipments to Central America, carried out with the assistance of the CIA, and that laundered money from drug trafficking and extortion-kidnapping was used to pay Argentines involved in counterinsurgency in Central America.[21] It is interesting to recall that Chile's DINA also contacted the CIA in 1974 about opening a Condor headquarters in Miami. That request was denied, but no further action was taken to forestall Condor.

Sánchez Reisse boasted about his freedom of movement in the United States, saying that his presence was authorized by the U.S. government, and declared that the CIA directly collaborated with his intelligence unit in Florida. He testified that Argentine intelligence and operations personnel were first sent to Central America in 1978, under the doctrine of "ideological frontiers" and with the approval of the United States.[22] It appears that the Argentines acted with the secret support of the U.S. intelligence apparatus during the Carter years.

Former contra "public relations" chief Chamorro noted the powerful ideological influence of the Argentine officers and CIA operatives on the Central Americans. The anti-Sandinistas were originally concerned with regaining their private property and oligarchic power and privilege, or pursuing revenge, he stated, but the messianic anticommunist ideology of the Argentines and the Americans began to reshape their rationale for the war. The Argentines fervently believed in the countersubversive struggle as a holy war and argued that Soviet and Cuban designs underlay the conflict. U.S. officers wanted to internationalize and sovietize the struggle in order to gain backing from (and intimidate) Congress.[23] They urged Chamorro and other Nicaraguans to make speeches linking the disorganized contras with the anti-Soviet rebels in Afghanistan and the international anticommunist movement. Gradually, contra propaganda portrayed the war in this light. Chamorro realized that, "[i]nstead of admitting that our objective was to overthrow the Nicaraguan government, we were instructed [by the CIA] to say that it was to create conditions for democracy. . . . In reality the *contras* were not working for freedom or democracy, but to go backwards in time, to a repressive, rightwing military government."[24] Chamorro left the contras in 1984 because he decided that the CIA-run war was a cynical, deceitful, and destructive enterprise that no longer reflected Nicaraguan interests or direction. He criticized the CIA for creating an illusory world that had nothing to do with the complex reality of Nicaragua and deplored the position that murder and torture were justified in the name of patriotism.[25]

The Role of Southern Cone Condor Organizations

General Guillermo Suárez Mason, the powerful commander of Argentina's First Army Corps, was instrumental in the creation of the Extraterritorial Task

Force (grupo de tareas exteriores or GTE), a unit of Battalion 601 that carried out secret intelligence operations outside of Argentina. Sanchéz Reisse said the GTE was based in Florida, with the authorization of the CIA.[26] Suárez Mason himself presided over the Fourth Congress of the Latin American Anticommunist League, the WACL affiliate, in 1980, and WACL reportedly donated U.S. $8 million to pay for the deployment of Argentine officers to Central America.[27] Suárez Mason fled Argentina after the transition to democracy in 1984, and, according to one human rights organization, Oliver North arranged a false visa for him to enter the United States. North had been discussing with him the formation of a continental counterinsurgency force,[28] a concept that, again, evokes Operation Condor.

Argentina's GTE was a key Condor unit commanded by Colonel Osvaldo Ribeiro, head of the counterinsurgency team in Central America and organizer of a secret torture and detention center in the Campo de Mayo military base near Buenos Aires.[29] The GTE had two objectives in Central America: pursuit of Argentine insurgents (some of whom were working with the Sandinistas) as well as assistance to and training of Central American officers.[30] In the first category, Argentine commanders sent a contra squad to Costa Rica in 1980, where it firebombed a radio station staffed by suspected Montoneros. The radio station had broadcast news about the dirty war in Argentina. Three Costa Ricans were killed.[31]

According to the former human rights commissioner of Honduras, Leo Valladares, the practice of disappearances became systematic in Honduras after the arrival of the Argentines, and his 1993 report included the names of thirteen key Argentine officers who worked with Battalion 3-16.[32] Ribeiro's chief of operations was Santiago Hoya, also known as Santiago Villegas. He worked closely with the contras and directed the establishment of a secret Honduran detention and torture center known as "La Quinta."[33] La Quinta, or the 5th Army School, was also where the Argentines carried out training in dirty war operations. Other Argentine officers in Central America included Alberto A. Valín, Mario Davico, Raúl Guglielminetti, and Rafael López Fader.

The Central American Struggles Become Internationalized

In a familiar pattern, the Honduran police and armed forces began an aggressive counterinsurgency campaign after the arrival of the Argentines. In 1979, Honduran colonel Amílcar Zelaya Rodríguez, commander of the police, formed a secret unit called Grupo de los 14 (Group of 14), a forerunner to Battalion 3-16. The fourteen included operatives who became notorious for their role in disappearances and torture, men such as Alejandro Hernández

Santos (linked by Honduran experts to the CIA), Billy Joya (who reportedly graduated from West Point), and Ramón Montañola. According to a former member of 3-16, the Group of 14 was charged with eliminating persons considered enemies of the state. In January 1981, Colonel Gustavo Alvarez Martínez, then head of the Honduran Fuerza de Seguridad Pública (FUSEP, Public Security Force), reorganized the group and reduced it to ten members.[34] Over the following months, more members were added and the group underwent counterintelligence training provided by U.S., Argentine, and Chilean instructors. The group was then divided into three teams and deployed to different cities, where they carried out disappearances and torture. By 1982, the organization became Departamento de Investigaciones Especiales (DIES, Department of Special Investigations), and in 1984 it was renamed Battalion 3-16. Despite the fact that a civilian was elected president in 1981 after a series of military regimes, the majority of the disappearances in Honduras occurred between 1981 and 1984 (184 by official count, some 2,000 according to human rights advocates[35]).

Alvarez Martínez, named head of the army in 1982, was a commanding figure in the counterinsurgency campaigns, one of the three most powerful men in the country (the other two, according to Honduran sources, were President Suazo Córdova and U.S. ambassador John Negroponte). Alvarez openly told outgoing Ambassador Jack Binns in 1981 that he admired the Argentines' dirty war tactics and that he intended to use the same ruthless methods in Honduras.[36] Known for his fierce anticommunism, Alvarez was closely linked to Negroponte, to the CIA, and to the U.S. military, which decorated him on several occasions and promoted his rapid rise in the military hierarchy. The ascendency of Alvarez marked the predominance of the hard-line sectors of the Honduran military over more professional and apolitical officers.[37] Alvarez was so close to the CIA station chief in Honduras, Donald Winters (1982–84), that Winters asked him to be the godfather of his adopted daughter. Ronald Reagan awarded Alvarez the Legion of Merit in 1983.[38]

Under Alvarez, FUSEP had carried out illegal acts and human rights abuses, and after he became head of the army, atrocities intensified. Alvarez had attended Argentine military academies between 1958 and 1962, when French counterinsurgency instructors were a powerful influence on the Argentine military,[39] and he retained close links to Argentine officers during the repression of the 1970s in that country. Alvarez also attended advanced courses at Fort Benning, Georgia, the counterinsurgency course at Fort Bragg, North Carolina, and the combined operations course at Fort Gulick in the Panama Canal Zone (School of the Americas, SOA).[40]

The naming of Alvarez as army chief prompted the resignation of Colonel Leonidas Torres Arias, then-head of the intelligence branch of the army. In 1982, Torres issued an extraordinary public declaration in Mexico in which he accused Alvarez of directly heading a death squad in Honduras. He said Alvarez exhibited "an extremist psychosis" that threatened democratic, reformist, and peaceful processes in Honduras, and warned that Alvarez was bringing the nation to the brink of a bloody and fratricidal war with its neighbor (Nicaragua). Torres condemned Alvarez for his use of repressive and criminal methods, specifically his aim "to annihilate physically and make disappear . . . all that fails to sustain his radical ideas," adding that his "repressive plans and physical extermination of all opposition . . . and his abandonment of Honduran neutrality" [41] violated Honduran law and negated military traditions. Torres's denunciation was accurate: Battalion 3-16 reported directly to Alvarez, and victims' testimonies and human rights studies show that he personally made decisions about who lived and who died.

Under CIA orders, Nicaraguan contra Ricardo "Chino" Lau became head of the counterintelligence section of the contras based in Honduras, a unit set up with the assistance of the CIA,[42] and he worked closely with Alvarez. Lau was a feared torturer and he took part in many abductions in Honduras. Formerly a National Guardsman under Somoza, Lau was a graduate of the SOA, where he took numerous courses in officer training, munitions, intelligence, and counterintelligence in the 1960s.[43] According to a former contra, Alvarez signed a secret agreement in early 1982 with the Fuerza Democrática Nicaragüense (Nicaraguan Democratic Force) or FDN, the key contra organization, establishing that the contra counterintelligence unit would work directly with the Dirección de Investigaciones Especiales (DIES, Directorate of Special Investigations), the forerunner to Battalion 3-16.[44] The Honduran military pledged to aid the contras and allow them free movement in Honduras. This bilateral agreement paralleled the secret arrangements that comprised Operation Condor.

The Role of the CIA

In the early 1980s, the Reagan administration stated publicly that its goal in Central America was limited, to stop arms traffic from Nicaragua to the Salvadoran rebels. But as CIA analyst David McMichael testified later, a secret plan "originated in the Latin American Bureau of the CIA (in the fall of 1981) and was adopted by the president and presented to the congress in late 1981. The plan was to introduce a covert force in Nicaragua of approximately 1500 men." The secret objective was to provoke a cross-border response by the Sandinistas and thereby cause their government to lose support.[45]

In 1982, Representative Edward Boland proposed, and the U.S. Congress passed, an amendment prohibiting the involvement of the U.S. government in the overthrow of the Sandinista government. Nevertheless, the Reagan administration pursued the war while seeking to hide the U.S. hand. The strategy was set back after the Argentine junta invaded the Falklands-Malvinas Islands in 1982, sparking a war with Britain. The Reagan administration sided with Britain and aided its naval operations with secret intelligence. Leopoldo Galtieri, head of the Argentine junta, had expected U.S. support for his invasion, given the regime's clandestine collaboration with the United States in Central America. After Argentina's defeat in that war, Galtieri withdrew most of the Argentine forces from Central America in retaliation. (Former human rights commissioner Valladares has said, however, that Argentine counterinsurgency experts continued to operate in Honduras until 1987, after the transition to democracy in Argentina. This situation illustrated the continuing parallel power and secret operations of the Argentine army, despite the transition from military rule.) The CIA gradually took over the management of the contras from the Argentines.

In 1982, Nicaraguan vice-interior minister Luis Carrión noted that the size and sophistication of the contra units had dramatically improved and that they were armed by "elements in the Honduras army and the CIA."[46] Another Sandinista official said that, according to witnesses who had been kidnapped and taken to Honduras by the contras (and who later escaped), "an American named Daniel and an Argentine named Felix" as well as Honduran military personnel were regularly in the contra camps.

In 1982, there were weekly meetings among the contra directorate, the CIA, and the Honduran military to discuss the progress of the war. Edgar Chamorro and other contra leaders met with U.S. Army colonel Raymond, a CIA officer; CIA station chief Donald Winters and his deputy John W. Mallet; Honduran colonel Calderini; and Argentines Ribeiro and Hoya. Duane Clarridge, CIA chief of Latin American operations, attended some meetings as well.[47] Several deserters from Honduran Battalion 3-16 referred to "Raymond," also known as "Papi," as the CIA officer with whom they coordinated, and Nicaraguan contras worked with Raymond as well. In this sense, the CIA, and especially Raymond, were central in the functioning of Condor structures in the region. Bob Woodward identified him as the chief of a CIA base in Tegucigalpa and a former Special Forces lieutenant colonel named Ray Doty.[48] A former leader of paramilitary training in Laos during the Vietnam war, "Raymond" was chief of the operational arm of the covert contra program and had a direct, top secret communications channel to CIA headquarters. A contra deserter named "Miguel" said that Raymond supervised all the CIA officers who worked with the contras. Every Monday, he said, Raymond received a report from counterintelligence chief "Chino" Lau, who told Raymond of all the operations carried out by his contra unit and the costs incurred. "Miguel" said that the FDN had presented written reports on all investigations and interrogations, and all death sentences carried out, until Raymond told Lau never again to include any reporting on persons captured and then killed by the contras.

Lau became so infamous for his human rights atrocities, according to "Miguel," that Raymond reassigned him from the counterintelligence unit to a clandestine force called the Death Squad.[49] "Miguel" told a U.S. reporter another chilling story about Raymond. When one prisoner was deemed innocent by "Miguel," Lau opposed his release and Raymond summoned "Miguel" to his office. Raymond told him he could not let the prisoner live because he might reveal sensitive information about the Hondurans, the contras, or the CIA. "Miguel" did have the prisoner killed, but according to the contra, the incident haunted him.

"Miguel" said he had helped to organize a death squad in Honduras with the assistance of the CIA, and he showed U.S. journalist Linda Drucker a manual the contras had used that gave instructions in kidnapping techniques. He said that the job of his counterintelligence unit was to abduct and interrogate not only guerrillas but also political opponents, student leaders, human rights activists, and unionists. "Miguel" said that "the gringos knew" about their dirty war operations and that, in fact, Colonel Raymond, his CIA contact, had congratulated him for a job well done.[50] "Miguel" said two CIA officers were present when the Hondurans and contras agreed that contra operatives would use Honduran military uniforms and identifications to hide their identities. Again, this sort of agreement paralleled Condor, and it illuminated the role of the CIA.

In 1983, a CIA officer known as "John Kirkpatrick," with counterinsurgency experience in the Phoenix Program in Vietnam, compiled a training course that culminated in an assassination manual that was distributed to the contras. It included ways to "neutralize" or assassinate selected political targets, carry out sabotage, blackmail, and mob violence, create martyrs by killing one's own allies, and otherwise engage in terrorist acts.[51] In fact, one section was entitled "Implicit and Explicit Terror." A second CIA booklet called *Freedom Fighters' Manual*, in comic book format, gave instructions in making Molotov cocktails and carrying out sabotage.[52] The assassination manual drew from material used for training U.S. Special Forces during the Vietnam war, and included passages that repeated word for word U.S. Army guerrilla warfare and counterinsurgency lessons from the 1960s. When news of the manual became public, the U.S. Congress was outraged, as was much of U.S. public opinion.[53] It was clear that, contrary to public statements by the administration, it was determined to overthrow the Sandinista government, outside the laws of war and ignoring congressional restraints. This realization led to the passage of the second Boland amendment in 1984, which outlawed aid to the contras in more specific language. The Reagan administration's expanded efforts to circumvent Congress resulted in the Iran-contra affair.[54]

Other fragments of information emerged about the involvement of the CIA in the contra war. CIA officers who worked closely with 3-16 and the contras, according to Honduran human rights advocates interviewed in 2002, included "Mr. Mike," "Jerry Clark," "William E. Clark," "Mr. Bill," and "Richard Smith," along with Raymond. In 1983, the Sandinistas announced that "Mike," the CIA station chief in Tegucigalpa, had approved the infiltration of two assassins into Nicaragua to kill Sandinista officials. They named the station chief as "Mike Tock."[55] The identity of "Mike" remains unclear, but CIA sources told reporter Christopher Dickey that "Mike" did serve as station chief until 1982.[56] Various Honduran sources said that "Mike" was "Mike Collins," "Mike Dobbs," or "Mike Dubbs."[57] In 1983, another contra, Jorge Ramírez Zelaya, was captured by the Sandinistas as he entered Nicaragua to carry out assassinations under a covert CIA operation code-named M-83 (for Managua-1983, the date when the CIA expected the overthrow of the Sandinistas). Ramírez Zelaya told an interviewer that money from the CIA was channeled through "Mike Tock."[58] He said in a press briefing organized by the Sandinistas that Mike Tock, CIA station chief in Honduras, and Alvarez Martínez had approved the M-83 operation.[59] *Baltimore Sun* reporters were told by a ranking diplomat at the U.S. Embassy in Tegucigalpa that there was a CIA officer named Michael Dubbs stationed there.[60] "Mr. Mike" appears as a key figure in other cases, such as the disappearance and execution of U.S. priest James Carney and the torture and interrogation of Honduran Inés Murillo, outlined presently.

In 1985, another former contra, José Ephren Mondragón Martínez, said he was forced to join the FDN but went on to say he had attended "courses in intelligence, counterinsurgency and psychology of war at an Argentine military school" between July and September 1983.[61] He admitted to leading a task force from Honduras that penetrated deep into Nicaragua, where it was ultimately captured by the Sandinistas. Later in 1985 Mondragón supplied more detail, speaking of receiving earlier specialized training in Argentina (in 1981) and training in "terrorist sabotage, clandestine operations, and counterinsurgencies" in Guatemala. Mondragón said that the Argentines and the CIA had taught him the use of explosives and that the CIA advised the contras to recruit new members through the kidnapping of peasants. Those who refused to join were shot or stabbed to death, he said, on orders of contra commander Enrique Bermúdez, who proclaimed that "one must plant terror." Mondragón said the contras kidnapped, killed, and raped Nicaraguans in the refugee camps in Honduras and that young Nicaraguan girls were "sexual merchandise," "raped night and day," while old women were made to cook and men "were treated like slaves." Overall, the Hondurans "governed like savages" in the refugee camps, he asserted.[62]

In 1985, Honduran human rights advocate Ramón Custodio accused U.S. personnel of involvement in the training of death squads. He cited a *Miami Herald* article that discussed the role of Green Berets in training Honduran military personnel at La Venta and also said the CIA had a role in the disappearance of 147 people.[63] That same year, Nicaragua brought the U.S. government before the World Court on charges of conducting illegal war operations against Nicaragua.[64]

In 1986, another contra defector named Mario Rene Fernández said he had received military training in the 5th army school of Tegucigalpa, first infantry battalion area, and that one course taught from a CIA manual was called "Troops trained in jungle and night operations."[65] The 5th school in Tegucigalpa was run by the Argentine military.[66] This defector said that a CIA officer named "Bill Johnson" (doubtless a code name) directly supervised and advised the contras, as did a Bolivian code-named "Ricardo."[67] A CIA officer admitted in a closed-door Senate hearing in 1988 that "Mr. Bill," a former army special forces officer, was a CIA trainer in Honduras, and said that he was killed in the April 1983 Beirut bombing of the U.S. Embassy.[68]

Battalion 3-16

Through the sworn testimonies of a number of former members and deserters from the fearsome Battalion 3-16, formed in 1984, we can piece together a fairly complete picture of the unit's functioning. General Luis Alonso Discua, a graduate of the SOA and former chief of 3-16, said publicly that in 1983 he was brought to the United States for two months to coordinate the battalion's activities with those of the contras.[69] Four deserters from 3-16 fled to Canada, where they lived for some years until their pasts were uncovered by the *Baltimore Sun.* Canada then expelled three of them for human rights crimes. The most infamous of the former Battalion 3-16 members was Florencio Caballero, who died in 1997. His testimony was pivotal for the proceedings of various human rights cases, including the disappearance of Angel Manfredo Velásquez Rodríguez, heard by the Inter-American Court of Human Rights.[70.] Caballero testified that some of his victims were innocent of the charges that led to their torture and death. He also insisted that he was an interrogator, not a torturer, but his former compatriots and his victims flatly contradicted this assertion and described him as a sadistic torturer.[71] Other defectors, José Valle and José Barrera, gave separate but similar accounts of the tortures used by 3-16 and the training provided by U.S. and Argentine instructors.[72]

Battalion 3-16 was divided into squadrons with different tasks: surveillance, abductions, and executions.[73] José Barerra, who gave a sworn statement to a Mexican notary in 1987, said that U.S. officials financed all the operations of 3-16, including the abductions and disappearances, and all the facilities of 3-16, including the clandestine detention centers.[74] Caballero, similarly, discussed CIA payments to the Honduran death squads in his testimony. Barerra, who had been a member of 3-16 for four years, named all the key operatives of the unit. He confirmed that Battalion 3-16 was the military unit responsible for abduction, torture, and assassination of more than 100 Hondurans. Barerra detailed his earlier participation in FUSEP, preceded by the Group of 10 and the Group of 14 (whose mission, he said, was "to eliminate those individuals that caused problems to the Armed Forces of Honduras and who were incorrigible communists"). He revealed that the Group of 14 was dissolved when the Honduran press discovered the death squad. One of the group's members had become drunk and was detained, and police found on his person photos of individuals who had been murdered. He had revealed the modus operandi of the group, which was to carry photos of targeted persons in order to identify and eliminate them. Barerra admitted that he was later assigned to execute his former comrade.[75]

Barerra's testimony confirmed the role of the CIA in the financing and training of Battalion 3-16. He said that eight CIA officers and four Argentines had taught 3-16 members combat maneuvers, surveillance, torture, explosives, interrogation, and interchange of prisoners. More important, Barerra said that he gradually realized that the payment of personnel, the maintenance of the clandestine cells, and, in general, the very existence of 3-16 was due to the CIA's financing and direct participation. Barerra named Raymond, or Papi, as the liaison between the CIA and 3-16, and said that Raymond visited the headquarters of 3-16 periodically; he named another Puerto Rican CIA officer who worked with 3-16 named Lieutenant Rivera, code named Javier.

Caballero testified that in 1979 or 1980, he learned of a massacre of some 150 Salvadorans by Honduran and Salvadoran forces,[76] an early combined operation. He said that Argentine and Chilean officers taught the Hondurans the methods of surveillance, abduction, and torture, beginning in 1979.[77] Caballero named Major Alexander Hernández as chief of the death squad that operated within the army intelligence apparatus—that is, Battalion 3-16—in charge of the disappearances and murders, clandestine detention centers, and safe houses,[78] and described in horrific detail the physical tortures used against captives. Caballero said that U.S. advisors taught "psychological methods" of coercive interrogation, such as putting rats in cells, forcing prisoners to stand for long periods of time, denying them sleep, and throwing icy water on them, and said that U.S. officers discouraged physical torture. (According to international human rights standards, however, such "psychological techniques" do constitute torture; they are aimed at destroying the will and spirit of a person.[79]) Moreover, Caballero told *Baltimore Sun* reporters, "the Americans knew everything we were doing. They saw what condition the victims were in—their marks and bruises. They did not do anything."[80] Other defectors confirmed that U.S. officers knew of the torture and raised no objections.

In 1988, Richard Stoltz, deputy director for Operations of the CIA, admitted to a Senate Committee that the CIA manual used to train 3-16 members in the early 1980s specified the use of coercive methods such as sensory deprivation, denial of sleep, forced standing, and isolation, thus confirming Caballero's account.[81] Stoltz told senators that Caballero did "attend a CIA human resources exploitation or interrogation course."[82] However, he denied that CIA officers looked the other way as their Honduran counterparts tortured and murdered prisoners. Similarly, the CIA inspector general's report of 1997 stated, "There is no information in CIA files indicating that CIA officers either authorized or were directly involved in human rights abuses."[83] That statement was not a denial, however; such evidence might have been taken out of CIA files or never put in. The inspector general's report did admit for the first time that the CIA knew about the systematic abuses committed by 3-16 members in the 1980s and did not report them.[84] In 1989, the Senate Select Committee on Intelligence discovered that the CIA had failed to inform committee members during the 1988 hearings of the 1963 *KUBARK Manual*, the CIA manual upon which the Honduran interrogation manual had been based.[85] The lineage of the 1983 manual showed that the methods advocated by U.S. military and intelligence instructors were not "mistakes" but an integral part of long-standing counterinsurgency doctrine.

Another 3-16 defector who issued a sworn statement, José Federico Valle López, spoke of his training in intelligence in 1980. Valle was part of a group of 120 trainees, including some sixty or seventy officers from Guatemala and El Salvador and contras from Nicaragua, who were taught methods of surveillance of unions, student organizations, and political parties. The classes were taught by Americans as well as Panamanians, Puerto Ricans, Argentines, and Chileans, he said, and the U.S. instructors "were in charge of giving courses on how to follow someone, surveillance, persecution, camouflage, photography, disguise, psychological interrogations, and handling of small arms," including bombs.[86] In 1981, Alvarez Martínez divided the group into squadrons and each squad was again divided into three teams: operations, surveillance, and security. Valle said his team's first act was the abduction of

Honduran Humberto Sánchez, who was suspected of collaboration with the Sandinistas. Sanchéz was seized along with his nine-year-old son, Valle said, and held for three months in a closet. He was tortured with the *capucha* (a rubber mask or hood used to suffocate a victim), electric shock, being buried alive, and other horrific methods. Sánchez was finally turned over to the contras, who killed him along with his son.[87] This double crime was carried out jointly by Honduran and Nicaraguan operatives, and, as such, replicated Condor operations.

Valle also clarified other well-known cases, including that of Felix Martínez, president of the union of university workers who had disappeared in 1982. After three months of torture and interrogation, Valle said, Martínez was turned over to the FDN (contras) and killed by multiple knife wounds. Valle revealed that Argentines also had interrogated Martínez. His body was found on the border between Honduras and Nicaragua. Valle also discussed the case of a disappeared Costa Rican woman whose surname was Padilla. She was detained-disappeared at the airport in Tegucigalpa, he said, transferred to the Intelligence School at Lepaterique, Honduras and finally delivered to the intelligence apparatus of El Salvador. These cases reflected Condor characteristics such as cross-border coordination of disappearances, torture, interrogation, and assassination by combined countersubversive teams.

Due to the atrocious human rights record of 3-16, the unit was nominally disbanded in 1988. U.S. officials expressed concern about the shutdown. In one cable, Secretary of State George Shultz asked, "If disbanded, completely or partially, by whom have its various functions been assumed? Also, what element within the military is presently responsible for counterintelligence functions?"[88] In fact, 3-16's operations were assumed by the Department of Counterintelligence. Targeted assassinations continued in Honduras into the 1990s.

The Role of CREM

In 1983, the U.S. military set up the Regional Center for Military Training (CREM) in Honduras as a means to upgrade the capabilities of the Salvadoran and Honduran militaries and the contra forces in counterinsurgency and irregular warfare. Some 4,000 troops were training there in 1984, and there were some 160 U.S. military instructors. The training center was also the site of a secret detention center that held disappeared prisoners from all the countries in the region.

In 1984, Alvarez Martínez was ousted in a "palace coup," and CIA station chief Winters was reassigned soon afterward. In a secret 1984 report to the new commander in chief of the Honduran army, Walter López Reyes, Lieutenant

Colonel Angel Ricardo Luque Portillo made an assessment of the CREM.[89] He reported that the United States had provided the infrastructure for the base, including a permanent radar surveillance system that covered its airspace and theaters of operation around the country; a system of telephone intervention through the use of microwaves; and a detention center for thirty prisoners. The United States also paid for the labor of some 320 workers, who built barracks, maintained the physical plant, and prepared food for the personnel of the Center. A secret intelligence network called the Center of Joint Operations (Centro de Operaciones Conjuntas) linked CREM to the Center of Operations of Task Force Bravo of the U.S. army (based at Palmerola), the intelligence directorate of the High Command of the Honduran armed forces, the minister of defense of El Salvador, and the High Command of the contra organization FDN. This communications network, and its U.S.-provided technological and logistical infrastructure, evoke Condortel, and illustrate the centrality of such systems for repressive operations in a geographic region. According to the secret report, the Center of Joint Operations collected, processed, and distributed intelligence information to its combat units through an intelligence network that extended across Honduras, El Salvador, and Nicaragua.

Luque's classified report also listed the prisoners in the detention center. One, Nicaraguan Melba Cáceres Mondragón, had been captured in a combined contra-3-16 operation. Her fate was publicly unknown at the time; a 1987 Human Rights Watch report said that after her abduction by 3-16 in 1983 she was taken to the detention center at INDUMIL (a Honduran secret torture and detention center), but her trail was lost afterward.[90] Other CREM prisoners named in the report included Francisco Osorto, captured in a combined operation by the armies of El Salvador and Honduras near the border; María Marta Ventura Ramos, a Salvadoran seized in Tegucigalpa by 3-16; Luis Alonso Romero Ortiz, a Guatemalan also seized in Tegucigalpa; and José Amilcar Maradiaga, captured in a combined 3-16 and FDN operation. There were numerous Hondurans in the detention center as well. Supervision of the prisoners was exercised by three officers—a Honduran, a Salvadoran, and a Nicaraguan contra. This secret multinational detention center thus resembled Condor parastatal structures—and it was set up and paid for by U.S. military and intelligence forces.

Luque's report made clear that the prisoners were "disappeared" and not legally held. In the report, he warned that human rights groups were asking questions and suggested that the prisoners be moved. He also urged the armed forces chief to "orient" the colonel in charge of an in-house investigative commission on the disappeared so that he would not reveal CREM's link to disappeared prisoners. Luque recommended that the Honduran military work with U.S. Task Force Bravo to transfer the Center of Joint Operations to Aguacate, Capire, or Llamales, and advised that PROMITEC initiate a program of "psychological action" to ensure that no leaks occurred and to shape public perceptions. This remarkable document revealed a great deal about the extralegal functioning of military and intelligence forces within parallel state structures and the central role of the United States in their operation.

Ironically, after Alvarez Martínez was ousted by López, the traditional hostility between the Salvadoran and Honduran armies resurfaced. Soon, the Hondurans refused to admit Salvadoran officers to CREM, and a key objective of U.S. government—to strengthen the Salvadoran army and prevent "another Nicaragua"—was thwarted.[91] López reduced the involvement of Honduras in Washington's counterinsurgency war against the Sandinistas. Nevertheless, the organization and functioning of CREM exposed the deep U.S. involvement in creating command and control structures in the region comparable to Operation Condor.

The Early 1980s in Central America: Terror Emerges

This section presents an abbreviated chronology of unfolding events in the counterinsurgency wars that intensified in the early 1980s: in effect, the results of the joint military planning and "black world" operations detailed in previous sections. In 1979, Sandinista interior minister Tomás Borge noted that the Honduran government was harboring counterrevolutionary Nicaraguans, including many former National Guardsmen and Somocistas, some of whom conducted sporadic raids into Nicaragua.[92] These data confirmed that the contras were functioning even before the Reagan administration came into office in 1981. However, the Nicaraguan revolution enjoyed deep popular support and the former National Guardsmen were despised; Carter administration officials believed that the early contras presented no threat to the Sandinista government.[93] Nicaraguan government pronouncements, in retrospect, were quite accurate in their descriptions of the growing counterrevolutionary effort and its foreign sponsors.

The civil war in El Salvador was worsening in the late 1970s as well. As repression intensified, thousands of Salvadorans crossed the porous border to Honduras in 1980, as many had before in times of trouble, to work the fields and eke out a living.[94] In May 1980, the Honduran press reported that a secret meeting had taken place among the high commands of the Honduran, Salvadoran, and Guatemalan militaries. A few days later, between 300 and 600 Salvadoran refugees, mainly women, children, and the aged, were murdered in a combined Honduran-Salvadoran military operation at Río Sumpul. While the Honduran military formed a cordon to block the movement of some

1,000 to 1,500 refugees, Salvadoran troops and paramilitaries from ORDEN tortured and massacred many of them and left the bodies for the vultures.[95] It was an early incidence of combined operations by the two militaries, which had been historical adversaries. The massacre was described in detail and denounced on June 18, 1980, by the Catholic Diocese of Copán,[96] but the Honduran military denied that it had occurred. It was the first of several massacres on the border over the next years, carried out by units from both countries.

Other stunning developments in 1980 marked the emergence of a new counterinsurgency era in Central America. The 1980 WACL meeting in Buenos Aires seems to have been a defining event in the exporting of the Condor system from the Southern Cone. The meeting brought together various right-wing forces, intelligence agents, and military officers, including many involved in Condor, to strategize about ways to accelerate the world anticommunist crusade. In March 1980, the Sandinista media announced that the CIA was interfering in Nicaragua and El Salvador and training former National Guard troops in Honduras.[97] That same month in El Salvador, Archbishop Oscar Romero, a conservative prelate who had sternly ordered the Salvadoran military to stop the repression, was assassinated. This case bore a strong similarity to a Condor "Phase III" assassination operation, as shown here.

The 1993 UN Truth Commission on El Salvador exhaustively investigated Romero's assassination and concluded that the extremist Salvadoran major Roberto D'Aubuisson gave the execution order, although the actual assassin was not conclusively identified.[98] D'Aubuisson's security team, acting as a death squad, had organized and supervised the crime. The UN commission named some officers who were involved, including Captain Alvaro Saravia, and cited documents seized in a raid against D'Aubuisson's compound in May, including a list of accusations against Romero "by a South American informant," and Saravia's diary. The diary included cryptic notes about the purchase of the types of arms and ammunition used by the assassination team,[99] and referred to the transfer of $120,000 as "contributions to Nicaraguans." According to journalist Christopher Dickey, the diary, suggestively, also included the name and phone number of "Col. Ricardo Lau,"[100] the contra commander. Moreover, Dickey reported, an exiled Salvadoran colonel later said that Lau's name was there because he had organized the assassination for $120,000.[101] If so, this act, involving Salvadoran and Nicaraguan operatives, would clearly conform to the profile of a "Phase III" assassination. (In September 2003, a lawsuit was filed against Saravia, former right-hand man of D'Aubuisson, accusing him of obtaining the weapons, vehicles, and other equipment for the assassination, of lending his personal driver to the assassin, and of paying the assassin for the crime, and Saravia was found guilty in 2004.[102])

Soon after Romero's assassination, four U.S. churchwomen on their way to the airport were stopped at a military checkpoint outside of San Salvador and then raped and murdered by a commando. The Carter administration cut off aid to El Salvador (temporarily), but later several high-ranking Reagan administration officials suggested publicly that the churchwomen had been involved in subversion. In April 1981, the first detention-disappearance of Salvadorans in Honduras—an operation that again reflected Condor methods—occurred. A group of Salvadoran refugees, including the former secretary of Archbishop Romero and several children, were seized and disappeared by a squad of men dressed in civilian clothes.[103] The Honduran government denied that the Salvadorans had ever entered the country and also denied knowledge of Costa Ricans, Nicaraguans, and Guatemalans who were reported disappeared by human rights groups in the same time period.[104] However, in June the U.S. ambassador reported information that FUSEP had secretly turned over fifteen Salvadorans to Salvadoran security forces and that Salvadoran officers had interrogated and tortured them in Tegucigalpa.[105]

In July 1981, the Sandinista government presented to the press four contra prisoners who admitted to infiltrating the country from Honduras to carry out assassinations. One of the four said that a contra leader, Fernando "El Negro" Chamorro, had received $50,000 in Miami from Argentina to finance military training in Argentina and Honduras (it is possible that these funds were handled through the Condor headquarters in Florida headed by Sánchez Reisse). The prisoner also said that his contra group drew up death lists of leaders of popular organizations in Nicaragua. Another described how his group had gouged out the eyes of a dying Sandinista.[106] The contras soon became infamous for their scorched earth tactics and the atrocious methods they used against civilians as well as combatants. In 1985, one told an interviewer that his job "was that of a terrorist" and that he was assigned to assassinate Sandinista officials.[107]

In August 1981, according to Edgar Chamorro, the leader who later left the contras, Vernon Walters (who at this time was special assistant to the secretary of state) and the CIA arranged a meeting in Guatemala City to further the integration of former Somocista National Guardsmen with the contras and to introduce the Argentine instructors to the Guatemalans.[108] In early 1982, the Sandinista government again charged the CIA with leading the counterrevolutionary assault against Nicaragua, organizing training camps across the border in Honduras, organizing contras in Miami, and masterminding a sabotage plot to destroy the country's industry.[109]

The Argentine link in the international effort to overthrow the Sandinista government attracted substantial attention in Argentina, where it was denied by the junta, as was the charge that the army had given the contras $50,000 to buy arms in Miami.[110] But evidence of the multinational conspiracy was accumulating. For example, in March 1982, Nicaraguan police arrested a contra defector, Noel Ernesto Vásquez, who said he had been recruited in Miami to serve as a doctor for a contra group based in Tegucigalpa. As he learned of the group's involvement in bombings and assassination plans in Nicaragua he decided to leave, but was threatened by a high-ranking Argentine official in the Honduran capital if he did so.[111]

Key Cases Replicating Condor Operations in Honduras and Guatemala

Several other cases illustrated the appearance of cross-border operations in Central America as well as the central role of the CIA. The case of Inés Murillo raised particular questions about CIA officer "Mr. Mike." Murillo, a young Honduran attorney and militant, was traveling with a Salvadoran friend in 1983 when they were seized by Battalion 3-16. She was held in a permanently lighted cell to disorient her, and she was tortured, starved, and interrogated for seventy-eight days. A declassified CIA document showed that after she had been detained a month, a CIA officer was sent to personally control her interrogation. An internal CIA report on Murillo stated that she was "blindfolded and seemed unconscious, asleep or simulating sleep. She had marks on her arms and legs that could have been from beatings . . . there was a vat with 55 gallons of water and he was told that her head was repeatedly submerged when she refused to answer questions."[112] Clearly, the CIA officer knew of her torture. In the 1980s, however, embassy officials claimed that they knew of no human rights abuses in Honduras, and the CIA denied condoning torture.

Murillo later spoke extensively with U.S. journalists[113] and CIA deputy director Richard Stoltz did not contradict or deny her account during his Senate testimony. Murillo said that between torture sessions, "Mr. Mike" would often come into her cell. She perceived that he passed written questions to her interrogators so that she would not hear his voice, and Caballero separately confirmed that "Mike" prepared questions for the prisoner. "He came and went as he pleased," Caballero said, "He had full access." Stoltz confirmed that "Mike" went frequently to INDUMIL, although Honduran civilian officials were not allowed entry to the site.[114] Murillo denounced two 3-16 "interrogators" in particular as her torturers, Caballero and Marco Tulio Regalado. Both had graduated from a CIA training course in interrogation on the same day that she was abducted. Stoltz denied that "Mike" gave 3-16 a green light to torture, however. Murillo was freed after her father warned Honduran officials that he would name a U.S. official in the embassy who knew where she was and after garnering support around the world for his daughter's release.[115]

"Mr. Mike" was also associated with the case of U.S. priest Father James Carney, who disappeared in Honduras in 1983. According to Caballero, "Mr. Mike" was in the room when Alvarez Martínez made the decision to execute Carney.[116] Carney was a Jesuit priest who had worked for many years with the poor in Honduras and who was transformed into "a Christian revolutionary," according to his autobiography. Eventually, he was expelled by the military regime, and he told family members that Alvarez personally hated him due to his defense of banana workers during a strike. Carney also told relatives he thought he was on a CIA blacklist.[117]

Father Carney joined a guerrilla column of some 100 persons that entered Honduras from Nicaragua in September 1983. It was intercepted by the Honduran military in the province of Olancho, Honduras. The U.S. military was conducting counterinsurgency exercises in the area and Army Rangers parachuted into Olancho after two guerrillas deserted and informed on their comrades.[118] U.S. news reports at the time said that U.S. army helicopters transported Honduran troops to Olancho for the operation, and a Honduran officer said that U.S. advisors played a command and control role in the sweep, relaying information by radio to ground troops.[119] In fact, in 2003, a former U.S. Special Forces officer named Eric Haney revealed that he had taken part in the ambush against the column and that he had killed a man whom he then discovered was someone he knew. The man was a former Delta Force trainee, a Nicaraguan who had become a naturalized U.S. citizen, David Báez.[120] Haney's account proved that U.S. commandos were involved in the firefight, strongly suggesting that U.S. commanders did indeed know what happened to Carney.

According to the accounts of several captured guerrillas, even before the routing of the column the Honduran military had distributed photographs of leader Reyes Mata and Carney to peasants in the area, who were told to report any sighting of the two.[121] After their capture, Reyes Mata died under torture and some forty of the guerrillas were subsequently tortured and killed, but the Honduran military said officially that Carney had starved to death in the jungle before the military ambushed the column.

Carney family members did their own investigation, however, and heard several more disturbing versions of Father Carney's death. Joseph Connolly, Carney's brother-in-law, interviewed sixteen members of the guerrilla group in 1983. They told Connolly that Carney was among those captured in a combined operation by the Honduran military, U.S. National Guardsmen, and troops from the U.S. Southern Command. Father Carney was tortured at the CIA/contra base at Aguacate, according to their accounts. Three Honduran military officers separately told him that Carney was tortured and then thrown, alive, from a helicopter provided by the U.S. government.[122] In 1995, the family asked the U.S. Embassy in Honduras to help them (as they had before to little effect) and specifically requested that Colonel Gerald Clark, military attaché at the time, be located. The embassy later told them that Clark had been killed in an auto accident in Panama.

U.S. officials have given varying versions of the death of Carney.[123] One declassified State Department document said that Honduran officials immediately informed the U.S. defense attaché office when the guerrillas were detected, but U.S. officials said at the time that they were not aware Carney was with them. For years embassy officials told the family that Carney had starved in the jungle. A 2002 affadavit by a Honduran Christian Democrat leader established definitively, however, that Carney was captured alive.[124] Moreover, declassified documents revealed that U.S. military intelligence received detailed reports on the seizure of the guerrillas, and that the defense attaché actually interrogated the guerrillas and prepared questions for his Honduran counterparts.[125] Caballero, who said he had interrogated Carney, told the Carney family that "there is not the slightest doubt" that U.S. officials knew of Carney's detention and death "because members of the CIA and Pentagon instructors training the contras were at the place where he was held."[126] Caballero also named three others who interrogated Carney, including Lieutenant Segundo Flores Murillo, a well-known member of 3-16; all three had been trained at the SOA.[127] Finally, a guerrilla deserter said that two U.S. military advisors, Lieutenant West Blank and Major Mark Kelvi, were present at Carney's interrogation.[128] The Carney family has not been able to ascertain his fate despite years of queries of the U.S. government, with significant congressional support for a full accounting.

Several other cases illustrated the role of Condor-like kidnap squads made up of 3-16 and contra members. Tomás Nativí was a university professor and labor union leader who was abducted from his bed by hooded, armed men on June 11, 1981, in the presence of his wife, Bertha Oliva. Oliva, who later became head of the Committee of the Relatives of the Detained-Disappeared (COFADEH), in time came to believe that the man who gave the orders was the notorious contra "Chino" Lau. She recognized his Nicaraguan accent, and he wore no black ski mask like the others. She pulled the mask off another assailant, whom she later identified as Alexander Hernández, the leader of 3-16. Oliva was beaten but left alive, possibly because she was pregnant, but she never saw her husband again.[129] It was significant that this death squad was commanded by a Nicaraguan contra in Honduran territory.

In another key case, José Eduardo Becerra Lanza, a university student and leader of the Student Federation of the School of Medicine, was "disappeared" as he returned from a baptism in the center of Tegucigalpa in 1982. His family appealed to various judicial and military authorities to no avail, despite the fact that various persons reported that he was alive and in military hands.[130] Much later, contra defector "Miguel" confessed his participation in the murder of Becerra.[131] He said that 3-16 chief Alexander Hernández turned Becerra and another Honduran student, Félix Martínez, over to his contra unit, under Alvarez's orders, for execution. Becerra had been tortured for forty days by Honduran officers. Alvarez had ordered that Becerra be killed immediately and his body hidden, but that Martínez had to be discovered dead with such horrible mutilations "that no other communist would want to see himself in his shoes."[132] Martínez was shot and stabbed sixty-nine times, and his disfigured body was found soon afterward. Becerra's body was not found until after the 1986 interview with "Miguel," the former contra, was published. Becerra's body showed signs of torture including gouged-out eyes, broken teeth, and mutilations.[133]

The final case presented here, reflecting characteristics of Condor, is that of Salvadoran doctor Héctor Oquelí and his companion, Guatemalan lawyer Gilda Flores. Oquelí had briefly served as deputy foreign minister in El Salvador and was an internationally known, moderate socialist. He was secretary of the Committee for Latin America and the Caribbean of the Socialist International. The two were kidnapped in Guatemala only twenty-four hours after arriving in the country in 1990 and were found dead the same day. In 1990, Salvadoran guerrillas, citing a presidential inquiry by Guatemalan president Vinicio Cerezo, accused the Salvadoran military attaché in Guatemala of planning the crime.[134] The UN Truth Commission found that the murders were carried out by Guatemalan and Salvadoran security forces acting jointly.[135] After the Guatemalan government failed to conduct a fair and impartial investigation, the Inter-American Commission on Human Rights (IACHR) took up the case. It concluded that many important leads had not been pursued and that much evidence had been lost or ignored, and it raised a number of questions for the Guatemalan government to investigate. For example, the IACHR report stated that the vehicle in which the two bodies were found had been reported stolen that morning, and the owner had said that the armed men who commandeered it showed police identifications.[136] This case clearly fit the profile of a Condor Phase III operation involving military intelligence from two or more countries. It has never been clarified.

This compressed historical sketch of the Central American crisis of the 1980s demonstrates that Argentine and U.S. military and intelligence personnel were instrumental in organizing a new Condor system in the region (a collaboration that merits a book-length study in its own right). Under the Reagan administration, U.S. officials trained, financed, and collaborated with Honduran army death squads under the auspices of Battalion 3-16, and directed the operations of the contras, a paramilitary force that carried out atrocities against civilians as a core strategy. High-ranking U.S. intelligence officers such as Vernon Walters and Duane Clarridge were pivotal figures, as were CIA officers such as Raymond and Mike. Argentine and U.S. forces encouraged combined operations through such mechanisms and structures as CREM, joint training of contra and Honduran units in extralegal methods, and shared intelligence and communications networks. Multinational "hunter-killer" squads on the Condor model appeared in Central America in 1980, and multilateral intelligence cooperation was evident in the abduction and assassination of noted figures and lesser-known activists.

The Reagan administration's military "solution" to the crisis in Central America, implemented with the active support of far-right Latin American forces, was based on a covert strategy that sanctioned the use of illegal parallel forces and atrocious methods. The carnage wrought in Central America during this decade provided sobering evidence of the destructive effects of counterinsurgency warfare and parallel structures on state and society in the region—and on the democratic process in the United States.

Notes

1. "Escuadrones de la muerte reaparecen mimetizados," *El Diario/La Prensa* (New York), October 13, 1994; North American Congress on Latin America (NACLA), "Mass Graves and Torture Chambers Found at Contra Base," *Report on the Americas*, Vol. 33, no. 2 (September/October 1999): 2. See also Comisionado Nacional de los Derechos Humanos, *Los hechos hablan por sí mismos: Informe preliminar sobre los desaparecidos en Honduras, 1980–1993*, 2nd. ed. (Tegucigalpa: Editorial Guaymuras, 2002) for details on individual cases. The case of another U.S. citizen killed in Honduras, a Nicaraguan American named David Arturo Báez Cruz, became known in 1998 when a declassified 1983 U.S. document mentioned that he was killed with Father James Carney. Interview with Father Joseph Mulligan, New York, November 1, 2002.

2. Author interview with analyst Longino Becerra, August 19, 2002, Tegucigalpa. See also Débora Munczek Soler, *El impacto psicológico de la represión política en los hijos de los desaparecidos asesinados en Honduras* (Tegucigalpa: COFADEH, 1996).

3. See Gary Cohn and Ginger Thompson, "Unearthed: Fatal Secrets," four-part series, *Baltimore Sun* (June 11–18, 1995) and Dieter Eich and Carlos Rincón, *The Contras: Interviews with Anti-Sandinistas* (San Francisco: Synthesis Publications, 1984), 46–47.

4. Gary Cohn and Ginger Thompson, "Unearthed: Fatal Secrets. When a Wave of Torture and Murder Staggered a Small U.S. Ally, Truth Was a Casualty," *Baltimore Sun*, June 11, 1995.

5. Author interview with Ramón Custodio, national commissioner of human rights, Honduras, on August 13, 2002, Tegucigalpa; written testimony of Florencio Ca-

ballero, 3-16 defector, in author's possession; U.S. Senate, Select Committee on Intelligence, "Honduran Interrogation Manual Hearing," June 16, 1988, 14.

6. A vast literature exists on the Central American crises of the 1980s and space limits prevent much background here. A sampling of books includes Raymond Bonner, *Weakness and Deceit: U.S. Policy and El Salvador* (New York: Times Books, 1984); Kenneth M. Coleman and George C. Herring, *The Central American Crisis: Sources of Conflict and the Failure of U.S. Policy* (Wilmington, Del.: Scholarly Resources, 1985; Marlene Dixon and Susanne Jonas, eds., *Revolution and Intervention in Central America* (San Francisco: Synthesis Publications, 1983); Eldon Kenworthy, *America/Americas: Myth in the Making of U.S. Policy toward Latin America* (University Park: Penn State University Press, 1995); Walter LaFeber, *Inevitable Revolutions: The United States in Central America*, 2nd ed. (New York: W. W. Norton, 1993); William LeoGrande, *Our Own Backyard: The United States in Central America 1977–1992* (Chapel Hill: University of North Carolina Press, 1998); Thomas W. Walker, ed., *Reagan versus the Sandinistas: The Undeclared War on Nicaragua* (Boulder, Colo.: Westview, 1987).

7. Nicaragua, Honduras, Guatemala, and El Salvador are the main focus of this section, since Costa Rica is an exception in important ways. This historical introduction draws from McSherry, "Civil Conflicts and the Role of the International Community: The Cases of Guatemala and El Salvador" (New York: Ralph Bunche Institute on the United Nations: Occasional Papers Series, Number 23, October 1994).

8. Daniel Siegel and Joy Hackel, "El Salvador: Counterinsurgency Revisited," in Michael Klare and Peter Kornbluh, eds., *Low Intensity Warfare: Counterinsurgency, Proinsurgency, and Antiterrorism in the Eighties* (New York: Pantheon, 1988), 113.

9. Christopher Dickey, *With the Contras* (New York: Simon & Schuster, 1985), 85.

10. Author interview with John J. Youle, former political counselor, U.S. Embassy, Montevideo (1977–81), conducted by telephone, July 24, 2003.

11. Edgar Chamorro, *Packaging the Contras: A Case of CIA Disinformation* (New York: Institute of Media Analysis, 1987), 2; Comisionado Nacional de los Derechos Humanos, *Los hechos hablan*, 357–380.

12. Claudine McCarthy, "Spies among Us: U.S. Retired CIA Agents Tout the Agency," *Sun Sentinel* (Florida), October 29, 1997.

13. Ariel C. Armony, *Argentina, the United States, and the Anti-Communist Crusade in Central America, 1977–1984* (Athens: Center for International Studies, Ohio University, 1997).

14. Armony, *Argentina*, 77; Goyo Dionis, "La aparición de osamentas en una antigua base militar de la CIA en Honduras reabre la participación argentino-norteamericano en ese país," Equipo Nizkor, Derechos Human Rights, SERPAJ Europa (September 7, 2001).

15. Armony, *Argentina*, 148–152; Jack Blum testimony to Senate Select Committee on Intelligence, October 23, 1996.

16. Chamorro, *Packaging the Contras*, 5.

17. Chamorro, *Packaging the Contras*, 5.

18. Chamorro, *Packaging the Contras*, 6; Interhemispheric Resource Center, "Group Watch: World Anticommunist League," at www.publiceye.org/research/Group_Watch/

Entries-129.htm; see also Luis Bruschtein, "Cavallo fue agente de los genocidios, el de los '70 y el de los '90," *Página/12* (Argentina), October 20, 2003.

19. "Si me mandan de regreso a la Argentina soy hombre muerto," *Siete Días* (Argentina), March 13, 1983.

20. Excerpts from transcript of November 6, 1982, interview with Héctor Francés (Estánislao Valdez)," in Chamorro, *Packaging the Contras*, 61; see also "Las revelaciones de Héctor Francés," *Nueva Presencia* (Honduras), June 17, 1983.

21. Armony, *Argentina*, 149–152; see also McSherry, *Incomplete Transition: Military Power and Democracy in Argentina* (New York: St. Martin's Press, 1997), 184–186.

22. Ana Barón, "La conexión Sánchez-Reisse—Suárez Mason—Guglielminetti," *Somos*, February 25, 1987, 20–22.

23. Chamorro, *Packaging the Contras*, 5–7.

24. Chamorro, *Packaging the Contras*, 57.

25. Chamorro, *Packaging the Contras*, 58.

26. Armony, *Argentina*, 148–152.

27. Samuel Blixen, "The Double Role of Drug-Trafficking in State Terrorism and Militarized Democracy," 2, on TNI website (www.tni.org.reports/drugs/folder1/blixen.htm).

28. Human Rights Watch, "Argentina Report 2001," chapter 11, "Role of the United States," November 2001, at www.hrw.org.

29. Human Rights Watch, "Argentina Report 2001," chapter 11, "Role of the United States," November 2001.

30. Blixen, "The Double Role."

31. Marta Gurvich and Robert Parry, "Nazi Echo: Argentina, Death Camps and the Contras," *Consortiumnews.com*, September 19, 1998, at www.consortiumnews.com.

32. Author interview with Leo Valladares, Tegucigalpa, August 15, 2002; Comisionado Nacional de los Derechos Humanos, *Los hechos hablan*, 350–357; see also Enrique Yeves, *La Contra: Una guerra sucia* (Buenos Aires: Grupo Editorial Zeta, S.A., 1990), 66–69.

33. Blixen, "The Double Role," 3.

34. Notes by 3-16 deserter whose identity is not revealed, obtained by author in Tegucigalpa, August 2002.

35. Author interview with Bertha Oliva, president of Comité de Familiares de Detenidos Desaparecidos en Honduras (COFADEH), Tegucigalpa, August 19, 2002.

36. Declassified State Department cable from U.S. Embassy in Tegucigalpa to Secretary of State, "Impressions of Col. Gustavo Alvarez," February 11, 1981.

37. *Tiempo* (Honduras), "Alvarez, el hombre de Estados Unidos en C.A.," April 2, 1984; declassified U.S. profile of Alvarez Martínez, CR M 83-14346, August 25, 1983, obtained by the author in Tegucigalpa. It appears to be a CIA document.

38. Presentation by Gary Cohn in "Notes from a Conference: The CIA in Honduras," organized by the Center for International Policy, May 7, 1997.

39. See McSherry, *Incomplete Transition*, 47–49.

40. U.S. profile of Alvarez, n.d., obtained by author in Honduras, August 2002.

41. Torres Arias, "Al pueblo y a las Fuerzas Armadas de Honduras," *Tiempo* (Honduras) (reprinted from *El Excelsior*, Mexico), September 6, 1982; Cohn and Thompson, "When a Wave," June 11, 1995.

42. Elizabeth Reimann, *Confesiones de un Contra: Historia de 'Moisés' en Nicaragua* (Buenos Aires: Legasa, 1986), 178.

43. Curriculum vitae of Ricardo Lau Castillo, obtained by author in Tegucigalpa, August 2002. See also Dickey, *With the Contras*, for references to Lau.

44. Linda Drucker, "'Contra' relata como ayudó a formar un secreto escuadrón de la muerte en Honduras," *Tiempo*, August 18, 1986. This article was a translation of the original in *The Progressive*, published in August 1986.

45. Declassified State Department document 02560, dated September 13, 1985, obtained by author in Tegucigalpa, August 2002.

46. Declassified State Department cable, "GRN Vice Min of Interior Reports on 'War' with Counterrevolution," July 15, 1982, obtained by author in Tegucigalpa, August 2002.

47. Chamorro, *Packaging the Contras*, 47–50.

48. Bob Woodward, *Veil: The Secret Wars of the CIA 1981–1987* (New York: Simon & Schuster, 1987), 230–231. The author obtained in Honduras a memo from "Comandantes de Fuerzas de Tareas, FDN y MISURAS, to the U.S. Embassy via Col. Raymond" asking for the incorporation of an anticommunist fighter named Gustavo Villoldo to their ranks. The memo, dated January 23, 1984, cited Villoldo's record in Bolivia and elsewhere, suggesting links to Condor.

49. Linda Drucker, "'Contra' relata como ayudó a formar un secreto escuadrón de la muerte en Honduras," *Tiempo* (August 18, 1986): 18–19.

50. Drucker, "'Contra' relata," 18.

51. Tayacán, "Psychological Operations in Guerrilla Warfare," copy in author's possession. See also Chamorro, *Packaging the Contras*, 55–57; Dickey, *With the Contras*, 254–257; Joel Brinkley, "CIA Primer Tells Nicaraguan Rebels How to Kill," *New York Times*, October 17, 1984. For a critique of the manual and the policy behind it from an anticommunist perspective, see Leon Wieseltier, "Our Man in Nicaragua: Tayacan, the Reaganite Revolutionary," *The New Republic*, November 19, 1984.

52. "Manual del Combatiente por la Libertad," copy in possession of author.

53. See, for example, Hedrick Smith, "CIA Manual: A Policy Is Undermined," *New York Times*, October 30, 1984.

54. For studies, see Lawrence E. Walsh, *Iran-Contra: The Final Report* (New York: Random House Times Books, 1993); Theodore Draper, *A Very Thin Line: The Iran-Contra Affairs* (New York: Hill and Wang, 1991).

55. Declassified State Department document, "GRN Claims to Thwart CIA plot," August 23, 1983.

56. Dickey, *With the Contras*, 126, 294.

57. Author interviews in Tegucigalpa, August 2002.

58. Eich and Rincón, *The Contras*, 39.

59. Declassified State Department document, from U.S. Embassy in Managua, to Secretary of State, August 23, 1983. In this document, Ramírez Zelaya is referred to as "José Ignacio" rather than Jorge, but it seems to be the same person.

60. Gary Cohn and Ginger Thompson, "Unearthed: Fatal Secrets: A Survivor Tells Her Story," *Baltimore Sun*, June 15, 1995.

61. Declassified State Department document, from U.S. Embassy in Managua to Secretary of State, dated March 20, 1985.

62. U.S. Embassy in Managua to Secretary of State, March 20, 1985.

63. Cable from U.S. Embassy to Secretary of State, "Human Rights Leader Accuses United States of Involvement in Training of 'Death Squads,'" May 9, 1985, obtained by author in Tegucigalpa, August 2002.

64. The court ruled that the indiscriminate mining by U.S. agents of harbors used by commercial ships and other unlawful uses of force against Nicaragua were clear violations of international law. See *Nicaragua v. United States of America*, Judgment of June 27, 1986, decisions (6), (7), and (8), 138–139. The Reagan administration withdrew the United States from the court's jurisdiction.

65. Declassified State Department document #02667, dated February 12, 1986.

66. Eich and Rincón, *The Contras*, 31.

67. Declassified State Department document #02667, dated February 12, 1986.

68. Gary Cohn and Ginger Thompson, "Torturers' Confessions," *Baltimore Sun*, June 13, 1995. The name Bill Johnson does not appear on Internet lists of those killed in Beirut (checked on internet by author in October 2002).

69. *Honduras This Week*, "Meet his gray eminence, John Negroponte," Online Edition 30, July 30, 2001.

70. See Corte Interamericana de Derechos Humanos, Caso Velásquez Rodríguez, Sentencia de 29 de Julio de 1988.

71. Cohn and Thompson, "Torturers' Confessions."

72. Cohn and Thompson, "Torturers' Confessions," and testimonies acquired by author in Tegucigalpa, August 2002.

73. Comité de Familiares Detenidos Desaparecidos (COFADEH), "Historia de un desertor del escuadrón de la muerte" (n.d.), 5. This is a Spanish translation of a May 1987 Americas Watch report.

74. Estados Unidos Mexicanos, Notaria Pública Num. 42, "Declaraciones, José Barerra Martínez," July 2, 1987, 5.

75. "Declaraciones." See also typed, unsigned thirty-three-page testimony, acquired in Tegucigalpa in 2002 by author, n.d.; the text was identified by a lawyer at the Comisionado Nacional de los Derechos Humanos as Caballero's testimony.

76. Federal Court of Canada, IMM-272-96 between Florencio Caballero and Minister of Citizenship and Immigration, November 13, 1996.

77. "En testimonio antes de morir Florencio Caballero involuncró a otros militares en violación a derechos humanos," *La Prensa* (Honduras), July 9, 1997.

78. Caballero testimony, in author's possession.

79. See Edward Peters, *Torture* (Philadelphia: University of Pennsylvania Press, 1985), 168–170; Tim Weiner, "CIA Taught, then Dropped, Mental Torture in Latin America," *New York Times*, January 29, 1997. A flurry of articles in 2002 and 2003 suggested that psychological coercion—and torture—were still being used by U.S. forces; see, for example, Matthew Brzezinski, "Hady Hassan Omar's Detention," *New York Times Magazine*, October 27, 2002, 50–55; Dana Priest and Barton Gellman, "U.S. Decries Abuse but Defends Interrogations; 'Stress and Duress' Tactics Used on Terrorism Suspects Held in Secret Overseas Facilities," *Washington Post*, December 26, 2002; Nat Hentoff, "The American Way of Torture: 'If We're Not in the Room, Who Is to Say?'" *Village Voice*, January 31, 2003 and "Our Designated Killers: Where Is the Outrage?" *Village Voice*, February 14, 2003. The 2004 torture scandal at Abu Ghraib laid any doubts to rest.

80. Cohn and Thompson, "Torturers' Confessions." See also thirty-three-page testimony by Caballero, n.d., in which he details the paymaster role of the CIA.

81. U.S. Senate, Select Committee on Intelligence, "Honduran Interrogation Manual Hearing," June 16, 1988, 25–27. These methods were used again in Iraq and elsewhere in the "war on terror."

82. U.S. Senate, Select Committee on Intelligence, "Honduran Interrogation Manual Hearing," June 16, 1988, 14.

83. Central Intelligence Agency Inspector General, "Report of Investigation: Selected Issues Relating to CIA Activities in Honduras in the 1980s," 96-0125-IG, August 27, 1997, 2.

84. Central Intelligence Agency, "Report of Investigation," 96-0125-IG, August 27, 1997, 2–3; see also Susan Peacock, "Secret CIA Report Admits 'Honduran Military Committed Hundreds of Human Rights Abuses' and 'Inaccurate' Reporting to Congress," press release, October 23, 1998; Human Rights Watch, "Report 2001: Argentina, The Role of the United States," 4, at www.hrw.org; Tim Golden, "Honduran Army's Abuses Were Known to CIA," *New York Times*, October 24, 1998; "Report: CIA Knew of Abuses in Honduras in '80s," *Miami Herald*, October 4, 1998.

85. Senate Select Committee on Intelligence, "Inquiry into Honduran Interrogation Training," July 10, 1989, 2, 11–12.

86. Testimony of José Federico Valle López, n.d., obtained by author in Tegucigalpa, August 2002.

87. Valle López testimony, 3.

88. Cable from secretary of state to U.S. Embassy, Tegucigalpa, "Disbanding of the 316th Military Intelligence Battalion," January 26, 1988, 2.

89. Lieutenant Colonel Angel Ricardo Luque Portillo, "Informe Especial," November 30, 1984. Obtained by author in Tegucigalpa, August 2002.

90. COFADEH, "Historia de un desertor del escuadrón de la muerte," Spanish translation of the 1987 Human Rights Watch report, May 1987, 13.

91. Committee on Foreign Affairs, U.S. House of Representatives, "Congress and Foreign Policy," 1984, 39.

92. Declassified State Department document #01092, dated November 9, 1979.

93. Jack R. Binns, *The United States in Honduras, 1980–1981: An Ambassador's Memoir* (Jefferson, N.C.: McFarland, 2000), 32.

94. Centro de Documentación (CODEH), *Los refugiados salvadoreños en Honduras*, booklet, n.d. (circa 1983).

95. CODEH, *Los refugiados*, 19–21; UN Security Council, "Report of the UN Truth Commission on El Salvador," S25500, 1 April 1993, 121.

96. To read the denunciation, see CODEH, *Los refugiados*, 36–40.

97. Declassified State Department #01118, dated March 1, 1980, obtained by author in Tegucigalpa, August 2002.

98. UN Security Council, "Report of the UN," 127–131.

99. UN Security Council, "Report of the UN," 129; CARECEN-N.Y., "The UN Truth Commission on Romero's Murder," at www.icomm.ca/carecen/page41.html, accessed by author in October 2002.

100. Dickey, *With the Contras*, 88.

101. Dickey, *With the Contras*, 88; Jonathan Marshall, Peter Dale Scott, and Jane Hunter, *The Iran-Contra Connection: Secret Teams and Covert Operations in the Reagan Era* (Boston: South End Press, 1987), 132.

102. The Center for Justice and Accountability filed the suit. William Branigin, "Suit Filed in '80 Death of Salvadoran Bishop," *Washington Post*, September 17, 2003.

103. Author interview with Ramón Custodio, National Commissioner of Human Rights, in Tegucigalpa, August 13, 2002; Center for International Policy, "The CIA in Honduras," notes from a conference on May 7, 1997; Comisionado Nacional de los Derechos Humanos, *Los hechos hablan*, 146–155.

104. Honduran government, "Anexo 'F': Listado de Personas que se dan por desaparecidas que no han ingresado al país, según información proporcionada por la Dirección General de Población y Política Migratoria," document obtained by author in Tegucigalpa, August 2002, n.d. on my copy.

105. Cable from U.S. Embassy to Secretary of State, "Reports of GOH Repression and Approach to Problem," June 17, 1981. In the cable, Ambassador Binns decried "increasing evidence of officially-sponsored/sanctioned assassinations." See also Sister Laetitia Bordes, "An Account of John Negroponte," letter sent by e-mail, August 2001; "EE.UU. desoyó violaciones a derechos humanos," *El Diario/La Prensa* (New York), October 31, 1995.

106. Declassified State Department document 01362, dated July 29, 1981, obtained by author in Tegucigalpa, August 2002. See also Eich and Rincón, *The Contras*, 23–25.

107. Eich and Rincón, *The Contras*, 38; for other accounts of contra atrocities, see Dickey, *With the Contras*, especially 180, 193, 230, 246; and Sam Dillon, *Commandos: The CIA and Nicaragua's Contra Rebels* (New York: Henry Holt, 1991).

108. Sworn declaration of Edgar Chamorro before the World Court, *Nicaragua vs. United States*, during the hearing regarding Nicaragua's charges of U.S. mining of its harbors, September 5, 1985, 300, note 8.

109. Declassified State Department document 01430, from U.S. Embassy in Managua to Secretary of State, January 13, 1982.

110. Declassified State Department document 01435, from U.S. Embassy in Buenos Aires to Secretary of State, January 15, 1982.

111. Declassified State Department document, from U.S. Embassy in Managua to Secretary of State, March 20, 1982.

112. Declassified document cited in Spanish-language article by Susan Peacock, "Los secretos de la CIA," *Clarín*, Zona, November 8, 1998.

113. See, for example, James LeMoyne, "Testifying to Torture," *New York Times Magazine*, June 5, 1988.

114. Cohn and Thompson, "A Survivor Tells Her Story."

115. Author interview with César Murillo, Tegucigalpa, August 19, 2002; Comisionado Nacional de los Derechos Humanos, *Los hechos hablan*, 282–285.

116. Leo Valladares Lanza and Susan C. Peacock, *In Search of Hidden Truths: An Interim Report on Declassification by the National Commissioner for Human Rights in Honduras* (Tegucigalpa: Comisionado Nacional de los Derechos Humanos en Honduras, 1998), 33.

117. Author interview with Pat Carney, Father Carney's brother, and Barbara Carney, Pat's wife, in Los Angeles, October 14, 2002.

118. Author interview with Longino Becerra, Honduran scholar, in Tegucigalpa, August 19, 2002; Valladares and Peacock, *In Search of Hidden Truths*, 37.

119. Valladares and Peacock, *In Search of Hidden Truths*, 46–47.

120. Juan O. Tamayo, "Ex-Green Beret's Sandinista Story Emerges 20 Years Later," *Miami Herald*, September 3, 2003. Tamayo confirmed with a former U.S. military officer in Honduras at the time that U.S. "advisors" took part in the operation. Two Delta Force commandos confirmed that Eric Haney, the officer who killed Báez, had been part of the group but criticized him for violating the Delta Force's oath of secrecy. Haney himself wondered whether Báez had been a CIA infiltrator in the column, saying that "the whole [operation] was handled by the CIA."

121. Declassified CIA report dated July 1995, in possession of author.

122. U.S. Embassy in Tegucigalpa, cable to Secretary of State, "Connolly/Carney family visit with ambassador concerning disappearance of Father James Francis Carney in 1983," May 24, 1995, 5; Center for International Policy, "Summary of the declassification request from the Honduran National Human Rights Commissioner to the U.S. Government," February 14, 1997, at www.us.net/cip/declass.htm.

123. For an excellent summary, see Valladares and Peacock, *In Search of Hidden Truths*, chapter 2.

124. Lucas Aguilera, who testified in 2002, said that he saw Carney in Nueva Palestina, Olancho, in military detention. Author interview with Father Joe Mulligan, November 1, 2002, New York.

125. Valladares and Peacock, *In Search of Hidden Truths*, 38–41; Marta Hernández, "Reportedly Slain Priest's Family Sues U.S. for Papers," *Los Angeles Times*, February 5, 1988.

126. Joseph S. Mulligan, S.J., "CIA: Murder Can't Be Ruled Out," *National Jesuit News*, April/May 1997.

127. Jean Brenner, "Help Hondurans Find Bodies of Disappeared U.S. Citizens," *Miami Herald*, April 13, 2000; Jack McKinney, "Close the School of the Americas," *Philadelphia Daily News*, May 2, 1997.

128. Valladares and Peacock, *In Search of Hidden Truths*, 56.

129. Author interview with Bertha Oliva, Tegucigalpa, August 19, 2002.

130. "Detenciones forzosas en Honduras," statement prepared by family members of José Eduardo Becerra, May 14, 1984; Longino Becerra, *Cuando las tarántulas atacan*, 6th ed. (Tegucigalpa: Baktun Editorial, 2002).

131. Drucker, "'Contra' relata."

132. Drucker, "'Contra' relata," 18. Free translation by author.

133. Author interview with Longino Becerra in Tegucigalpa, August 19, 2002.

134. Foreign Broadcast Information Service, FBIS-LAT-90-102 (25 May 1990): 7.

135. UN Security Council, "Report of the UN," 96–101.

136. Inter-American Commission on Human Rights, Organization of American States, "Annual Report 1991, chapter 3, Reports on Individual Cases," February 4, 1992.

8
Conclusions

UNTIL THE LATE 1990S, the principal commanders and operatives of Operation Condor denied that the transnational system had ever existed. Condor was a top-secret organization, one whose very existence was classified. Yet as one Bolivian miner, persecuted by the Banzer regime, put it, "Like a monster that leaves tracks of blood and destruction in its way, Plan Condor left behind tracks and proof that can't be erased by their executors."[1]

This book has shown that Operation Condor was a top-secret component of a larger inter-American counterinsurgency strategy—led, financed, and overseen by Washington—to prevent and reverse social and political movements in Latin America in favor of structural change. It is interesting to note that Pinochet's defense lawyer made a similar argument in 2004: that Condor had existed, but that it was a legitimate counterterror alliance comparable to Interpol or the European antiterror agreement.[2] Contreras had portrayed the Condor system that way in his letter of invitation to the November 1975 Condor conference, calling it "something similar to Interpol, but dedicated to Subversion." Clearly, though, unlike Interpol, the Condor system was a criminal operation that used terrorist practices to eliminate political adversaries, and extinguish their ideas, outside the rule of law.

During the Cold War, military, intelligence, and police commanders built and worked within parallel, or parastatal, structures to carry out counterterrorist campaigns in the shadows, concealed from domestic and international view. I have used the conceptual construct of the parallel state to highlight the secret forces and infrastructure developed as a hidden part of the state to carry out covert counterinsurgency wars. A vast parallel infrastructure of secret detention centers and clandestine killing machinery enabled the military states to avoid national and international law and scrutiny, and facilitated their use of disappearance, torture, and assassination out of the public eye. Anticommunist officials adopted extreme "black world" measures to solidify or reorient the existing political and socioeconomic systems in the hemisphere and to advance the power and privilege of anticommunist, pro-U.S. elites. As Operation Condor expanded, it became an extremist global network linking messianic military institutions, intelligence forces, right-wing civilians, paramilitary death squads, Masonic lodges such as Propaganda-Due (P-2), former Nazis, and other dangerous antidemocratic forces that mounted aggressive campaigns against all manner of political opposition. The Condor system used the methods of terror to advance the countersubversive cause.

The crimes of Operation Condor in the terrifying 1970s have continued to haunt the region long after the end of the Cold War. The counterinsurgents reshaped and transformed conventional armies into lethal killing machines that respected no laws or limits, with commanders who deliberately chose to kill their political opponents, secretly and without due process. As one astute observer of Latin America once wrote, "Today there are a number of influential soldiers and officers . . . who have themselves either tortured and murdered, or given the order for others to do so. They were told that such killing was not a crime, but a duty to preserve national security. That is an experience that corrupts men."[3]

Many Condor commanders and operatives, and other veterans of the region's dirty wars, continued to wield power in their societies and block democratizing measures long after transitions from military rule. Others became common criminals, engaged in kidnapping-extortion, theft and larceny, and drug trafficking. The legacy of Operation Condor was also reflected in the still-unsolved cases of thousands of disappeared persons in Latin America, including children, whose families still mourn.

The emergence of court cases in Latin America, Europe, and the United States in recent years, seeking to hold Condor officers accountable, is evocative of previous efforts to track down and prosecute Nazi criminals from the World War II era, efforts that continue to this day. Such trials have been condemned by conservative forces in the world, which counsel immunity from prosecution for crimes committed on the Western side during the Cold War. But the evidence suggests that the monumental terror and trauma visited upon Latin American societies during that epoch can only be healed through a process of truth and justice.

The history presented here undoubtedly is incomplete, a partial exhumation of Operation Condor. A more complete rendering could be provided by the U.S. government, with its enormous intelligence, defense, and diplomatic archives, if the will existed. Unfortunately, powerful forces within the U.S. government apparently believe that the full historical record is too revealing, too shocking, or too incriminating to allow public disclosure. When President Bill Clinton ordered the declassification of government documents relevant to Spanish judge Baltasar Garzón's inquiries in 1998, the Pentagon and especially the CIA ferociously resisted compliance, and the declassification on Argentina in 2002 contained no documents from these two branches of the U.S. security apparatus. The impression left by such secrecy is that the CIA and the Pentagon have the most to hide. Yet like Condor itself, U.S. clandestine warfare and covert operations left a trail behind.

The Parallel State

This book has documented the key characteristics of Operation Condor: its specialization in cross-border and foreign operations against exiles; its multinational character; its precise and selective targeting of dissidents; its parastatal structure; its advanced technology; and its use of criminal syndicates and extremist organizations to carry out operations. I have shown that counterinsurgency warfare, conducted in the shadows by secret armies and paramilitary forces using unlawful and atrocious strategies and tactics, deeply transformed the targeted states and societies. By creating and mobilizing a parastatal apparatus, the counterinsurgents gave the state vast new powers and erased any semblance of government accountability to the citizenry. The state was reconstituted as a predator against its own people, using "industrial repression" to quell political opposition and enforce conformity. Intelligence organizations proliferated and delved deep into the lives of ordinary persons. Terrorized citizens were forced to choose between loyalty to the state and the risk of disappearance, torture, or death. State power was expanded, reinforced, and buttressed by invisible parastatal structures, and the rights of citizens were obliterated; counterinsurgency states controlled the lives of their people through terror.

I have shown that the concept of the parallel state, as developed in this study, provides a useful means to understand the hidden apparatus of terror and social control of the military states, with the assistance, financing, and advice of the U.S. security establishment. Paramilitary and parapolice groups operated in the nebulous zone between military command and partial autonomy, creating terror, eliminating democratic rights, precluding activities seen as threatening to elites, and keeping the population fearful and politically inert. They also afforded the state deniability. In Latin America, parastatal structures allowed military and intelligence forces to carry out illegal acts that were visible on the one hand, and deniable on the other. Military rulers could attribute the waves of torture, disappearance, and assassination throughout the region to "out-of-control death squads" or internal disputes within the left. The military states were well served by the deniability and enhanced repressive power provided by the parallel state. They were able to maintain, at least partially and in some cases, an appearance of moderation and legitimacy, and avoid the damage that accompanied world criticism of widespread, public human rights abuses. Meanwhile, parastatal structures dramatically expanded the ability of the military states to spread terror and destroy resistance throughout, and outside of, their countries. The parallel state was an important tool with which the national security states achieved and wielded total power over their societies.

In this book I have analyzed the parallel state in operation at the international, state, and individual levels. Powerful global actors, notably the United States, combined forces with national elites and military-security institutions in Latin America to carry out the anticommunist crusade. The U.S. government was the predominant designer of the continental security agenda, and Washington exerted heavy influence in its implementation. I have also shown that Condor's roots can be traced to earlier parastatal structures in Europe.

A review of early Cold War history in Europe demonstrated that parallel organizations created there, under the auspices of NATO and the U.S. government, bore striking similarities to Operation Condor—and in several cases were directly linked to Condor. Covert anticommunist commandos formed to combat Soviet incursions that never came turned instead to subversion of legal political parties, manipulation of elections, and undermining of communist, leftist, and popular forces in many countries. The European "stay-behind" armies recruited from fascist and terrorist circles and from hard-right sectors of state military and intelligence forces. Key figures in Western governments led these forces centrally, but secretly; they were unknown to many elected officials and to other constitutional branches of government. The U.S. government developed stay-behind units in Vietnam as well. The formation and use of such secret armies, outside normal military chains of command and civilian control, presaged Operation Condor, and showed that covert structures such as Condor were not anomalies, nor ad hoc, transitory forces, but crucial components of a secret anticommunist strategy sanctioned by Western leaders.

This book has also shown that counterinsurgency was undertaken in countries where power seemed to be shifting from elite, pro-capitalist, and pro-U.S. forces in the Third World to non-elite social sectors with an interest in restructuring political and economic power. Military intervention in former colonies and quasi-colonies by Western powers was not unprecedented, of course. Washington had interfered in the politics of the Caribbean since the nineteenth century, and the protection and advancement of long-term economic and political interests in Latin America dominated U.S. hemispheric policy after 1898. After World War II, U.S. intervention, imbued with virulent ideological overtones, became largely covert rather than overt. The effects were even deeper and more destructive than in earlier times.

As leftist and nationalist leaders won elections throughout Latin America in the 1960s and 1970s, and new revolutionary and progressive movements emerged, U.S. security strategists feared that the informal U.S. economic and political empire in the hemisphere was threatened. Localized elites similarly feared the threat to their traditional dominance. U.S. policy served, in most cases, to strengthen traditional elites and military-security forces, while leftist and progressive social movements and individuals were crushed. The concept of the parallel state allows the observer to connect the state and system levels of analysis and analyze the coincident interests of national and international actors. The conceptual framework offered here allows us to understand why the world's most powerful liberal democracy would sponsor and collaborate with repressive dictatorships that brutalized their own societies. Seeking to protect and expand U.S. economic, political, and security interests, Washington turned to reactionary forces worldwide whose most important asset was anticommunism.

As Washington sought to preserve its hegemony in the hemisphere, local elites and military forces in Latin America sought to strengthen themselves and weaken the social forces that challenged them. The anti-left campaign swept through the region, and beginning in the 1960s, repressive, right-wing military governments seized power and established national security states in almost all of Latin America. Leftist governments were subverted through multinational action in Bolivia, Chile, and later, Nicaragua. Counterinsurgency war was a means to demobilize popular movements, terrorize society, and solidify military power in these countries. Social change in the interest of disadvantaged sectors of society was halted, the economic power of traditional elite classes reasserted, and inequitable class divisions reinforced. In many cases, military institutions became autonomous actors with their own interests in advancing their power.

In February 1974, commanders of South America's police held a key preliminary meeting of the Condor network in Buenos Aires, where they agreed to fuse their countersubversive operations and coordinate repression across borders. In November 1975, Operation Condor was formalized at the level of the region's militaries and intelligence organizations. As stated by a Chilean appeals court, the military regimes created an extraofficial, noninstitutional organism to unify their secret police in their crusade against leftists. In 1976,

Condor organizers extended, upgraded, and modernized the transnational system. Operating from a nucleus of such intelligence organizations as DINA (Chile), SIDE and Batallion 601 (Argentina), OCOA (Uruguay), DOPS, DOI-CODI, OBAN, and the SNI (Brazil), and La Técnica (Paraguay), among others, at times in concert with neofascist and terrorist groups such as Milicia and Triple A (Argentina), CORU (Cuban exiles), Ordine Nuovo and Avanguardia Nazionale (Italy), the Condor apparatus picked off major democratic leaders such as Carlos Prats, Bernardo Leighton, Zelmar Michelini, Héctor Gutiérrez Ruiz, and Orlando Letelier. Condor "disappeared," tortured, and murdered hundreds of other lesser-known community leaders, social activists, dissidents, critics, and members of nonviolent leftist organizations as well as guerrillas.

Condor served important functions for the military regimes and their sponsors in Washington. It allowed the militaries to remove safe havens for exiles and eliminate them covertly, while maintaining a quasi-legal face to the world; it camouflaged state use of criminal and terrorist methods which would have reduced domestic and international tolerance for the regimes; it inhibited action by human rights groups, families, and critics to identify and counteract the covert transnational system; and it implanted uncertainty, disorientation, and terror in target societies. Condor, as a parastatal organization, magnified and extended the power of the military states.

As E. V. Walter argued, terror was used to engineer compliant behavior in these societies, and to impose political paralysis, thereby consolidating the power of the counterinsurgents across a vast geographical area of South America. Later, in the 1980s, Condor methods and operations were replicated in Central America. Throughout it all—with the partial exception of the Carter era—U.S. officials worked closely with the Latin American military and intelligence forces that carried out the carnage. During the Nixon and Ford years, the State Department and the National Security Council, both led by Henry Kissinger, provided political support for the Condor states as well.

In 1997, former Honduran national commissioner for human rights Leo Valladares asked a series of incisive questions about U.S. policy in the region:

> Can the U.S. spend millions of dollars to defend democracy using undemocratic means? Can the CIA determine who is good and who is bad in foreign lands? Can the United States sustain democratic governments using terrorism of the state? Can the United States have confidence in undemocratic allies? Can the U.S. foment terrorism in order to defend its own democracy and national interest?[4]

U.S. promotion of clandestine warfare, "unofficial" military and intelligence units, and covert operations—including the use of terror—in the world deeply damaged not only the target societies, but also the U.S. democratic process itself, as officials maneuvered to avoid constitutional oversight, deceived and manipulated Congress and the U.S. public, and degraded constitutional rights and freedoms through obsessive secrecy. Most seriously, the complicity of the U.S. government in crimes against humanity in Latin America was a perversion of the principles and values broadly supported by the U.S. public.

Operation Condor and the Role of the United States

Operation Condor, the transnational arm of the parallel state, and its operations were consistent with U.S. counterinsurgency and counterterror doctrine and training. Indeed, U.S. post–September 11 military and intelligence strategies and tactics in Afghanistan and Iraq included the methods of disappearance,[5] torture,[6] extrajudicial transfer across borders,[7] incommunicado detention,[8] extrajudicial execution,[9] and military rule[10] to achieve counterterror objectives. In the United States, government agencies rounded up and imprisoned thousands of immigrants, and several U.S. citizens, without the right to counsel; set up vast new domestic surveillance programs; and planned the use of military tribunals.[11] These are not measures normally associated with democratic governments. After 9/11, key political and military leaders were, again, willing to jettison observance of the rule of law and human rights[12]; the ends, again, justified the means.

UN human rights commissioner Mary Robinson sharply criticized Washington in September 2002 for eroding civil liberties at home and human rights standards worldwide after the September 11 attack.[13] The *New York Times* called the Bush administration's policy of unilaterally decreeing indefinite military detention for "enemy combatants"—without judicial review or due process of law—a "formula for totalitarianism."[14] A legal brief filed by former federal officials, including two former secretaries of the navy, contested the administration's claim that federal courts had no jurisdiction over the detention of noncitizens at the military prison in Guantánamo, stating: "If no constitutional rights applied to offshore detainees, then the government would be free *to create a parallel system of extraterritorial courts and extraterritorial prisons to punish extraterritorial crimes without legal oversight or constraint.*"[15] The reference to the parallel system evoked counterinsurgency doctrine and the concept of the parallel state as analyzed in this book. Washington's rapid adoption—or continuation—of such methods mirrored its promotion and acceptance of similar methods—employed by Condor and the military states—during the Cold War.

In late 2003, news reports revealed the existence of a secret commando team of U.S. Special Forces and CIA paramilitaries, possibly including foreigners as well, called Task Force 121. The hunter-killer squadron was engaged in a cross-border, regional mission to pursue, and kill, "high-value targets" in the Middle East. While officials stated that details about the force were classified, it clearly evoked the Condor model.[16] Indeed, the George W. Bush administration presided over the construction of vast, worldwide parallel structures, including secret prisons in Iraq, Qatar, Afghanistan, and elsewhere in the "war on terror." Suspects were transported across borders on covert aircraft and essentially "disappeared." A former CIA officer insisted that such extrajudicial kidnappings were not illegal, arguing, "There is a long history of this. It has been done for decades." Similarly, a State Department officer testified that if "a terrorist suspect is outside of the United States, the CIA helps to catch and send him to the United States or a third country." When "rendered" to third countries, U.S. specialists developed interrogation questions with their counterparts and then watched the interrogation through a two-way mirror.[17] The use of such practices in the present, again, added significance to the evidence of U.S. collaboration with Operation Condor in the 1970s.

Assessing the Role of the U.S. Government in Condor

Philip Agee, the former CIA officer, explained the methods of the CIA in Latin America this way: "[The CIA] contracted Brazilians in Brazil, Chileans in Chile. They weren't U.S. citizens, under the protection of the State Department, but local people who worked for the CIA. The CIA was behind the repressive operations. Persons like me never got their hands dirty. We motivated local agents and gave them money, equipment, and they did the rest; they got their hands dirty."[18]

Given this modus operandi, what can we conclude about the U.S. relationship to Operation Condor? Undoubtedly there is much that remains hidden. But a number of dots can be connected. It is clear that the CIA helped organize the transnational intelligence networks that comprised Condor and that Condor continued to be a CIA-backed program, with the approval of Washington. An intricate web of evidence from multiple sources indicates that U.S. military and intelligence forces were deeply involved in the creation and functioning of the cross-border hunter-killer program known as Condor.

We have established a number of relationships between U.S. military and intelligence forces and Condor, which can be categorized as Preparation/Instigation, Logistical Support, and Direct Operational Support.

Preparation/Instigation

During the Cold War, and especially after the Cuban revolution, U.S. officials took the lead in revitalizing and upgrading inter-American security structures. The U.S. security establishment trained, indoctrinated, financed, and advised military, police, and intelligence forces in Latin America. In the early 1960s, the Conferences of American Armies assembled military and intelligence personnel from Latin America and the United States to share tactics and intelligence on the "subversive threat," establish combined intelligence organizations, develop a hemispheric security strategy, and otherwise cooperate with one another to control and purge their societies of leftist activists and ideas. The School of the Americas (SOA) was also a central vehicle for welding the armies together and combining their forces to create a unified continental anticommunist force. An SOA official privately told a journalist in 1995 that the school "systematically encouraged the transplantation of military structures into, and facilitated the propagation of military power and objectives against, legitimate civilian governments."[19] The shared programs, ideologies, strategies, and organizations developed in the 1960s laid the groundwork for Operation Condor in the 1970s.

As early as 1959, U.S. military and intelligence officers in Colombia recommended the formation of hunter-killer teams and the creation of secret underground units to use "paramilitary, sabotage, and/or terrorist" methods against the enemy, units that strongly resembled later Condor squads. U.S. commanders taught and used the same methods in Southeast Asia and in Europe during the same period, and some of the same individuals were involved. As Michael McClintock has pointed out, new patterns of repression and the organizational forms to carry them out emerged in the Americas in the 1960s, closely associated with U.S. security programs. The national security states of the 1960s, '70s, and '80s, and the parastatal structures they constructed, including Condor, were tightly linked to U.S. doctrine and training and to the inter-American counterinsurgency regime.

The CIA basically coordinated all counterinsurgency in Latin America throughout the Cold War, an era that began in Latin America in Guatemala in the early 1950s. The CIA created, financed, and directed a right-wing parallel force to subvert the government of Jacobo Arbenz from Honduras in 1954. It organized a parallel army from within Cuban exile communities after 1959 to invade Cuba in the Bay of Pigs operation, and used members of this force as a resource for decades to come. CIA officer E. Howard Hunt played a central role in both Guatemala and the Bay of Pigs operations and was later involved in the Watergate break-in. He retained close ties to the Cuban exiles. As former FBI agent and Watergate burglar Gordon Liddy explained:

> Mr. Hunt informed me he had played a major role in the aborted attempt to overthrow Fidel Castro that has come to be known historically as the Bay of Pigs

> episode. He told me that there were still many very well-trained, trained by the Central Intelligence Agency, very pro-American, anti-Castro Cubans in Miami, and that he knew them well, that he believed that they would be available, indeed eager, to engage in special operations, special missions on behalf of the special group of which Mr. Hunt and I were members [the "Plumbers" of the Nixon administration] . . . we referred to them as our Cuban assets.[20]

Many Bay of Pigs veterans joined the U.S. Special Forces after the defeat of the invasion of Cuba, or served as CIA contract agents in later operations. In effect, the CIA had its own covert, parallel army in the Cuban exiles, to act as cut-outs (intermediaries to conceal the U.S. role) and to implement controversial or illegal operations. Cuban exiles have appeared and reappeared in many of the covert operations of the U.S. government up to the present time. Their many links to Condor were suggestive of a covert CIA role in the transnational parastatal apparatus. Such operatives as the Novo brothers and Orlando Bosch worked with the CIA at the Bay of Pigs in the 1960s and with Condor in the 1970s; others reappeared with the CIA in Central America in the 1980s. The counterrevolutionary movement in the Americas was integrated, even though its specific targets shifted over time.

U.S. forces worked behind the scenes with the Latin American military and intelligence forces that comprised the Condor Group, providing resources, administrative assistance, intelligence, and financing. U.S. officers performed an enabling role among the Latin American military and intelligence forces that organized Operation Condor. In the late 1960s and early 1970s, CIA and military officers worked to meld the intelligence forces of the region together into one organization and urged their counterparts to undertake cross-border surveillance and pursuit of political opponents. The CIA arranged meetings of South American police and military officers—including some who ran death squads—to establish contacts and facilitate the transfer and sharing of repressive techniques, including torture methods, among the region's intelligence forces. These alliances and connections were the foundation for Operation Condor, and U.S. security forces essentially acted as host and patron, while remaining in the background.

As Condor took shape in 1973 and 1974, U.S. officers worked closely with the Condor Group's leaders. The CIA station chief in Santiago offered advice and organizational assistance to Manuel Contreras of Chile to set up the DINA apparatus, and CIA officers played a similar role in the organization of other intelligence and operations bodies that became Condor members. The CIA station chief in Santiago served as a bridge between the Brazilian intelligence organization SNI and DINA, and enlisted the Brazilians to help Contreras organize the Chilean intelligence organization. Contreras was a CIA asset, and other top Condor figures—such as Amaurí Prantl of Uruguay and Osvaldo Ribeiro of Argentina—worked closely with the CIA as well. The CIA trained Condor operatives such as Hugo Campos Hermida, and many other Condor officers, such as Raúl Eduardo Iturriaga Neumann and Armando Fernández Larios, attended the SOA or other U.S. training centers, where a ruthless counterrevolutionary culture was fostered. In these ways, U.S. forces laid the groundwork for Operation Condor.

Logistical Support

In this category, we can place the various forms of support that U.S. forces supplied to the Condor apparatus or to the military and intelligence organizations that comprised the Condor Group. This assistance included providing advanced computers to Condor to modernize intelligence operations and communications; training Condor officers; financing the militaries and intelligence agencies that made up the axis of Condor; sharing intelligence (lists of persons to detain, photos and reports on suspects) and coordinating intelligence information; and advising Condor Group officers and forces. Intelligence documents recovered in the Paraguayan Archives show regular intelligence coordination and interchange between Latin American intelligence bodies that participated in Condor and the CIA and FBI. Additionally, U.S. military and intelligence officers had intimate knowledge of Condor operations and did not raise any objections (as we have seen, some State Department and embassy officials did). U.S. officials provided invaluable political support to Condor during the Nixon and Ford administrations. The Kissinger State Department watched as Condor disappearances and extrajudicial executions continued, and rescinded the one known demarche to ambassadors that would have relayed criticism of Condor assassinations to the military states. State Department officials defended the Uruguayan regime in 1976 as Congress tried to limit military aid to Latin American dictatorships. Several 1980 documents show that a U.S. security official knew of illegal Condor transfers and "permanent disappearances" in advance and did not object. He clearly was accepted within the top echelons of the Condor apparatus in Argentina. In Central America in the 1980s, U.S., Argentine, and Chilean intelligence instructors taught death squad personnel from several countries methods of surveillance, interrogation, torture, and abduction.

U.S. military and intelligence documents from the 1970s wrote approvingly of Condor as a "countersubversive" or "anti-Marxist" organization. Such documents—relatively few of which have been declassified—demonstrated that U.S. military and intelligence forces were fully informed of key Condor operations, such as the abductions of PVP (Partido por la Victoria del Pueblo) members in Argentina, and of internal discussions within the Condor apparatus. To the Condor officers, all this showed that the top ranks of the U.S. government clearly sanctioned Operation Condor.

Direct Operational Involvement

In this category is the evidence that U.S. forces went beyond a liaison or enabler role and directly collaborated with Condor in an operational role. Clearly, this is the most sensitive, and secret, level of U.S. collaboration with Condor, and the one that remains the most opaque. There is still much we do not know.

Probably the most concrete evidence of a secret U.S. role in Condor was the Condor Group's use of the Panama Canal Zone telecommunications center to coordinate operations. Acting as an unofficial partner, or secret sponsor, of the Condor system, the United States greatly expanded Condor's lethal reach via the continental communications system. Moreover, U.S. personnel could monitor Condor communications through this channel, indicating U.S. knowledge of Condor hunter-killer operations and intelligence. This access to the secure U.S. telecommunications system showed that covert, operational support for Condor was authorized at high levels of the U.S. government. While it is still unclear who approved Condor's use of the U.S. network, this intelligence relationship demonstrated that Condor was considered a key covert operation that served the interests of Washington.

In several known cases, U.S. personnel collaborated with Condor abductions and interrogations. U.S. officials in Argentina participated in the effort to capture Chilean Jorge Isaac Fuentes Alarcón in Paraguay, notifying the Chilean security forces of his interrogation and initiating an investigation of Fuentes's contacts in the United States, thus acting as part of the Condor system. DINA agent Juan Muñoz Alarcón testified shortly before his murder that U.S. officials played a central role in the Chilean Condor structure. The abductions of U.S. citizens Charles Horman and Frank Teruggi in Chile may have been approved and/or facilitated by U.S. military and/or intelligence forces. State Department investigators suspected so in 1976. The role of U.S. intelligence is still murky in these cases, as is the role of U.S. officials and agencies in Phase III assassinations (Michelini/Gutiérrez-Ruiz and Letelier/Moffitt), and troubling questions have not been resolved. Recall that the Chilean ambassador told a Washington journalist in 1978 that the United States was a member of Condor, citing Vernon Walters and his trip to Asunción. Walters met with Contreras in Washington in 1975 immediately before the DINA commander's trips to numerous South American capitals to organize Condor networks, and in 1976 he met with Contreras again a month before the Letelier/Moffitt assassinations. The general and top CIA officer took his secrets with him to the grave. Leandro Sánchez Reisse, an Argentine intelligence officer, stated before a U.S. Senate subcommittee in 1987 that the U.S. CIA and DIA were linked to an "Intelligence Advisory Committee" of Condor intelligence organizations.

Argentine officers established a Condor base in Florida in the 1970s, and set up front companies to channel funds and weapons to Argentine intelligence units working with the CIA in Central America and elsewhere in Latin America in the early 1980s. Condor officers Sánchez Reisse and Battaglia bragged about their freedom to conduct operations in the United States, and Sánchez Reisse told the U.S. Senate subcommittee in 1987 that he had worked directly with the CIA in Florida. Former contra collaborators testified that they had received $50,000 in Argentine funds in Florida, possibly through Sánchez Reisse's operation. It has since been well documented that Oliver North and the CIA were seeking untraceable ways to finance the contras in the 1980s, to bypass congressional prohibitions. The evidence suggests that the Condor system was one such channel, and the Reagan administration's obsession with overthrowing the Sandinistas supplies a motive for its collaboration with Condor operations in the United States in the 1980s. Also in the 1980s, in Central America, CIA and military personnel were directly involved in setting up and financing a new Condor-like system. Working with Condor veterans from Argentina, U.S. military and intelligence forces helped organize and finance anticommunist death squads and a secret, parallel infrastructure to centralize command and control of the dirty wars in Central America.

In sum, the evidence, while still incomplete, allows us to state quite conclusively that Washington not only collaborated with Operation Condor and took advantage of the Condor system to advance perceived U.S. interests, but also played an indispensable role in its genesis and functioning. The CIA and the Pentagon were instrumental in organizing the early foundations of Condor, and, as the Condor system coalesced and expanded, U.S. military and intelligence forces provided it with crucial technological infrastructure and cooperation, and sanctioned, encouraged, and at times actively collaborated with it. Indeed, the U.S. relationship to Condor was undoubtedly more substantial than acknowledged thus far, but the refusal of the Defense Department and CIA to declassify relevant files continues to inhibit efforts to clarify the facts.

It is important to reiterate that some U.S. officials and many members of Congress raised strong objections to U.S. counterinsurgency strategies and alliances with brutal militaries and dictators, and to Operation Condor. But high-ranking U.S. policymakers, and national security policy as a whole, placed anticommunism and counterrevolution squarely at the top of U.S. priorities during the Cold War. It was a policy that fostered and encouraged the widespread use of extreme and illegal methods in the anticommunist crusade in Latin America.

The military dictatorships that formed the Condor Group have passed into history. Some Condor officers have served prison time and many others have been charged with crimes. But despite a number of important judicial processes in several countries, many of the families of Condor victims still have little or no information about what happened to their loved ones. Most Condor commanders and operatives still refuse to shed light on the fates of Condor victims. Justice has not yet been done. Today, as the twenty-first century unfolds, the mentalities and methods of Operation Condor persist. The legacy of Operation Condor still casts a long shadow over Latin America, the United States, and the world.

Notes

1. José Antonio Aruquipa, "Banzer's Involvement in Operation Condor," *Bolivian Times*, January 17, 2002.

2. Maxine Lowy, "Pinochet in the Clutches of the Condor," *Memoria y Justicia*, July 2004, at http://www.memoriayjusticia.cl/english/en_rights-OpCondor.htm.

3. James LeMoyne, "Testifying to Torture," *New York Times Magazine* (June 5, 1988): 66.

4. "The CIA in Honduras," notes from a conference hosted by the Center for International Policy, Washington, D.C., May 7, 1997.

5. Afghan tribal leaders protested en masse in January 2003, after one of their colleagues was pulled from his car by American men in unmarked vehicles, pushed into one of the vehicles, and taken away. The leader had been en route to a meeting with government officials. In the protest, which took place after the leader had been missing for two weeks, the tribal leaders said hundreds of similar detentions had been carried out by U.S. forces. "This is what we expected during the Soviet time here, not with the Americans," one said. See Marc Kaufman, "Afghans Protest Clan Leader's Detention," *Washington Post*, January 12, 2003. In 2004, it became clear that thousands of Iraqis and other suspects were being held in secret U.S. detention centers worldwide.

6. U.S. officials admitted to *Washington Post* reporters that they used "stress and duress" techniques in Afghanistan (Human Rights Watch called it "torture lite") such as depriving sleep, using twenty-four-hour lights in cells, holding prisoners in painful positions for hours, and withholding medicine and painkilling drugs from wounded prisoners. U.S. officers also transferred prisoners to countries where torture was practiced, with lists of questions prepared by U.S. officials. At the CIA's secret interrogation

base at Bagram, Afghanistan, two prisoners died of blunt force trauma, classified as homicide by U.S. pathologists, in 2002. The Abu Ghraib revelations removed any lingering doubts regarding U.S. use of torture. See, for example, Dana Priest and Barton Gellman, "U.S. Uses Tough Tactics on Silent Terrorists," *Washington Post*, December 26, 2002; Peter Slevin, "U.S. Pledges to Avoid Torture: Pledge on Terror Suspects Comes amid Probes of Two Deaths," *Washington Post*, June 27, 2003; Tania Branigan, "Ex-Prisoners Allege Rights Abuses by U.S. Military," *Washington Post*, August 19, 2003; Amnesty International, "Iraq: Torture Not Isolated—Independent Investigation Vital," press release, April 30, 2004; Dana Milibank, "U.S. Tries to Calm Furor Caused by Photos," *Washington Post*, May 1, 2004.

7. See, for example, Amnesty International, "USA/Malawi: Another Unlawful Transfer to U.S. Custody?" June 25, 2003; DeNeen L. Brown, "Ex-Detainee Details Fearful Path to Syria: Torture Followed Handover by American 'Removal' Unit," *Washington Post*, November 12, 2003; Clifford Krause, "Qaeda Pawn, U.S. Calls Him. Victim, He Calls Himself." *New York Times*, November 15, 2003.

8. The Guantánamo detention facility was a prime example. Hundreds of foreigners, including three juveniles, were held in small cages for years without access to lawyers or family. Although U.S. officials denied ill treatment, photos were broadcast worldwide of hooded and shackled prisoners, and a significant number attempted suicide. In 2004, prisoners who were released described torture suffered at the hands of U.S. units. See, for example, Tania Branigan, "3 Likely to Be Freed From Guantánamo: Rights Groups Urge Children's Release under International Law," *Washington Post*, August 23, 2003; John Mintz, "Britons Allege Guantánamo Abuse in Letter to Bush," *Washington Post*, May 14, 2004.

9. See, for example, Dana Priest, "CIA Killed U.S. Citizen in Yemen Missile Strike," *Washington Post*, November 8, 2002; Dexter Filkins, "Flaws in U.S. Air War Left Hundreds of Civilians Dead," *New York Times*, July 21, 2002; Craig S. Smith, "After a Commando Operation, Questions about Why and How 21 Afghans Died," *New York Times*, January 28, 2002. In the last case, villagers said they found the bodies of more than a dozen men who had been shot and burned. Two other bodies had their hands tied with tough white plastic strips. A destroyed truck had a piece of paper stuck on its windshield with a U.S. flag and the words "God Bless America"; a handwritten message said "Have a nice day. From Damage, Inc."

10. After invading Iraq and routing its government, U.S. forces set up a system of military rule (with a civilian proconsul overseeing the occupation), hand picked an advisory body of Iraqis, discouraged elections, and resisted the transfer of power to Iraqis. As the U.S. presidential election drew closer, and the war became more unpopular, the Bush administration changed course and declared that on June 30, 2004, a handover of power would occur, giving limited sovereignty to Iraqis. The hand-picked leader of the new administration had close ties to the CIA.

11. These tribunals were criticized by lawyers' groups such as the American Bar Association and the National Association of Criminal Defense Lawyers, as well as human rights organizations, as dangerous, unfair, and misguided. Their procedures included the use of secret evidence; secret proceedings; absence of an impartial jury; monitoring of attorney-client communications; forcing of lawyers to disclose client

information to security officials; absence of civilian review; and imposition of gag rules on public comments by lawyers on the trials. Conservative columnist William Safire wrote that after 9/11 the president had "assumed what amounts to dictatorial power to jail or execute aliens." Safire, "Seizing Dictatorial Power," *New York Times*, November 15, 2001.

12. In fact, some U.S. officials of the 1970s were again in government: Donald Rumsfeld and Richard Cheney served in the Nixon administration, and, of course, George W. Bush's father served as CIA director in 1976.

13. Julia Preston, "Departing Rights Commissioner Faults U.S.," *New York Times*, September 12, 2002.

14. Editors, "'Enemy Combatants' in Court," *New York Times*, April 26, 2004.

15. Emphasis added. Linda Greenhouse, "The Imperial Presidency and the Constraints of the Law," *New York Times*, April 18, 2004.

16. Thom Shanker and Eric Schmitt, "Secret Unit Hunts Saddam, Bin Laden," *New York Times*, November 8, 2003; Seymour Hersh, "'Phoenix' Arises in Iraq: Moving Targets," *New Yorker*, December 8, 2003.

17. Dana Priest and Joe Stephens, "Secret World of U.S. Interrogation," *Washington Post*, May 11, 2004.

18. "Revelan que la CIA contrataba agentes para aplicar torturas," *Primera Linea* (Chile), October 10, 2001.

19. W. E. Gutman, "Politics of Assassination," *Z Magazine* (September 1995).

20. Mark Lane, *Plausible Denial: Was the CIA Involved in the Assassination of JFK?* (New York: Thunder's Mouth Press, 1991): 204–205. See also E. Howard Hunt, *Undercover: Memoirs of an American Secret Agent* (London: W. H. Allen, 1975), 129–133 and the second half of the book, on Watergate.

Bibliography

Scholarly Works

Abramovici, Pierre. "Latin America: The 30 Years' Dirty War," *Le Monde Diplomatique* (August 2001).

Agee, Philip. "Exposing the CIA," in Philip Agee and Louis Wolf, eds., *Dirty Work: The CIA in Western Europe*. Pp. 40–62. London: Zed Press, 1978.

Allodi, Federico. "Somoza's National Guard: A Study of Human Rights Abuses, Psychological Health and Moral Development," in Ronald Crelinsten and Alex P. Schmid, eds., *The Politics of Pain: Torturers and Their Masters*. Pp. 118–123. Boulder, Colo.: Westview, 1995.

Almada, Martín. *Paraguay: La cárcel olvidada, el país exiliado*. Asunción: Imprenta Salesiana, 1993.

Andersen, Martin Edwin. *Dossier Secreto: Argentina's Desaparecidos and the Myth of the 'Dirty War.'* Boulder, Colo.: Westview, 1993.

———. "Kissinger and the 'Dirty War,'" *The Nation* (October 31, 1987): 477–480.

Andrew, Christopher. *For the President's Eyes Only: Secret Intelligence and the American Presidency from Washington to Bush*. New York: Harper Collins, 1995.

Arboleya, Jesús. *The Cuban Counterrevolution*. Athens: Center for International Studies, Ohio University, 2000.

Arce, Luz. *The Inferno: A Story of Terror and Survival in Chile*. Trans. Alba Skar. Madison: University of Wisconsin Press, 2004.

Armony, Ariel C. *Argentina, the United States, and the Anti-Communist Crusade in Central America, 1977–1984*. Athens: Center for International Studies, Ohio University, 1997.

Ballester, Horacio P., José Luis García, Carlos Mariano Gazcón, and Augusto B. Rattenbach. "El sistema interamericano de defensa como paradigma de la seguridad nacional." *Revista Cruz del Sur*, Instituto Latinoamericano de Estudios Geopolíticos, Vol. 3, no. 7 (December 1985): 5–14.

Barahona de Brito, Alexandra. *Human Rights and Democratization in Latin America: Uruguay and Chile.* New York: Oxford University Press, 1997.

Barry, Tom. *Low-Intensity Conflict: The New Battlefield in Central America.* Albuquerque, N.M.: The Resource Center, 1986.

Bartov, Omer. "Industrial Killing: World War I, The Holocaust, and Representation," presentation at Rutgers University, March 1997, at muweb.millersville.edu/~holocon/bartov.html.

———. *Mirrors of Destruction: War, Genocide, and Modern Identity.* New York: Oxford University Press, 2000.

———. *Murder in Our Midst: The Holocaust, Industrial Killing, and Representation.* New York: Oxford University Press, 1996.

Becerra, Longino. *Cuando las tarántulas atacan*, 6th ed. Tegucigalpa, Honduras: Baktun Editorial, 2002.

Beit-Hallahmi, Benjamin. *The Israeli Connection: Who Israel Arms and Why.* New York: Pantheon, 1987.

Berger, D. H. "The Use of Paramilitary Activity as a Policy Tool: An Analysis of Operations Conducted by the U.S. CIA, 1949–1951." Decatur, Ga.: Marine Corps Command and Staff College, n.d.

Binns, Jack R. *The United States in Honduras, 1980–1981: An Ambassador's Memoir.* Jefferson, N.C.: McFarland, 2000.

Black, George. "The Cold War's Devils Were on Both Sides," *Los Angeles Times*, November 29, 1990.

———. "Delle Chiaie: From Bologna to Bolivia; A Terrorist Odyssey," *The Nation*, Vol. 244 (April 26, 1987): 525–531.

Blasier, Cole. "Security: The Extracontinental Dimension," in Kevin J. Middlebrook and Carlos Rico, eds., *The United States and Latin America in the 1980s.* Pp. 523–564. Pittsburgh, Pa.: University of Pittsburgh Press, 1988.

———. "The Soviet Union," in Morris J. Blachman, William M. Leogrande, and Kenneth Sharpe, eds., *Confronting Revolution: Security through Diplomacy in Central America.* Pp. 256–270. New York: Pantheon, 1986.

Blixen, Samuel. *El Vientre del Cóndor: Del archivo del terror al caso Berríos*, 2nd ed. Montevideo, Uruguay: Ediciones de Brecha, 1995.

———. *Seregni: La mañana siguiente*, 2nd ed. Montevideo: Ediciones de Brecha, 1997.

Boccia Paz, Alfredo, Myrian Angélica González, and Rosa Palau Aguilar. *Es mi informe: Los archivos secretos de la Policía de Stroessner.* Asunción, Paraguay: CDE, 1994.

Bonasso, Miguel. *El presidente que no fue: Los archivos ocultos del peronismo*, 2nd ed. Buenos Aires: Planeta, 2002.

Bonner, Raymond. *Weakness and Deceit: U.S. Policy and El Salvador.* New York: Times Books, 1984.

Branch, Taylor and Eugene M. Propper. *Labyrinth.* New York: Viking Press, 1982.

Calloni, Stella. *Los años del lobo: Operación Cóndor*, 2nd ed. Buenos Aires: Peña Lillo, Ediciones Continente, 1999.

———. "The Horror Archives of Operation Condor," *Covert Action Bulletin*, no. 50 (Fall 1994): 7–61.

Campbell, Bruce B. and Arthur D. Brenner, eds. *Death Squads in Global Perspective: Murder with Deniability*. New York: St. Martin's Press, 2000.

Castro, Daniel. *Revolution and Revolutionaries*. Wilmington, Del.: Scholarly Resources, 1999.

Catholic Church, Archdiocese of São Paulo. *Torture in Brazil*. Trans. Jaime Wright. Austin: University of Texas Press, 1998.

Chamorro, Edgar. *Packaging the Contras: A Case of CIA Disinformation*. New York: Institute of Media Analysis, 1987.

Child, John. *Unequal Alliance: The Inter-American Military System, 1938–1978*. Boulder, Colo.: Westview, 1980.

Christie, Stuart. *Stefano Delle Chiaie: Portrait of a Black Terrorist*. London: Anarchy Magazine/Refract Publications, 1984.

Clarridge, Duane, with Digby Diehl. *A Spy for All Seasons: My Life in the CIA*. New York: Scribner, 1997.

Cockburn, Leslie. *Out of Control: The Story of the Reagan Administration's Secret War in Nicaragua, the Illegal Arms Pipeline, and the Contra Drug Connection*. New York: Altantic Monthly Press, 1987.

Cockcroft, James. *Latin America*, 2nd ed. Chicago: Nelson-Hall, 1996.

CODEPU, Equipo DIT-T. *Más allá de las fronteras: Estudios sobre las personas ejecutadas o desaparecidas fuera de Chile, 1973–1990*. Santiago, Chile: LOM Ediciones, 1996.

———. *La gran mentira: El caso de las listas de los 119*. Santiago, Chile: CODEPU, 1994.

Cohen, Stanley and Daphan Golan. *The Interrogation of Palestinians during the Intifada: Ill-Treatment, 'Moderate Physical Pressure' or Torture?* Jerusalem: B'TSELEM, Israeli Information Center for Human Rights in the Occupied Territories, 1991.

Coleman, Kenneth M. and George C. Herring. *The Central American Crisis: Sources of Conflict and the Failure of U.S. Policy*. Wilmington, Del.: Scholarly Resources, 1985.

Comblin, José. *The Church and the National Security State*. Maryknoll, N.Y.: Orbis Books, 1979.

Comisión Nacional de Verdad y Reconciliación. *Informe Rettig*. Vols. 1 and 2. Santiago: Chilean Government and Ediciones del Ornitorrinco, 1991.

Comisión Nacional sobre la Desaparición de Personas. *Nunca más*. Buenos Aires: Eudeba, 1984.

Comisionado Nacional de los Derechos Humanos de Honduras. *Boletín Informativo*, Vol. 3, no. 484 (January 20, 1997).

———. *Los hechos hablan por si mismos, Informe preliminar sobre los desaparecidos en Honduras 1980–1993*, 2nd ed. Tegucigalpa, Honduras: Editoriales Guaymuras, 2002.

Constable, Pamela and Arturo Valenzuela. *A Nation of Enemies: Chile under Pinochet*. New York: W. W. Norton, 1991.

Corn, David. "Kissinger's Back . . . As 9/11 Truth Seeker," *The Nation* (November 27, 2002).

Crelinsten, Ronald D. "In Their Own Words: The World of the Torturer," in Ronald D. Crelinsten and Alex P. Schmid, eds., *The Politics of Pain: Torturers and Their Masters*. Pp. 35–64. Boulder, Colo.: Westview, 1995.

———. "The Discourse and Practice of Counter-Terrorism in Liberal Democracies," *Australian Journal of Politics and History*, Vol. 44, no. 3 (September 1998): 389–413.

Davis, Darién J. "The Arquivos das Policias Politicais of the State of Rio de Janeiro," *Latin America Research Review*, Vol. 31, no. 1 (1996): 99–104.

Dickey, Christopher. *With the Contras*. New York: Simon & Schuster, 1985.

Dillon, Sam. *Commandos: The CIA and Nicaragua's Contra Rebels*. New York: Henry Holt, 1991.

Dinges, John. *The Condor Years*. New York: New Press, 2004.

———. "The Dubious Document," *Columbia Journalism Review*, Vol. 38, no. 5 (January 2000): 10.

Dinges, John and Saul Landau. *Assassination on Embassy Row*. New York: Pantheon Books, 1980.

Dixon Marlene and Susanne Jonas, eds. *Revolution and Intervention in Central America*. San Francisco: Synthesis Publications, 1983.

Doe, John. "Phoenix Program," in Harold V. Hall and Leighton C. Whitaker, eds., *Collective Violence: Effective Strategies for Assessing and Intervening in Fatal Group and Institutional Aggression*. New York: CRC Press, 1999.

Draper, Theodore. *A Very Thin Line: The Iran-Contra Affairs*. New York: Hill and Wang, 1991.

Eich, Dieter and Carlos Rincón. *The Contras: Interviews with Anti-Sandinistas*. San Francisco: Synthesis Publications, 1984.

Fall, Bernard B. "Counterinsurgency: The French Experience," seminar at Industrial College of the Armed Forces, Washington, D.C., 18 January 1963, published as number L63–109, Industrial College of the Armed Forces.

———. "The Theory and Practice of Insurgency and Counterinsurgency," *Naval War College Review* (April 1965), at www.nwc.navy.mil/press/Review/1998/winter/art5-w98.htm.

Fischer, Mary A. "Teaching Torture," *Gentlemen's Quarterly* (June 1997): 182–240.

Fraga, Rosendo. *Ejército: Del escarnio al poder (1973–1976)*. Buenos Aires: Grupo Editorial Planeta, 1988.

Freed, Donald with Fred Landis. *Death in Washington: The Murder of Orlando Letelier*. Westport, Conn.: Lawrence Hill, 1980.

Galula, David. *Counterinsurgency Warfare: Theory and Practice*. New York: Praeger, 1964.

García Rivas, J. Víctor. *Confesiones de un torturador*. Barcelona: Editorial Laia, 1981.

Garst, Rachel. "Military Intelligence and Human Rights in Guatemala: The Archivo and the Case for Intelligence Reform," Washington, D.C.: Washington Office on Latin America (WOLA), March 30, 1995.

Gasparini, Juan. *La pista suiza*. Buenos Aires: Editorial Legasa, 1986.

Gilio, María Esther. *The Tupamaro Guerrillas: The Structure and Strategy of the Urban Guerrilla Movement*. New York: Saturday Review Press, 1972.

Gill, Lesley. *The School of the Americas: Military Training and Political Violence in the Americas*. Durham, N.C.: Duke University Press, 2004.

Giraldo, Javier. *Colombia: Genocidal Democracy*. Monroe, Maine: Common Courage Press, 1996.

———. "Corrupted Justice and the Schizophrenic State in Colombia," *Social Justice*, Vol. 26, no. 4 (1999): 31–54.

González, Mónica and Edwin Harrington. *Bomba en una calle de Palermo*. Santiago, Chile: Editorial Emisión, 1987.

González Janzen, Ignacio. *La Triple A*. Buenos Aires: Editorial Contrapunto, 1986.

Graebner, Norman A., ed. *The National Security: Its Theory and Practice 1945–1960*. New York: Oxford University Press, 1986.

Guzmán, Nancy. *Romo: Confesiones de un torturador*. Santiago, Chile: Planeta, 2002.

Halperin, Morton, Jerry Berman, Robert Borosage, and Christine Marwick. *The Lawless State: The Crimes of the U.S. Intelligence Agencies*. New York: Penguin Books, 1976.

Halperín Donghi, Tulio. *The Contemporary History of Latin America*. Trans. John Charles Chasteen. Durham, N.C.: Duke University Press, 1993.

Haritos-Fatouros, Mika."The Official Torturer: A Learning Model for Obedience to the Authority of Violence," in Ronald D. Crelinsten and Alex P. Schmid, eds., *The Politics of Pain: Torturers and Their Masters*. P. 130. Boulder, Colo.: Westview, 1995.

Haugaard, Lisa. "Recently Declassified Army and CIA Manuals Used in Latin America: An Analysis of Their Content," Washington, D.C.: Latin America Working Group, Memorandum, 1997.

Hauser, Thomas. *The Execution of Charles Horman*. New York: Harcourt, Brace, Jovanovich, 1978.

Hayden, Patrick. "The War on Terrorism and the Just Use of Military Force," in Patrick Hayden, Tom Lansford, and Robert P. Watson, eds., *America's War on Terror*. Pp. 105–121. Burlington, Vt.: Ashgate Publishing, 2004.

Heinz, Wolfgang S. "The Military, Torture and Human Rights: Experiences from Argentina, Brazil, Chile and Uruguay," in Ronald Crelinsten and Alex P. Schmid, eds., *The Politics of Pain: Torturers and Their Masters*. Pp. 65–97. Boulder, Colo.: Westview, 1995.

Hersh, Seymour M. *Chain of Command: The Road from 9/11 to Abu Ghraib*. New York: HarperCollins, 2004.

———. *The Price of Power: Kissinger in the Nixon White House*. New York: Summit Books, 1983.

Hitchens, Christopher. "Kissinger's Green Light to Suharto," *The Nation* (February 18, 2002).

———. *The Trial of Henry Kissinger*. London: Verso, 2002.

Holt, Pat. *Secret Intelligence and Public Policy: A Dilemma of Democracy*. Washington, D.C.: Congressional Quarterly Press, 1995.

Horowitz, Irving Louis, ed. *The Rise and Fall of Project Camelot*. Cambridge, Mass.: The MIT Press, 1967.

Huggins, Martha K. *Political Policing: The United States and Latin America*. Durham, N.C.: Duke University Press, 1998.

Huggins, Martha K., Mika Haritos-Fatouros, and Philip G. Zimbardo. *Violence Workers: Police Torturers and Murderers Reconstruct Brazilian Atrocities*. Berkeley: University of California Press, 2002.

Human Rights Watch (HRW). *Colombia's Killer Networks: The Military-Paramilitary Partnership and the United States*, November 1996. New York.

———. *The Ties that Bind: Colombia and Military-Paramilitary Links*, Vol. 12, no. 1 (February 2000).

Hunt, E. Howard. *Undercover: Memoirs of an American Secret Agent.* London: W. H. Allen, 1975.

Immerman, Richard H. *The CIA in Guatemala: The Foreign Policy of Intervention.* Austin: University of Texas Press, 1982, 5th printing 1990.

Irusta M., Gerardo. *Espionaje y servicios secretos en Bolivia y el Cono Sur: Nazis en la Operación Cóndor*, 2nd ed. La Paz, Bolivia, 1997.

Johnson, Chalmers. *Blowback: The Costs and Consequences of American Empire.* New York: Henry Holt, 2000.

Johnson, Kermit D. *Ethics and Counterrevolution.* Lanham, Md.: University Press of America, 1998.

Jonas, Susanne. "Contradictions of Revolution and Intervention in Central America in the Transnational Era: The Case of Guatemala," in Marlene Dixon and Susanne Jonas, eds., *Revolution and Intervention in Central America.* Pp. 288–289. San Francisco: Synthesis Publications, 1983.

———. *The Battle for Guatemala: Rebels, Death Squads, and U.S. Power.* Boulder, Colo.: Westview, 1991.

Kenworthy, Eldon. *America/Americas: Myth in the Making of U.S. Policy toward Latin America.* University Park: Penn State University Press, 1995.

Klein, Herbert S. *Bolivia: The Evolution of a Multi-Ethnic Society*, 2nd ed. New York: Oxford, 1992.

Ko'aga Rone'eta. "La 'Operación Cóndor': El terrorismo de estado de alcance transnacional," at www.derechos.org/koaga/vii/2/cuya.html (1996).

Komisar, Lucy. "Documented Complicity," *The Progressive* (1999).

———. "Kissinger Declassified," *The Progressive* (May 1999).

Kornbluh, Peter. "Kissinger and Pinochet," *The Nation* (March 29, 1999).

———. "Prisoner Pinochet: The Dictator and the Quest for Justice," *The Nation* (December 21, 1998): 15

———. *The Pinochet File: A Declassified Dossier on Atrocity and Accountability.* New York: New Press, 2003.

Kwitney, Jonathan. "The CIA's Secret Armies in Europe," *The Nation*, Vol. 254, no. 13 (April 6, 1992).

LaFeber, Walter. *Inevitable Revolutions: The United States in Central America.* New York: W. W. Norton, 1983.

Landau, Saul. *The Dangerous Doctrine: National Security and U.S. Foreign Policy* (A PACCA Book). Boulder, Colo.: Westview, 1988.

———. "They Educated the Crows: An Institute Report on the Letelier-Moffitt Murders." Washington D.C.: Transnational Institute, 1978.

Lane, Mark. *Plausible Denial: Was the CIA Involved in the Assassination of JFK?* New York: Thunder's Mouth Press, 1991.

Langguth, A. J. *Hidden Terrors: The Truth about U.S. Police Operations in Latin America.* New York: Pantheon, 1978.

Lasswell, Harold D. "The Garrison State," *The American Journal of Sociology*, Vol. 46, no. 4 (1941): 455–468.

———. "The Garrison-State Hypothesis Today," in Samuel P. Huntington, ed., *Changing Patterns of Military Politics*. Pp. 51–70. New York: The Free Press, 1962.

Latin American Working Group (a project of the National Council of Churches). "Inspector General's Report on Army Manuals a Feeble Response; What the Recently Declassified Manuals Contain." Washington, D.C.: LAWG, 1997.

Leeds, Elizabeth. "Cocaine and Parallel Politics in the Brazilian Urban Periphery: Constraints on Local-Level Democratization," *Latin American Research Review*, Vol. 31, no. 3 (1996): 47–84.

Leffler, Melvyn P. *The Specter of Communism: The United States and the Origins of the Cold War, 1917–1953.* New York: Hill and Wang, 1994.

LeoGrande, William. *Our Own Backyard: The United States in Central America 1977–1992.* Chapel Hill: University of North Carolina, 1998.

Lernoux, Penny. *Cry of the People.* New York: Doubleday, 1980.

Lewis, Paul. "The Right and Military Rule," in Sandra McGee Deutsch and Ronald H. Dolkart, eds., *The Argentine Right.* Pp. 147–180. Wilmington, Del.: Scholarly Resources, 1993.

Loveman, Brian, and Thomas M. Davies, eds. *Che Guevara and Guerrilla Movements*, 3rd ed. Wilmington, Del.: Scholarly Resources, 1997a.

———. *The Politics of Antipolitics*, 3rd ed. Wilmington, Del.: Scholarly Resources, 1997b.

Malamud Goti, Jaime. "State Terror and Memory of What?" *University of Arkansas at Little Rock Law Review*, Vol. 21, no. 1 (Fall 1998): 107–118.

Mariano, Nilson Cezar. *Operación Cóndor: Terrorismo de Estado en el Cono Sur.* Buenos Aires: Lohlé-Lumen, 1998.

Marshall, Jonathan, Peter Dale Scott, and Jane Hunter. *The Iran-Contra Connection: Secret Teams and Covert Operations in the Reagan Era.* Boston: South End Press, 1987.

Marton, Kati. *The Polk Conspiracy: Murder and Cover-Up in the Case of CBS News Correspondent George Polk.* New York: Farrar, Straus & Giroux, 1990.

Mason, T. David and Dale A. Krane, "The Political Economy of Death Squads: Toward a Theory of the Impact of State-Sanctioned Terror," *International Studies Quarterly*, Vol. 33 (1989): 175–198.

McClintock, Michael. *The American Connection.* Volume I: *State Terror and Popular Resistance in El Salvador.* London: Zed Books, 1985.

———. "American Doctrine and Counterinsurgent State Terror," in Alexander George, ed., *Western State Terrorism.* Pp. 121–154. New York: Routledge, 1991.

———. *Instruments of Statecraft: U.S. Guerrilla Warfare, Counterinsurgency, Counterterrorism, 1940–1990.* New York: Pantheon Books, 1992.

McNamara, Robert S. with Brian VanDeMark. *In Retrospect: The Tragedy and Lessons of Vietnam.* New York: Random House, Times Books, 1995.

McPherson, Sandra B. "The Misuse of Psychological Techniques under U.S. Government Auspices: Interrogation and Terrorism Manuals," in Harold V. Hall and Leighton C. Whitaker, eds., *Collective Violence: Effective Strategies for Assessing and Intervening in Fatal Group and Institutional Aggression.* Pp. 621–632. New York: CRC Press, 1999.

McSherry, J. Patrice. "Analyzing Operation Condor: A Covert Inter-American Structure," paper presented at the 22nd International Congress of Latin American Studies Association (LASA), Miami, March 2000.

———. "Hidden Cold War History: Operation Condor's Structures and Operations," paper prepared for 23rd International Congress of Latin American Studies Association (LASA), Washington, D.C., September 2001.

———. *Incomplete Transition: Military Power and Democracy in Argentina.* New York: St. Martin's Press, 1997.

———. "Operation Condor and the Inter-American Military System," paper presented at the 25th International Congress of Latin American Studies Association (LASA), Las Vegas, October 2004.

———. "Operation Condor as a Hemispheric 'Counterterror' Organization," in Cecilia Menjívar and Néstor Rodríguez, eds., *When States Kill: Latin America, the U.S., and Technologies of Terror.* Austin: University of Texas Press, 2005.

———. "Operation Condor: Clandestine Inter-American System," *Social Justice*, Vol. 26, no. 4 (Winter 1999): 144–174.

———. "Tracking the Origins of a State Terror Network: Operation Condor," *Latin American Perspectives*, Vol. 29, no. 1 (2002): 38–60.

Meilinger de Sannemann, Gladys. *Paraguay en el Operativo Cóndor: Represión e intercambio clandestino de prisioneros políticos en el Cono Sur*, 3d. ed. Asunción: Ministerio de Educación y Culto, 1993.

———. *Paraguay y la 'Operación Cóndor' en los 'Archivos del Terror.'* Asunción: A. R. Impresiones, 1994.

Metz, Steven. "A Flame Kept Burning: Counterinsurgency Support after the Cold War," *Parameters* (Autumn 1995): 31-41.

Milgram, Stanley. *Obedience to Authority: An Experimental View.* New York: Harper and Row, 1974.

Mine, Douglas Grant. "The Assassin Next Door, Part II," *Miami New Times*, October 12, 2000.

Munczek Soler, Débora. *El impacto psicológico de la repressión política en los hijos de los desaparecidos asesinados en Honduras.* Tegucigalpa, Honduras: COFADEH, 1996.

Nelson-Pallmeyer, Jack. *School of Assassins.* New York: Orbis Books, 1997.

Nevares, Henry. "Antecedentes sobre las conferencias de ejércitos americanos: Trabajo y presentación efectuado por el delegado del ejército de los EEUU," Santiago, Chile: Secretaría Permanente, XVI Conferencia de Ejércitos Americanos, 1985.

Nickson, R. Andrew. "Paraguay's Archivo del Terror," *Latin America Research Review*, Vol. 30, no. 1 (1995): 125–129.

Nisbet, Robert A. "Project Camelot: An Autopsy," in Philip Rieff, ed., *On Intellectuals: Theoretical Studies, Case Studies.* Pp. 283–313. Garden City, N.Y.: Doubleday, 1969.

Nordlinger, Eric, response to Gabriel Almond. "The Return to the State," *American Political Science Review*, Vol. 82, no. 3 (September 1988): 875–902.

North American Congress on Latin America (NACLA). "Mass Graves and Torture Chambers Found at Contra Base," *Report on the Americas*, Vol. 33, no. 2 (September/October 1999): 2.

Olmsted, Kathryn. *Challenging the Secret Government: The Post-Watergate Investigations of the CIA and FBI.* Chapel Hill: University of North Carolina Press, 1996.

Ostrovsky, Victor and Claire Hoy. *By Way of Deception: The Making and Unmaking of a MOSSAD Officer.* New York: St. Martin's Press, 1990.

Paret, Peter and John Shy. "The Theory and the Threat," in T. N. Greene, ed., *The Guerrilla and How to Fight Him.* New York: Praeger, 1962.

Paterson, Thomas G., ed. *Major Problems in American Foreign Policy.* Volume II: *Since 1914,* 3rd ed. Lexington, Ky.: D. C. Heath, 1989.

Paterson, Thomas G. and J. Garry Clifford. *America Ascendant: U.S. Foreign Relations since 1939.* Lexington, Ky.: D. C. Heath, 1995.

Paterson, Thomas G. and Robert J. McMahon, eds. *The Origins of the Cold War,* 3rd ed. Lexington, Ky.: D. C. Heath, 1991.

Peregrino Fernández, Rodolfo. *Autocrítica policial.* Buenos Aires: El Cid Editor/Fundación para la Democracia en Argentina, 1983.

Pérez Esquivel, Adolfo. "Prólogo," in Stella Calloni, ed., *Los años del lobo: Operación Condor,* 2nd ed. Pp. 7–10. Buenos Aires: Ediciones Continente, 1999.

Peters, Edward. *Torture.* Philadelphia: University of Pennsylvania Press, 1985.

Phillips, David Atlee. *The Night Watch.* New York: Atheneum, 1977.

Pinetta, Santiago. *López Rega: El final de un brujo.* Buenos Aires: Editorial Abril, documento de *Siete Días,* 1986.

PIT-CNT [labor union confederation of Uruguay]. *Desaparecidos: La coordinación represiva.* Montevideo, Uruguay: Editorial Espacio, 1998.

Policzer, Pablo. "Organizing Coercion in Authoritarian Chile." Ph.D. dissertation, MIT, Cambridge, Mass., 2001.

Powers, Thomas. "Inside the Department of Dirty Tricks," *Atlantic Monthly,* Vol. 244, no. 2 (August 1979): 33–64.

Pyle, Christopher. *Military Surveillance of Civilian Politics, 1967–1970.* New York: Garland, 1986.

Rabe, Stephen. *Eisenhower and Latin America: The Foreign Policy of Anticommunism.* Chapel Hill: University of North Carolina Press, 1988.

Reimann, Elizabeth. *Confesiones de un Contra: Historia de 'Moisés' en Nicaragua.* Buenos Aires: Legasa, 1986.

Rempe, Dennis M. "Guerrillas, Bandits, and Independent Republics: U.S. Counterinsurgency Efforts in Colombia 1959–1965," from *Small Wars and Insurgencies,* Vol. 6, no. 3 (Winter 1995): 304–327. Published by Frank Cass, London. (www.derechos.net/paulwolf/colombia/ smallwars.htm)

Resende-Santos, João. "The Origins of Security Cooperation in the Southern Cone," *Latin American Politics and Society,* Vol. 44, no. 4 (Winter 2002): 89–128.

Rodríguez, Felix I. and John Weisman. *Shadow Warrior: The CIA Hero of a Hundred Unknown Battles.* New York: Simon & Schuster, 1989.

Rojas Baeza, Paz. "Antecedentes de la violación a los derechos humanos en América Latina en la segunda mitad de este siglo," manuscript, July 1996.

Roubatis, Yiannis and Karen Wynn. "CIA Operations in Greece," in Philip Agee and Louis Wolf, eds., *Dirty Work: The CIA in Western Europe.* London: Zed Press, 1978.

Rowse, Arthur E. "Gladio: The Secret U.S. War to Subvert Italian Democracy," *Covert Action Quarterly*, no. 49 (1994).

Ryan, Jeffrey. "Turning on their Masters: State Terrorism and Unlearning Democracy in Uruguay," in Néstor Rodríguez and Cecilia Menjívar, eds., *When States Kill: Latin America, the U.S., and Technologies of Terror*. Austin: University of Texas Press, 2005.

Schlesinger, Stephen and Stephen Kinzer. *Bitter Fruit: The Untold Story of the American Coup in Guatemala*. New York: Doubleday, 1983.

Schmitz, David. *Thank God They're on Our Side*. Chapel Hill: University of North Carolina Press, 1999.

Schraeder, Peter J. *United States Foreign Policy toward Africa: Incrementalism, Crisis and Change*. Cambridge, UK: Cambridge University Press, 1994.

Schwartz, Benjamin. "Permanent Interests, Endless Threats: Cold War Continuities and NATO Enlargement," *World Policy Journal*, Vol. 14, no. 3 (Fall 1997).

Scobell, Andrew and Brad Hammitt, "Goons, Gunmen, and Gendarmerie: Toward a Reconceptualization of Paramilitary Formations," *Journal of Political and Military Sociology*, Vol. 26, no. 2 (Winter 1998): 213–227.

Scott, Peter Dale and Jonathan Marshall. *Cocaine Politics: Drugs, Armies, and the CIA in Central America*. Berkeley: University of California Press, 1991.

Sheehan, Neil, Hendrick Smith, E. W. Kenworthy, and Fox Butterfield. *The Pentagon Papers*. New York: New York Times/Bantam Books, 1971.

Siegel, Daniel and Joy Hackel. "El Salvador: Counterinsurgency Revisited," in Michael Klare and Peter Kornbluh, eds., *Low Intensity Warfare: Counterinsurgency, Proinsurgency, and Antiterrorism in the Eighties*. Pp. 112–135. New York: Pantheon, 1988.

Simpson, Christopher. *Blowback: America's Recruitment of Nazis and Its Effects on the Cold War*. New York: Macmillan, Collier Books, 1988.

Singer, Daniel. "The Gladiators," *The Nation*, Vol. 251, no. 20 (1990).

Sivak, Martín. *El asesinato de Juan José Torres: Banzer y el mercosur de la muerte*. Buenos Aires: Ediciones del Pensamiento Nacional, 1998.

Slack, Keith M. "Operation Condor and Human Rights: A Report from Paraguay's Archive of Terror," *Human Rights Quarterly*, Vol. 18 (1996): 492–506.

Smith, Gaddis. *The Last Years of the Monroe Doctrine*. New York: Hill and Wang, 1994.

Staub, Ervin. "Torture: Psychological and Cultural Origins," in Ronald D. Crelinsten and Alex P. Schmid, eds., *The Politics of Pain: Torturers and Their Masters*. Pp. 99–111. Boulder, Colo.: Westview, 1995.

Stepan, Alfred. *Rethinking Military Politics*. Princeton, N.J.: Princeton University Press, 1988.

Stohl, Michael and George Lopez, eds. *Dependence, Development, and State Repression*. Stamford, Conn.: Greenwood Press, 1989.

———. *Government Violence and Repression*. Stamford, Conn.: Greenwood Press, 1986.

———. *The State as Terrorist*. Stamford, Conn.: Greenwood Press, 1987.

———. *Terrible beyond Endurance? The Foreign Policy of State Terrorism*. Stamford, Conn.: Greenwood Press, 1988.

Stokes, Doug. "US Military Doctrine and Colombia's War of Terror," *Znet*, September 25, 2002.

Streeter, Stephen. *Managing the Counterrevolution: The United States and Guatemala, 1954–1961.* Athens: Center for International Studies, Ohio University, 2000.

Valentine, Douglas. *The Phoenix Program.* New York: William Morrow, 1990.

Valladares Lanza, Leo and Susan C. Peacock. *In Search of Hidden Truths: An Interim Report on Declassification by the National Commissioner for Human Rights in Honduras.* Tegucigalpa, Honduras: Comisionado Nacional de los Derechos Humanos en Honduras, 1998.

Vandenbrouke, Lucien. *Perilous Options: Special Operations as an Instrument of U.S. Foreign Policy.* New York: Oxford, 1993.

Verdugo, Patricia. *Chile, Pinochet, and the Caravan of Death.* Coral Gables, Fla.: University of Miami, North-South Center Press, 2001.

Walker, Thomas W., ed. *Reagan versus the Sandinistas: The Undeclared War on Nicaragua.* Boulder, Colo.: Westview, 1987.

Walsh, Lawrence E. *Iran-Contra: The Final Report.* New York: Random House, Times Books, 1993.

Walter, E. V. *Terror and Resistance: A Study of Political Violence.* New York: Oxford University Press, 1969.

Weeks, Greg. "Fighting the Enemy within: Terrorism, the School of the Americas, and the Military in Latin America," *Human Rights Review* vol. 5, no. 1 (October–December 2003): 12–27.

Weinstein, Martin. *Uruguay: Democracy at the Crossroads.* Boulder, Colo.: Westview, 1988.

Weschler, Lawrence. *A Miracle, A Universe: Settling Accounts with Torturers.* New York: Penguin Books USA, 1990.

Willan, Philip. *Puppet Masters: The Political Use of Terrorism in Italy.* London: Constable, 1991.

Woodhouse, C. M. *The Rise and Fall of the Greek Colonels.* New York: Franklin Watts, 1985.

Woodward, Bob. *Veil: The Secret Wars of the CIA 1981–1987.* New York: Simon & Schuster, 1987.

Yeves, Enrique. *La Contra: Una guerra sucia.* Buenos Aires: Grupo Editorial Zeta, S.A., 1990.

Zoglin, Katie. "Paraguay's Archive of Terror: International Cooperation and Operation Condor," *Inter-American Law Review,* Vol. 32, no. 1 (Winter–Spring 2001): 57–82.

U.S. Government Documents

Note: The declassified documents available on the State Department's Chile Declassification Project and Argentina Project (www.foia.state.gov), cited in the notes, are not listed again here.

U.S. Army. Escuela de las Américas, Ejército de los EEUU, Fuerte Gulick, Panama, "FM 31-16, Operaciones de contra-guerrilla," June 1968 (replaced FM 31-16 of February 16, 1963).

———. *Vietnam Studies: U.S. Army Special Forces 1961–1971*, Part Two, "The Middle Years: 1965–1968. Chapter IV. The CIDG [Civilian Irregular Defense Group] Program Begins to Mature." At www.ehistory.com/vietnam/books/spfor/0077.cfm. (Accessed by author in May 2003.)

U.S. Congress. Letter from Thirty-Four Congressional Representatives to President Clinton (requesting declassification of U.S. documents related to human rights violations in Honduras). Washington, D.C. (December 3, 1996).

U.S. Congress. Office of Joseph P. Kennedy. "Report on the School of the Americas." Washington, D.C. (March 6, 1997).

U.S. Government Accounting Office (GAO). "School of the Americas: U.S. Military Training for Latin American Countries (Report 08/22/96, GAO/NSIAD-96-178). Washington, D.C. (1996).

U.S. Intelligence Oversight Board (Anthony S. Harrington, General Lew Allen, Jr., USAF [Ret.], Ann Z. Caracristi, and Harold W. Pote). "Report on the Guatemala Review." June 28, 1996.

U.S. Senate. Committee on Foreign Relations. "Drugs, Law Enforcement and Foreign Policy, A Report," prepared by the Subcommittee on Terrorism, Narcotics and International Operations, December 1988.

———. Staff Report of the Select Committee to Study Governmental Operations with Respect to Intelligence Activities. "Covert Action in Chile 1963–1973." Washington, D.C.: Government Printing Office, 1976.

U.S. State Department. "United States Overseas Internal Defense Policy" (SECRET), September, 1962.

Archives

Archives of Centro de Estudios Legales y Sociales (CELS), Buenos Aires, Argentina.

Archives of Servicio para la Paz y Justicia (SERPAJ), Buenos Aires, Argentina.

Archives of Servicio para la Paz y Justicia (SERPAJ), Montevideo, Uruguay.

"Archives of Terror," Asunción, Paraguay.

Archives of the Comisionado Nacional de los Derechos Humanos, Tegucigalpa, Honduras.

Arquivo Ana Lagôa of the Universidade Federal de São Carlos, São Carlos, Brazil.

National Security Archive, Washington, D.C.

Periodicals

Argentina: *Ambito Financiero, Clarín, La Nación, Página/12.*

Bolivia: *Bolivia Press, La Razón, Bolivia Times.*

Brazil: *Correio Popular, Jornal do Brasil, Fohla de São Paulo, O Globo, Senhor.*
Chile: *El Mercurio, El Mostrador, La Nación, La Tercera, Qué Pasa, Santiago Times.*
Paraguay: *Noticias, ABC Color.*
United States: *El Diario/La Prensa, InterPress Service, Miami Herald, NACLA Report on the Americas, The Nation, Newsweek, New York Times, The Progressive, San Francisco Chronicle, Washington Post.*
Uruguay: *Brecha, El Observador, La República, Posdata.*
Materials from Amnesty International, Equipo Nizkor, Human Rights Watch, National Security Archive, *Latinamerica Press.*

Index

About the Author

J. Patrice McSherry is associate professor of political science and director of the Latin American and Caribbean Studies Program at Long Island University in New York. She has been awarded two Fulbright grants (for fieldwork in Argentina in 1992 and Uruguay in 2005), and is the author of *Incomplete Transition: Military Power and Democracy in Argentina* (1997) and numerous scholarly articles on Operation Condor, military regimes, civil-military relations, and U.S. foreign policy. She is associate editor for Latin America for *Journal of Third World Studies.*